Microsoft® Access™ 2007 Data Analysis

Microsoft® Access™ 2007 Data Analysis

Michael Alexander

Wiley Publishing, Inc.

Microsoft® Access™ 2007 Data Analysis
Published by
Wiley Publishing, Inc.
10475 Crosspoint Boulevard
Indianapolis, IN 46256
www.wiley.com

Published simultaneously in Canada

ISBN: 978-0-470-10485-9

10 9 8 7 6 5

Library of Congress Cataloging-in-Publication Data Available from Publisher

For Mary, Ethan, and Emma

About the Author

Michael Alexander is a Microsoft Certified Application Developer (MCAD) with more than 14 years experience consulting and developing office solutions. He currently lives in Plano, TX where he serves as a Senior Program Manager for a top technology firm. In his spare time he runs a free tutorial site, `www.datapigtechnologies.com`, where he shares basic Access and Excel tips to the Office community.

Credits

Acquisitions Editor
Katie Mohr

Development Editor
Kelly Talbot

Technical Editor
Todd Meister

Production Editor
Angela Smith

Copy Editor
Travis Henderson

Editorial Manager
Mary Beth Wakefield

Production Manager
Tim Tate

Vice President and Executive Group Publisher
Richard Swadley

Vice President and Executive Publisher
Joseph B. Wikert

Project Coordinator
Patrick Redmond

Graphics and Production Specialists
Jennifer Mayberry, Barbara Moore, Rashelle Smith

Quality Control Technician
John Greenough

Proofreading
Lisa Stiers

Indexing
Aptara

Anniversary Logo Design
Richard J. Pacifico

Contents

Acknowledgments

A big thank you to Katie Mohr for taking a chance on this project and being such a wonderful project manager. Many thanks to Kelly Talbot, Todd Meister, and the brilliant team of professionals who helped bring this book to fruition. A special thank you to Mary who puts up with all my crazy projects.

Introduction

If you were to ask a random sampling of people what data analysis is, most would say that it is the process of calculating and summarizing data to get an answer to a question. In one sense, they are correct. However, the actions they are describing represent only a small part of the process known as data analysis.

For example, if you were asked to analyze how much revenue in sales your company made last month, what would you have to do in order to complete that analysis? You would just calculate and summarize the sales for the month, right? Well, where would you get the sales data? Where would you store the data? Would you have to clean up the data when you got it? How would you present your analysis: by week, by day, by location? The point being made here is that the process of data analysis is made up of more than just calculating and summarizing data.

A more representative definition of data analysis is the process of systematically collecting, transforming, and analyzing data in order to present meaningful conclusions. To better understand this concept, think of data analysis as a process that encapsulates four fundamental actions: collection, transformation, analysis, and presentation.

- **Collection:** Collection encompasses the gathering and storing of data—that is, where you obtain your data, how you will receive your data, how you will store your data, and how you will access your data when it comes time to perform some analysis.
- **Transformation:** Transformation is the process of ensuring your data is uniform in structure, free from redundancy, and stable. This

generally entails things like establishing a table structure, cleaning text, removing blanks, and standardizing data fields.

- **Analysis:** Analysis is the investigation of the component parts of your data and their relationships to your data source as a whole. You are analyzing your data when you are calculating, summarizing, categorizing, comparing, contrasting, examining, or testing your data.
- **Presentation:** In the context of data analysis, presentation deals with how you make the content of your analysis available to a certain audience. That is, how you choose to display your results. Some considerations that go along with presentation of your analysis include the platform you will use, the levels of visibility you will provide, and the freedom you will give your audience to change their view.

As you think about these four fundamental actions, think about this reality: Most analysts are severely limited to one tool—Excel. This means that all of the complex actions involved in each of these fundamentals are mostly being done with and in Excel. What's the problem with that? Well Excel is not designed to do many of these actions. However, many analysts are so limited in their toolsets that they often end up in hand-to-hand combat with their data, creating complex workarounds and inefficient processes.

What this book will highlight is that there are powerful functionalities in Access that can help you go beyond your two-dimensional spreadsheet and liberate you from the daily grind of managing and maintaining redundant analytical processes. Indeed, using Access for your data analysis needs can help you streamline your analytical processes, increase your productivity, and analyze the larger datasets that have reached Excel's limitations.

Throughout this book, you will come to realize that Access is not a dry database program used only for storing data and building departmental applications. Access possesses strong data analysis functionalities that are easy to learn and certainly applicable to many types of organizations and data systems.

What to Expect from This Book

Within the first three chapters, you will be able to demonstrate proficiency in Access, executing powerful analysis on large datasets that have long since reached Excel's limitations. Within the first nine chapters, you will be able to add depth and dimension to your analysis with advanced Access functions, building complex analytical processes with ease. By the end of the book, you will be able to create your own custom functions, perform batch analysis, and develop automated procedures that essentially run on their own.

After completing this book, you will be able to analyze large amounts of data in a meaningful way, quickly slice data into various views on the fly, automate redundant analysis, save time, and increase productivity.

What to Not Expect from This Book

It's important to note that there are aspects of Access and data analysis that are outside the scope of this book. While this book does cover the fundamentals of Access, it is always in the light of data analysis and it is written from a data analyst's point of view. This is not meant to be an all-encompassing book on Access. That being said, if you are a first-time user of Access, you can feel confident that this book will provide you with a solid introduction to Access that will leave you with valuable skills you can use in your daily operations.

This book is not meant to be a book on data management theory and best practices. Nor is it meant to expound on high-level business intelligence concepts. This is more of a "technician's" book, providing hands-on instruction that introduces Access as an analytical tool that can provide powerful solutions to common analytical scenarios and issues.

Finally, while this book does contain a chapter that demonstrates various techniques to perform a whole range of statistical analysis, it is important to note that this book does not cover statistics theory, methodology, or best practices.

Skills Required for This Book

In order to get the most out of this book, it's best that you have certain skills before diving into the topics highlighted in this book. The ideal candidate for this book will have:

- Some experience working with data and familiarity with the basic concepts of data analysis such as working with tables, aggregating data, and performing calculations.
- Experience using Excel with a strong grasp of concepts such as table structures, filtering, sorting and using formulas.
- Some basic knowledge of Access; enough to know it exists and to have opened a database once or twice.

How This Book Is Organized

Part I: Fundamentals of Data Analysis in Access

Part I, which includes Chapters 1, 2, and 3, provides a condensed introduction to Access. Here, you will learn some of the basic fundamentals of Access, along with the essential query skills required throughout the rest of the book. Topics covered in this Part are: relational database concepts, query basics, using aggregate queries, action queries, and Crosstab queries.

Part II: Basic Analysis Techniques

Part II will introduce you to some of the basic analytical tools and techniques available to you in Access. Chapter 4 covers data transformation, providing examples of how to clean and shape raw data to fit your needs. Chapter 5 provides in-depth instruction on how to create and utilize custom calculations in your analysis. Chapter 5 also shows you how to work with dates, using them in simple date calculations, or performing advanced time analysis. Chapter 6 introduces you to some conditional analysis techniques that allow you to add logic to your analytical processes.

Part III: Advanced Analysis Techniques

Part III will demonstrate many of the advanced techniques that truly bring your data analysis to the next level. Chapter 7 covers the fundamentals SQL statements. Chapter 8 picks up from there and introduces you to subqueries and domain aggregate functions. Chapter 9 demonstrates many of the advanced statistical analysis you can perform using subqueries and domain aggregate functions. Chapter 10 provides you with an in-depth look at using PivotTables and PivotCharts in Access.

Part IV: Automating Data Analysis

Part IV takes you beyond manual analysis with queries and introduces you to the world of automation. Chapter 11 gives you an in-depth view of how macros can help increase you productivity by running batch analysis. Chapter 12 demonstrates how a little coding with Visual Basic for Applications (VBA) can help enhance data analysis. Chapter 13 offers some final thoughts and tips on query performance, database corruption, and how to get help in Access.

Part V: Appendixes

Part V includes useful reference materials that will assist you in your everyday dealings with Access. Appendix A details many of the built-in Access functions that are available to data analysts. Appendix B provides a high-level overview of VBA for those users who are new to the world of Access programming. Appendix C highlights and explains many of the Access error codes you may encounter while analyzing your data.

Companion Database

The examples demonstrated throughout this book can be found in the companion database. This sample database is located at `www.wiley.com/go/access2007dataanalysis`.

Microsoft® Access™ 2007 Data Analysis

CHAPTER

1

The Case for Data Analysis in Access

When you ask most people which software tool they use for their daily data analysis, the answer you most often get is Excel. Indeed, if you were to enter the key words *data analysis* in an Amazon.com search, you would get a plethora of books on how to analyze your data with Excel. Well if so many people seem to agree that using Excel to analyze data is the way to go, why bother using Access for data analysis? The honest answer: to avoid the limitations and issues that plague Excel.

This is not meant to disparage Excel or its wonderful functionalities. Many people have used Excel for years and continue to use it every day. It is considered to be the premier platform for performing and presenting data analysis. Anyone who does not understand Excel in today's business world is undoubtedly hiding that shameful fact. The interactive, impromptu analysis that Excel can perform makes it truly unique in the industry.

However, it is not without its limitations, as you will see in the following section.

Where Data Analysis with Excel Can Go Wrong

Years of consulting experience have brought me face to face with managers, accountants, and analysts who all have had to accept one simple fact: their analytical needs had outgrown Excel. They all met with fundamental issues that stemmed from one or more of Excel's three problem areas: scalability, transparency of analytical processes, and separation of data and presentation.

Scalability

Scalability is the ability for an application to develop flexibly to meet growth and complexity requirements. In the context of this chapter, scalability refers to the ability of Excel to handle ever-increasing volumes of data. Most Excel aficionados will be quick to point out that as of Excel 2007, you can place 1,048,576 rows of data into a single Excel worksheet. This is an overwhelming increase from the limitation of 65,536 rows imposed by previous versions of Excel. However, this increase in capacity does not solve all of the scalability issues that inundate Excel.

Imagine that you are working in a small company and you are using Excel to analyze your daily transactions. As time goes on, you build a robust process complete with all the formulas, pivot tables, and macros you need to analyze the data that is stored in your neatly maintained worksheet.

As your data grows, you will first notice performance issues. Your spreadsheet will become slow to load and then slow to calculate. Why will this happen? It has to do with the way Excel handles memory. When an Excel file is loaded, the entire file is loaded into RAM. Excel does this to allow for quick data processing and access. The drawback to this behavior is that each time something changes in your spreadsheet, Excel has to reload the entire spreadsheet into RAM. The net result in a large spreadsheet is that it takes a great deal of RAM to process even the smallest change in your spreadsheet. Eventually, each action you take in your gigantic worksheet will become an excruciating wait.

Your pivot tables will require bigger pivot caches, almost doubling your Excel workbook's file size. Eventually, your workbook will be too big to distribute easily. You may even consider breaking down the workbook into smaller workbooks (possibly one for each region). This causes you to duplicate your work.

In time, you may eventually reach the 1,048,576-row limit of your worksheet. What happens then? Do you start a new worksheet? How do you analyze two datasets on two different worksheets as one entity? Are your formulas still good? Will you have to write new macros?

These are all issues that need to be dealt with.

Of course, you will have the Excel power-users, who will find various clever ways to work around these limitations. In the end, however, they will always be just workarounds. Eventually even these power-users will begin to think less about the most effective way to perform and present analysis of their data and more about how to make something fit into Excel without breaking their formulas and functions. Excel is flexible enough that a proficient user can make most things fit into Excel just fine. However, when users think only in terms of Excel, they are undoubtedly limiting themselves, albeit in an incredibly functional way!

In addition, these capacity limitations often force Excel users to have the data prepared for them. That is, someone else extracts large chunks of data from a large database and then aggregates and shapes the data for use in Excel. Should the serious analyst always be dependant on someone else for his or her data needs? What if an analyst could be given the tools to access vast quantities of data without being reliant on others to provide data? Could that analyst be more valuable to the organization? Could that analyst focus on the accuracy of the analysis and the quality of the presentation instead of routing Excel data maintenance?

Access is an excellent, many would say logical, next step for the analyst who faces an ever-increasing data pool. Since an Access table takes very few performance hits with larger datasets and has no predetermined row limitations, an analyst will be able to handle larger datasets without requiring the data to be summarized or prepared to fit into Excel. Since many tasks can be duplicated in both Excel and Access, an analyst who is proficient at both will be prepared for any situation. The alternative is telling everyone, "Sorry, it is not in Excel."

Another important advantage of using Access is that if ever a process that is currently being tracked in Excel becomes more crucial to the organization and needs to be tracked in a more enterprise-acceptable environment, it will be easier to upgrade and scale up if it is already in Access.

NOTE An Access table is limited to 256 columns but has no row limitation. This is not to say that Access has unlimited data storage capabilities. Every bit of data causes the Access database to grow in file size. An Access database has a file size limitation of 2 gigabytes. In comparison, Excel 2007 has a limit of 1,048,576 rows and 16,384 columns regardless of file size.

Transparency of Analytical Processes

One of Excel's most attractive features is its flexibility. Each individual cell can contain text, a number, a formula, or practically anything else the user defines. Indeed, this is one of the fundamental reasons Excel is such an effective tool for data analysis. Users can use named ranges, formulas, and macros to create an intricate system of interlocking calculations, linked cells, and formatted summaries that work together to create a final analysis.

So what is the problem with that? The problem is that there is no transparency of analytical processes. Meaning it is extremely difficult to determine what is actually going on in a spreadsheet. Anyone who has had to work with a spreadsheet created by someone else knows all too well the frustration that comes with deciphering the various gyrations of calculations and links being used to perform some analysis. Small spreadsheets that are performing modest analysis are painful to decipher, whereas large, elaborate, multi-worksheet workbooks are virtually impossible to decode, often leaving you to start from scratch.

Even auditing tools that are available with most Excel add-in packages provide little relief. Figure 1-1 shows the results of a formula auditing tool run on an actual workbook used by a real company. This is a list of all the formulas in this workbook. The idea is to use this list to find and make sense of existing formulas. Notice that line 2 shows that there are 156 formulas. Yeah, this list helps a lot; good luck.

Formula Report for: C:\MyProject\ProjectWorkz.xls
Number of formulas: 156

Address	Row	Column	Formula
AF9	9	32	='Customer Input'!AK$10
D15	15	4	='Customer Input'!AK$12
D17	17	4	='RFQ Input'!$I23
D18	18	4	='RFQ Input'!$I13
D19	19	4	='RFQ Input'!$I15
D20	20	4	=CONCATENATE('RFQ Input'!$I17,", ",'RFQ Input'!$I19," ",'RFQ Input'!$I21)
I24	24	9	='Customer Input'!AK$10
D27	27	4	=CONCATENATE("Dear ",$D17,":")
D57	57	4	=IF('RFQ Input'!$AA$47="TPM Project Mgr",'Customer Input'!$J$12,'Customer Input'!$J$24)
D58	58	4	=IF('RFQ Input'!$AA$47="TPM Project Mgr","TPM Project Manager",'Customer Input'!$J$26)
G60	60	7	=CONCATENATE('Customer Input'!$J$16)
AF65	65	32	='Customer Input'!AK$10
D65	65	4	=$D18
D66	66	4	=$D15
D71	71	4	='RFQ Input'!$B52
AF71	71	32	=IF(OR($T71=0,$AB71=0),0,$T71*$AB71)
AF86	86	32	=IF(SUM(AF71:AJ85)<0.1,0,SUM($AF71:$AJ85))
AF89	89	32	=IF(OR($T89=0,$AB89=0),0,$T89*$AB89)
AF94	94	32	=IF(SUM(AF89:AJ93)<0.1,0,SUM($AF89:$AJ93))
D97	97	4	='RFQ Input'!$B78
T97	97	20	='RFQ Input'!$R78
W97	97	23	='RFQ Input'!$U78

Figure 1-1: Formula auditing tools don't help much in deciphering spreadsheets.

Compared to Excel, Access might seem rigid, strict, and unwavering in its rules. No, you can't put formulas directly into data fields. No, you can't link a data field to another table. To many users, Excel is the cool gym teacher who enables you to do anything, whereas Access is the cantankerous librarian who has nothing but error messages for you. However, all this rigidity comes with a benefit.

Since only certain actions are allowable, you can more easily come to understand what is being done with a set of data in Access. If a dataset is being edited, a number is being calculated, or any portion of the dataset is being affected as a part of an analytical process, you will readily see that action. This is not to say that users can't do foolish and confusing things in Access. However, you definitely will not encounter hidden steps in an analytical process such as hidden formulas, hidden cells, or named ranges in dead worksheets.

Separation of Data and Presentation

Data should be separate from presentation; you do not want the data to become too tied into any one particular way of presenting it. For example, when you receive an invoice from a company, you don't assume that the financial data on that invoice is the true source of your data. It is a presentation of your data. It can be presented to you in other manners and styles on charts or on web sites, but such representations are never the actual source of the data. This sounds obvious, but it becomes an important distinction when you study an approach of using Access and Excel together for data analysis.

What exactly does this concept have to do with Excel? People who perform data analysis with Excel, more often than not, tend to fuse the data, the analysis, and the presentation together. For example, you will often see an Excel Workbook that has 12 worksheets, each representing a month. On each worksheet, data for that month is listed along with formulas, pivot tables, and summaries. What happens when you are asked to provide a summary by quarter? Do you add more formulas and worksheets to consolidate the data on each of the month worksheets? The fundamental problem in this scenario is that the worksheets actually represent data values that are fused into the presentation of your analysis. The point being made here is that data should not be tied to a particular presentation, no matter how apparently logical or useful it may be. However, in Excel, it happens all the time.

In addition, as previously discussed, because all manners and phases of analysis can be done directly within a spreadsheet, Excel cannot effectively provide adequate transparency to the analysis. Each cell has the potential of holding formulas, being hidden, and containing links to other cells. In Excel, this blurs the line between analysis and data and makes it difficult to determine exactly what is going on in a spreadsheet. Moreover, it takes a great deal of effort in the way of manual maintenance to ensure that edits and unforeseen changes don't affect previous analyses.

Access inherently separates its analytical components into Tables, Queries, and Reports. By separating these elements, Access makes data less sensitive to changes and creates a data analysis environment where you can easily respond to new requests for analysis without destroying previous analyses.

Many who use Excel will find themselves manipulating its functionalities to approximate this database behavior. If you find yourself in this situation, you must consider that if you are using Excel's functionality to make it behave like a database application, perhaps the real thing just might have something to offer. Utilizing Access for data storage and analytical needs would enhance overall data analysis and would allow the Excel power-users to focus on the presentation in their spreadsheets.

In the future, there will be more data, not less. Likewise, there will be more demand for complex data analysis, not less. Power-users are going to need to add some tools to their repertoire in order to get away from being simply spreadsheet mechanics. Excel can be stretched to do just about anything, but maintaining such creative solutions can be a tedious manual task. You can be sure that the sexy part of data analysis is not in routine data management within Excel. Rather it is in the creating of slick processes and utilities that will provide your clients with the best solution for any situation.

Deciding Whether to Use Access or Excel

After such a critical view of Excel, it is important to say that the key to your success in the sphere of data analysis will not come from discarding Excel altogether and exclusively using Access. Your success will come from proficiency with both applications and the ability to evaluate a project and determine the best platform to use for your analytical needs. Are there hard-and-fast rules that you can follow to make this determination? The answer is no, but there are some key indicators in every project that you can consider as guidelines to determine whether to use Access or Excel. These indicators are the size of the data, the data's structure, the potential for data evolution, the functional complexity of the analysis, and the potential for shared processing.

Size of Data

The size of your dataset is the most obvious consideration you will have to take into account. Although Excel can handle more data than in previous versions, it is generally a good rule to start considering Access if your dataset begins to approach 100,000 rows. The reason for this is the fundamental way Access and Excel handle data.

When you open an Excel file, the entire file is loaded into RAM to ensure quick data processing and access. The drawback to this behavior is that Excel requires a great deal of RAM to process even the smallest change in your spreadsheet. You may have noticed that when you try to perform an AutoFilter on a large formula-intensive dataset, Excel is slow to respond, giving you a Calculating indicator in the status bar. The larger your dataset is, the less efficient the data crunching in Excel will be.

Access on the other hand does not follow the same behavior as Excel. When you open an Access table, it may seem as though the whole table is opening for you, but in reality Access is storing only a portion of data into RAM at a time. This ensures the cost-effective use of memory and allows for more efficient data crunching on larger datasets. In addition, Access allows you to make use of Indexes that enable you to search, sort, filter, and query extremely large datasets very quickly.

Data Structure

If you are analyzing data that resides in a table that has no relationships with other tables, Excel is a fine choice for your analytical needs. However, if you have a series of tables that interact with each other, such as a Customers table, an Orders table, and an Invoices table, you should consider using Access. Access is a relational database, which means it is designed to handle the intricacies of interacting datasets. Some of these are the preservation of data integrity, the prevention of redundancy, and the efficient comparison and querying of data between the datasets. You will learn more about the concept of table relationships in Chapter 2.

Data Evolution

Excel is an ideal choice for quickly analyzing data that is being used as a means to an end, such as a temporary dataset that is being crunched to obtain a more valuable subset of data. The result of a pivot table is a perfect example of this kind of one-time data crunching. However, if you are building a long-term analytical process with data that has the potential of evolving and growing, Access is a better choice. Many analytical processes that start in Excel begin small and run fine, but as time passes these processes grow in both size and complexity until they reach the limits of Excel's capabilities. The message here is that you should use some foresight and consider future needs when determining which platform is best for your scenario.

Functional Complexity

There are far too many real-life examples of analytical projects where processes are brute forced into Excel even when its limitations have been reached. How many times have you seen a workbook that contains an analytical process encapsulating multiple worksheets, macros, pivot tables, and formulas that add, average, count, look up, and link to other workbooks? The fact is that when Excel-based analytical processes become overly complex, they are difficult to manage, difficult to maintain, and difficult to translate to others. Consider using Access for projects that have complex, multiple-step analytical processes.

Shared Processing

Although it is possible to have multiple users work on one central Excel spreadsheet located on a network, ask anyone who has tried to coordinate and manage a central spreadsheet how difficult and restrictive it is. Data conflicts, loss of data, locked out users, and poor data integrity are just a few examples of some of the problems you will encounter if you try to build a multiple user process with Excel. Consider using Access for your shared processes. Access is better suited for a shared environment for many reasons, some of which are: the ability for users to concurrently enter and update data, inherent protection against data conflicts, prevention of data redundancy, and protection against data entry errors.

An Excel User's Guide to Access: Don't Panic!

Many seasoned managers, accountants, and analysts at some point come to realize that just because something can be done in Excel that does not necessarily mean Excel is the best way to do it. This is the point when they decide to open Access for the first time. When they do open Access, the first object that looks familiar to them is the Access table. In fact, Access tables look so similar to an Excel spreadsheet that most Excel users try to use tables just like a spreadsheet. However, when they realize that they can't type formulas directly into the table or duplicate most of the behavior and functionality of Excel, most of them wonder just what exactly the point of using Access is.

When many Excel experts find out that Access does not behave or look like Excel, they write Access off as being too difficult or taking to much time to learn. However, the reality is that many of the concepts behind how data is stored and managed in Access are concepts with which the user is already familiar. Any Excel user has already learned such concepts in order to perform and present complex analysis. Investing a little time up front to see just how Access can be made to work for you can save a great deal of time later in automating routine data processes.

Throughout this book, you will learn various techniques in which you can use Access to perform much of the data analysis you are now performing exclusively in Excel. This section is a brief introduction to Access from an Excel expert's point of view. Here, you will focus on the big-picture items in Access. If some of the Access terms mentioned here are new or not terribly familiar, be patient. They will be covered more in depth as the book progresses.

Tables

What will undoubtedly look most familiar to you are Access tables. Tables appear almost identical to spreadsheets with the familiar cells, rows, and columns. However, the first time you attempt to type a formula in one of the cells, you will see that Access tables do not possess Excel's flexible, multi-purpose nature that allows any cell to take on almost any responsibility or function.

The Access table is simply a place to store data, such as numbers and text. All of the analysis and number crunching happens somewhere else. This way, data will never be tied to any particular analysis or presentation. The data is in its raw form, leaving it up to users to determine how they want to analyze or display it. If an Excel user only uses Access tables, that user can still immensely increase his or her effectiveness and productivity.

Queries

You may have heard of Access queries but have never been able to relate to them.

Consider this: In Excel, when you use AutoFilter, a VLookup formula, or Subtotals, you are essentially running a query. So what is a query? A query is a question you pose against your data in order to get an answer or a result. The answer to a query can be a single data item, a Yes/No answer, or many rows of data. In Excel, the concept of querying data is a bit nebulous as it can take the form of the different functionalities, such as formulas, AutoFilters, and PivotTables.

In Access, a query is an actual object that has its own functionalities. A query is separate from a table in order to ensure that data is never tied to any particular analysis. You will cover queries extensively in subsequent chapters. Your success in using Microsoft Access to enhance your data analysis will depend on your ability to create all manners of both simple and complex queries.

Reports

Access reports are an incredibly powerful component of Microsoft Access that allows data to be presented in a variety of styles. Access reports, in and of themselves, provide an excellent illustration of one of the main points of this book: data should be separate from the analysis and presentation. The report serves as the presentation layer for a database, displaying various views into the data within. Acting as the presentation layer for your database, reports are inherently disconnected from the way your data is stored and structured. As long as the report receives the data it requires in order to accurately and cleanly present its information, it will not care where the information came from.

Access reports can have mixed reputations. On the one hand, they can provide clean-looking PDF-esque reports that are ideal for invoices and form letters. On the other hand, Access reports are not ideal for showing the one-shot displays of data that Excel can provide. However, Access reports can easily be configured to prepare all manners of report styles, such as crosstabs, matrices, tabular layouts, and subtotaled layouts.

Macros and VBA

Just as Excel has macro and VBA functionality, Microsoft Access has its equivalents. This is where the true power and flexibility of Microsoft Access data analysis resides. Whether you are using them in custom functions, batch analysis, or automation, macros and VBA can add a customized flexibility that is hard to match using any other means. For example, you can use macros and VBA to automatically perform redundant analyses and recurring analytical processes, leaving you free to work on other tasks. Macros and VBA also enable you to reduce the chance of human error and to ensure that analyses are preformed the same way every time. Starting in Chapter 11, you will explore the benefits of macros and VBA and how you can use them to schedule and run batch analysis.

Summary

Although Excel is considered the premier tool for data analysis, Excel has some inherent characteristics that often lead to issues revolving around scalability, transparency of analytic processes, and confusion between data and presentation. Access has a suite of analytical tools that can help you avoid many of the issues that arise from Excel.

First, Access can handle very large datasets and has no predetermined row limitation. This allows for the management and analysis of large datasets without the scalability issues that plague Excel. Access also forces transparency of the separation of data and presentation by separating data into functional objects (such as tables, queries, and reports) and by applying stringent rules that protect against bad processes and poor habits.

As you continue through this book, it is important to remember that your goal is not to avoid Excel altogether. Your goal is to broaden your toolset and to understand that Access often offers functionality that both enhances your analytical processes and makes your life easier.

CHAPTER

2

Access Basics

When working with Access for the first time, it is tempting to start filling tables right away and querying data to get fast results, but it's important to understand the basics of the relational database concept before pounding away at data. A good understanding of how a relational database works will help you take full advantage of Access as a powerful data analysis solution. This chapter covers the fundamentals of Access and methods to bring data into the program.

Access Tables

Upon opening Access, you notice that the Database window, shown in Figure 2-1, contains a task pane on the left. Using the topmost drop-down box, change the navigation category to All Access Objects. You will get six sections. Each section represents one of the six database objects: Tables, Queries, Forms, Reports, Macros, and Modules. The Tables selection is appropriately at the top of the list, because it is the precise location where your data will be stored. All other database objects will refer to the tables in your database for data, whether asking questions of the data or creating reports based on the data. This section covers the basics to get you working with Access tables.

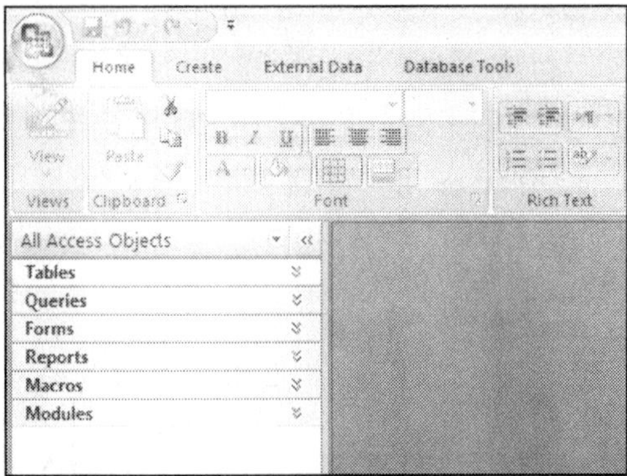

Figure 2-1: The navigation pane on the left enables you to navigate through the six types of database objects: Tables, Queries, Forms, Reports, Macros, and Modules.

Table Basics

One way to think of a table is as a collection of data concerning a specific type of entity (such as customers, branches, transactions, products, and so on). You want each of these entities to have its own unique table. Among the many advantages to storing your data using this approach is eliminating or significantly decreasing duplicate information. Later in the chapter, you will learn about the dangers inherent in storing data with excessive duplications.

Opening a Table in the Datasheet View

Open your sample database and go to the Tables section in the navigation pane. Double-click the CustomerMaster table. When the table opens, it is in the Datasheet view. In this view, you are able to directly view and edit the contents of the table. As you can see in Figure 2-2, the names of the columns are at the top.

CustomerMaster

Customer_Number	Branch_Num	Customer_Name	Address1
103838	301301	CORRUL Corp.	13 HUSSLUY MALL RD
103923	301301	ANYTHA Corp.	4556 CUNSTATASAUN RI
103950	301301	RHFUSU Corp.	604 DUKALB AND WAY
103962	301301	MUUZEO Corp.	4120 DUNNALLY AVE SW
103983	301301	NABCO Corp.	4600 ULD ANAUN PT RD
103995	301301	UNESTU Corp.	MATT IVUY
104071	301301	ALTUC Corp.	554 FARST ST
104145	301301	TORAEA Corp.	5421 REBUSTS RD
104229	301301	CARTUM Corp.	3542 HWY 52 STE B5
104270	301301	ATLANT Corp.	4200 HWY 4614 SUASH
104492	301301	HALLSG Corp.	142 W TAYLUS
104506	301301	ATLANT Corp.	602 SULAG DR
104518	301301	VALCAN Corp.	52 ULD RECK QAORY RD
104539	301301	PRATT Corp.	440 WUTTLOKE PKWY
104607	301301	PLANTU Corp.	ATTN CHRAS
104631	301301	SUASHW Corp.	645 CUNTRAL HAGH REA
104653	301301	CYCLES Corp.	401 KUNWUPD RD

Record: 1 of 9253 No Filter Search

Figure 2-2: Opening the table in Datasheet view will allow you to view and edit the data stored in the table.

Identifying Important Table Elements

The table is comprised of rows, with each row representing a single instance of the table name or entity. In CustomerMaster, each row represents a single distinct customer with which the firm does business. The proper database terminology for a row is *record*.

The table is also comprised of columns, with each column representing a particular piece of information common to all instances of the table's entity. In CustomerMaster, each column represents some attribute of the customer that you want to record. The proper database terminology for a column is *field*.

TIP **The number of records in a table is visible at the bottom left of the Datasheet view, next to the record selectors.**

Opening a Table in the Design View

Through the Design view of a table, you are able to set the field names and data types. To get to the Design view of the CustomerMaster table, go to the Home tab and select View → Design View as demonstrated in Figure 2-3.

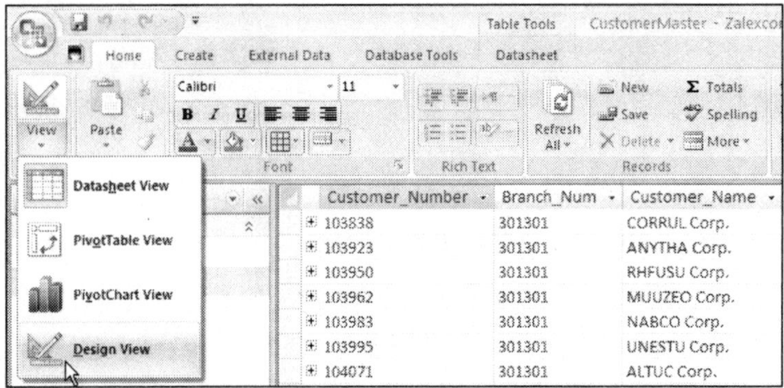

Figure 2-3: Opening the CustomerMaster table in the Design view.

As you can see in Figure 2-4, the Design view shows you the fields that comprise the CustomerMaster table in an easy-to-manage view.

Note how each field has a Field Name and a Data Type. The Field Name is the descriptive text string given to that particular column of a table. It is what appears at the top of the table when it is in the Datasheet view. The Data Type of the field ensures that only a certain type of data is allowed in the field. If a data type is tagged as a Number, Access does not enable you to enter any text into that field. By setting the data type of each column, you go a long way to ensuring the integrity and consistency of the data.

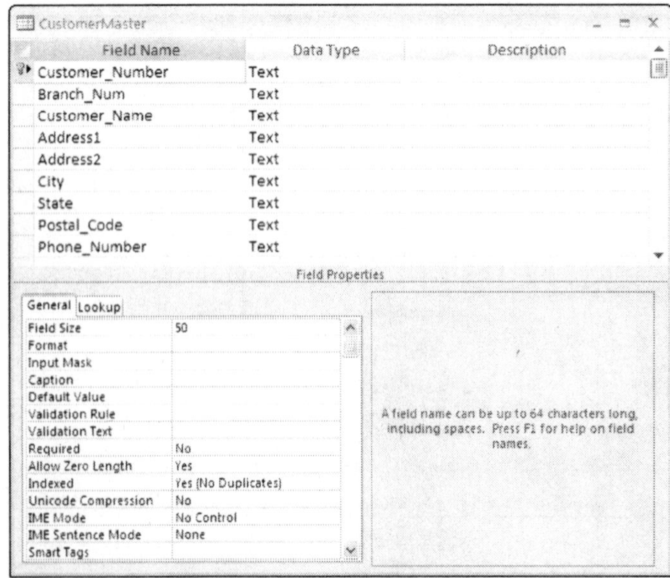

Figure 2-4: Opening the table in the Design view enables you to add field names or change existing ones.

TIP **It's good practice not to put any spaces in your field names. When constructing queries or referring to tables in VBA code, spaces in the field names can lead to problems. If you need to indicate a space in your field name, use the underscore character (_). Keep in mind that your field names cannot include a period (.), an exclamation point (!), an accent grave (`), or brackets ([ ]).**

Exploring Data Types

The concept of the data type is crucial not only to understanding Access, but also to unlocking the power of the programming language behind Access, VBA. Quite simply, computers process and store data, and that data is categorized by its type.

With the Design view of the CustomerMaster table open, select the Data type section of the first field and click the drop-down arrow. A list of predefined data type choices becomes visible. These data types are: Text, Memo, Number, Date/Time, Currency, AutoNumber, Yes/No, OLE Object, Hyperlink, and Attachment.

NOTE **When in Design View, you will also see a data type selection called Lookup Wizard. This selection is actually not a data type at all. It's actually a mechanism used to activate the Lookup Wizard in order to create lookup fields. The Lookup Wizard is not within the scope of this book.**

- **Text:** Any combination of letters, numbers, spaces, and characters is text. This is by far the most common data type. Although text can be a number, it should not be a number used in a calculation. Examples of common uses of the Text data type are customer names, customer numbers (using customer numbers in calculations would have no meaning), and addresses. The maximum number of characters allowed in a Text field is 255 characters.
- **Memo:** If you need to store text data that exceeds the 255-character limit of the Text field, the Memo field should be used. Long descriptions or notes about the record can be stored in fields of this type.
- **Number:** This type is for all numerical data that will be used in calculations, except currency (which has its own data type). Actually, Number is several data types under one heading. When you select Number as a data type in the Design view of the table, you go to the Field Size field at the top of the General tab. When you select the drop-down arrow, you get the following options: Byte, Integer, Long

Integer, Single, Double, Replication ID, and Decimal. Probably the most commonly used field sizes of the Number data type are Long Integer and Double. Long Integer should be selected if the numbers are whole numbers that do not have any non-zeros to the right of the decimal point. Double should be selected if decimal numbers need to be stored in that field.

- **Date/Time:** Another data type often used in calculations is Date/Time. To record the time that certain events occur is among the more important uses of this data type. Recording dates and times enables you to compare data by time durations, be it months, years, or another unit. In the business world, the date field can be crucial to analysis, especially in identifying seasonal trends or year-over-year comparisons.
- **Currency:** A special calculation data type, Currency is ideal for storing all data that represents amounts of money.
- **AutoNumber:** This data type is actually a Long Integer that is automatically and sequentially created for each new record added to a table. The AutoNumber can be one mechanism by which you can uniquely identify each individual record in a table. You will not enter data into this field.
- **Yes/No:** There are situations where the data that needs to be represented is in a simple Yes/No format. Although you could use the Text data type for creating a True/False field, it is much more intuitive to use the Access native data type for this purpose.
- **OLE Object:** This data type is not encountered very often in data analysis. It is used when the field must store a binary file, such as a picture or sound file.
- **Hyperlink:** When you need to store an address to a web site, this is the preferred data type.
- **Attachment:** This data type is new to Access. When you set a field to the Attachment type, you can attach images, spreadsheet files, documents, charts, and other types of supported files to the records in your database. You can also configure the field to view and edit attached files.

Before Creating a Table

Before you begin creating a table, there are some questions that need answering:

- What is the name of the table?
- What is the entity for which you would like to collect and store data?
- What are the names and types of columns or fields?
- Which attributes of this particular entity do you need to record / store?
- What are the appropriate data types of these fields?
- How can you identify each instance of the entity uniquely?

Keep in mind that to take full advantage of Access, you may have to split data that was previously stored in one large dataset into separate tables. For example, think of a flat-file list of invoice details in Excel. Typically, this list would repeat Invoice Header information for each individual detail of that invoice. In order to eliminate as much of the duplicate data as possible, you would divide the single list into two logical parts; InvoiceHeaders and InvoiceDetails. Each unique Invoice will be listed only once in the InvoiceHeader table. All of the details for that invoice will be in the InvoiceDetails table. Given this structure, Access will be able to recognize a relationship between the two tables.

Creating a Table with Design View

Access provides several methods for creating a table. The ideal way to create a table in Access is with the Design view. Why? The Design view allows for a compact work area so you can add fields, reposition fields, and assign attributes easily.

Imagine that the Human Resources department asks you to create a simple list of employees in Access. To create a table in the Design view, go to the application ribbon and select the Create tab and then the Table Design button. This opens an empty table called Table1 in Design view.

Adding Fields

The idea here is to create a list of fields that describe employee attributes. Among the more common attributes in this situation are the following: EmployeeNumber, FirstName, LastName, Address, City, State, Zip, and HourlyWage. You begin by entering the names of the columns going down the list. When you have entered all of the required column names, your dialog box should look like Figure 2-5.

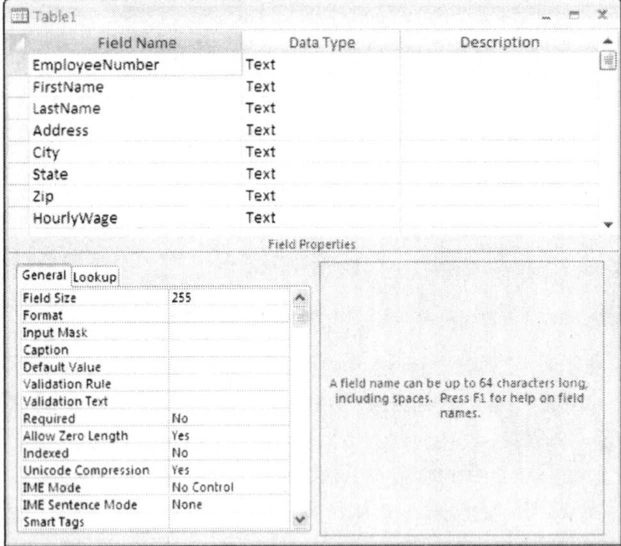

Figure 2-5: Enter the column names you want to see in your table.

Adjusting Data Types

As you entered the field names, the data types defaulted to the most common data type, Text. You now want to set the data type for each field or at least change the data type of each non-text field.

Choosing the correct data type for the first field, EmployeeNumber, may be initially confusing. With the word *Number* in the field, you might think that Number would be the logical choice for the data type. Actually, the rule of thumb is that if the field will not be used in a calculation, it is best to set its data type to Text. Because there is no logical reason to perform a calculation on an employee's EmployeeNumber, the EmployeeNumber data type should remain Text. Another reason for using the Text data type for the field EmployeeNumber is that there could be a need to use alphabetic or other characters in the field.

As you go through the field names, it should be fairly obvious that you will want to set all of the fields to Text except for HourlyWage. This field will almost certainly be used in calculations, and it will represent a monetary value, so you should change the data type to Currency.

At this point, your Design view should look similar to Figure 2-6.

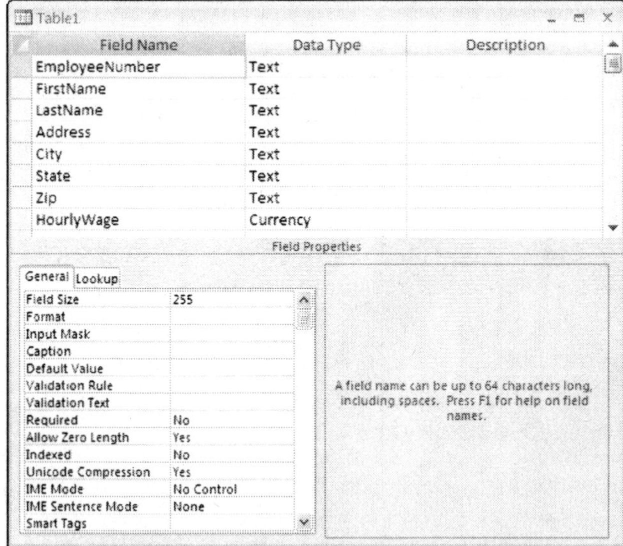

Figure 2-6: You have created your first table!

Now you can save and name your table. Click the Office Icon and select Save As. This opens the Save As dialog box where you will give your newly created table an appropriate name like Employees or Employee-Master. Keep in mind that at this point, this table has no data in it. You can begin entering employee information directly into the table through the Datasheet view. For tables with a small number of records, you can enter your records manually. However, most sets of data are quite large, so other techniques of bringing data into Access are introduced later in the chapter.

NOTE **When you save a table, you may be prompted to set a primary key. Primary keys are explained later. In most cases, Access will try to choose one for you. It's generally good practice to accept Access' recommendation to create a primary key if you do not already have one on mind.**

TRICKS OF THE TRADE: SAVE TIME WITH TABLE TEMPLATES

Access 2007 comes with a number of templates that enable you to get up and running quickly. Although these templates may not fit all of your needs precisely, you can easily do some tweaking to make them yours. To get to the built-in templates, click Table Templates on the Create tab.

Field Properties

When working with data in tables, you may encounter situations that require the data be restricted or adhere to some default specifications in particular columns. You can define these requirements by using the field properties.

The field properties affect how the data is stored and presented, among other things. The list of field properties that are available to you is dependent on the data type chosen for that field. Some field properties are specific to Text fields, and others are specific to Number fields. The field properties can be found in the Design view as illustrated in Figure 2-7. As you click each field, you will see the field properties for that field.

Some of the most important field properties to note are:

- **Field Size:** You encountered the Field Size property before, when working with the Number data type. This property also exists for the common Text data type. It enables you to set a maximum size limit on data entered in that column. For the Text data type, size refers to the length (number of characters and spaces) of the Text data in that column. For example, looking at the Employees table, you see a field for State. Your firm tells you that the names of states should be recorded using their two-letter designation. If you set the field size to 2 for the State column, the user will be unable to type any text that is longer than two characters. So with Access, you are not only able to force a certain data type in a particular column, you can also customize that individual column to accept data only in the rigid format that you specify.
- **Format:** This property enables you to set the precise manner in which Access displays or prints the data that is located in its Tables. As with Field Size, the format available to select depends on the data type of that column. For example, with a Currency field, you can display the data in a form that uses a dollar sign, a Euro sign, or no sign at all. The data itself will not be changed with these settings, just how the data is displayed. Another very useful function of Format is with Date/Time data types. Whether you want to display data in the long format or short format, this property enables you to set that option.

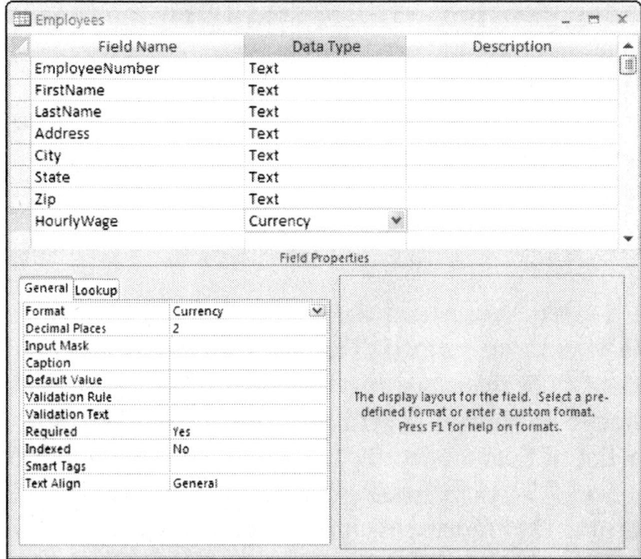

Figure 2-7: You can find the field properties in Design view beneath the field names.

- **Input Mask:** This feature can be useful in data entry situations. Where Format controls how data is displayed, Input Mask controls how data is entered into a particular field. Input Mask is available for the following data types: Text, Number, Date/Time, and Currency. For example, if a user needs to enter a telephone number, Input Mask can create the characters and structure with which you are all familiar. As the user types, the number automatically assumes a phone number format: (###) ###-####.
- **Decimal Places:** In number fields, you can set the number of decimal places to the right of the decimal point that will be recorded. There is an Auto setting, which defers to the Format setting to determine the correct number of places. Apart from Auto, you are able to select 0 to 15 for the number of decimal places.
- **Default Value:** An important database concept, the default value can help save time in the data entry process. The default value is automatically placed in that column every time a new record is added. Defaults can be overridden, so it is not forcing your column to have only that particular value.

- **Required:** Another important property, Required simply forces a user to enter some value, using the proper data type, in the designated field. A new record will not be added if the Required field is not properly filled. As with Input Mask, this property is an excellent mechanism for asserting more control over the data entry process.

Primary Key

Earlier, when designing a table, you asked three questions to determine just how your new table was to be created. The third question specified that you need a way to identify or reference every record. There needs to be some unique text or number column that will have no duplicate values. One example of this is a list of Social Security numbers. Each person has one and only one unique Social Security number. By definition, you cannot have a Social Security number that represents two people. This unique column is what you call a *primary key*, and it is the mechanism by which you relate different tables to each other.

To set the primary key, right-click on the chosen field and select Primary Key. When you set it, Access automatically determines whether that particular field has any null (or blank) values or duplicate data (data duplicating in multiple records for a single field). If there are blanks or duplicates, Access informs you with an error message. You must fill in the blanks with unique values and remove any duplicates if that column is indeed to become the primary key for the table.

TIP **Access provides its own automatic primary key with the AutoNumber data type. The AutoNumber simply increments one for each record added, so there will be no duplicates. However, it is preferable to use actual data for a primary key and not just some number that indicates the records position in a table.**

If every Employee has a unique Employee number, that is ideal for a primary key. If you have a situation where there is no unique single column, consider using a combination of columns that together make up a unique record. You can set multiple columns to be the primary key; this is called a *compound key*. This has the effect of combining separate columns to represent a single, unique value.

TRICKS OF THE TRADE: SORTING AND FILTERING FOR ON-THE-FLY ANALYSIS

There is inherent functionality within Access that enables you to sort and filter the contents of your tables on-the-fly. With this functionality, you can perform quick, impromptu data analysis with just a few clicks of the mouse.

With Access 2007, the sorting and filtering functionality has an Excel feel to it. To get a sense of what this means, open a table in the Datasheet view and select the column you want to sort or filter. Then click the drop-down arrow next to that column's field name.

For example, if you wanted to find any employee with the last name of Pitirsen, you could click the drop-down arrow under the Last_Name field, select Text Filters, and then select Equals as demonstrated in Figure 2-8. This opens a Custom Filter dialog box where you can simply enter the name that you are filtering.

Click here to activate the Sorting and Filtering menu

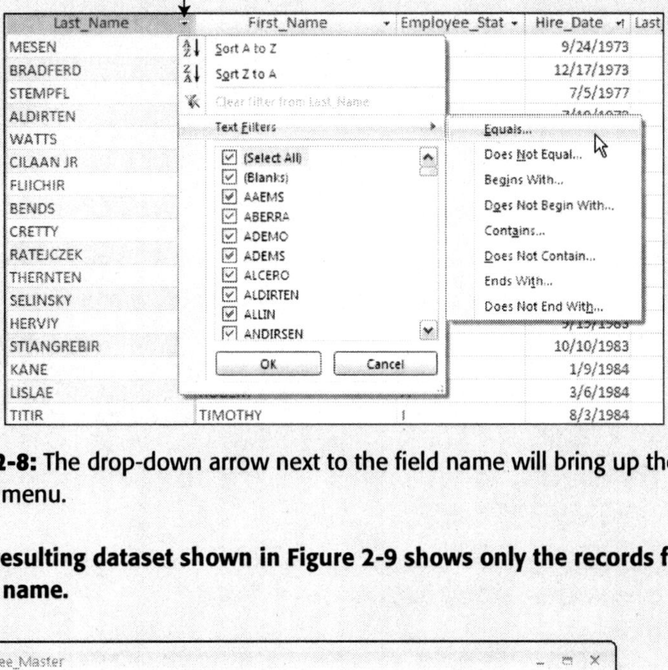

Figure 2-8: The drop-down arrow next to the field name will bring up the sorting and filtering menu.

The resulting dataset shown in Figure 2-9 shows only the records for the filtered name.

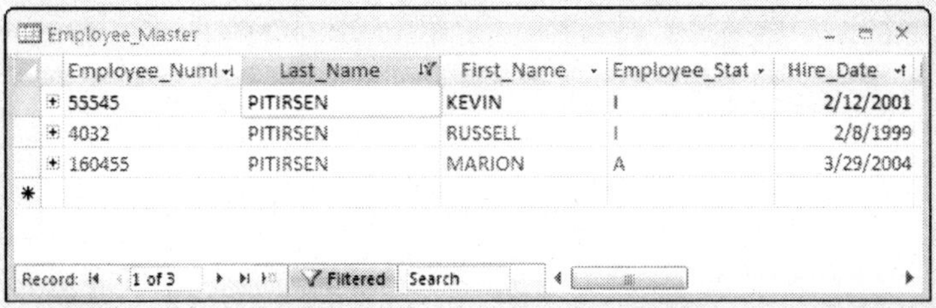

Figure 2-9: There are three employees with the last name of "Pitirsen".

To remove the filter, simply click the dropdown arrow next to the filtered column's field name and select Clear Filter from *x*, where *x* equals the field name.

Getting Data into Access

Now that you have covered tables, you are ready to bring data from outside sources into Access. Apart from creating a table from scratch and manually entering the data, the two main methods for bringing data into Access are importing and linking.

Importing

With importing, you are making a copy of the data and filling a newly created table with the copied data. After importing, the data is disconnected from the source from which it was imported. If any future changes are made to the outside source, they will not be reflected in the Access data. This is also true in the other direction, in that changes to your Access data will have no affect on the original source. After importing a table, it is common to treat that Access data as the true data source. Any updating, appending, or deleting will be done to the Access data. Then when it is time to analyze the data, you can be sure it reflects the latest, most accurate version of that data.

Linking

When you link a table to Access, you are creating a pointer to another data source. When the Access database is opened, it establishes links to its outside data source and displays the data as if it were a regular local Access table. However, linked data does not reside in Access. The data is physically located on another computer, server, or other source. If you change the data in the Access table, the true data source will reflect that change. If you change the original data source, when you reopen your linked table, those changes will be reflected.

Things to Remember About Importing Data

Whether you choose importing or linking data can depend on the situation. When you import data, it resides directly in the Access file, so operations on that data perform much more quickly. With linked tables, you can be dependant on the speed of the connection with the data source or the speed of the database engine at the other end.

An important point to remember is that when importing data you can select to create a new table or import your data into an existing table. If you choose to create a new table, Access makes a copy of the data to import and then attempts to determine the column names and field data types. Access may make an incorrect assumption about the data type, but you can go back and make the necessary changes. If you choose to import data into an existing table, you must make sure that the data types of the fields are compatible. If you attempt to import a text string into a number field, an error will occur.

WARNING **It's important to remember that Access does not let go of disk space on its own. This means that as time passes all the file space taken up by the data you imported will be held by your Access file, regardless of whether the data is actually still there. In that light, it's critical that you perform a compact -and-repair operation on your Access database regularly to ensure that your database does not grow to an unmanageable size or, even worse, become corrupted. To compact and repair your database, click the Office icon and select Manage → Compact and Repair Database.**

Importing Data from an Excel Spreadsheet

You can import data from a wide variety of sources into Access tables: Excel spreadsheets, text files, or other database tables. Access provides a set of easy-to-use Import wizards that will guide you through the process of importing data.

In this example, you will import data from an Excel workbook provided with the sample files for this book.

1. Go to the application ribbon and select the External Data tab.
2. Click the Excel icon in the Import group as illustrated in Figure 2-10.
3. Select the Excel file containing the data you want to import. In this case, select the Excel file called Employee_Master2. Choose the selection next to Import the source data into a new table in the current database, and then click the OK button. This activates the Import Spreadsheet Wizard.
4. Go through each screen of the Import Spreadsheet Wizard, answering the questions posed and clicking Next.

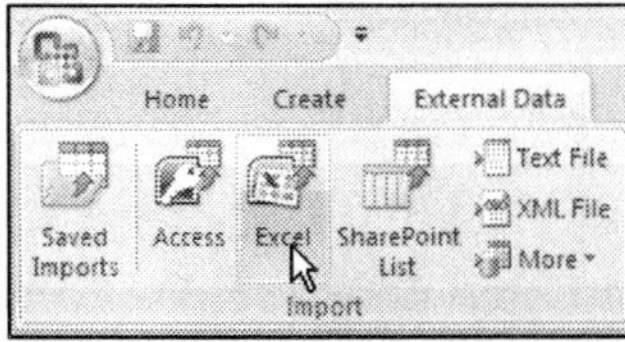

Figure 2-10: Import data from an Excel spreadsheet.

When you step through the entire Wizard, you have an Access table that contains the same data as in the source Excel file.

There are a couple of things worth noting about the Import Spreadsheet Wizard. The wizard enables you to specify the first line of the dataset as the column headings. As long as you are importing a properly formatted Excel file, this option can save time. Another extremely useful feature is the ability to select a column to serve as the primary key of the table. The wizard also offers to create a primary key adding an AutoNumber field.

NOTE **If you select a column to serve as the primary key, the Import Spreadsheet Wizard will perform a test on the column, to ensure against blank entries or duplicate values. If there are blanks or duplicate values in the chosen column, the wizard will inform you that it cannot set that column to primary key and the table is imported anyway.**

Importing Data from a Text File

Similar to the data imported from spreadsheets, the data in text files must be in a consistent format for the wizard to extract the information correctly. Typically, the data in text files is delimited (separated) by commas. Access will properly interpret this and separate the data located between the commas into their appropriate fields. Usually someone in I.T. will prepare a text file of data for the analyst, or it can be the output of a mainframe application.

Understanding the Relational Database Concept

Now that you have covered tables and brought some data into the database, you can turn your focus to one of the more useful features of Access: relationships. Access relationships are the mechanism by which separate tables are related to each other. The idea behind relationships is the Relational Database Concept. Before you begin to directly create relationships between Access tables, take a closer look at the concept behind relational database systems.

Why Is This Concept Important?

This concept is important because it is the theoretical framework from which most database programs are designed. If you want to understand just how databases work, you need to understand this concept. You are learning Access, among other reasons, because the data storage and data manipulation capacity of Excel is insufficient for your analysis needs. The concept that dictates just how data is stored and structured is the Relational Database Concept. Even though you may have no intention of becoming a database administrator, having some understanding about how the data that you would like to analyze has been stored and structured will increase your performance and productivity. It will also promote better communication between you and the I.T. department and the database administrator, since now you will be able to understand at least some of the vocabulary of the database language.

Excel and the Flat-File Format

Before you cover the proper techniques for storing data in Access, examine the common data storage scenario that led to the problems that the concept attempts to address. Even if they are not aware of the term flat-file format, most Excel users are very adept at working with data that has been stored in it. In fact, most people in general are familiar with the concept because it is used in so many things that you encounter every day. The flat-file, of course, organizes data into rows and columns.

There are data analysis scenarios that are not terribly complex in which a flat-file representation of the data to be analyzed is adequate. However, most data-analysis scenarios require analyzing data that is much more multi-dimensional. One of the main reasons that the flat-file can prove inadequate is that it is two-dimensional. Real-world business data rarely falls into a convenient, two-dimensional format. Of course, it can be forced into that format by the Excel guru who wants all analysis to fit into the spreadsheet. Take a look at a typical example of a flat-file. Figure 2-11 shows a typical flat-file list of invoices.

Customer_Name	Address1	City	State	Invoice_Number	Invoice_Date	Sales_Amount
CORRUL Corp.	13 HUSSLUY MALL RD	CARROLLTON	GA	27812618	12/16/2004	$140.09
CORRUL Corp.	13 HUSSLUY MALL RD	CARROLLTON	GA	26507793	7/8/2004	$112.39
CORRUL Corp.	13 HUSSLUY MALL RD	CARROLLTON	GA	25251995	1/28/2004	$112.39
CORRUL Corp.	13 HUSSLUY MALL RD	CARROLLTON	GA	26507793	7/8/2004	$140.09
CORRUL Corp.	13 HUSSLUY MALL RD	CARROLLTON	GA	26940942	9/3/2004	$112.39
CORRUL Corp.	13 HUSSLUY MALL RD	CARROLLTON	GA	26940942	9/3/2004	$140.09
CORRUL Corp.	13 HUSSLUY MALL RD	CARROLLTON	GA	27378702	10/29/2004	$112.39
CORRUL Corp.	13 HUSSLUY MALL RD	CARROLLTON	GA	27378702	10/29/2004	$140.09
CORRUL Corp.	13 HUSSLUY MALL RD	CARROLLTON	GA	27812618	12/16/2004	$112.39
CORRUL Corp.	13 HUSSLUY MALL RD	CARROLLTON	GA	26078955	5/12/2004	$112.39
CORRUL Corp.	13 HUSSLUY MALL RD	CARROLLTON	GA	25656619	3/25/2004	$140.09
CORRUL Corp.	13 HUSSLUY MALL RD	CARROLLTON	GA	25251995	1/28/2004	$140.09
CORRUL Corp.	13 HUSSLUY MALL RD	CARROLLTON	GA	25656619	3/25/2004	$112.39
CORRUL Corp.	13 HUSSLUY MALL RD	CARROLLTON	GA	26078955	5/12/2004	$140.09
ANYTHA Corp.	4556 CUNSTATASAUN F	ATLANTA	GA	27314610	10/20/2004	$194.05
ANYTHA Corp.	4556 CUNSTATASAUN F	ATLANTA	GA	27535362	11/16/2004	$194.05
ANYTHA Corp.	4556 CUNSTATASAUN F	ATLANTA	GA	27096178	9/28/2004	$194.05

Figure 2-11: Data is usually stored in an Excel spreadsheet using the flat-file format.

In order to get the customer information for each invoice, there are several fields for customer-specific information such as customer name, address, city, and so on. Since most firms sell to customers more than once, for each invoice the same customer information has to be repeated. Duplicate information is one of the main drawbacks of the flat-file format.

What is wrong with duplicate data? Initially, the duplicate data may not appear to be a potential source of future problems, but upon further examination, you discover the shortcomings. First is the size of the file. Duplicate data wastes space, both on the computer hard drive, where the file is stored, and in the computer's memory, where the data resides when it is being used. Although the enormous amount of memory that is standard with today's machines goes a long way to handling these demands, you are wasting valuable computer space and resources. The duplicate information is not valuable. In fact, it leads to problems.

One of the main problems that can arise from too much duplicate data occurs when that data needs to be updated. In the previous example, there are several invoices for CORRUL Corp. You can also see that you have to repeat the information about the customer for each instance of an invoice. Imagine a scenario where the customer information might change. For example, the customer acquires new office space, and you want to reflect this change of location in your data. Looking at the preceding list, you see that you will have to update the change in several different places. You need to ensure that every invoice will correctly map back to its relevant customer information.

Although there are excellent functions that find and replace data in Excel, there is still a danger that you might not make all of the updates correctly. Whenever you are changing duplicate information, there is always the risk of introducing unintentional errors. This could significantly affect your data analysis. For example, imagine that customer CORRUL Corp. moved not just to a different address, but a different city. Figure 2-12 demonstrates how easy it is to incorrectly update the data.

Customer_Name	Address1	City	State	Invoice_Number	Invoice_Date	Sales_Amount
CORRUL Corp.	4120 DUNNALLY AVE S\	ATLANTA	GA	27812618	12/16/2004	$140.09
CORRUL Corp.	4121 DUNNALLY AVE S\	ATLANTA	GA	26507793	7/8/2004	$112.39
CORRUL Corp.	4122 DUNNALLY AVE S\	ATLANTA	GA	25251995	1/28/2004	$112.39
CORRUL Corp.	4123 DUNNALLY AVE S\	ATLANTA	GA	26507793	7/8/2004	$140.09
CORRUL Corp.	4124 DUNNALLY AVE S\	ATLANTA	GA	26940942	9/3/2004	$112.39
CORRUL Corp.	4125 DUNNALLY AVE S\	ATLANTA	GA	26940942	9/3/2004	$140.09
CORRUL Corp.	4126 DUNNALLY AVE S\	ATLANTA	GA	27378702	10/29/2004	$112.39
CORRUL Corp.	4127 DUNNALLY AVE S\	ATLANTA	GA	27378702	10/29/2004	$140.09
CORRUL Corp.	4128 DUNNALLY AVE S\	ATLANTA	GA	27812618	12/16/2004	$112.39
CORRUL Corp.	4129 DUNNALLY AVE S\	ATLANTA	GA	26078955	5/12/2004	$112.39
CORRUL Corp.	4130 DUNNALLY AVE S\	ATLANTA	GA	25656619	3/25/2004	$140.09
CORRUL Corp.	4131 DUNNALLY AVE S\	ATLANTA	GA	25251995	1/28/2004	$140.09
CORRUL Corp.	4132 DUNNALLY AVE S\	ATLANTA	GA	25656619	3/25/2004	$112.39
CORRUL Corp.	13 HUSSLUY MALL RD	CARROLLTON	GA	26078955	5/12/2004	$140.09
ANYTHA Corp.	4556 CUNSTATASAUN I	ATLANTA	GA	27314610	10/20/2004	$194.05
ANYTHA Corp.	4556 CUNSTATASAUN I	ATLANTA	GA	27535362	11/16/2004	$194.05
ANYTHA Corp.	4556 CUNSTATASAUN I	ATLANTA	GA	27096178	9/28/2004	$194.05

Figure 2-12: The last record of CORRUL Corp. was not correctly updated to the new address.

If the City data is not properly updated everywhere, when you attempt a by city filter/analysis, you will not get accurate results. Some of the invoice records could reflect the incorrect state locations of the customer. The attributes of data can and often do change. If these changes are not accurately recorded, your data analysis is providing an incorrect picture of the actual situation.

Splitting Data into Separate Tables

Data must be consistent if analysis is to have any true value in the decision-making process. Duplicate data is the bane of consistent data. If an entity is changed in one place, it must be changed in every place. Would it not be more logical and efficient if you could create the name and information of a customer only once? Would it not be great to simply have some form of customer reference number instead of creating the same customer information repeatedly? Then that customer reference could send you to another list where the information is unique and written once.

This is the idea behind the relational database concept. You have separate, carefully designed, unique lists of data, and you relate them to each other by using their unique identifiers (primary keys).

Excel users may not realize it, but they have made great efforts to make the data on their spreadsheets relational. They use (or overuse) VLOOKUP or HLOOKUP to match data from separate lists that have some data field or key in common. Although much is possible with these functions, they do have their limitations. Besides, the functions are not very intuitive and are trying to solve a problem that Access was designed from the ground up to address. When Excel users use these functions to bring data from separate lists onto a single row, they are emulating a relationship of that data. The problem is that the data has not really been related; it has simply been shown how it could relate to each other in the confines of a particular spreadsheet tab. A different tab may choose to relate the data completely differently.

The problem for the analyst is that if there are relationships between the data that are consistent or even permanent, it is easier to somehow reflect this in a behind-the-scenes representation of the data. Some of the data relationships can be quite complex, and forcing the analyst to remember and manually enforce all of them detracts from analysis and increases the possibility of mistakes.

Foreign Keys

To set relationships between tables, you take a primary key field from one table and use it to relate that entity to records in another table. When the primary key is used in a different table to establish relationships, it is called a *foreign key*. In the TransactionMaster table, there is a Customer_Number field. This relates the records from the primary key field of the same name in the CustomerMaster table, thus making it a foreign key in the TransactionMaster table.

Relationship Types

Three types of relationships can be set in a relational database:

- **One-to-one relationship:** For each record in one table, there is one and only one matching record in a different table. It is as if two tables have the exact same primary key. Typically, data from different tables in a one-to-one relationship will be combined into one table.
- **One-to-many relationship:** For each record in one table, there may be zero, one or many records matching in a separate table. For example, you might have an invoice header table related to an invoice detail table. The invoice header table has a primary key, Invoice Number. The invoice detail table will use the Invoice Number for every record representing a detail of that particular invoice. This is certainly the most common type of relationship you will encounter.
- **Many-to-many relationship:** Used decidedly less often, this relationship cannot be defined in Access without the use of a mapping table. This relationship states that records in both tables can have any number of matching records in the other table.

In the sample database that came with this book, relationships have already been established between the tables. Take a look at some of these relationships to get a better idea of how they can be set and changed. Go to the application ribbon and select the Database Tools tab. Then select Relationships to view the existing relationships for this database. As shown in Figure 2-13, the tables are represented with lines between them signifying the relationships.

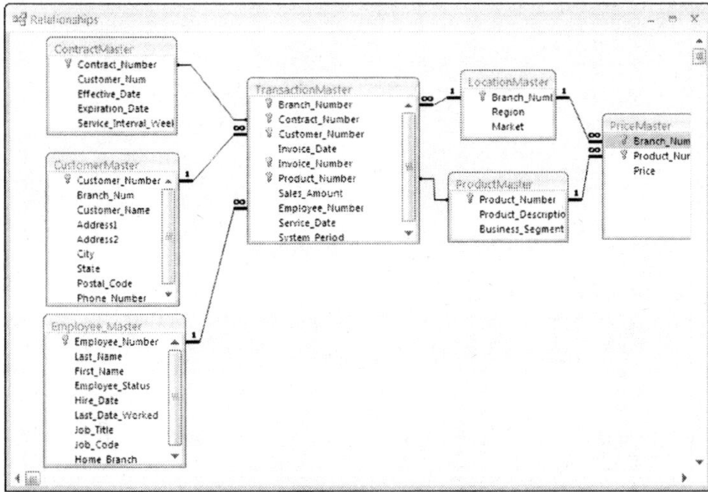

Figure 2-13: A one-to-many relationship between tables can be identified by the infinity symbol on the line connecting the tables.

> **TIP** You may have noticed that some of the objects you see in the figures here seem to have broken free from the tabbed layout. In Access 2007, the default display layout for the various objects in a database is the tabbed documents view. You can easily switch to the classic overlapping windows view by taking the following steps:
>
> 1. Click the Office icon on the upper left-hand corner.
> 2. Click Access Options. This activates the Access Options dialog box.
> 3. Click the Current Database button.
> 4. Select Overlapping Windows in the Application Options section, under Document Window Options.
> 5. Click OK.

In the Relationships window, you can add tables by right-clicking the display and selecting Show Table. After your tables have been added, relationships can be established by dragging one field from one table to a field in another table. This opens the Edit Relationships dialog box, shown in Figure 2-14.

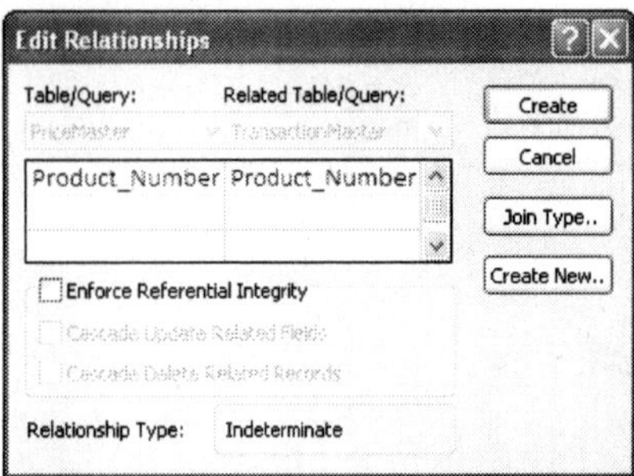

Figure 2-14: Based on the use of primary keys and foreign keys, the Edit Relationships dialog box attempts to guess the kind of relationship that you want to establish.

You can also edit an existing relationship by right-clicking the line connecting the two tables and selecting Edit Relationships.

Referential Integrity

In addition to establishing relationships between tables, you are able to enforce certain rules that guide these relationships. For example, if you have an Invoice table with a Customer_Number foreign key, you will not be able to add an invoice for a customer number that does not exist in the other table. You must add the new customer to the customer table before the new foreign key can be placed in the invoice table. Also, if you attempt to delete a customer from a table when there are matching invoices for that customer, an error will occur. Referential integrity enables you to use Access to maintain the relationships that you have created.

By selecting the Enforce Referential Integrity check box in the Edit Relationships dialog box, you tell Access to first verify that a valid relationship exists between the two tables. Other conditions that need to be met to establish referential integrity are:

- The field that is used to match the two tables must be a primary key in one of those tables.
- The field that is used to match the two tables must be of the same data type.
- After the validity of the relationship has been established, referential integrity will be continuously enforced until switched off.

Cascading Updates and Deletes

The main purpose of referential integrity is two-fold: first, to prevent changing a primary key value for which there are matching foreign key values in a second table, and second, to prevent deleting a primary key value for which there are matching foreign key values. These two rules of referential integrity can be overridden by clicking either Cascade Update Related Fields or Cascade Delete Related Records.

Query Basics

When the data is in Access and the relationships between the tables have been established, you are ready to start analyzing the data. In this section, you are going to focus on what is perhaps the most common type of query: the select query. You will see the concept behind the query and a few examples that illustrate just how easy it is to create queries in Access.

What Is a Query?

By definition, a query is a question. For your purposes, it is a question about the data that is stored in tables. Queries can be exceedingly simple, like asking what all of the data in a table is. Queries can also be quite complex, testing for different criteria, sorting in certain orders, and performing calculations. In Access, there are two main types of queries: select and action. The select query is perhaps the most common type. This query simply asks a question of the data and returns the results. No changes are made to the data whatsoever. You can always run select queries and never worry that the actual data is being altered. The action query actually manipulates and changes the data in a table. The action query can add records, delete records, or change (update) information in existing records.

Creating Your First Select Query

Quite often, when you are working with or analyzing data, it is preferable to work with smaller sections of the data at a time. The tables contain all the records pertaining to a particular entity, but perhaps for your purposes you need to examine a subset of that data. Typically, the subsets are defined by categories or criteria. The select query enables you to determine exactly which records will be returned to you.

If you thought that creating queries required learning a programming language or some other technological hurdle, you are mistaken. Although it is possible to create queries using the programming language of databases (SQL), Access provides a graphical interface that is easy to use and quite user-friendly. This graphical interface has been called the QBE (Query by Example) or QBD (Query by Design) in the past. Now Microsoft calls it the Query Design view. In the Query Design view, tables and columns are visually represented, making it easy to visualize the *question* you would like to ask of the data.

Go up to the application ribbon and select the Create tab. From there, select Query Design. The Show Table dialog box now opens on top of a blank Query Design interface, as shown in Figure 2-15. The white grid area you see in the Query Design view is often called the query grid.

When creating your *question* of the data, the first thing you must determine is from which tables you need to retrieve data. The Show Table dialog box enables the user to select one or more tables. As you can see in Figure 2-15, there are also tabs for Queries and Both. One of the wonderful features of queries is that you are not limited to just querying directly from the table. You can create queries of other queries.

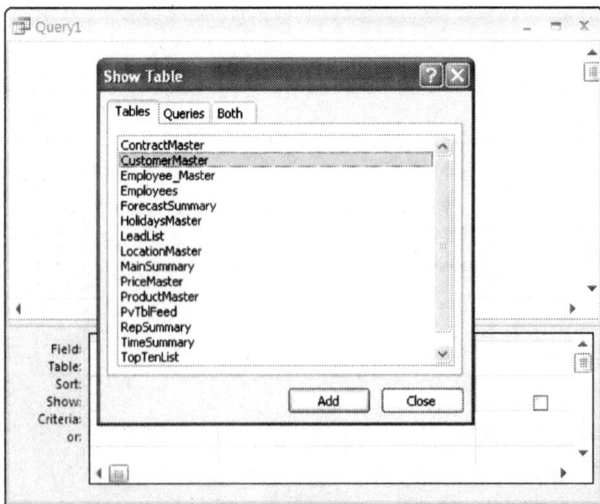

Figure 2-15: The Show Table dialog box enables you to select the tables or queries to add to the Query Design view.

For this first query, select the CustomerMaster table, either by selecting the table in the list and clicking Add or by double-clicking on the table in the list. Now that you have selected the table from which you want to retrieve data, you can close the Show Table dialog box and select the fields of that table that you would like to retrieve.

The Query Design view is divided into two sections. The top half shows the tables or queries from which the query will retrieve data. The bottom half (often called the query grid) shows the fields from which the query will retrieve data. You will notice in Figure 2-16 that the CustomerMaster table shown at the top half of the Query Design view lists all the fields but has an asterisk at the top of the list. The asterisk is the traditional database symbol that means that all fields from that table will be in the output.

For this example, select the following three fields: Branch_Num, Customer_Name, and State. To select fields, you can either double-click the field or click it once and drag it down to the bottom half (the query grid). Each field that you add to the query grid will be included in the output of the query. Figure 2-17 shows you how your query should look after selecting the output fields.

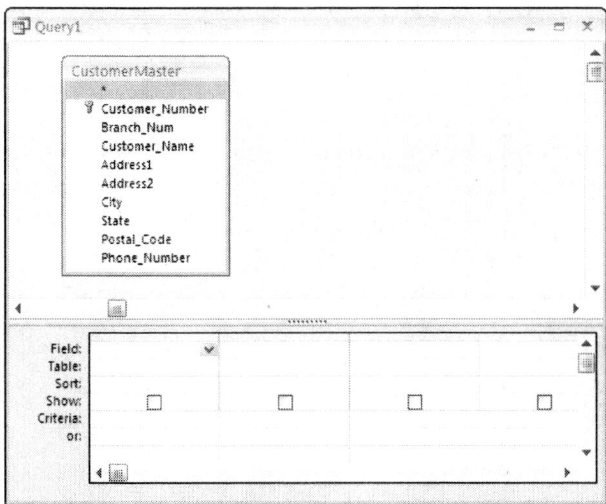

Figure 2-16: The Query Design view enables you to query all fields easily.

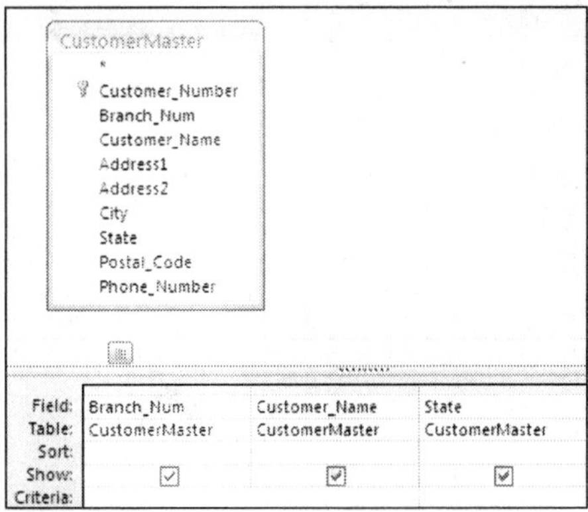

Figure 2-17: The lower half, or query grid, shows the output fields of the select query.

At this point, you have all you need to run the query. To run the query, click the Run button located on the Design tab. As you can see in Figure 2-18, the output from a query looks similar to a regular table after it is open.

NOTE **To return to the Query Design view, simply click View on the Home tab and then select Design View.**

Sorting Query Results

Now examine how you can sort the results of this query. Just as you sorted in Excel, you are going to select a column and choose between an ascending sort and a descending sort. In the query grid, notice the Sort row of the grid. This is where you can select either one or multiple sort columns. If you select multiple sort columns, the query will sort the results in order of left to right.

Branch_Num	Customer_Name	State
301301	CORRUL Corp.	GA
301301	ANYTHA Corp.	GA
301301	RHFUSU Corp.	GA
301301	MUUZEO Corp.	GA
301301	NABCO Corp.	GA
301301	UNESTU Corp.	GA
301301	ALTUC Corp.	GA
301301	TORAEA Corp.	GA
301301	CARTUM Corp.	GA
301301	ATLANT Corp.	GA
301301	HALLSG Corp.	GA
301301	ATLANT Corp.	GA
301301	VALCAN Corp.	GA
301301	PRATT Corp.	GA
301301	PLANTU Corp.	GA

Figure 2-18: The Datasheet view of a query shows the results of the query.

Go to the State column and click your mouse on the Sort section. As shown in Figure 2-19, a drop-down box appears, enabling you to select either Ascending or Descending for that particular column.

Select Ascending and rerun the query. When you ran the query before, the states were in no particular order. After setting the sort order of the State column to ascending, the query output simply looks better and more professionally formatted, as seen in Figure 2-20.

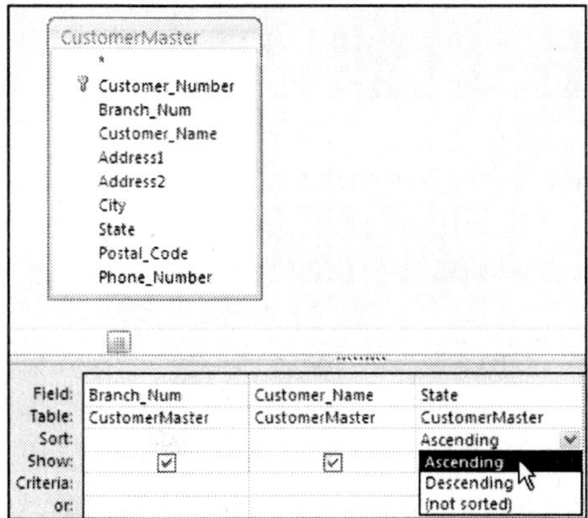

Figure 2-19: The sort order options for a column are provided by the Query Design view.

Branch_Num	Customer_Name	State
601310	LUUNOR Corp.	AL
601310	CORTUK Corp.	AL
601310	PHUNAX Corp.	AL
601310	PAKECN Corp.	AL
601310	CALLUW Corp.	AL
601310	CATYOF Corp.	AL
601310	TRACKS Corp.	AL
601310	GABBUN Corp.	AL
601310	GUUSGA Corp.	AL
601310	TALOPU Corp.	AL
601310	BORBUA Corp.	AL
601310	PLANTA Corp.	AL
601310	SRMOGG Corp.	AL
601310	BAG40T Corp.	AL
601310	EABAQN Corp.	AL

Figure 2-20: The results of the query are now sorted in ascending order by the State field.

Filtering Query Results

Next, you'll examine how you can filter the query output so that you retrieve only the specific records to analyze. As in Excel, in Access this filter is also called Criteria. Note the Criteria row in the query grid. This is where you will enter the value or values for which you would like to query. When entering a value in the Criteria section, all records that match it are returned in the query output. When entering text, you must enclose the text string with quotation marks. You can either place them there yourself or type your text and click another part of the query grid. Access then automatically places quotation marks around your criteria if the field you are filtering is a text field.

In the example demonstrated in Figure 2-21, your manager wants to see the list of customers from California. Since California is designated by the abbreviation CA in the table, that is exactly what you will enter in the Criteria row of the State column.

After you run the query, you will notice that fewer records are returned. This is obvious from looking at the Record Selector at the bottom of the query output window. A quick scan of the results verifies that indeed only records with CA in the State column were returned, as shown in Figure 2-22.

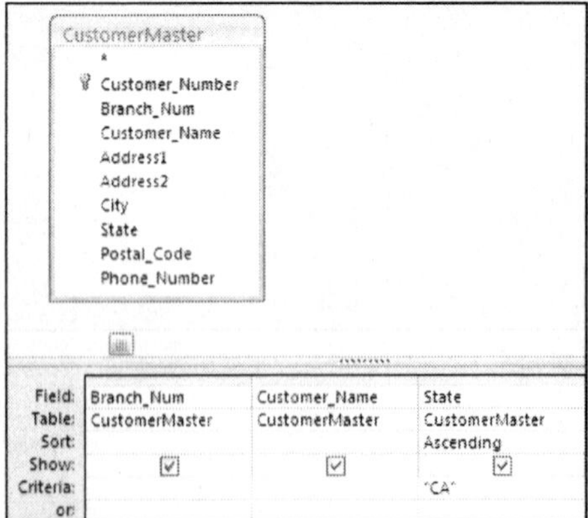

Figure 2-21: The Criteria section is where you type in a value for which you want to filter the data.

Branch_Num	Customer_Name	State
701717	SULUSZ Corp.	CA
501717	HULAXH Corp.	CA
501717	DANRED Corp.	CA
501718	FUDUSA Corp.	CA
701715	CALSAN Corp.	CA
701715	ANTUS Corp.	CA
701715	HORRAS Corp.	CA
201717	LAMUTA Corp.	CA
501717	CATYOF Corp.	CA
501717	DAOLAC Corp.	CA
201717	TUQQAA Corp.	CA
803717	RUTSI Corp.	CA
201717	JUSDAN Corp.	CA
701717	SAORUZ Corp.	CA
701715	MEESE Corp.	CA

Figure 2-22: The results of the query will be all records that match the criteria.

TIP **You can sort and filter query results just as if they were a Table. Simply click the drop-down arrow next to each of the column headings to active the sorting and filtering context menu.**

Querying Multiple Tables

Next you'll see how you can perform a query on multiple tables. Remember that you split your data into separtate tables. You used Relationships to define the logical relationships between the data. Now you will query from the tables based on the relationships that were established.

For example, say you want to see the customer transactions from California. A quick examination of the TransactionMaster reveals that there is no State field on which you can filter. However, you see that there is a Customer_Number field. In your Access relationships, you defined a one-to-many relationship between the Customer_Number primary key in CustomerMaster and the Customer_Number foreign key in the TransactionMaster table. Another way to think of it is filtering the TransactionMaster indirectly by filtering a table that is related to it and using those results to determine which TransactionMaster records to return.

In the query that you already have opened, add the TransactionMaster table so you can include some fields from that table in your query output. Right-click the top half of the Query Design view and select Show Table. Double-click the TransactionMaster table to add it to the Query Design view. You will notice that the previously established relationship is automatically represented, as shown in Figure 2-23. You can see the one-to-many relationship, indicating possible multiple records in TransactionMaster for each individual customer in the CustomerMaster table.

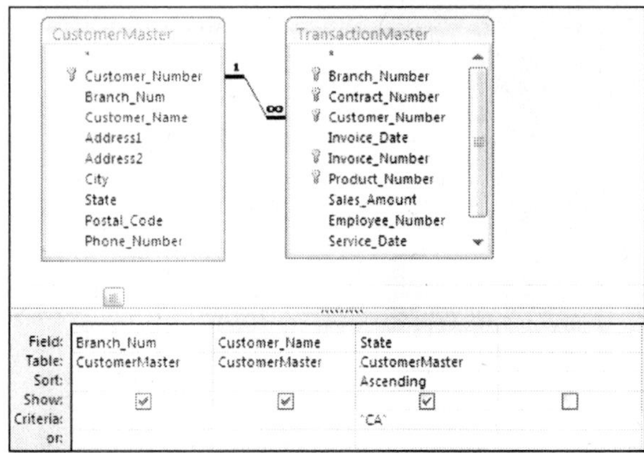

Figure 2-23: The relationship between the two tables is visually represented.

You must now select the fields from your newly added table, which you need to appear in the query output. Examine the individual invoices and invoice amounts that were issued to customers from California. Select the following three fields from the TransactionMaster table: Invoice_Number, Invoice_Date, and Sales_Amount. As you can see in Figure 2-24, the field names from the two tables are brought together in the query grid.

As you can see in Figure 2-25, you now have the invoice data matched with its appropriate customer data. Although there is repeating data, as with your flat-file examples, there is a significant difference. The repeating data is being read from a single source, the CustomerMaster table. If a value were to change in the CustomerMaster table, that changed value would be repeated in your query results. You have overcome potential update errors inherent with duplicate data.

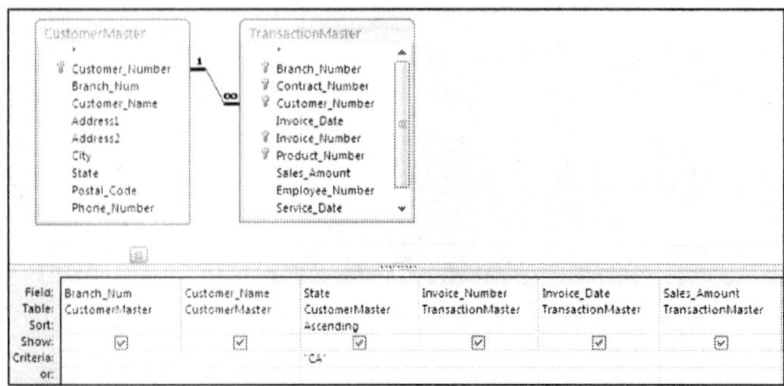

Figure 2-24: Fields from two tables are brought together to create a new dataset.

Branch_Num	Customer_Name	State	Invoice_Number	Invoice_Date	Sales_Amount
806708	NATAUN Corp.	CA	26043638	4/30/2004	$154.55
501717	FULAXE Corp.	CA	27482724	11/22/2004	$181.28
501717	FULAXE Corp.	CA	27043671	9/20/2004	$181.28
501717	FULAXE Corp.	CA	26611302	7/26/2004	$181.28
501717	FULAXE Corp.	CA	26073101	5/31/2004	$181.28
501717	FULAXE Corp.	CA	25599140	3/17/2004	$181.28
501717	FULAXE Corp.	CA	1919209	1/16/2004	$181.28
701715	FLUSAN Corp.	CA	27592015	11/23/2004	$185.27
701715	LUTSCH Corp.	CA	2395208	10/8/2004	$175.00
701715	FLUSAN Corp.	CA	26935083	8/31/2004	$185.27
701715	LUTSCH Corp.	CA	25473175	2/19/2004	$175.00
701715	FLUSAN Corp.	CA	26501868	7/7/2004	$185.27
701715	FLUSAN Corp.	CA	26288243	6/9/2004	$185.27
701715	FLUSAN Corp.	CA	26073026	5/17/2004	$185.27

Figure 2-25: The results of the query have successfully brought together and matched data from two separate tables.

Refining the Query

You can narrow your results down even further by filtering the query results according to a certain date. As you can see, there are several rows of criteria cells. These enable you to enter multiple criteria from which to filter. One thing to keep in mind is that each separate criteria row functions as its own separate set of criteria. Take a look at how this works.

Click the Criteria cell in the Invoice_Date column and type **4/20/2004**. When you click outside that cell, you will notice that number signs (#) now surround the date as shown in Figure 2-26. When running this query, only results matching the two criteria (State = 'CA' and Invoice_Date = 4/20/2004) are returned.

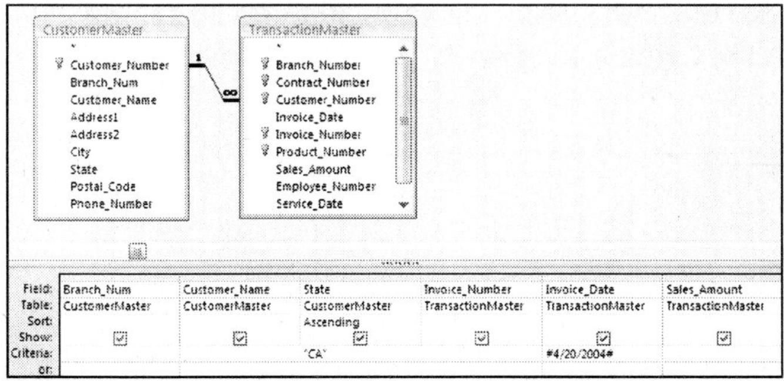

Figure 2-26: The number signs that surround the date identify the criteria as being a Date/Time data type.

Now look at using multiple criteria for a single field. For example, say you want to bring in invoices for the data 11/19/2004 as well as 4/20/2004. You will want to add the new criteria line below the existing criteria. This will have the effect of testing the records for either one criteria or the other.

Since you want to limit your query to only results from California, you must retype **"CA"** on your new Criteria line. If you do not do that, the query will think that you want all invoices from California on 4/20/2004 or invoices from all states on 11/19/2004. The criteria lines will be evaluated individually. Add "CA" to the state column under the existing "CA", as shown in Figure 2-27.

After running the query, you can see your results have been refined even further. You have only those invoices from California that were issued on November 19, 2004 and April 20, 2004. To use multiple criteria in a query, you are not limited to using the separate criteria lines. By using operators, you can place your multiple criteria on the same line.

Using Operators in Queries

You can filter for multiple criteria on any given field by using operators. The following operators enable you to combine multiple values in different logical contexts so you can create complex queries:

- **Or:** Either condition can be true. Multiple criteria values for one field can either be separated on different criteria lines or combined in one cell with the use of the `Or` operator. For example, using your query you can filter for both California and Colorado by typing **"CA" or "CO"** in the Criteria field.

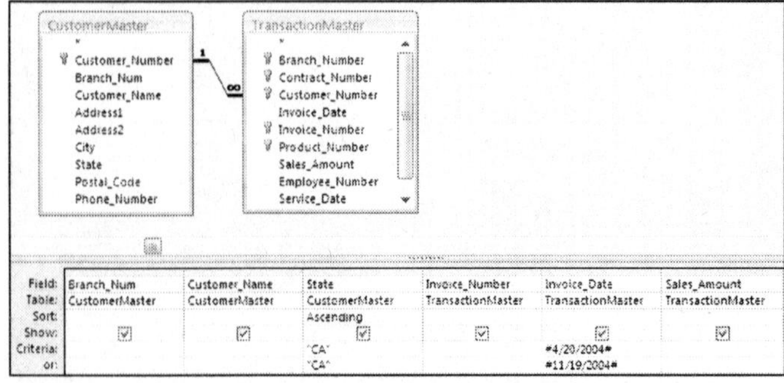

Figure 2-27: Each line of criteria will be evaluated separately.

- **Between:** Tests for a range of values. For example, using your query you can filter for all invoices between 4/20/2004 and 11/19/2004 instead of testing just for those particular dates by typing **Between #4/20/2004# and #11/19/2004#** in the Criteria field.
- **Like:** Tests for string expressions matching a pattern. For example, you can filter for all records with a customer number that begins with the number 147 by typing **Like "147*"** in the Criteria field. The asterisk is the wild card character, which can signify any character or combination of characters.
- **In:** Similar to `Or`. Tests for all records that have values contained in parentheses. For example, you can filter for both California and Colorado by typing **In ("CA", "CO")** in the Criteria field.
- **Not:** Opposite of writing a value in Criteria. All records not matching that value will be returned. For example, you can filter for all states except California by typing **Not "CA"** in the Criteria field.
- **Is Null:** Filters all records that have the database value Null in that field.
- **=, <, >, <=, >=, and <>:** The traditional mathematical operators allow you to construct complex criteria for fields that are used in calculations.

For example, suppose you want to further refine your query so that only invoice amounts over $200 will be returned in the results. As shown in Figure 2-28, use the greater-than operator to filter the Sales_Amount.

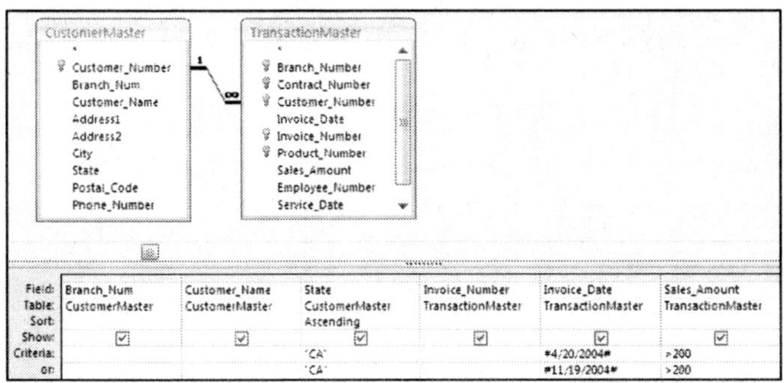

Figure 2-28: You can use operators to test for ranges of values.

After running the query, you can see that you narrowed your results down to just six records. These are the only records that match the multiple criteria that were designated in the query grid. Figure 2-29 shows the query results.

Branch_Num	Customer_Name	State	Invoice_Number	Invoice_Date	Sales_Amount
701717	VOFBC Corp.	CA	27592107	11/19/2004	$221.39
201717	ANAQAE Corp.	CA	27537772	11/19/2004	$214.17
701717	LECKHU Corp.	CA	27537829	11/19/2004	$221.39
501718	FUDUSA Corp.	CA	25914426	4/20/2004	$209.92
201717	ORRUWT Corp.	CA	27537779	11/19/2004	$214.17
501718	DUWHOM Corp.	CA	25914420	4/20/2004	$204.78

Figure 2-29: Here are your query results.

TRICKS OF THE TRADE: OUTPUT TO EXCEL WITHOUT SAVING ANYWHERE

After creating a query, you can select a set of records and quickly bring those to Excel without the need to save the query or create a temporary file.

First, you select the rows or columns you are interested in. Next, you click the highlighted square around the chosen cells (as demonstrated in Figure 2-30), and you drag them directly onto an Excel spreadsheet.

Query1

Branch_Num	Customer_Name	State	Invoice_Number	Invoice_Date	Sales_Amount
701717	VOFBC Corp.	CA	27592107	11/19/2004	$221.39
201717	ANAQAE Corp.	CA	27537772	11/19/2004	$214.17
701717	LECKHU Corp.	CA	27537829	11/19/2004	$221.39
501718	FUDUSA Corp.	CA	25914426	4/20/2004	$209.92
201717	ORRUWT Corp.	CA	27537779	11/19/2004	$214.17
501718	DUWHOM Corp.	CA	25914420	4/20/2004	$204.78
*					

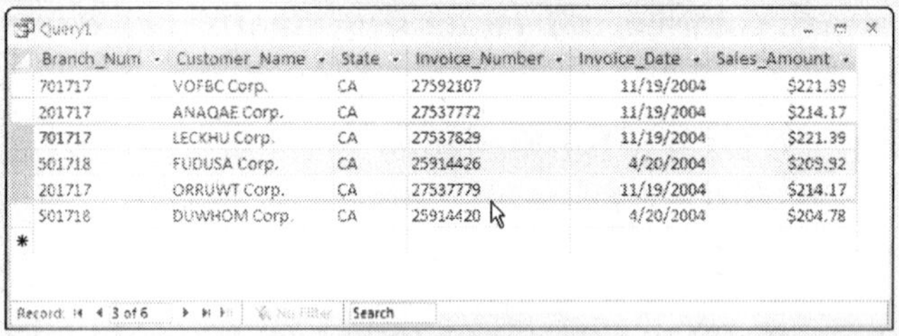

Record: 3 of 6 No Filter Search

Figure 2-30: Clicking on the orange border around a set of selected cells enables you to drag them directly into an Excel spreadsheet.

The data you selected is output to a spreadsheet with labels. Figure 2-31 demonstrates how this looks. This nifty trick enables you to do some on-the-fly analysis between Access and Excel without saving a gaggle of temporary files.

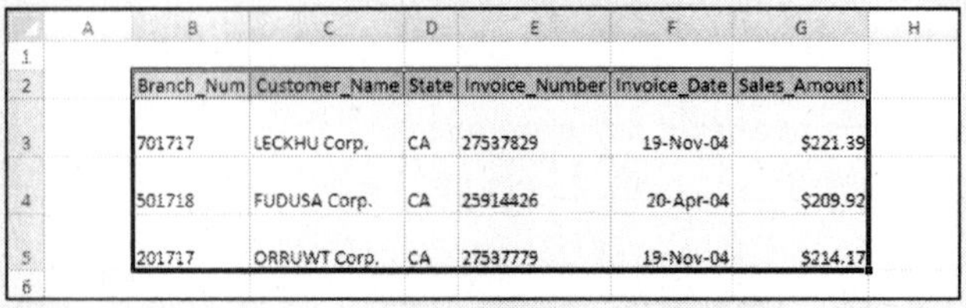

	A	B	C	D	E	F	G	H
1								
2		Branch_Num	Customer_Name	State	Invoice_Number	Invoice_Date	Sales_Amount	
3		701717	LECKHU Corp.	CA	27537829	19-Nov-04	$221.39	
4		501718	FUDUSA Corp.	CA	25914426	20-Apr-04	$209.92	
5		201717	ORRUWT Corp.	CA	27537779	19-Nov-04	$214.17	
6								

Figure 2-31: Your data has been output to Excel!

Exporting Query Results

Now that you have covered the basics of creating queries, you need to be able to export these results to Excel or another format. The simplest way to do this in Access is to right-click the query after it has been saved. Select Export and choose the appropriate file type. The query will take a snapshot of the data and save the results in the requested format.

Summary

The fundamental tools in Access are Tables and Queries. A table is a collection of data concerning a specific type of entity such as customers, branches, transactions, and products. Access enables you to build relationships between your tables and enforce certain rules that guide these relationships. This reduces the chance for error and allows for easy analysis across multiple tables.

A query is a question about the data that is stored in the tables. The results of a query are separate from the data. If the data in the table is changed and the query is run again, you would most often get different results. The most common query is the select query. With a select query, you can extract a dataset or individual data items. You can also utilize the built-in operators to apply filters and sorting to your queries.

CHAPTER

3

Beyond Select Queries

Retrieving and displaying specific records with a select query is indeed a fundamental task in analyzing data. However, it's just a small portion of what makes up data analysis. The scope of data analysis is broad and includes grouping and comparing data, updating and deleting data, performing calculations on data, and shaping and reporting data. Access has built-in tools and functionality designed specifically to handle each one of these tasks.

In this chapter, you will take an in-depth look at the various tools available to you in Access and how they can help you go beyond select queries.

Aggregate Queries

An *aggregate query*, sometimes referred to as a *group-by query*, is a type of query you can build to help you quickly group and summarize your data. With a select query, you can only retrieve records as they appear in your data source. However, with an aggregate query, you can retrieve a summary snapshot of your data that will show you totals, averages, counts, and more.

Creating an Aggregate Query

To get a firm understanding of what an aggregate query does, take the following scenario as an example. You have just been asked to provide the sum of total revenue by period. In response to this request, start a query in Design view and bring in the System_Period and Sales_Amount fields as shown in Figure 3-1. If you run this query as is, you will get every record in your dataset instead of the summary you need.

TIP **Here's a quick reminder on how to start a query in Access 2007. Go to the application ribbon, select the Create tab, and then select Query Design. This opens the Show Table dialog box on top of a blank Query Design view. Select the table or tables with which you need to work, and you're on your way. Feel free to refer to Chapter 2 for a quick refresher on the basics of Access queries.**

In order to get a summary of revenue by period, you will need to activate Totals in your design grid. To do this, go to the ribbon and select the Design tab and then click the Totals button. As you can see in Figure 3-2, after you have activated Totals in your design grid, you will see a new row in your grid called Totals. The Totals row tells Access which aggregate function to use when performing aggregation on the specified fields.

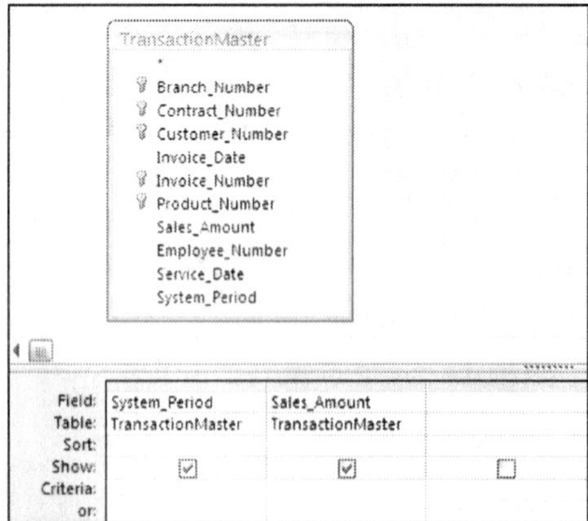

Figure 3-1: Running this query will return all the records in your dataset, not the summary you need.

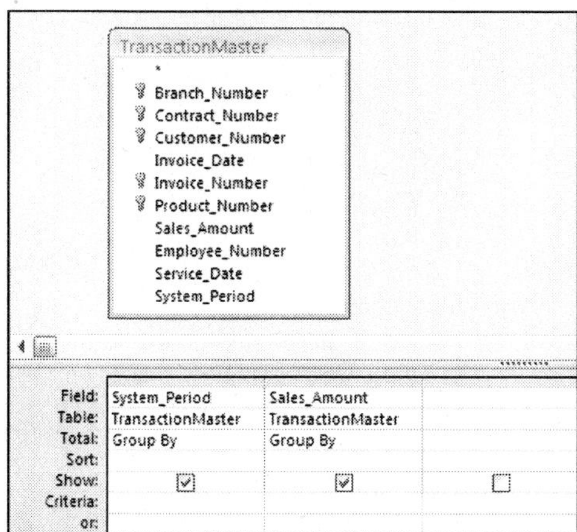

Figure 3-2: Activating Totals in your design grid will add a Totals row to your query grid that defaults to "group by".

You will notice that the Totals row contains the words "group by" under each field in your grid. This means that all similar records in a field will be grouped to provide you with a unique data item. You will cover the different aggregate functions in depth later in this chapter.

The idea here is to adjust the aggregate functions in the Totals row to correspond with the analysis you are trying to perform. In this scenario, you need to group all the periods in your dataset, and then sum the revenue in each period. Therefore, you will need to use the `Group By` aggregate function for the System_Period field, and the `Sum` aggregate function for the Sales_Amount field.

Since the default selection for Totals is the `Group By` function, no change is needed for the System_Period field. However, you will need to change the aggregate function for the Sales_Amount field from `Group By` to `Sum`. This tells Access that you want to sum the revenue figures in the Sales_Amount field, not group them. To change the aggregate function, simply click the Totals drop-down list under and the Sales_Amount field, shown in Figure 3-3, and select Sum. At this point, you can run your query.

As you can see in Figure 3-4, the resulting table gives a summary of your dataset, showing total revenue by period.

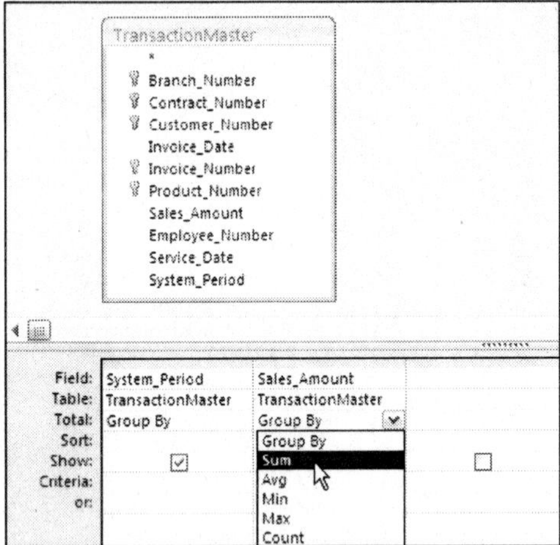

Figure 3-3: Change the aggregate function under the Sales_Amount field to `Sum`.

System_Period	SumOfSales_Amount
200401	$681,865.93
200402	$1,116,917.74
200403	$657,612.02
200404	$865,499.74
200405	$925,803.97
200406	$868,931.46
200407	$640,587.94
200408	$1,170,263.89
200409	$604,552.87
200410	$891,255.01
200411	$949,606.37
200412	$887,666.43

Figure 3-4: After you run your query, you have a summary showing you total revenue by period.

TRICKS OF THE TRADE: CREATE ALIASES FOR YOUR COLUMN NAMES

Notice that in Figure 3-4, Access automatically changed the name of the Sales_Amount field to SumOfSales_Amount. This is a normal courtesy extended by Access to let you know that the figures you see here are a result of summing the Sales_Amount field. This may be convenient in some cases, but if you need to distribute these results to other people, you may want to give this field a more seemly name. This is where aliases come in handy.

An alias is an alternate name you can give to a field in order to make it easier to read the field's name in the query results. There are two methods to create an alias for your field.

- **Method 1: The first method is to preface the field with the text you would like to see as the field name, followed by a colon. Figure 3-5 demonstrates how you would create aliases to ensure your query results have user-friendly column names. Running this query will result in a dataset with a column called Period and column called Total Revenue.**

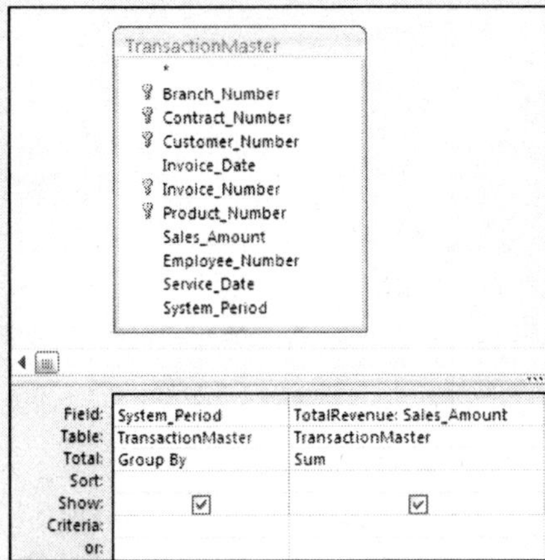

Figure 3-5: In this example, you are creating an alias called Total Revenue.

- **Method 2: The second method is to right-click the field name and select Properties. This activates the Property Sheet dialog box for Field Properties. In this dialog box, simply enter the desired alias into the Caption input, as shown here in Figure 3-6.**

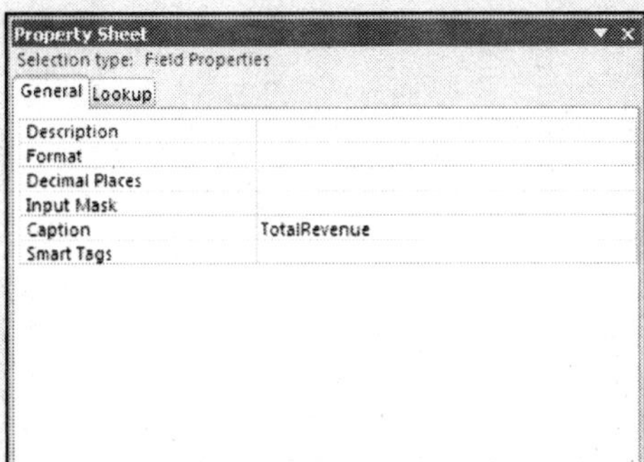

Figure 3-6: Using the Property Sheet dialog box for Field Properties is an alternate way of defining an alias for your field.

WARNING **Be aware that if you do use the Field Properties dialog box to define your alias, there will be no clear indication in your query's DDesign view, or in your query's SQL string that you are using an alias. This may lead to some confusion for anyone using your queries. For this reason, it is generally better to use the first method to define an alias.**

About Aggregate Functions

In the example shown in Figure 3-3, you selected the `Sum` aggregate function from the Totals drop-down list. Obviously, you could have selected any one of the 12 functions available. Indeed, you will undoubtedly come across analyses where you will have to use a few of the other functions available to you. In this light, it is important to know what each one of these aggregate functions implicates for your data analysis.

Group By

The `Group By` aggregate function aggregates all the records in the specified field into unique groups. Here are few things to keep in mind when using the `Group By` aggregate function.

- **Access will perform the `Group By` function in your aggregate query before any other aggregation.** If you are using a `Group By` function along with another aggregate function, the `group by` function will be executed first. The example shown in Figure 3-4, illustrates this concept. Access will group the System_Period field before summing the Sales_Amount field.
- **Access treats multiple Group By fields as one unique item.** To illustrate this point, create a query that looks similar to the one shown in Figure 3-7. As you can see after running the query, Access counted all the transactions that were logged in the 200401 System_Period.

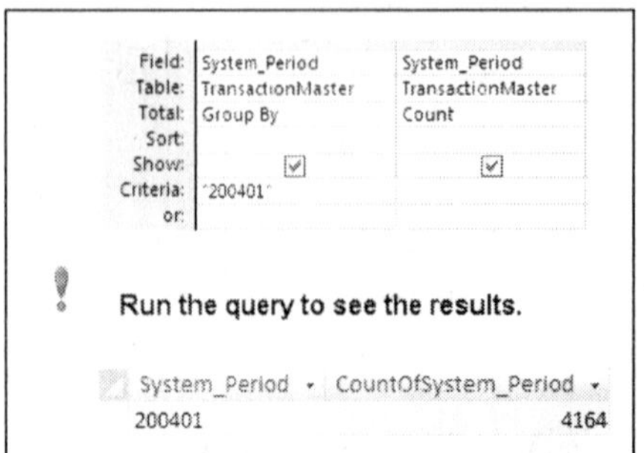

Figure 3-7: After you run this query, you will have a summary showing you that there are 4,164 records in System_Period 200401.

Field:	System_Period	Product_Number	System_Period
Table:	TransactionMaster	TransactionMaster	TransactionMaster
Total:	Group By	Group By	Count
Sort:			
Show:	☑	☑	☑
Criteria:	"200401"		
or:			

Run the query to see the results.

System_Period	Product_Number	CountOfSystem_Period
200401	16000	1087
200401	30300	1052
200401	70700	879
200401	81150	178
200401	87000	472
200401	90830	496

Figure 3-8: This query results in a few more records, but if you add up the counts in each group, they will total to 4,164.

- Now return to the Query Design view and add Product_Number as shown here in Figure 3-8. This time, Access treats each combination of System_Period and Product_Number as a unique item. Each combination is grouped before the records in each group are counted. The benefit here is that you have added a dimension to your analysis. Not only do you know how many transactions per Product_Number were logged in 200401, but also if you add up all the transactions, you will get an accurate count of the total number of transactions logged in 200401.
- **Access sorts each Group By field in ascending order.** Unless otherwise specified, any field tagged as a Group By field will be sorted in ascending order. If your query has multiple Group By fields, each field will be sorted in ascending order starting with the left-most field.

Sum, Avg, Count, StDev, Var

These aggregate functions all perform mathematical calculations against the records in your selected field. It is important to note that these functions exclude any records that are set to null. In other words, these aggregate functions ignore any empty cells.

- **Sum:** `Sum` calculates the total value of all the records in the designated field or grouping. This function only works with the following data types: AutoNumber, Currency, Date/Time, and Number.

- **Avg:** `Avg` calculates the Average of all the records in the designated field or grouping. This function only works with the following data types: AutoNumber, Currency, Date/Time, and Number.
- **Count:** `Count` simply counts the number of entries within the designated field or grouping. This function works with all data types.
- **StDev:** `StDev` calculates the standard deviation across all records within the designated field or grouping. This function only works with the following data types: AutoNumber, Currency, Date/Time, and Number.
- **Var:** `Var` calculates the amount by which all the values within the designated field or grouping vary from the average value of the group. This function only works with the following data types: AutoNumber, Currency, Date/Time, and Number.

Min, Max, First, Last

Unlike other aggregate functions, these functions evaluate all the records in the designated field or grouping and return a single value from the group.

- **Min:** `Min` returns the value of the record with the lowest value in the designated field or grouping. This function will only work with the following data types: AutoNumber, Currency, Date/Time, Number, and Text.
- **Max:** `Max` returns the value of the record with the highest value in the designated field or grouping. This function only works with the following data types: AutoNumber, Currency, Date/Time, Number, and Text.
- **First:** `First` returns the value of the first record in the designated field or grouping. This function works with all data types.
- **Last:** `Last` returns the value of the last record in the designated field or grouping. This function works with all data types.

Expression, Where

One of the steadfast rules of aggregate queries is that every field must have an aggregation performed against it. However, there will be situations where you will have to use a field as a utility. That is, use a field to simply perform a calculation or apply a filter. These fields are a means to get to the final analysis you are looking for, rather than part of the final analysis. In these situations, you will use the `Expression` function or the `Where` clause. The `Expression` function and the `Where` clause are unique in that they don't perform any grouping action per se.

- **Expression:** The `Expression` aggregate function is generally applied when you are utilizing custom calculations or other functions in an aggregate query. `Expression` tells Access to perform the designated custom calculation on each individual record or group separately.

  Create a query in Design view that looks like the one shown in Figure 3-9. Note that you are using two aliases in this query: Revenue for the Sales_Amount field and Cost for the custom calculation defined here. Using an alias of Revenue gives the sum of Sales_Amount a user-friendly name.

  Now you can use [Revenue] to represent the sum of Sales_Amount in your custom calculation. The `Expression` aggregate function ties it all together by telling Access that [Revenue]*.33 will be performed against the resulting sum of Sales_Amount for each individual System_Period group. Running this query returns the total Revenue and Cost for each System_Period group.

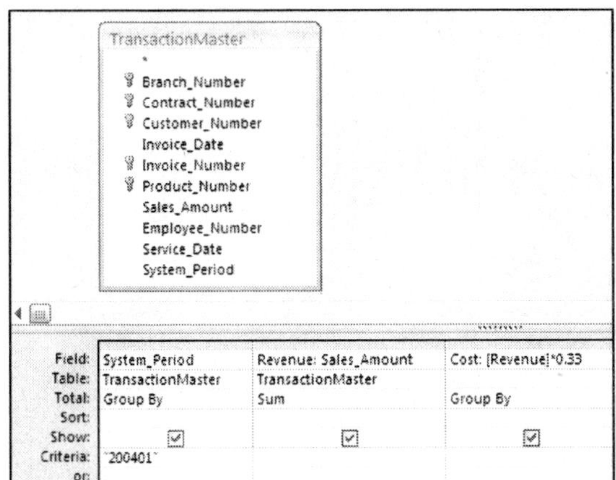

Figure 3-9: The `Expression` aggregate function enables you to perform the designated custom calculation on each System_Period group separately.

- **Where:** The `Where` clause enables you to apply a criterion to a field that is not included in your aggregate query, effectively applying a filter to your analysis. To see the `Where` clause in action, create a query in Design view that looks like the one shown in Figure 3-10.

  As you can see in the Total row, you are grouping Product_Number and summing Sales_Amount. However, System_Period has no aggregation selected because you only want to use it to filter one specific period. You have entered **200401** in the criteria for System_Period. If you run this query as is, you will get the following error message: "You tried to execute a query that does not include the specified expression 'System_Period' as part of an aggregate function."

  To run this query successfully, click the Totals drop-down list for the System_Period field and select Where from the selection list. At this point, your query should look similar to the one shown in Figure 3-11. With the `Where` clause specified, you can successfully run this query.

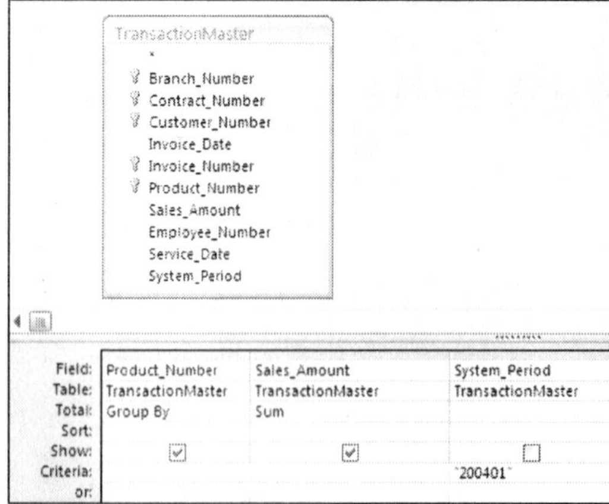

Figure 3-10: Running this query will cause an error message because you have no aggregation defined for System_Period.

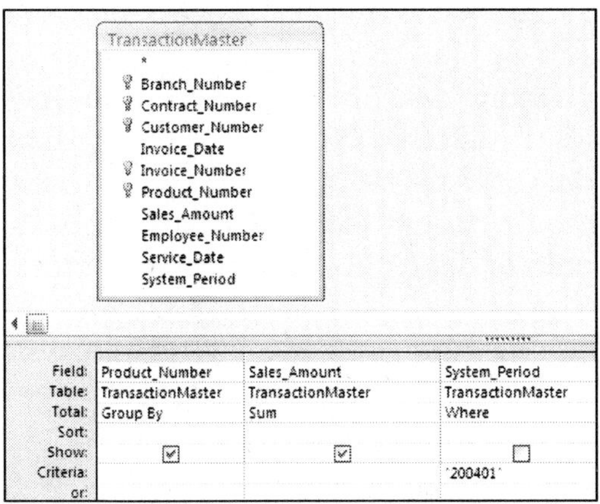

Figure 3-11: Adding a `Where` clause remedies the error and allows you to run the query.

NOTE **Here is one final note about the `Where` clause. Notice in Figure 3-11 that the check box in the Show row has no check in it for the System_Period. This is because fields that are tagged with the `Where` clause cannot be shown in an aggregate query. Therefore, this check box must remain empty. If you select the Show check box of a field with a `Where` clause, you will get an error message stating that you cannot display the field for which you entered `Where` in the Total row.**

Action Queries

You can think of an action query the same way you think of a select query. Like a select query, an action query extracts a dataset from a data source based on the definitions and criteria you pass to the query. The difference is that when an action query returns results it does not display a dataset; instead, it performs some action on those results. The action it performs depends on its type.

NOTE **Unlike select queries, you cannot use action queries as a data source for a form or a report, as they do not return a dataset that can be read.**

There are four types of action queries: make-table query, delete query, append query, and update query. Each query type performs a unique action that you will cover in this section.

Why Use Action Queries?

As mentioned before, along with querying data, the scope of data analysis includes shaping data, changing data, deleting data and updating data. Access provides action queries as data analysis tools to help you with these tasks. Unfortunately, too many people do not make use of these tools; instead, opting to export small chunks of data to Excel in order to perform these tasks.

This may be fine if you are performing these tasks as a one-time analysis with a small dataset. However, what do you do when you have to carry out the same analysis on a weekly basis, or if the dataset you need to manipulate exceeds the limits of Excel? In these situations, it would be impractical to routinely export data into Excel, manipulate the data, and then re-import the data into Access. Using action queries, you can increase your productivity and reduce the chance of errors by carrying out all your analytical process within Access.

Make-Table Queries

A *make-table* query creates a new table consisting of data from an existing table. The table that is created consists of records that have met the definitions and criteria of the make-table query.

Why Use a Make-Table Query?

In simple terms, if you create a query and would like to capture the results of your query in its own table, you can us a make-table query to create a hard table with your query results. You can then use your new table in some other analytical process.

What Are the Hazards of Make-Table Queries?

When you build a make-table query, you will have to specify the name of the table that will be created when the make-table query is run. If you give the new table the same name as an existing table, the existing table will be overwritten. If you accidentally overwrite another table with a make-table query, you will not be able to recover the old table. Be sure that you name the tables created by your make-table queries carefully as to avoid overwriting existing information.

The data in a table made by a make-table query is not, in any way, linked to its source data. This means that the data in your new table will not be updated when data in the original table is changed.

Creating a Make-Table Query

You have been asked to provide the Marketing department with a list of customers along with information about each customer's service interval. To meet this task, create a query in the Query Design view that looks similar to the one shown here in Figure 3-12.

Go up to the ribbon, select the Design tab, and then select the Make Table button. This activates the Make Table dialog box, shown in Figure 3-13. Enter the name you would like to give to your new table in the Table Name input box. For this example, type **CustomerIntervals**. Be sure not to enter the name of a table that already exists in your database, as it will be overwritten.

After you have entered the name, click the OK button to close the dialog box, and then run your query. At this point, Access will throw up the warning message shown in Figure 3-14 in order to alert you that you will not be able to undo this action. Click Yes to confirm and create your new table.

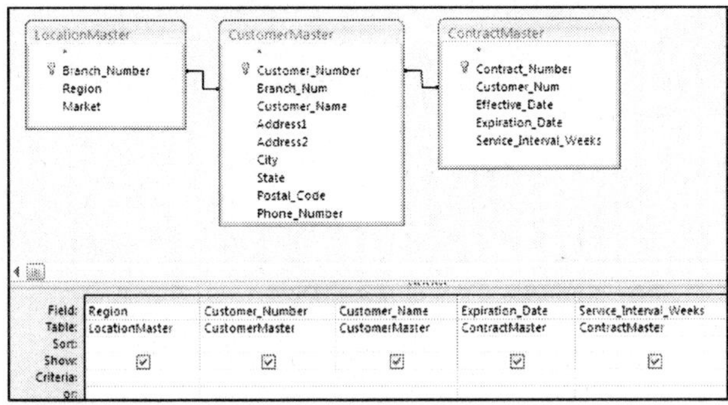

Figure 3-12: Create this query in Design view.

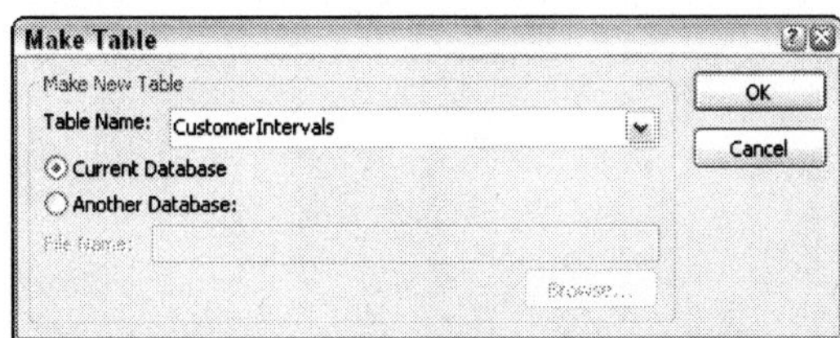

Figure 3-13: Enter the name of your new table.

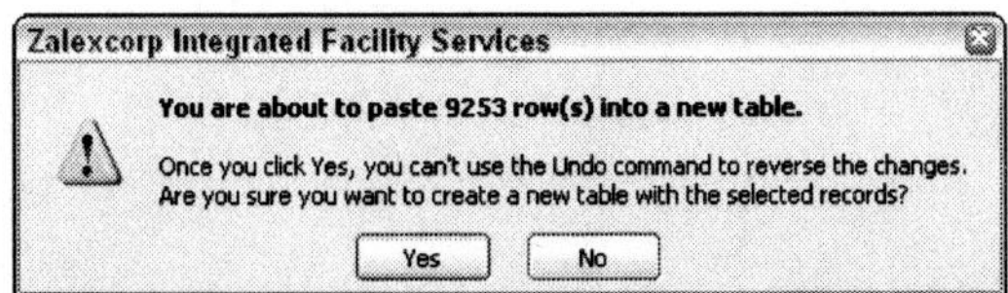

Figure 3-14: Click Yes to run your query.

When your query has completed, you will find a new table called CustomerIntervals in your Table objects.

TIP **Notice that in Figure 3-15 you defined a column with an alias of Customer. After the alias, you simply entered All in quotes. When you run the query, your new table has a column named Customer in which the value for every record is All. This example illustrates that when running a make-table query, you can create your own columns on the fly by simply creating an alias for the column and defining its contents after the colon.**

TRICKS OF THE TRADE: TURNING AGGREGATE QUERY RESULTS INTO HARD DATA

The results of aggregate queries are inherently not updatable. This means you will not be able to edit any of the records returned from an aggregate query. This is because there is no relationship between the aggregated data and the underlying data. However, you can change your aggregate query into a make-table query and create a hard table with your aggregate query's results. With your new hard table, you will be able to edit to your heart's content.

To illustrate how this works, create the query shown in Figure 3-15 in Design view. Then change the query into a make-table query, enter a name for your new table, and then run it.

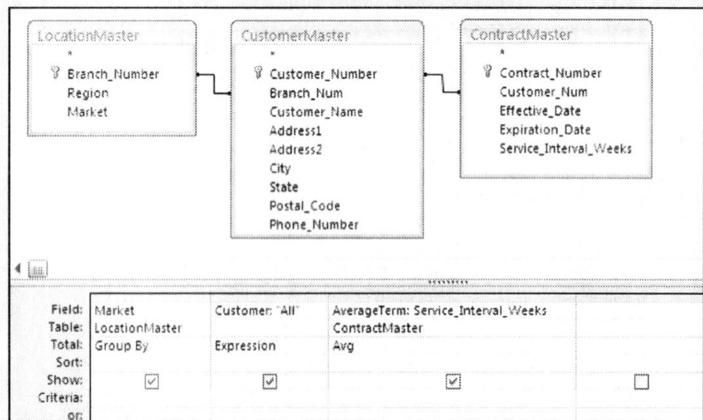

Figure 3-15: Running this query as a make-table enables you to edit the aggregate query's results.

Delete Queries

A *delete* query deletes records from a table based on the definitions and criteria you specify. That is, a delete query affects a group of records that meet a specified criterion that you apply.

Why Use a Delete Query?

Although you can delete records by hand, there are situations where using a delete query is more efficient. For example, if you have a very large dataset, a delete query will delete your records faster that a manual delete. In addition, if you want to delete certain records based on several complex criteria, you will want to utilize a delete query. Finally, if you need to delete records from one table based on a comparison to another table, a delete query is the way to go.

What Are the Hazards of Delete Queries?

Like all other action queries, you will not be able to undo the effects of a delete query. However, a delete query is much more dangerous than the other action queries because there is no way to remedy accidentally deleted data.

Given the fact that deleted data cannot be recovered, you should get into the habit of taking one of the following actions in order to avoid a fatal error.

- Run a select query to display the records you are about to delete. Review the records to confirm that these records are indeed the ones you want to delete, and then run the query as a delete query.
- Run a select query to display the records you are about to delete, then change the query into a make-table query. Run the make-table query to make a backup of the data you are about to delete. Finally, run the query again as a delete query to delete the records.
- Make a backup of your database before running your delete query.

Creating a Delete Query

The Marketing department has informed you that the CustomerIntervals table you gave them includes records that they do not need. They want you to delete all the customers that have an Expiration_Date earlier than January 1, 2006. In order to meet this task, design a query based on the CustomerIntervals table you created a moment ago. Bring in the Expiration_Date field and enter **<#1/1/2006#** in the Criteria row. Your design grid should look like the one shown here in Figure 3-16.

Perform a test by running the query. Review the records that are returned, and take note that 567 records meet your criteria. You now know that 567 will be deleted if you run a delete query based on these query definitions.

Return to the Design view. Go up to the ribbon, select the Design tab, and then select the Delete button. Now run your query again.

At this point, Access will throw up a message, as shown in Figure 3-17, telling you that you are about to delete 567 rows of data and warning you that you will not be able to undo this action. This is the number you were expecting to see, as the test you ran earlier returned 567 records. Since everything checks out, click Yes to confirm and delete the records.

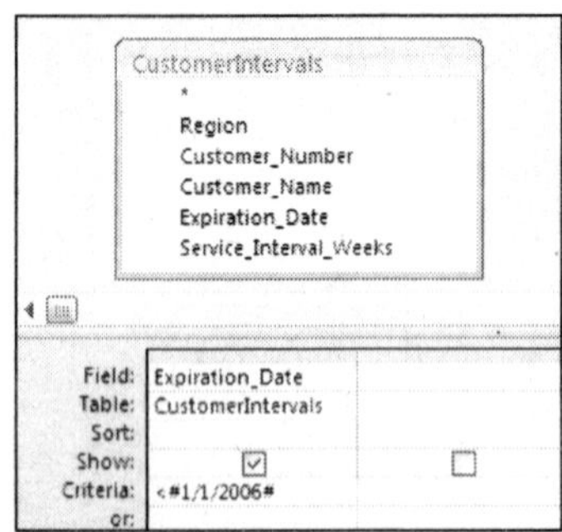

Figure 3-16: This query will select all records with an expiration date earlier than January 1, 2006.

Zalexcorp Integrated Facility Services

You are about to delete 567 row(s) from the specified table.

Once you click Yes, you can't use the Undo command to reverse the changes.
Are you sure you want to delete the selected records?

Show Help >>

Yes No

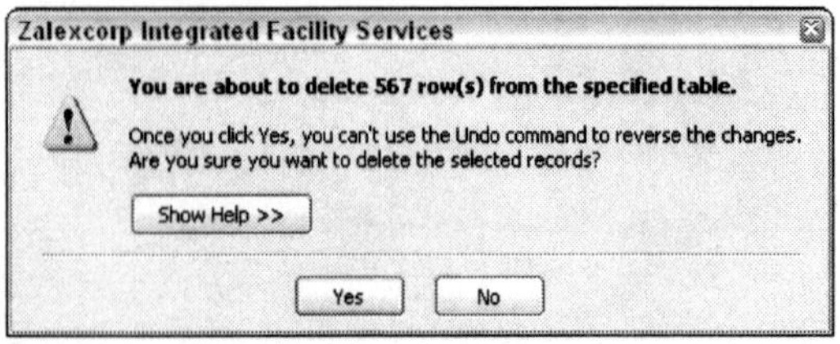

Figure 3-17: Click Yes to continue with your delete action.

NOTE If you are working with a very large dataset, Access may throw up a message telling you that the "undo command won't be available because the operation is too large or there isn't enough free memory."

Many people mistakenly interpret this message to mean that this operation can't be done because there is not enough memory. This message is simply telling you that Access will not be able to give the option of undoing this change if you choose to continue with the action.

This is the case when you try to delete, append, and update queries.

TRICKS OF THE TRADE: DELETING RECORDS FROM ONE TABLE BASED ON THE RECORDS FROM ANOTHER

You will encounter many analyses where you will have to delete records from one table based on the records from another. This is relatively easy to do. However, many users get stuck on this because of one simple mistake.

The query in Figure 3-18 looks simple enough. It is telling Access to delete all records from the CustomerIntervals table if the region in the region field is found in the LocationMaster table.

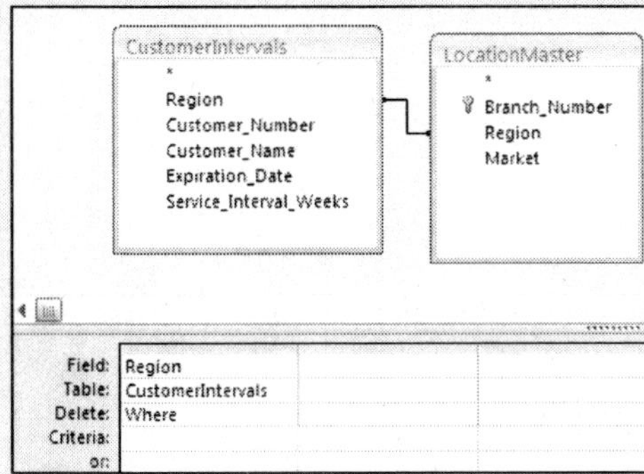

Figure 3-18: This delete query seems like it should run fine, but there is something wrong.

If you run this query, Access throws up the message shown in Figure 3-19. This message is asking you to specify which table contains the records you want to delete.

(continued)

TRICKS OF THE TRADE: DELETING RECORDS FROM ONE TABLE BASED ON THE RECORDS FROM ANOTHER *(Continued)*

Zalexcorp Integrated Facility Services

Specify the table containing the records you want to delete.

OK Help

Figure 3-19: Access does not know which table contains the records you want deleted.

This message stumps many Access users. Unfortunately, this message does not clearly state what you need to do in order to remedy the mistake. Nevertheless, the remedy is a simple one.

First, clear the query grid by deleting the Region field. Next, double-click the asterisk (*) in the CustomerIntervals table. This explicitly tells Access that the CustomerIntervals table contains the records you want to delete. Figure 3-20 demonstrates the correct way to build this query.

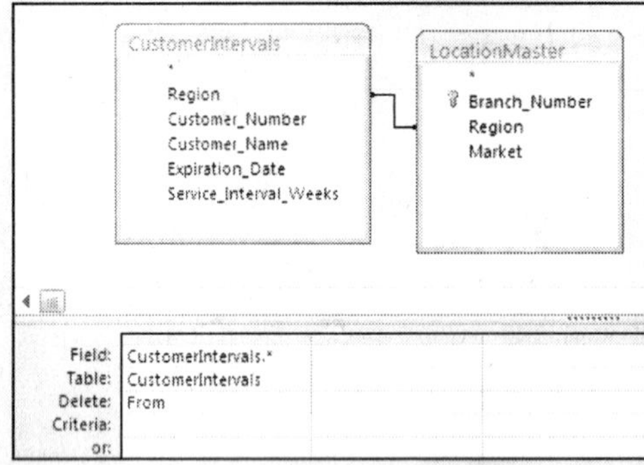

Figure 3-20: This is the correct way to build this query.

Append Queries

An *append* query appends records to a table based on the definitions and criteria you specify in your query. In other words, with an append query, you can add the results of your query to the end of a table, effectively adding rows to the table.

Why Use an Append Query?

With an append query, you are essentially copying records from one table or query and adding them to the end of another table. In that light, append queries come in handy when you need to transfer large datasets from one existing table to another. For example, if you have a table called Old Transactions where you archive your transaction records, you can add the latest batch of transactions from the New Transactions table by simply using an append query.

What Are the Hazards of Append Queries?

The primary hazard of an append query is losing records during the append process. That is, not all of the records you think you are appending to a table actually make it to your table. There are generally two reasons why records can get lost during an append process.

- **Type Conversion Failure:** This failure occurs when the character type of the source data does not match that of the destination table column. For example, imagine that you have a table with a field called Cost. Your Cost field is set as a TEXT character type because you have some entries that are tagged as TBD (to be determined), because you don't know the cost yet. If you try to append that field to another table whose Cost field is set as a NUMBER character type, all the entries that have TBD will be changed to Null, effectively deleting your TBD tag.
- **Key Violation:** This violation occurs when you are trying to append duplicate records to a field in the destination table that is set as a primary key or is indexed as No Duplicates. In other words, when you have a field that prohibits duplicates, Access will not allow you to append any record that is a duplicate of an existing record in that field.

Another hazard of an append query is that the query will simply fail to run. There are two reasons why an append query will fail:

- **Lock Violation**: This violation occurs when the destination table is open in Design view or is open by another user on the network.
- **Validation Rule Violation**: This violation occurs when a field in the destination table has one of the following properties settings:
  - **Required Field is set to Yes:** If a field in the destination table has been set to Required Yes and you do not append data to this field, your append query will fail.
  - **Allow Zero Length is set to No:** If a field in the destination table as been set to Zero Length No and you do not append data to this field, your append query will fail.

- **Validation Rule set to anything:** If a field in the destination table has a validation rule and you break the rule with your append query, your append query will fail. For example, if you have a validation rule for the Cost field in your destination table set to >0, then you cannot append records with a quantity less than or equal to zero.

Luckily, Access will clearly warn you if you are about to cause any of these errors. Figure 3-21 demonstrates this warning message.

As you can see, this warning message tells you that you cannot append all the records due to errors. It goes on to tell you exactly how many records will not be appended because of each error. In this case, two records will not be appended because of key violations. You have the option of clicking Yes or No. The Yes button will ignore the warning and append all records minus the two with the errors. The No button will cancel the query, which means that no records will be appended.

Keep in mind that like all other action queries, you will not be able to undo your append query once you have pulled the trigger.

TIP **If you can identify the records you recently appended in your destination table, you could technically undo your append action by simply deleting the newly append records. This would obviously be contingent upon you providing yourself a method of identifying appended records. For example, you could create a field that contains some code or tag that identifies the appended records. This code can be anything from a date to a simple character.**

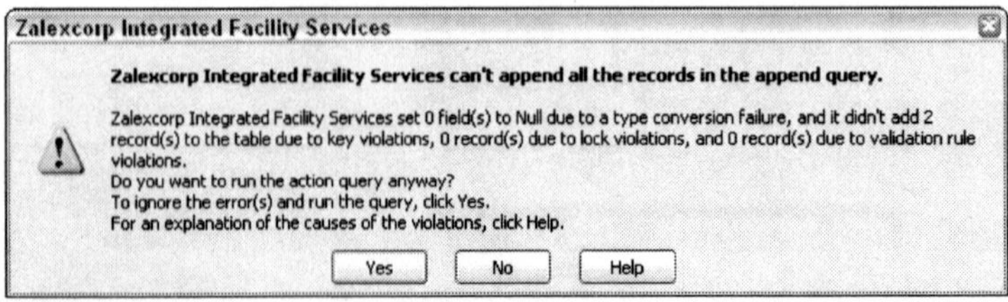

Figure 3-21: This warning message tells you that you will lose two records during the append process.

Creating an Append Query

The Marketing department contacts you and tells you that they made a mistake. They actually do need the customers that have an Expiration_Date earlier than January 1, 2006. They want you to add back the records you deleted. To do this, you will have to append the customers that have an Expiration_Date earlier than January 1, 2006 to the CustomerIntervals table.

In order to meet this task, create a query in the Query Design view that looks similar to the one shown in Figure 3-22.

Go to the ribbon, select the Design tab, and then select the Append button. This activates the Append dialog box shown in Figure 3-23. In the Table Name input box, enter the name of the table to which you would like to append your query results. For this example, enter **CustomerIntervals**.

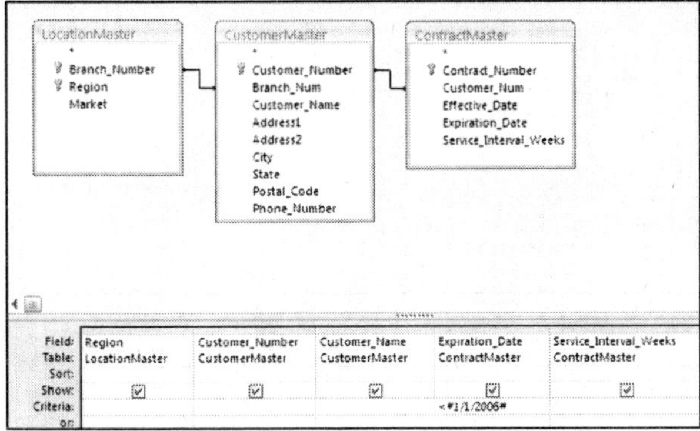

Figure 3-22: This query selects all records with an expiration date earlier than January 1, 2006.

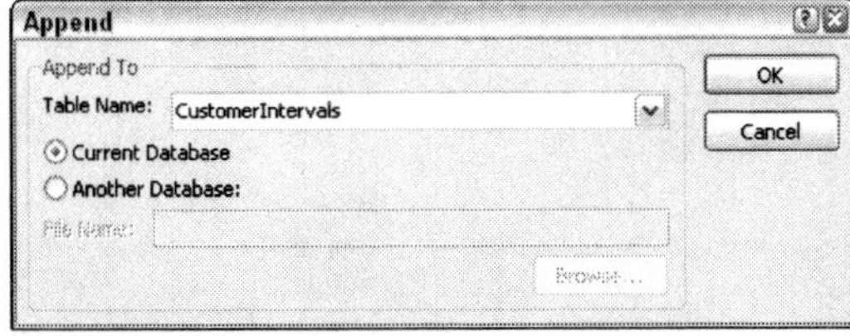

Figure 3-23: Enter the name of the table to which you would like to append your query results.

When you have entered your destination table's name, click the OK button. You will notice that your query grid has a new row called Append To under the Sort row. Figure 3-24 shows this new row.

The idea is to select the name of the field in your destination table where you would like append the information resulting from your query. For example, the Append To row under the Region field shows the word *Region*. This means that the data in the Region field of this query will be appended to the Region field in the CustomerIntervals table.

Now you can run your query. After you run your query, Access will throw up a message, shown in Figure 3-25, telling you that you are about to append 567 rows of data and warning you that you will not be able to undo this action. Click Yes to confirm and append the records.

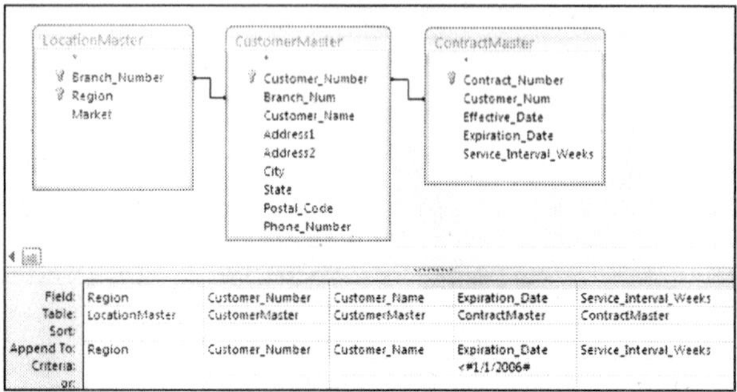

Figure 3-24: In the Append To row, select the name of the field in your destination table where you would like to append the information resulting from your query.

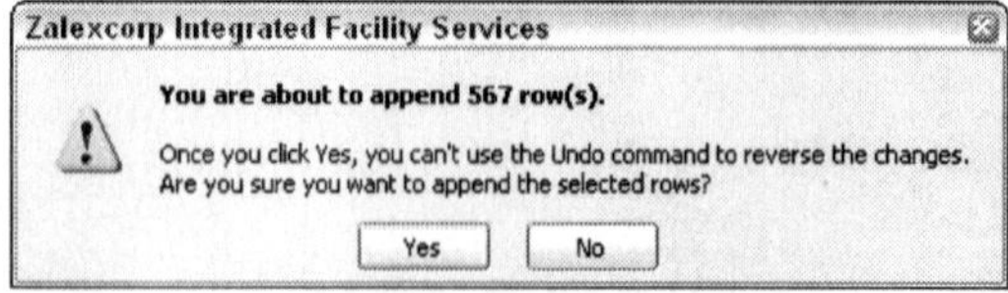

Figure 3-25: Click Yes to continue with your append action.

TRICKS OF THE TRADE: ADDING A TOTALS ROW TO YOUR DATASET

Your manager wants you to create a revenue summary report that shows the total revenue of all the employees in each market. He also wants to see the total revenue for each market. Instead of giving your manager two separate reports, you can give him one table that has employee details and market totals. This is an easy, two-step process:

1. **Make an Employees Summary. Create a query in the Query Design view that looks similar to the one shown here in Figure 3-26. Note that you are creating an alias for both the Last_Name field and the Sales_Amount Field. Change the query into a make-table query and name your table RevenueSummary. Run this query.**

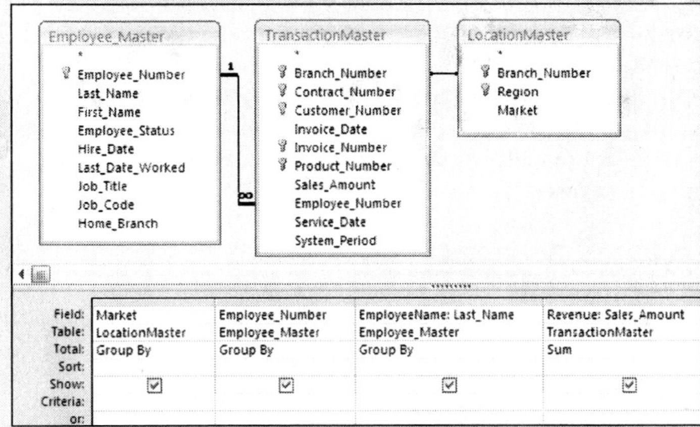

Figure 3-26: Run this query as a make-table query to make a table called RevenueSummary.

2. **Append the Market Totals. Now use the RevenueSummary table you just created to summarize revenue by Market. To do this, create a query in the Query Design view that looks similar to the one shown here in Figure 3-27.**

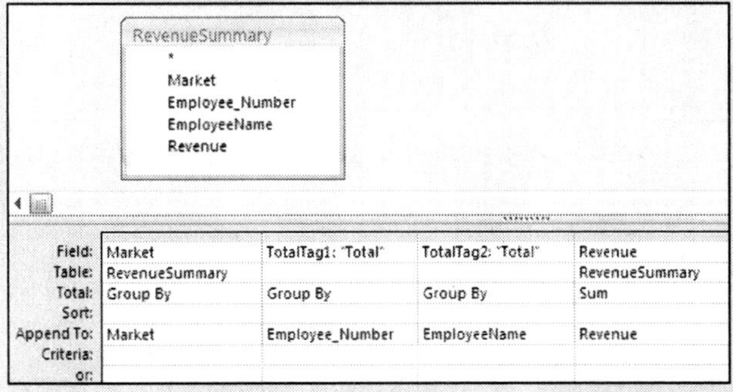

Figure 3-27: Run this market summary query as an append query and append it to the RevenueSummary table.

(continued)

TRICKS OF THE TRADE: ADDING A TOTALS ROW TO YOUR DATASET *(Continued)*

Take a moment and look at the query in Figure 3-27. You will notice that you are making two custom fields: Total Tag1 and Total Tag3. You are filling these fields with the word *Total*. This ensures that the summary lines you append to the RevenueSummary table are clearly identifiable, as they will have the word *Total* in the Employee_Number field and the Employee Name field.

Change the query into an append query and append these results to the RevenueSummary table.

Now you can open the RevenueSummary table and sort by Market and Employee_Number. As you can see in Figure 3-28, you have successfully created a table that has a total revenue line for every employee and a total revenue line for each market; all in one table.

Market	Employee_Number	EmployeeName	Revenue
BUFFALO	1416	CERMACHEIL	$1,120.57
BUFFALO	160133	MALISKI	$6,520.94
BUFFALO	160234	FOX	$151.36
BUFFALO	160235	STOFFERD	$336.00
BUFFALO	164550	TEMADY	$8,603.51
BUFFALO	2053	SMATH	$12,793.24
BUFFALO	3224	BEACE	$520.65
BUFFALO	4401	DIAST	$68,761.43
BUFFALO	4455	PIDLANIR	$2,244.97
BUFFALO	45641	EIGILLO	$30,779.12
BUFFALO	52311	SLAVIN	$4,198.09
BUFFALO	52562	CYGANAK	$30,696.44
BUFFALO	55051	SELINSKY	$114.52
BUFFALO	5601	WHATFAILD	$15,897.30
BUFFALO	56102	WANEGREDZKI	$67,690.02
BUFFALO	56405	BICKIR	$83,525.72
BUFFALO	6064	STANSEN	$56,877.03
BUFFALO	6146	BEWMAN	$661.83
BUFFALO	64100	CELIS	$35,045.26
BUFFALO	6442	KIASACK	$359.58
BUFFALO	6462	BIQGISS	$23,312.43
BUFFALO	6644	COX	$268.74
BUFFALO	Total	Total	$450,478.72

Figure 3-28: Sort by market and employee number to see each employee in a market, and the market total.

Update Queries

When you build a make-table query, you will have to specify the name of the table that will be made when the make-table query is run. If you give the new table the same name as an existing table, the existing table will be overwritten. If you accidentally write over another table with a make-table query, you will not be able to recover the old table. Be sure that you name the tables created by your make-table queries carefully as to avoid overwriting existing information.

The data in a table made by a make-table query is not in any way linked to its source data. This means that the data in your new table will not be updated when data in the original table is changed.

Why Use an Update Query?

The primary reason to use update queries is to save time. There is no easier way to edit large amounts of data at one time than with an update query. For example, imagine you have a Customers table that includes the customer's zip code. If the zip code 32750 has been changed to 32751, you can easily update your Customers table to replace 32750 with 32751.

What Are the Hazards of Update Queries?

As is the case with all other action queries, you must always take precautions to ensure that you are not in a situation where you cannot undo the effects of an update query. Get into the habit of taking one of the following actions in order to give yourself a way back to the original data in the event of a misstep.

- Run a select query to display, then change the query into a make-table query. Run the make-table query to make a backup of the data you are about to update. Finally, run the query again as an update query to delete the records.
- Make a backup of your database before running your update query.

CROSS REFERENCE **To see more potential hazards of using update queries, see the section "A Word on Updatable Datasets" below.**

Creating an Update Query

You have just received word that the zip code for all customers in the 32750 zip code has been changed to 32751. In order to keep your database accurate, you will have to update all the 32750 zip codes in your Customer-Master table to 32751. Create a query in the Query Design view that looks similar to the one shown here in Figure 3-29.

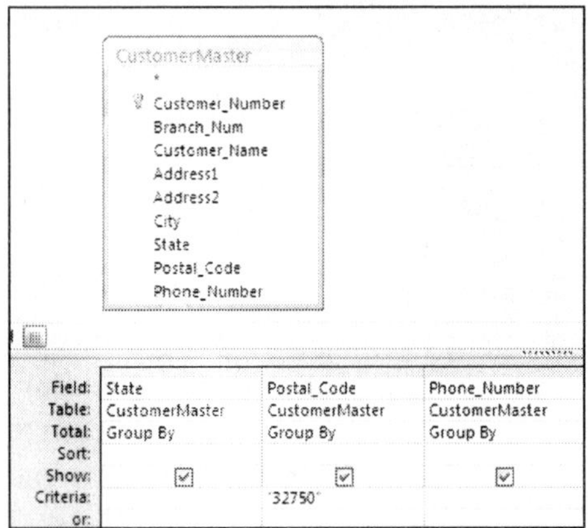

Figure 3-29: This query will select all customers that are in the 32750 zip code.

Perform a test by running the query. Review the records that are returned, and take note that 13 records meet your criteria. You now know that 13 records will be updated if you run an update query based on these query definitions.

Return to the Design view. Go up to the ribbon and select the Design tab. From there, select the Update button. You will notice that your query grid has a new row called Update To. The idea is to enter the value to which you would like to update the current data. In this scenario, shown in Figure 3-30, you want to update the zip code for the records you are selecting to 32751.

Run the query. Access will throw up the message shown in Figure 3-31, telling you that you are about to update 13 rows of data and warning you that you will not be able to undo this action. This is the number you were expecting to see, as the test you ran earlier returned 13 records. Since everything checks out, click Yes to confirm and update the records.

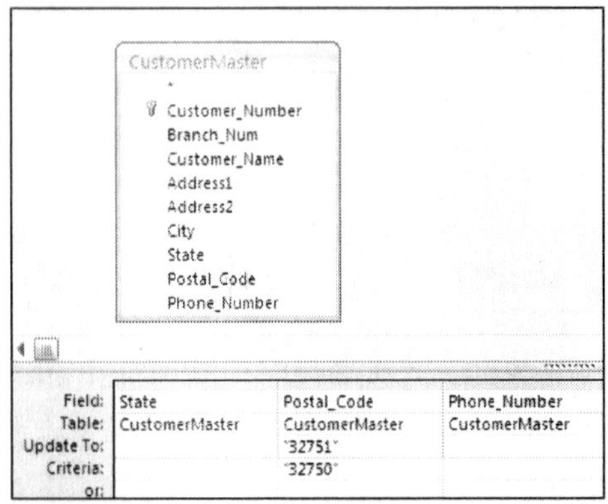

Figure 3-30: In this query, you are updating the zip code for all customers that have a code of 32750 to 32571.

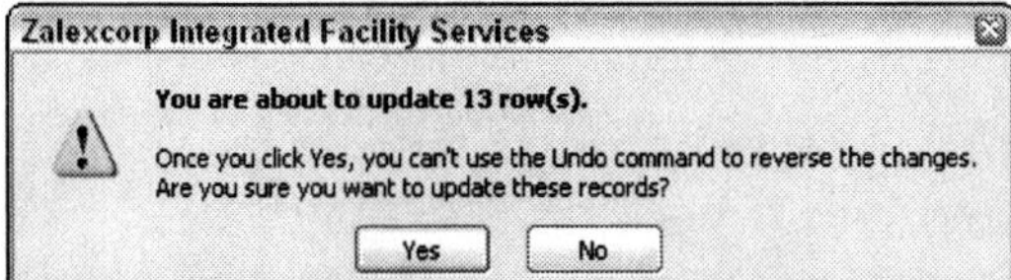

Figure 3-31: Click Yes to continue with your update action.

TRICKS OF THE TRADE: USING EXPRESSIONS IN YOUR UPDATE QUERIES

You will come across situations where you will have to execute record-specific updates. That is, you are not updating multiple records with one specific value; instead, you are updating each record individually based on an expression.

To demonstrate this concept, start a query in Design view base on the RevenueSummary table you created during "Tricks of the Trade: Adding a Totals Row to your Dataset". Build your query like the one shown in Figure 3-32.

This query is telling Access to update the Employee Name for all employees in the RevenueSummary table to the concatenated value of their [Last_Name] in the EmployeeMaster table, a comma, and their [First_Name] in the EmployeeMaster table.

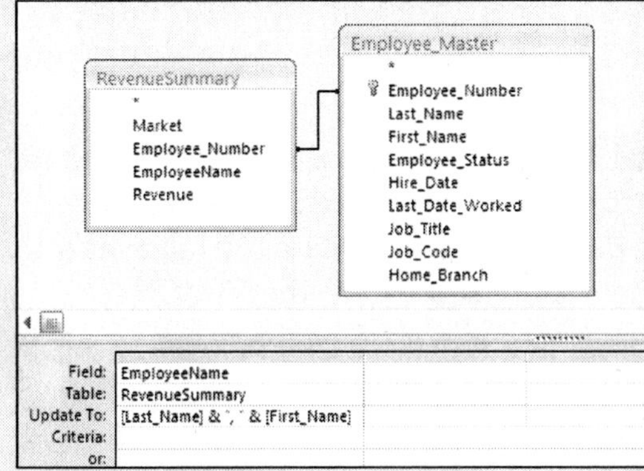

Figure 3-32: This update query is using an expression to make record-specific updates.

After you run this query, each employee will have his or her full name in the Employee Name field of the RevenueSummary table. For example, the name of employee number 104 in the RevenueSummary table will be updated from WIBB to WIBB, MAURICE.

Remember, this is just one example of an expression you can use to update your records. You can use almost any expression with an update query, ranging from mathematical functions to string operations.

A Word on Updatable Datasets

Not all datasets are updatable. That is, you may have a dataset that Access cannot update for one reason or another. If your update query fails, you will get one of these messages: "Operation must use an updatable query" or "This Recordset is not updateable".

Your update query will fail if any one of the following applies:

- **Your query is using a join to another query:** To work around this issue, create a temporary table that you can use instead of the joined query.
- **Your query is based on a crosstab query, an aggregate query, a Union query, or a sub query that contains aggregate functions:** To work around this issue, create a temporary table that you can use instead of the query.
- **Your query is based on three or more tables and there is a many-to-one-to-many relationship:** To work around this issue, create a temporary table that you can use without the relationship.
- **Your query is based on a table where the Unique Values property is set to Yes:** To work around this issue, set the Unique Values property of the table to No.
- **Your query is based on a table on which you do not have Update Data permissions, or is locked by another user:** To work around this issue, ensure you have permissions to update the table, and that the table is not in Design view or locked by another user.
- **Your query is based on a table in a database that is open as read-only or is located on a read-only drive:** To work around this issue, obtain write access to the database or drive.
- **Your query is based on a linked ODBC table with no unique index or a Paradox table without a primary key:** To work around this issue, add a primary key or a unique index to the linked table.
- **Your query is based on a SQL pass-through query:** To work around this issue, create a temporary table that you can use instead of the query.

Crosstab Queries

A *crosstab query* is a special kind of aggregate query that summarizes values from a specified field and groups them in a matrix layout by two sets of dimensions, one set down the left side of the matrix and the other set listed across the top of the matrix. Crosstab queries are perfect for analyzing trends over time, or providing a method for quickly identifying anomalies in your dataset.

The anatomy of a crosstab query is simple. You need a minimum of three fields in order to create the matrix structure that will become your crosstab: the first field makes up the row headings, the second field makes up the column headings, and the third field makes up the aggregated data in the center of the matrix. The data in the center can represent a `Sum`, `Count`, `Average`, or any other aggregate function. Figure 3-33 demonstrate the basic structure of a crosstab query.

There are two methods to create a crosstab query: using the Crosstab Query Wizard and creating a crosstab query manually using the query design grid.

Using the Crosstab Query Wizard

To activate the Crosstab Query Wizard, go to the ribbon, select the Create tab, and then select the Query Wizard button. This brings up the New Query dialog box shown in Figure 3-34. Select Crosstab Query Wizard from the selection list and then click the OK button.

Region Name	QTR1	QTR2	QTR3	QTR4
Region A	data	data	data	data
Region B	data	data	data	data
Region C	data	data	data	data

Figure 3-33: This is the basic structure of a crosstab query.

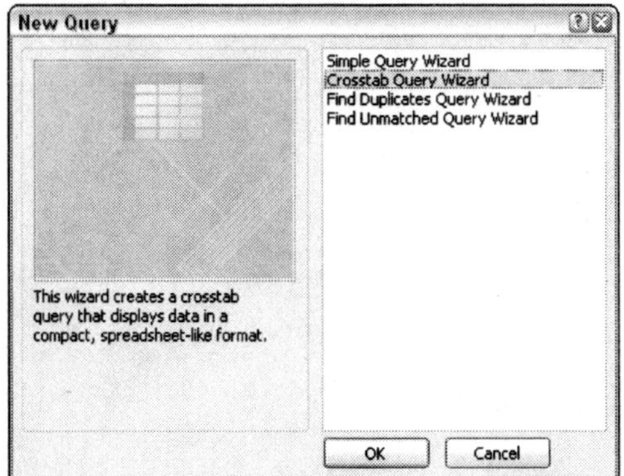

Figure 3-34: Select Crosstab Query Wizard from the New Query dialog box.

The first step in the Crosstab Query Wizard is to identify the data source you will be using. As you can see in Figure 3-35, you can choose either a query or a table as your data source. In this example, you will be using the TransactionMaster table as your data source. Select TransactionMaster and then click the Next button.

The next step is to identify the fields you would like to use as the row headings. Select the Product_Number field and click the button with the > symbol on it to move it to the Selected Items list. At this point, your dialog box should look like Figure 3-36. Note the Product_Number field is shown in the sample diagram at the bottom of the dialog box.

You can select up to three fields to include in your crosstab query as row headings. Remember that Access treats each combination of headings as unique items. That is, each combination is grouped before the records in each group are aggregated.

The next step is to identify the field you would like to use as the column heading for your crosstab query. Keep in mind there can be only one column heading in your crosstab. Select the Invoice_Date field from the field list. Again, note in Figure 3-37 that the sample diagram at the bottom of the dialog box updates to show the Invoice_Date.

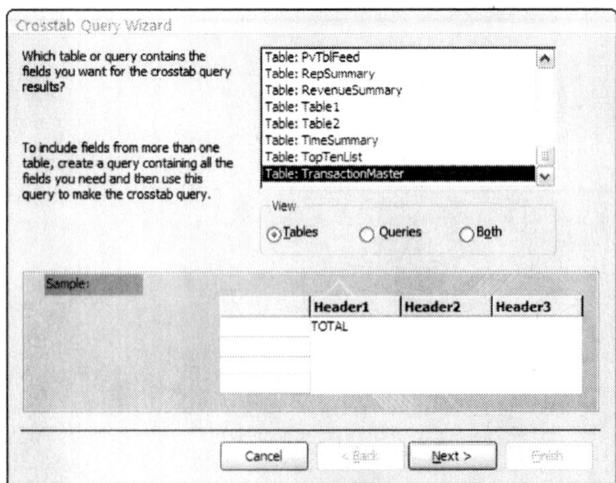

Figure 3-35: Select the data source for your crosstab query.

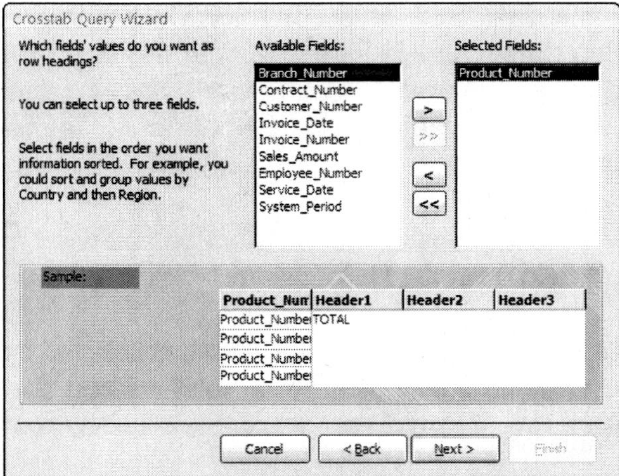

Figure 3-36: Select the Product_Number field then click the Next button.

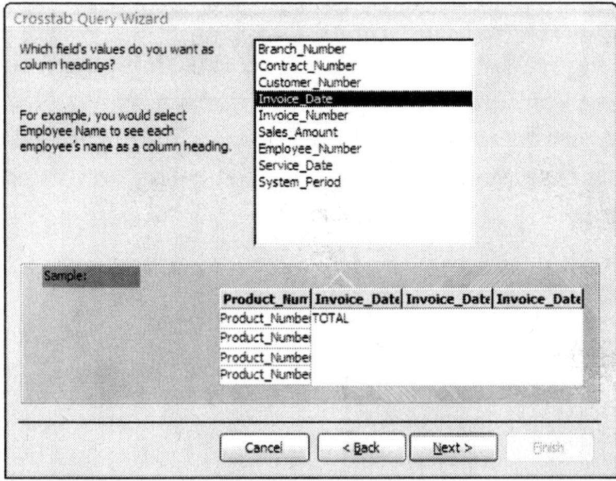

Figure 3-37: Select the Invoice_Date field then click the Next button.

NOTE **If the field that is being used as a column heading includes data that contains a period (.), an exclamation mark (!), or a bracket ([or]), those characters will be changed to an underscore character (_) in the column heading. This does not happen if the same data is used as a row heading. This behavior is by design, as the naming convention for Field names in Access prohibits use of these characters.**

If your column heading is a date field, as the Invoice_Date is in this example, you will see the step shown here in Figure 3-38. In this step, you will have the option of specifying an interval to group your dates by. Select Quarter here and notice that the sample diagram at the bottom of the dialog box updates accordingly.

You're almost done. In the second to last step, shown in Figure 3-39, you will identify the field you want to aggregate, and the function you want to use. Select the Sales_Amount field from the Fields list and then select Sum from the Functions list.

Note the check box next to Yes, include row sums. This box is selected by default to ensure that your crosstab query includes a Total column that contains the sum total for each row. If you do not want this column, clear the check box.

If you look at the sample diagram at the bottom of the dialog box, you will get a good sense of what your final crosstab query will do. In this example, your crosstab calculates the sum of the Sales_Amount field for each Product_Number by quarter.

The final step, shown in Figure 3-40, is to name your crosstab query. In this example, you are naming your crosstab Product Summary by Quarter. After you name your query, you have the option of viewing your query or modifying the design. In this case, you want to view your query results so simply click the Finish button.

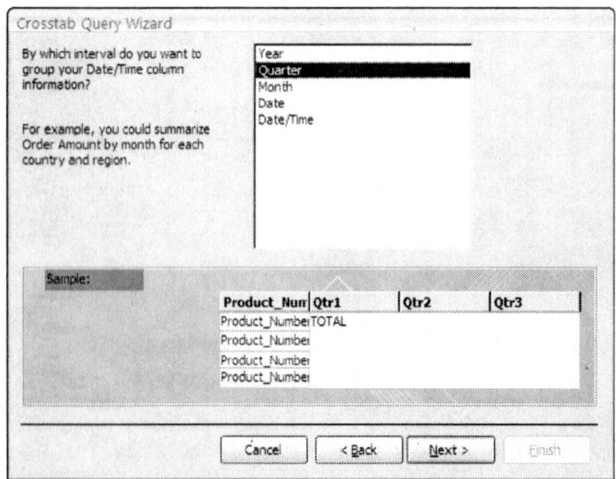

Figure 3-38: Select Quarter and then click the Next button.

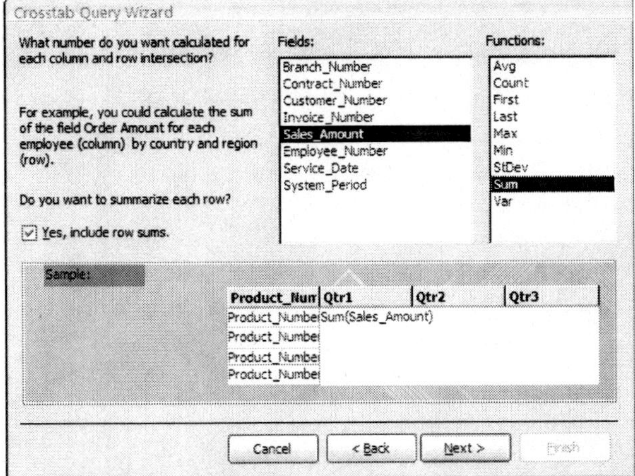

Figure 3-39: Select the Sale_Amount and Sum, and then click the Next button.

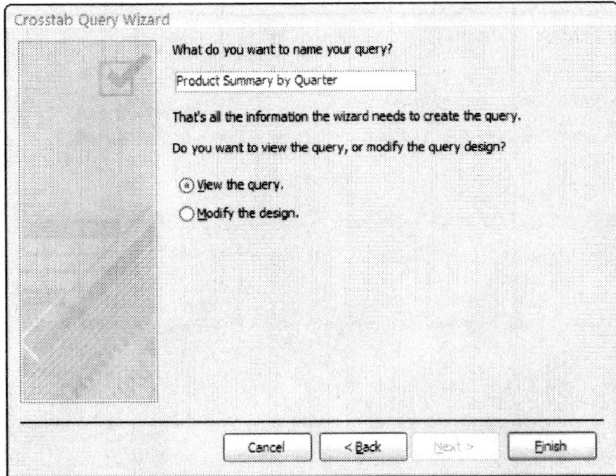

Figure 3-40: Select Finish to see your query results.

In just a few clicks, you have created a powerful look at the revenue performance of each product by quarter. See Figure 3-41.

Product_Number	Total Of Sales_Amount	Qtr 1	Qtr 2	Qtr 3	Qtr 4
16000	$2,361,161.41	$563,800.21	$621,715.87	$600,810.41	$574,834.92
30300	$2,627,798.02	$612,496.21	$691,440.40	$674,592.20	$649,269.21
70700	$2,178,932.11	$533,128.55	$567,392.96	$552,382.16	$526,028.44
81150	$1,138,595.78	$257,218.54	$290,074.98	$297,252.21	$294,050.05
87000	$1,190,911.60	$288,795.91	$310,668.86	$303,084.76	$288,362.07
90830	$1,276,790.55	$293,195.50	$325,277.88	$329,788.62	$328,528.56

Figure 3-41: A powerful analysis in just a few clicks.

TRICKS OF THE TRADE: TURNING YOUR CROSSTAB QUERY INTO HARD DATA

You will undoubtedly encounter scenarios where you will have to convert your crosstab query into hard data in order to use the results on another analysis. A simple trick in doing this is to use your saved crosstab query in a make-table query to create a new table with your crosstab results.

Start by creating a new select query in Design view and add your saved crosstab query. You are using the Product Summary by Quarter crosstab you just created (see Figure 3-42). Bring in the fields you will want to include in your new table.

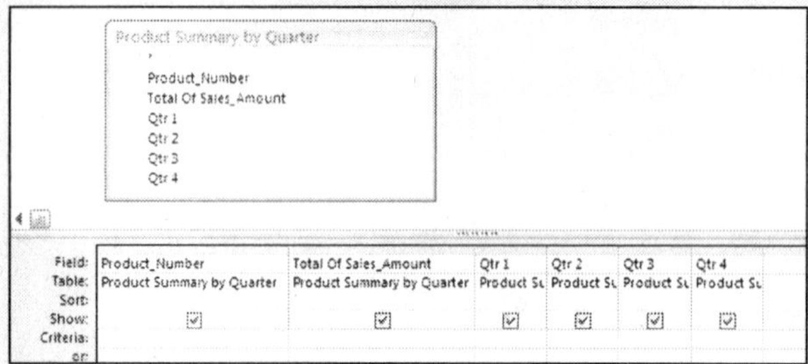

Figure 3-42: Create a select query using the crosstab query as your source data.

At this point, simply convert your query into a make-table query and run it. After you run your make-table, you will have a hard table that contains the results of your crosstab.

Creating a Crosstab Query Manually

Although the Crosstab Query Wizard makes it easy to create a crosstab in just a few clicks, it does come with its own set of limitations that may inhibit your data analysis efforts. These are the limitations you will encounter when using the Crosstab Query Wizard:

- You can only select one data source on which to base your crosstab. This means that if you need to crosstab data residing across multiple tables, you will need to take extra steps to create a temporary query to use as your data source.
- There is no way to filter or limit your crosstab query with criteria.

- You are limited to only three row headings.
- You cannot explicitly define the order of your column headings.

The good news is that you can create a crosstab query manually through the query design grid. As you will learn in the sections to follow, creating your crosstab manually allows you greater flexibility in your analysis.

Using the Query Design Grid to Create Your Crosstab Query

Create the aggregate query shown here in Figure 3-43. Note that you are using multiple tables to get the fields you need. One of the benefits of creating a crosstab query manually is that you don't have to use just one data source. You can use as many sources as you need in order to define the fields in your query.

Next, go to the ribbon and select the Design tab. From the Design tab, select the Crosstab button. At this point, you will notice that a row has been added to your query grid called Crosstab, as shown in Figure 3-44. The idea is to define what role each field will play in your crosstab query. Under each field in the Crosstab row, select where the field will be a Row Heading, a Column Heading, or a Value. Run the query to see your crosstab in action.

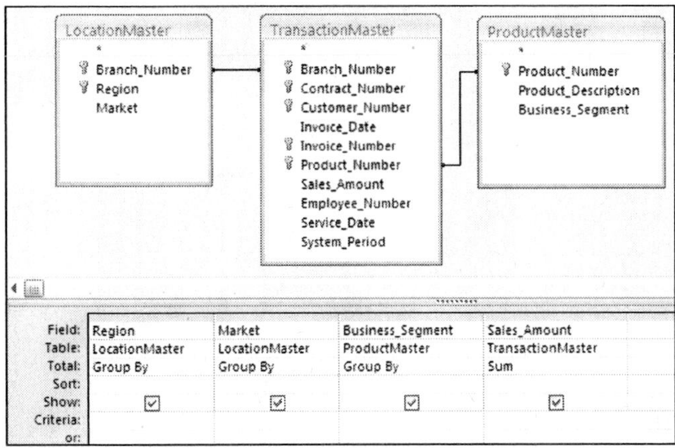

Figure 3-43: Create an aggregate query as shown here.

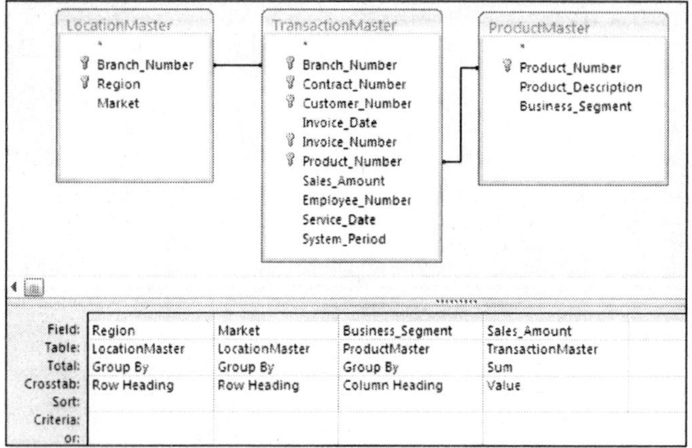

Figure 3-44: Set each field's role in the Crosstab row.

TRICKS OF THE TRADE: CREATING A CROSSTAB VIEW WITH MULTIPLE VALUE FIELDS

One of the rules of a crosstab query is that you cannot have more than one Value field. However, there is a trick to work around this limitation and analyze more than one metric with the same data groups. To help demonstrate how this works, create a crosstab query as shown in Figure 3-45 and save it as Crosstab-1. Your Column Heading is a custom field that will give you the region name and the word Revenue next to it.

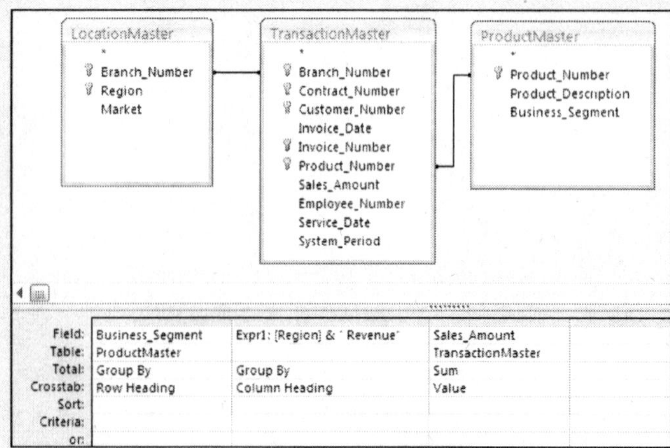

Figure 3-45: This crosstab will give you a revenue metric.

Next, create another crosstab query as shown in Figure 3-46 and save it as Crosstab-2. Again, your Column Heading is a custom field that will give you the region name and the word "Transactions" next to it.

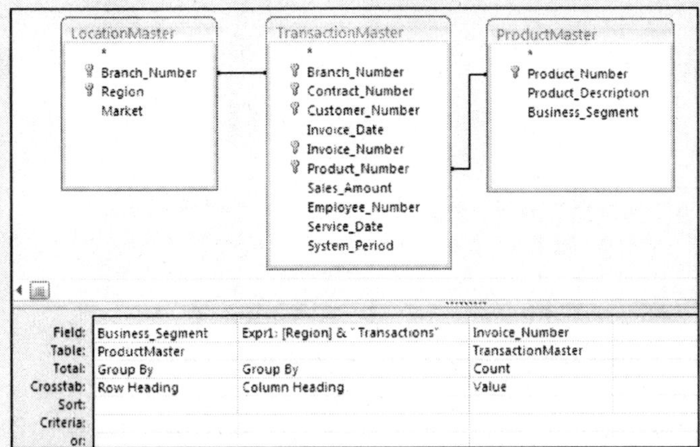

Figure 3-46: This crosstab will give you a transaction count metric.

Finally, create a select query that will join the two crosstab queries on the Row Heading. In the example shown here in Figure 3-47, the Row Heading is the Business_Segment field. Bring in all the fields in the appropriate order. When you run this query, the result will be an analysis that incorporates both crosstab queries, effectively giving you multiple value fields.

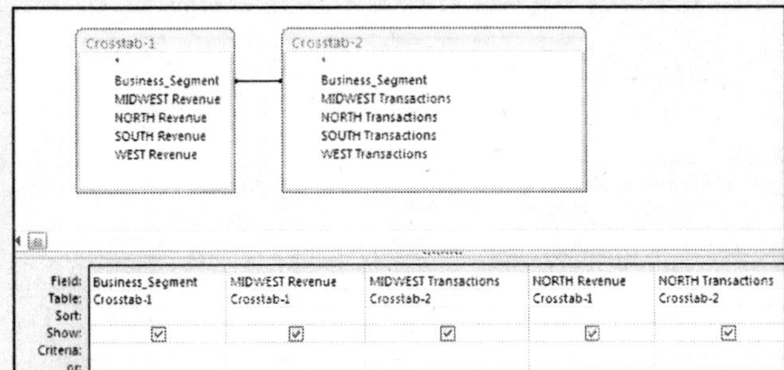

Figure 3-47: This crosstab will give you a transaction count metric.

When building your crosstab in the query grid, keep the following in mind:

- You must have a minimum of one Row Heading, one Column Heading, and one Value field.
- You cannot define more than one Column Heading.
- You cannot define more than one Value Heading.
- You are NOT limited to only three Row Headings.

NOTE Keep in mind that if you have more than one Row Heading, you will have to create a join on each Row Heading.

Customizing Your Crosstab Queries

As useful as crosstab queries can be, you may find that you need to apply some of your own customizations in order to get the results you need. In this section, you will explore a few of the ways you can customize your crosstab queries to meet your needs.

Defining Criteria in a Crosstab Query

The ability to filter or limit your crosstab query is another benefit of creating a crosstab query manually. To define a filter for your crosstab, simply enter the criteria as you normally would for any other aggregate query. Figure 3-48 demonstrates this concept.

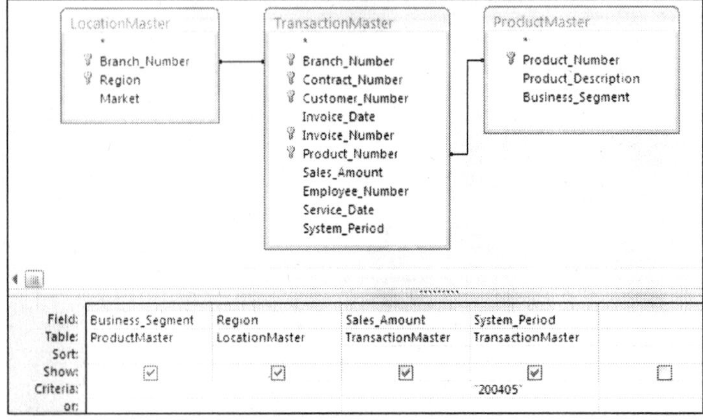

Figure 3-48: You can define a criterion to filter your crosstab queries.

Changing the Sort Order of Your Crosstab Column Headings

By default, crosstab queries sort their Column Headings in alphabetical order. For example, the crosstab query in Figure 3-49 will produce a dataset where the Column Headings read in this order: Midwest, North, South, West.

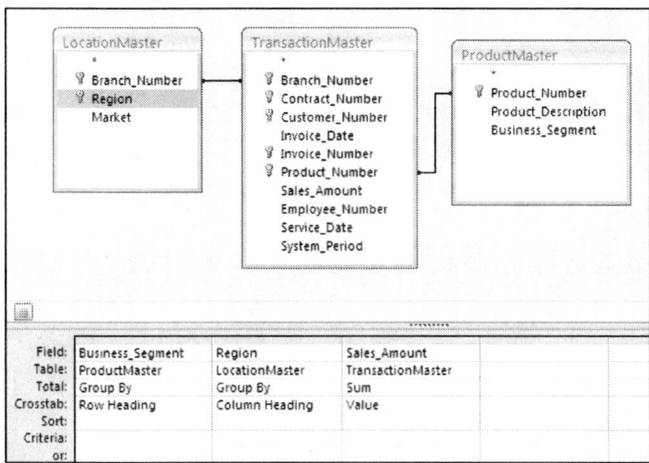

Figure 3-49: This crosstab will display all regions as columns in alphabetical order.

This may be fine in most situations, but if your company headquarters is in California, the executive management may naturally want to see the West region first. You can explicitly specify the column order of a crosstab query by changing the Column Headings attribute in the Property Sheet dialog box.

To get to the Column Headings attribute, open the query in Design view. Next, right-click in the grey area above the white query grid and select Properties. This activates the Property Sheet dialog box, shown in Figure 3-50. Here, you can enter the order you would like to see the column headings by changing the Column Headings attribute.

TIP **Adjusting the Column Headings attribute comes in handy when you are struggling with showing months in month order instead of alphabetical order. Simply enter the month columns in the order you would like to see them. For example: "Jan","Feb","Mar","Apr","May","Jun","Jul","Aug","Sep","Oct","Nov","Dec"**

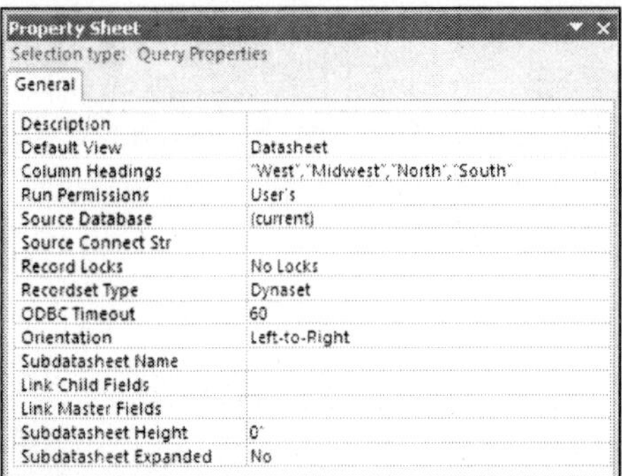

Figure 3-50: The Column Headings attribute is set to have the column headings read in this order: West, Midwest, North, South.

When working with the Column Headings attribute keep the following in mind:

- You must enter each column name in quotes and separate each column with commas.
- Accidentally misspelling a column name results in that column being excluded from the crosstab results and a dummy column with the misspelled name being included with no data in it.
- You must enter every column you want included in your crosstab report. Excluding a column from the Column Headings attribute will exclude that column from the crosstab results.
- Clearing the Column Headings attribute ensures that all columns are displayed in alphabetical order.

Summary

Data analysis often goes beyond selecting small extracts of data. The scope of data analysis also includes grouping and comparing data, updating and deleting data, performing calculations on data, and shaping and reporting data. Unfortunately, many Excel users don't realize that Access has built-in tools and functionality designed specifically to handle each one of these tasks.

Aggregate queries enable you to quickly group and summarize data, aggregating the returned dataset into totals, averages, counts, and more. Similarly, crosstab queries summarize values and group them in a matrix layout, perfect for analyzing trends over time, or providing a method for quickly identifying anomalies in your dataset.

Action queries go beyond just selecting data by actually performing some action on the returned results. The action that is performed depends on the type of action query you are using. There are four types of action queries: make-table query, delete query, append query, and update query.

A *make-table* query creates a new table consisting of the data resulting from the query. A *delete* query deletes records from a table based on the definitions and criteria you specify in the query. An *append* query appends records to a table based on the definitions and criteria you specify in your query. In other words, with an append query, you can add the results of your query to the end of a table, effectively adding rows to the table. An *update* query allows you to edit large amounts of data at one time.

Utilizing the tools and functionality outlined in this chapter will help you carry out all your analytical process *within* Access, saving you time, increasing your productivity, and reducing the chance for error.

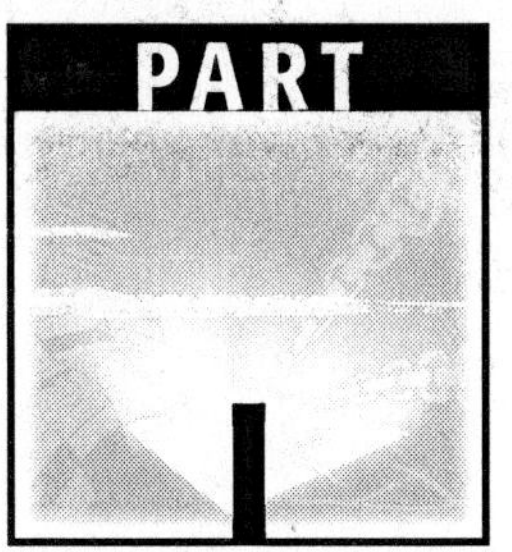

Fundamentals of Data Analysis in Access

CHAPTER

4

Transforming Your Data with Access

Data transformation generally entails certain actions that are meant to clean your data — actions such as establishing a table structure, removing duplicates, cleaning text, removing blanks, and standardizing data fields.

You will often receive data that is unpolished or raw. That is to say, the data may have duplicates, there may be blank fields, there may be inconsistent text, and so on. Before you can perform any kind of meaningful analysis on data in this state, it's important to go through a process of data transformation, or data cleanup.

Although many people store their data in Access, few use it for data transformation purposes, oftentimes preferring instead to export the data to Excel, perform any necessary cleanup there, and then import the data to Access. The obvious motive for this behavior is familiarity with the flexible Excel environment. However, exporting and importing data simply to perform such easy tasks can be quite inefficient, especially if you are working with large datasets.

This chapter introduces some of the tools and techniques in Access that make it easy for you to clean and massage your data without turning to Excel.

Finding and Removing Duplicate Records

Duplicate records are absolute analysis killers. The effect duplicate records have on your analysis can be far-reaching, corrupting almost every metric, summary, and analytical assessment you produce. It is for this reason that finding and removing duplicate records should be your first priority when you receive a new dataset.

Defining Duplicate Records

Before you jump into your dataset to find and remove duplicate records, it's important to consider how you define a duplicate record. To demonstrate this point, look at the table shown in Figure 4-1, where you see 11 records. Out of the 11 records, how many are duplicates?

If you were to define a duplicate record in Figure 4-1 as a duplication of just the SicCode, you would find 10 duplicate records. That is, out of the 11 records shown, one record has a unique SicCode whereas the other 10 are duplications. Now, if you were to expand your definition of a duplicate record to a duplication of both SicCode and PostalCode, you would find only two duplicates: the duplication of PostalCodes 77032 and 77040. Finally, if you were to define a duplicate record as a duplication of the unique value of SicCode, PostalCode, and CompanyNumber, you would find no duplicates.

This example shows that having two records with the same value in a column does not necessarily mean you have a duplicate record. It's up to you to determine which field or combination of fields will best define a unique record in your dataset.

SicCode	PostalCode	CompanyNumber	DollarPotential	City	State	Address
1389	77032	11147805	$9,517.00	houston	tx	6000 n sem heirten pk
1389	77032	11147848	$9,517.00	houston	tx	43410 e herdy rd
1389	77042	11160116	$7,653.00	houston	tx	40642 rachmend ave
1389	77051	11165400	$9,517.00	houston	tx	5646 heimis rd
1389	77057	11173241	$9,517.00	houston	tx	2514 san filape st ste
1389	77060	11178227	$7,653.00	houston	tx	100 n sem heirten pk
1389	77073	11190514	$9,517.00	houston	tx	4660 rankan rd # 400
1389	77049	11218412	$7,653.00	houston	tx	4541 mallir read 6
1389	77040	13398382	$18,379.00	houston	tx	3643 wandfirn rd
1389	77040	13399102	$18,379.00	houston	tx	3643 wandfirn rd
1389	77077	13535097	$7,653.00	houston	tx	44160 wisthiamir rd st

Figure 4-1: Are there duplicate records in this table? It depends on how you define one.

When you have a clear idea what field, or fields, best make up a unique record in your table, you can easily test your table for duplicate records by attempting to set them as a primary or combination key. To demonstrate this test, open the LeadList table in Design view, then tag the CompanyNumber field as a primary key. If you try to save this change, you will get the error message shown in Figure 4-2. This message means there is some duplication of records in your dataset that needs to be dealt with.

Finding Duplicate Records

If you have determined that your dataset does indeed contain duplicates, it's generally a good idea to find and review the duplicate records before removing them. Giving your records a thorough review will ensure you don't mistake a record as a duplicate and remove it from your analysis. You may find that you are mistakenly identifying valid records as duplications, in which case you will need to include another field in your definition of what makes up a unique record.

The easiest way to find the duplicate records in your dataset is to run the Find Duplicates Query Wizard. To start this wizard, go up to the application ribbon and select the Create tab. There you will find the Query Wizard button, which when clicked will activate the New Query dialog box shown in Figure 4-3. Here you can select Find Duplicates Query Wizard and then click the OK button.

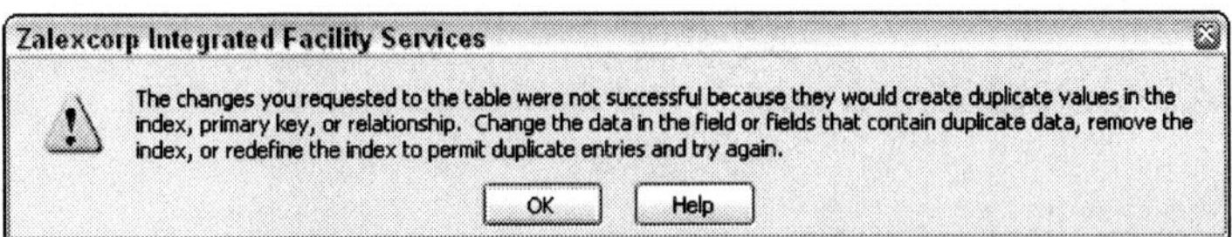

Figure 4-2: If you get this error message when trying to set a primary key, you have duplicate records in your dataset.

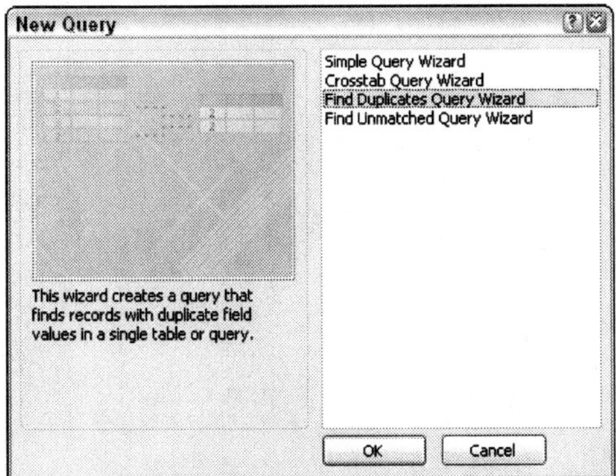

Figure 4-3: Select the Find Duplicates Query Wizard and then click the OK button.

At this point, you must select the particular dataset you will use in your Find Duplicate query. Note that you can use queries as well as tables. Select the LeadList table, as shown in Figure 4-4.

Next, you must identify which field, or combination of fields, best defines a unique record in your dataset. In the example shown in Figure 4-5, the CompanyNumber field alone defines a unique record. Click Next.

The next step, shown in Figure 4-6, is to identify any additional fields you would like to see in your query. Click the Next button.

In the final step, shown in Figure 4-7, finish off the wizard by naming your query and clicking the Finish button.

After you click Finish, your new Find Duplicates query opens immediately for your review. Figure 4-8 shows the resulting query.

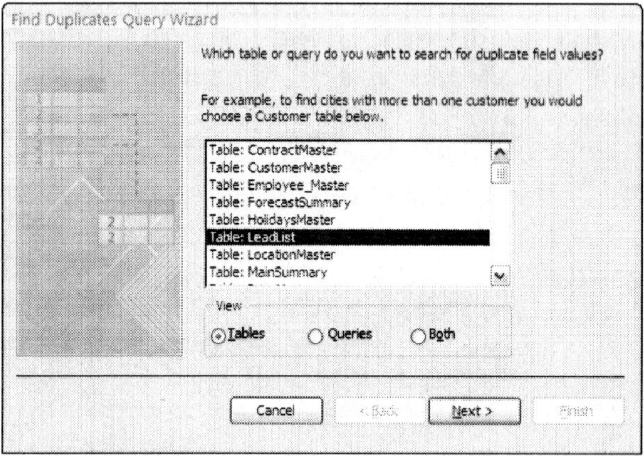

Figure 4-4: Select the dataset in which you want to find duplicates, then click Next.

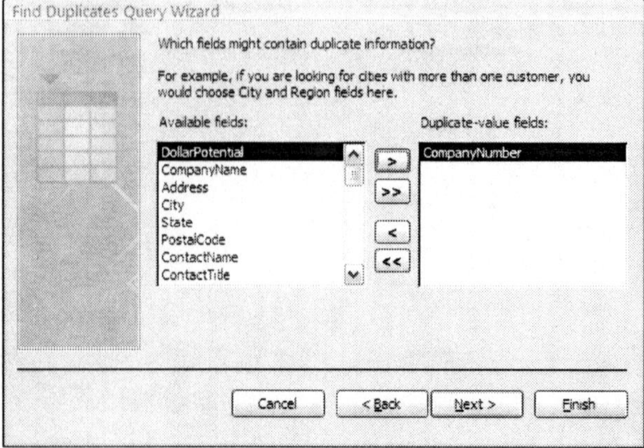

Figure 4-5: Select the field or fields that make up a unique record in your dataset.

Find Duplicates Query Wizard

Do you want the query to show fields in addition to those with duplicate values?

For example, if you chose to look for duplicate City values, you could choose CustomerName and Address here.

Available fields:

CompanyName
ContactName
ContactTitle
Phone
Fax
SicCode
SicDescription
Segment

Additional query fields:

DollarPotential
Address
City
State
PostalCode

Cancel | < Back | Next > | Finish

Figure 4-6: Select the field or fields you want to see in your query.

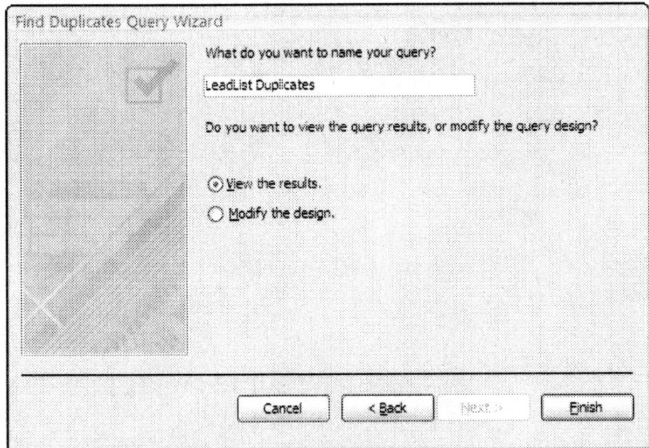

Figure 4-7: Name your query and click Finish.

CompanyNumber	DollarPotential	Address	City	State	PostalCode
10625840	$47,039.00	1100 landirs rd	n little rock	ar	72117
10625840	$47,039.00	1100 landirs rd	n little rock	ar	72117
11145186	$60,770.00	5364 lost fwy	houston	tx	77029
11145186	$60,770.00	5364 lost fwy	houston	tx	77029
11145186	$60,770.00	5364 lost fwy	houston	tx	77029
11145186	$60,770.00	5364 lost fwy	houston	tx	77029
11166089	$60,770.00	6632 biffalo spiidway	houston	tx	77054
11166089	$60,770.00	6632 biffalo spiidway	houston	tx	77054
11166089	$60,770.00	6632 biffalo spiidway	houston	tx	77054
11166089	$60,770.00	6632 biffalo spiidway	houston	tx	77054
11220179	$60,770.00	40420 tilge rd	houston	tx	77095
11220179	$60,770.00	40420 tilge rd	houston	tx	77095
11220179	$60,770.00	40420 tilge rd	houston	tx	77095
11220179	$60,770.00	40420 tilge rd	houston	tx	77095

Figure 4-8: Your Find Duplicates query.

NOTE **The records shown in your Find Duplicates query are not only the duplications. They include one unique record plus the duplication. For example, in Figure 4-8, you will notice that there are four records tagged with the CompanyNumber 11145186. Three of the four are duplicates that can be removed, while one should remain as a unique record.**

Removing Duplicate Records

If you are working with a small dataset, removing the duplicates can be as easy as manually deleting records from your Find Duplicates query. However, if you are working with a large dataset, your Find Duplicates query may result in more records than you care to manually delete. Believe it when someone tells you that manually deleting records from a 5,000-row Find Duplicates query is an eyeball-burning experience. Fortunately, there is an alternative to burning out your eyeballs.

The idea is to remove duplicates en masse by taking advantage of Access' built-in protections against duplicate primary keys. To demonstrate this technique, right-click on the LeadList table and select Copy. Next, right-click again and select Paste. At this point, the Paste Table As dialog box, shown in Figure 4-9, activates.

Name your new table LeadList_NoDups and select Structure Only from the Paste Options section. This creates a new empty table that has the same structure as your original.

Next, open your new LeadList_NoDups table in Design view and set the appropriate field or combination of fields as primary keys. Again, it's up to you to determine which field or combination of fields best define a unique record in your dataset. As you can see in Figure 4-10, the CompanyNumber field alone defines a unique record; therefore only the CompanyNumber field will be set as a primary key.

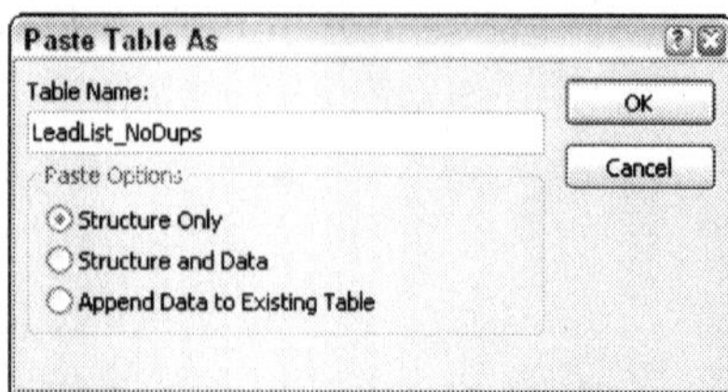

Figure 4-9: Activate the Paste Table As dialog box to copy your table's structure into a new table called LeadList_NoDups.

Pause here a moment and review what you have so far. At this point, you should have a table called LeadList and a table called LeadList_NoDups. The LeadList_NoDups table is empty and has the CompanyNumber field set as a primary key.

The last step is to create an Append query that appends all records from the LeadList table to the LeadList_NoDups table. When you run the Append query, you will get a message similar to the one shown in Figure 4-11.

Because the CustomerNumber field in the LeadList_NoDups table is set as the primary key, Access will not allow duplicate customer numbers to be appended. In just a few clicks, you have effectively created a table free from duplicates. You can now use this duplicate-free table as the source for any subsequent analysis!

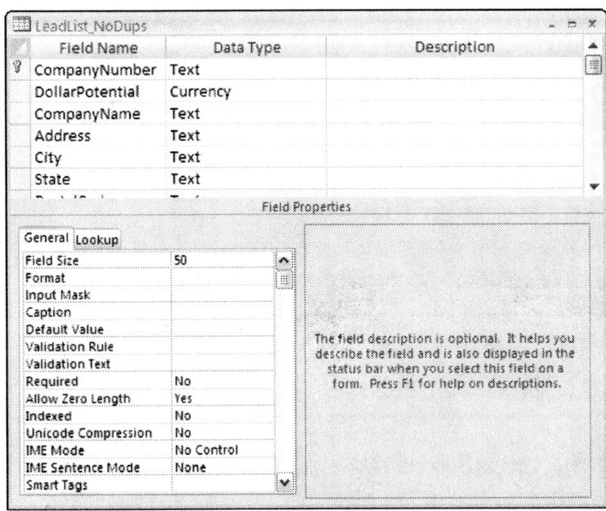

Figure 4-10: Set as a primary key the field or fields that best define a unique record.

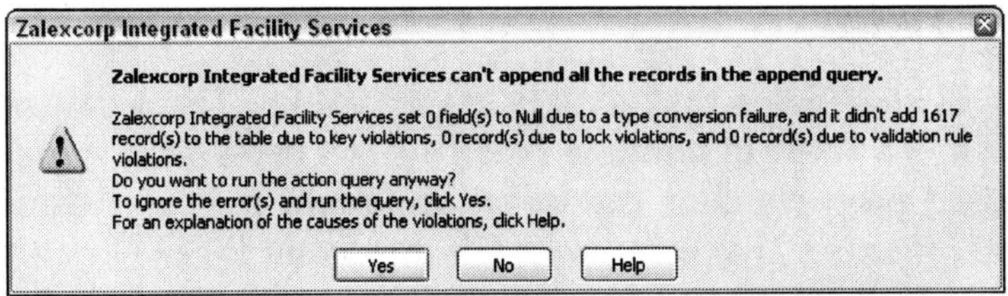

Figure 4-11: Now you can append all records excluding the duplicates.

TRICKS OF THE TRADE: REMOVING DUPLICATES WITH ONE MAKE-TABLE QUERY

Start a Make-Table query in Design view using, as the data source, the dataset that contains the duplicates. Right-click the grey area above the white query grid and select Properties. This activates the Property Sheet dialog box shown in Figure 4-12.

All you have to do here is change the Unique Values property to Yes. Close the Property Sheet dialog box and run the query.

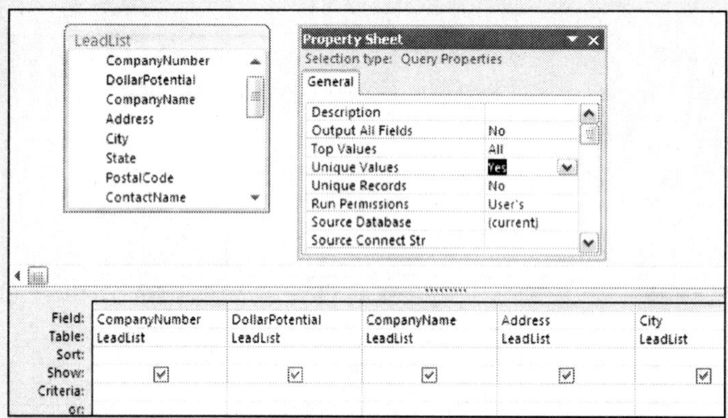

Figure 4-12: Running a Make-Table query with the Unique Values property set to Yes will ensure that your resulting table contains no duplicates.

Common Transformation Tasks

You will find that many of the unpolished datasets that come to you will require the same transformation actions. In that light, this section covers some of the most common transformation tasks you will have to perform.

Filling in Blank Fields

Oftentimes, you will have fields that contain empty values. These values are considered Null — a value of nothing. Nulls are not necessarily a bad thing. In fact, if used properly, they can be an important part of a well-designed relational database. That being said, it is important to note that an excessive amount of Null values in your data can lead to an unruly database environment. Too many Nulls in a database make querying and coding for your data more difficult as you will have to test for Nulls in almost every action you take.

Your job is to decide whether to leave the Nulls in your dataset or fill them in with an actual value. When deciding this, you should consider the following general guidelines:

- **Use Nulls Sparingly:** Working with, and coding for, a database is a much less daunting task when you don't have to test for Null values constantly.
- **Use alternatives when possible:** A good practice is to represent missing values with some logical missing value code whenever possible.
- **Never use Null values in number fields:** Use zeros instead of Nulls in a currency or a number field that will be used in calculations. Any mathematical operation that is performed using a field containing even one Null value will result in a Null answer (the wrong answer).

Filling in the Null fields in your dataset is as simple as running an Update query. In the example shown in Figure 4-13, you are updating the Null values in the DollarPotential field to zero.

It's important to note that there are actually two kinds of blank values: Null and empty string (""). When filling in the blank values of a text field, include the empty string as a criterion in your Update query to ensure that you don't miss any fields. In the example shown in Figure 4-14, you are updating the blank values in the Segment field to "Other."

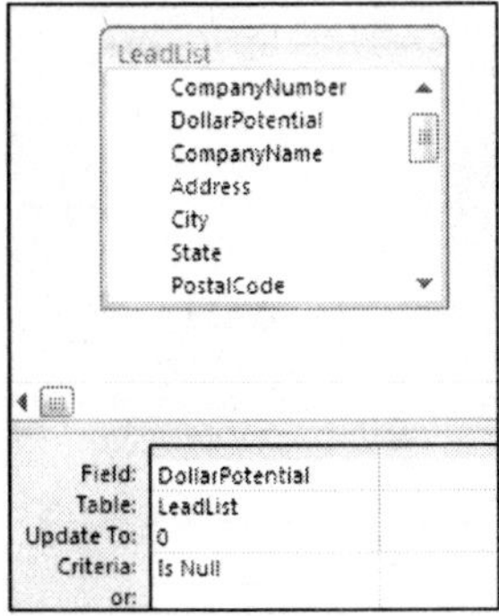

Figure 4-13: This query will update the Null values in the DollarPotential field to a value of zero.

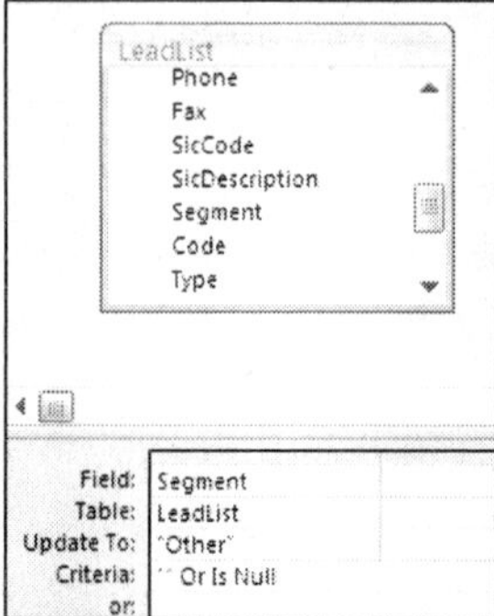

Figure 4-14: This query updates blank values in the Segment field to a value of "Other."

Concatenating

It's always amazing to see anyone export data out of Access and into Excel, only to concatenate (join two or more character strings end to end) and then re-import the data back into Access. You can easily concatenate any number of ways in Access with a simple Update query.

Concatenating Fields

Look at the Update query shown in Figure 4-15. In this query, you are updating the MyTest field with the concatenated row values of the Type field and the Code field.

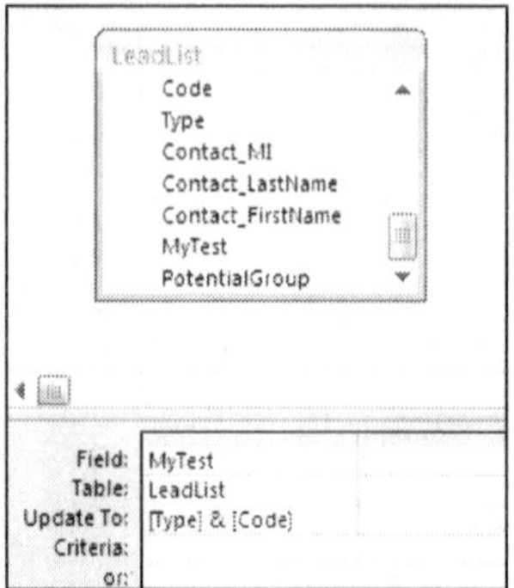

Figure 4-15: This query concatenates the row values of the Type field and the Code field.

TIP **It's a good idea to create a test field in order to test the effects of your data transformation actions before applying changes to the real data.**

Take a moment to analyze the following query breakdown:

- `[Type]`: This tells Access to use the row values of the Type field.
- `&`: The ampersand is a character operator that joins strings together.
- `[Code]`: This tells Access to use the row values of the Code field.

Figure 4-16 shows the results of this query.

WARNING **When running Update queries that perform concatenations, make sure the field you are updating is large enough to accept the concatenated string. For example, if the length of your concatenated string is 100 characters long, and the Field Size of the field you are updating is 50 characters, your concatenated string will be cut short without warning.**

Augmenting Field Values with Your Own Text

You can augment the values in your fields by adding your own text. For example, you may want to concatenate the row values of the Type field and the Code field, but separate them with a colon. The query in Figure 4-17 does just that.

Code	Type	MyTest
100199	DB	DB100199
200	DB	DB200
100199	DB	DB100199
100199	DB	DB100199
100199	DB	DB100199
100199	DB	DB100199
100199	DB	DB100199
100199	DB	DB100199
100199	DB	DB100199
100199	DB	DB100199
200	DB	DB200
100199	DB	DB100199
200	DB	DB200
200	DB	DB200
200	DB	DB200
100199	DB	DB100199

Figure 4-16: The MyTest field now contains the concatenated values of the Type field and the Code field.

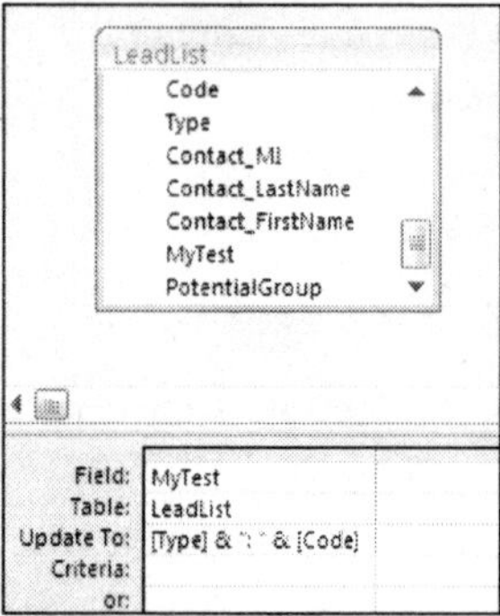

Figure 4-17: This query concatenates the row values of the Type field and the Code field and separates them with a colon.

Take a moment to analyze the following query breakdown:

- `[Type]`: This tells Access to use the row values of the Type field.
- &: The ampersand is a character operator that joins strings together.
- `": "`: This text will add a colon and a space to the concatenated string.
- `[Code]`: This tells Access to use the row values of the Code field.

Figure 4-18 shows the results of this query.

NOTE **When specifying your own text in a query, you must enclose the text in quotes.**

Code	Type	MyTest
100199	DB	DB: 100199
200	DB	DB: 200
100199	DB	DB: 100199
100199	DB	DB: 100199
100199	DB	DB: 100199
100199	DB	DB: 100199
100199	DB	DB: 100199
100199	DB	DB: 100199
100199	DB	DB: 100199
100199	DB	DB: 100199
200	DB	DB: 200
100199	DB	DB: 100199
200	DB	DB: 200
200	DB	DB: 200
200	DB	DB: 200
100199	DB	DB: 100199

Figure 4-18: The MyTest field now contains the concatenated values of the Type field and the Code field, separated by a colon.

Changing Case

Making sure the text in your database has the correct capitalization may sound trivial, but it's important. Imagine you receive a customer table that has an address field where all the addresses are lowercase. How is that going to look on labels, form letters, or invoices? Fortunately, for those who are working with tables containing thousands of records, Access has a few built-in functions that make changing the case of your text a snap.

The LeadList table shown in Figure 4-19 contains an Address field that is in all lowercase letters.

To fix the values in the Address field, you can use the `StrConv` function, which is a function that converts a string to a specified case.

The Update query shown in Figure 4-20 converts the values of the Address field to the proper case.

NOTE **You can also use the `Ucase` and `Lcase` functions to convert your text to upper- and lowercase text. These functions are highlighted in Appendix A of this book.**

ABOUT THE STRCONV FUNCTION

```
StrConv(string to be converted, conversion type,)
```

To use the `StrConv` function, you must provide two required arguments: the string to be converted, and the conversion type.

The string to be converted is simply the text you are working with. In a query environment, you can use the name of a field to specify that you are converting all the row values of that field.

The conversion type tells Access whether you want to convert the specified text to all uppercase, all lowercase, or proper case. There is a set of constants that identify the conversion type:

- **Conversion type 1 converts the specified text to uppercase characters.**
- **Conversion type 2 converts the specified text to lowercase characters.**
- **Conversion type 3 converts the specified text to proper case. That is, the first letter of every word is uppercase.**

Examples:

`StrConv("My Text",1)` **would be converted to "MY TEXT".**

`StrConv("MY TEXT",2)` **would be converted to "my text".**

`StrConv("my text",3)` **would be converted to "My Text".**

Address	City	State	PostalCode
46 gin criaghten w ebrems dr	agawam	ma	01001
426 bewlis rd	agawam	ma	01001
651 sheimekir ln	agawam	ma	01001
44 almgrin dr	agawam	ma	01001
35 mall ln	brimfield	ma	01010
460 fillir rd	chicopee	ma	01020
320 mimeraal dr ste 4	chicopee	ma	01020
4010 shiradan st	chicopee	ma	01022
5046 wistevir rd	chicopee	ma	01022
40 meple st	east longmeadow	ma	01028
242 biich st	holyoke	ma	01040
42 whatang ferms rd	holyoke	ma	01040
100 whatniy ave	holyoke	ma	01040
242 biich st	holyoke	ma	01040
4566 mean st	holyoke	ma	01040

Figure 4-19: The address field is in all lowercase letters.

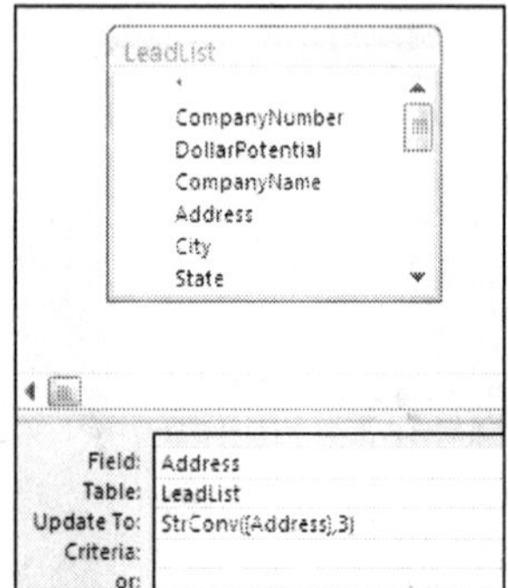

Figure 4-20: Use the StrConv function to convert the address to proper case.

TRICKS OF THE TRADE: SORTING BY CAPITALIZATION

Ever needed to sort on the capitalization of the values in a field? The query in Figure 4-21 demonstrates a trick that sorts a query where all the values whose first letter is lowercase are shown first.

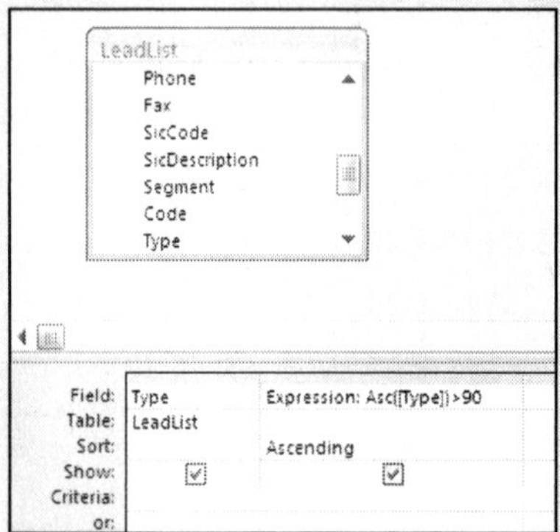

Figure 4-21: This query returns a dataset where all the values beginning with a lowercase letter are shown first.

How does this work? The `Asc` function is used to convert a string to its ASCII code. For example, `Asc("A")` would return 65 because 65 is the ASCII code for the uppercase letter A.

If you pass an entire word to the `Asc` function, it will only return the ASCII code for the first letter. Now in ASCII codes, uppercase letters A–Z are respectively represented by codes 65–90, whereas the lowercase letters a–z are respectively represented by codes 97–122.

The function `Asc([Type])>90` is asking the question, "Is the ASCII code returned by the string greater than 90?" The answer will be either True or False (-1 or 0). If the answer is true, then the first letter of the string is lowercase; otherwise, the first letter is uppercase.

Figure 4-22 shows the results of the query with the Expression field displayed.

Type	Expression
db	-1
db	-1
db	-1
db	-1
db	-1
DB	0
DB	0
DB	0
DB	0
DB	0
DB	0
DB	0
DB	0
DB	0
DB	0

Figure 4-22: This query is sorted in ascending order on the Expression field. Sorting this field in descending order displays values starting with uppercase letters first.

Removing Leading and Trailing Spaces from a String

When you receive a dataset from a mainframe system, a data warehouse, or even a text file, it is not uncommon to have field values that contain leading and trailing spaces. These spaces can cause some abnormal results, especially when you are appending values with leading and trailing spaces to other values that are clean. To demonstrate this, look at the dataset in Figure 4-23.

This is intended to be an Aggregate query that displays the sum of the dollar potential for California, New York, and Texas. However, the leading spaces are causing Access to group each state into two sets, preventing you from discerning the accurate totals.

State	SumOfDollarPotential
ca	$26,561,554.00
ny	$7,483,960.00
tx	$13,722,782.00
ca	$12,475,489.00
ny	$827,563.00
tx	$7,669,208.00

Figure 4-23: The leading spaces are preventing an accurate aggregation.

You can easily remove leading and trailing spaces by using the `Trim` function. Figure 4-24 demonstrates how you would update a field to remove the leading and trailing spaces by using an Update query.

NOTE **Using the `Ltrim` function removes only the leading spaces, whereas the `Rtrim` function removes only the trailing spaces. These functions are highlighted in Appendix A of this book.**

Finding and Replacing Specific Text

Imagine that you work in a company called BLVD, Inc. One day, the president of your company informs you that abbreviation blvd on all addresses is now deemed an infringement on your company's trademarked name, and must be changed to Boulevard as soon as possible. How would you go about meeting this new requirement? Your first thought may be to use the built-in Find and Replace functionality that exists in all Office applications. However, when your data consists of hundreds of thousands of rows, the Find and Replace function will only be able to process a few thousand records at a time. This clearly would not be very efficient.

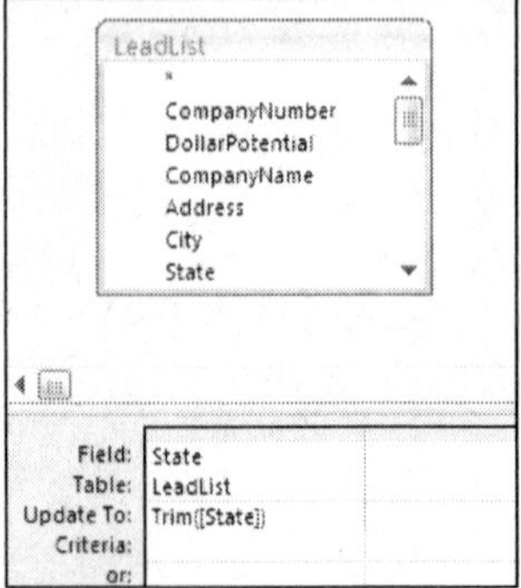

Figure 4-24: Simply pass the field name through the `Trim` function in an Update query to remove the leading and trailing spaces.

ABOUT THE REPLACE FUNCTION

`Replace(Expression, Find, Replace[, Start[, Count[, Compare]]])`

There are three required arguments in a `Replace` function and three optional arguments:

- `Expression` **(required): This is the full string you are evaluating. In a query environment, you can use the name of a field to specify that you are evaluating all the row values of that field.**
- `Find` **(required): This is the substring you need to find and replace.**
- `Replace` **(required): This is the substring used as the replacement.**
- `Start` **(optional): The position within substring to begin the search; default is 1.**
- `Count` **(optional): Number of occurrences to replace; default is all occurrences.**
- `Compare` **(optional): The kind of comparison to use; see Appendix A for details.**

For example:

`Replace("Pear", "P", "B")` **would return "Bear".**

`Replace("Now Here", " H", "h")` **would return "Nowhere".**

`Replace("Microsoft Access", "Microsoft ", "")` **would return "Access".**

The `Replace` function is ideal in a situation like this. As you can see in the following sidebar, the `Replace` function replaces a specified text string with a different string.

Figure 4-25 demonstrates how you would use the `Replace` function to meet the requirements in the scenario above.

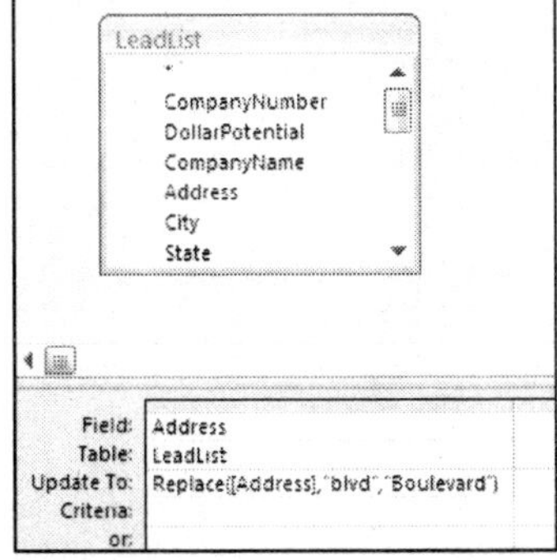

Figure 4-25: This query finds all instances of blvd and replaces them with Boulevard.

Adding Your Own Text in Key Positions Within a String

When transforming your data, you will sometimes have to add your own text in key positions within a string. For example, in Figure 4-26, you see two fields. The Phone field is the raw phone number received from a mainframe report, whereas the MyTest field is the same phone number transformed into a standard format. As you can see, the two parentheses and the dash were added in the appropriate positions within the string to achieve the correct format.

The edits demonstrated in Figure 4-26 were accomplished by using the `Right` function, the `Left` function, and the `Mid` function in conjunction with each other. See the sidebar below for more information on these functions.

TIP **In a `Mid` function, if there are fewer characters in the text being used than the length argument, the entire text will be returned. For example, `Mid("go",1,10000)` will return "go". As you will see later in this chapter, this behavior comes in handy when you are working with nested functions.**

Figure 4-27 demonstrates how the MyTest field was updated to the correctly formatted phone number.

Phone	MyTest
5165056000	(516) 505-6000
5164035400	(516) 403-5400
5066165444	(506) 616-5444
3455234200	(345) 523-4200
3455643000	(345) 564-3000
4402542666	(440) 254-2666
4404254000	(440) 425-4000
4403162400	(440) 316-2400
4406666060	(440) 666-6060
4401426366	(440) 142-6366
4406651235	(440) 665-1235
3454354055	(345) 435-4055
4404456066	(440) 445-6066
4403341000	(440) 334-1000
4404104020	(440) 410-4020
4401156404	(440) 115-6404

Figure 4-26: The phone number has been transformed into a standard format by adding the appropriate characters to key positions within the string.

ABOUT THE RIGHT, LEFT, AND MID FUNCTIONS

The `Right`, `Left`, and `Mid` functions allow you to extract portions of a string starting from different positions:

- **The `Left` function returns a specified number of characters starting from the leftmost character of the string. The required arguments for the `Left` function are the text you are evaluating and the number of characters you want returned. For example, `Left("70056-3504", 5)` returns five characters starting from the leftmost character ("70056").**
- **The `Right` function returns a specified number of characters starting from the rightmost character of the string. The required arguments for the `Right` function are the text you are evaluating and the number of characters you want returned. For example, `Right("Microsoft", 4)` returns four characters starting from the rightmost character ("soft").**
- **The `Mid` function returns a specified number of characters starting from a specified character position. The required arguments for the `Mid` Function are the text you are evaluating, the starting position, and the number of characters you want returned. For example, `Mid("Lonely", 2, 3)` returns three characters starting from the second character, or character number 2 in the string ("one").**

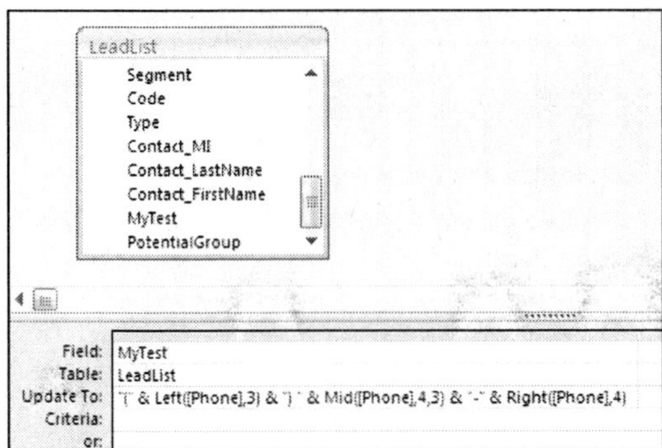

Figure 4-27: This query updates the MyTest field with a properly formatted phone number.

Take a moment to analyze the query breakdown below.

QUERY BREAKDOWN

- **"(": This text adds an open parenthesis to the resulting string.**
- **&: The ampersand is a character operator that joins strings together.**
- `Left([Phone],3)`**: This function extracts the left three characters of the [Phone] field.**
- **&: The ampersand is a character operator that joins strings together.**
- **") ": This text adds a close parenthesis and a space to the resulting string.**
- **&: The ampersand is a character operator that joins strings together.**
- `Mid([Phone],4,3)`**: This function extracts the three characters of the [Phone] field starting from character number four.**
- **&: The ampersand is a character operator that joins strings together.**
- **"-": This text will add a dash to the resulting string.**
- **&: The ampersand is a character operator that joins strings together.**
- `Right([Phone],4)`**: This function extracts the right four characters of the [Phone] field.**

TRICKS OF THE TRADE: PADDING STRINGS TO A SPECIFIC NUMBER OF CHARACTERS

You may encounter a situation where key fields are required to be a certain number of characters in order for your data to be able to interface with peripheral platforms such as ADP or SAP.

For example, imagine that the CompanyNumber field shown in Figure 4-28 must be 10 characters long. Those that are not 10 characters must be padded with enough leading zeros to create a 10-character string.

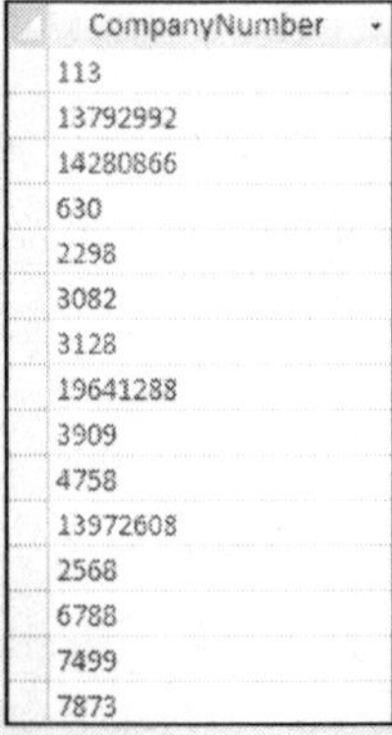

CompanyNumber
113
13792992
14280866
630
2298
3082
3128
19641288
3909
4758
13972608
2568
6788
7499
7873

Figure 4-28: You need to pad the values in the CompanyNumber field with enough leading zeros to create a 10-character string.

The secret to this trick is to add 10 zeros to every company number, regardless of the current length, then pass them through a `Right` function that will extract only the right 10 characters. For example, company number 29875764 would first be converted to 000000000029875764, then would go into a `Right` function that extracted out only the right 10 characters; `Right("000000000029875764",10)`. This would leave you with 0029875764.

Although this is essentially two steps, you can accomplish this with just one Update query. Figure 4-29 demonstrates how this is done. This query first concatenates each company number with "0000000000", and then passes that concatenated string through a `Right` function that extracts only the right 10 characters.

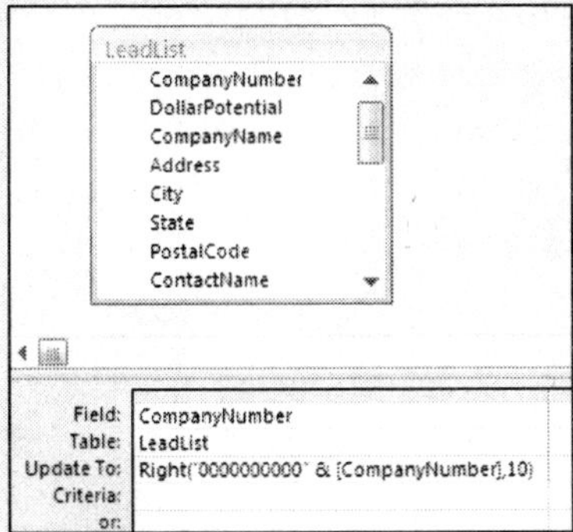

Figure 4-29: This query updates each value in the CompanyNumber field to a 10-character string with leading zeros.

Figure 4-30 shows the results of this query.

CompanyNumber
0000000113
0013792992
0014280866
0000000630
0000002298
0000003082
0000003128
0019641288
0000003909
0000004758
0013972608
0000002568
0000006788
0000007499
0000007873

Figure 4-30: The CompanyNumber field now contains 10-character company numbers.

Parsing Strings Using Character Markers

Have you ever had a dataset where two or more distinct pieces of data were jammed into one field and separated by commas? For example, a field called Address may have a string that represents Address, City, State, Zip. In a proper database, this string would be parsed into four fields.

In Figure 4-31, you can see that the values in the ContactName field are strings that represent Last name, First name, Middle initial. You will need to parse this string into three separate fields.

Although this is not a straightforward undertaking, it can be done fairly easily with the help of the `Instr` function, which is detailed in the following sidebar.

If the `Instr` function only returns a number, how can it help you? Well, the idea is to use the `Instr` function with the `Left`, `Right`, or `Mid` functions in order to extract a string. For example, instead of using a hard-coded number in your `Left` function to pass it the required length argument, you can use a nested `Instr` function to return that number. For example, `Left("Alexander, Mike",9)` is the same as `Left ("Alexander, Mike", Instr("Alexander, Mike", ",")-1)`.

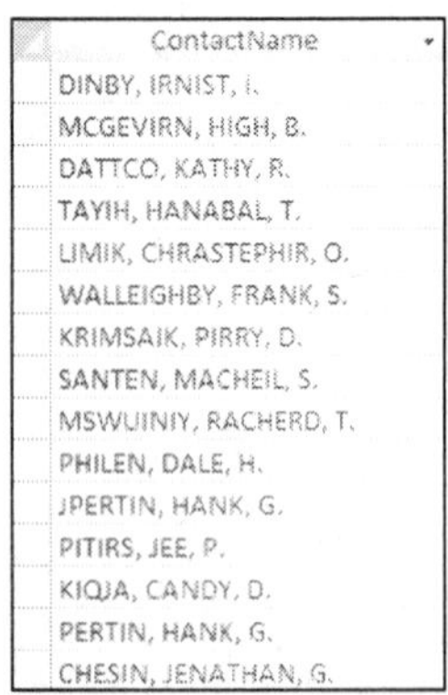

ContactName
DINBY, IRNIST, I.
MCGEVIRN, HIGH, B.
DATTCO, KATHY, R.
TAYIH, HANABAL, T.
LIMIK, CHRASTEPHIR, O.
WALLEIGHBY, FRANK, S.
KRIMSAIK, PIRRY, D.
SANTEN, MACHEIL, S.
MSWUINIY, RACHERD, T.
PHILEN, DALE, H.
JPERTIN, HANK, G.
PITIRS, JEE, P.
KIQJA, CANDY, D.
PERTIN, HANK, G.
CHESIN, JENATHAN, G.

Figure 4-31: You need to parse the values in the ContactName field into three separate fields.

ABOUT THE INSTR FUNCTION

`Instr(Start, String, Find, Compare)`

The `Instr` function searches for a specified string in another string and returns its position number. There are two required arguments in an `Instr` function and two optional arguments.

- `Start` **(optional): This is the character number to start the search; default is 1.**
- `String` **(required): This is the string to be searched.**
- `Find` **(required): This is the string to search for.**
- `Compare` **(optional): This specifies the type of string comparison.**

For example:

`InStr("Alexander, Mike, H",",")` **would return 10 because the first comma of the string is character number 10.**

`InStr(11,"Alexander, Mike, H",",")` **would return 16 because the first comma from character number 11 is character number 16.**

NOTE **When you are nesting an `Instr` function inside of a `Left`, `Right`, or `Mid` function, you may have to add or subtract a character, depending on what you want to accomplish. For example:**

`Left("Zey, Robert", Instr("Zey, Robert", ","))` **returns "Zey,".**

Why is the comma included in the returned result? The `Instr` function returns `4` because the first comma in the string is the fourth character. The `Left` function then uses `4` as a length argument, effectively extracting the left four characters: "Zey,".

If you want a clean extract without the comma, you will have to modify your function to read like this:

```
Left("Zey, Robert", Instr("Zey, Robert", ",")-1)
```

Subracting `1` from the `Instr` function leaves you with `3` instead of `4`. The `Left` function then uses `3` as the length argument, effectively extracting the left three characters: "Zey".

The easiest way to parse the contact name field, shown in Figure 4-31, is to use two Update queries.

WARNING **This is a somewhat tricky process, so you will want to create and work in test fields. This ensures that you give yourself a way back from any mistakes you may make.**

Query 1

The first query, shown in Figure 4-32, parses out the last name in the ContactName field and updates the Contact_LastName field. It will then update the Contact_FirstName field with the remaining string.

If you open the LeadList table, you will be able to see the impact of your first Update query. Figure 4-33 shows your progress so far.

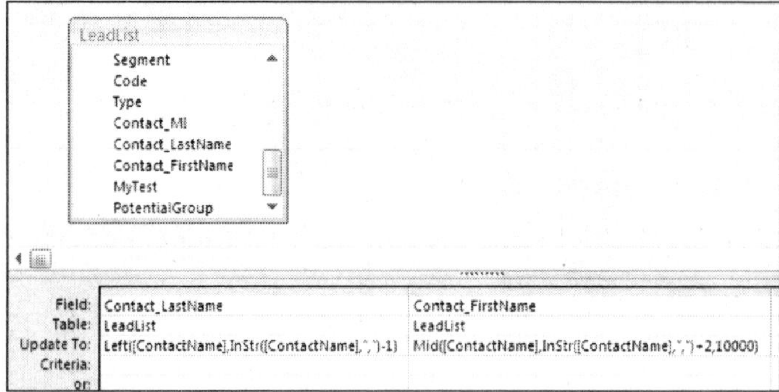

Figure 4-32: This query updates the Contact_LastName and Contact_FirstName fields.

Contact_LastName	Contact_FirstName
DINBY	IRNIST, I.
MCGEVIRN	HIGH, B.
DATTCO	KATHY, R.
TAYIH	HANABAL, T.
LIMIK	CHRASTEPHIR, O.
WALLEIGHBY	FRANK, S.
KRIMSAIK	PIRRY, D.
SANTEN	MACHEIL, S.
MSWUINIY	RACHERD, T.
PHILEN	DALE, H.
JPERTIN	HANK, G.
PITIRS	JEE, P.
KIQJA	CANDY, D.
PERTIN	HANK, G.
CHESIN	JENATHAN, G.

Figure 4-33: Check your progress so far.

Query 2

The second query, shown in Figure 4-34, updates the Contact_FirstName field and the Contact_MI.

After you run your second query, you can open your table and see the results, shown in Figure 4-35.

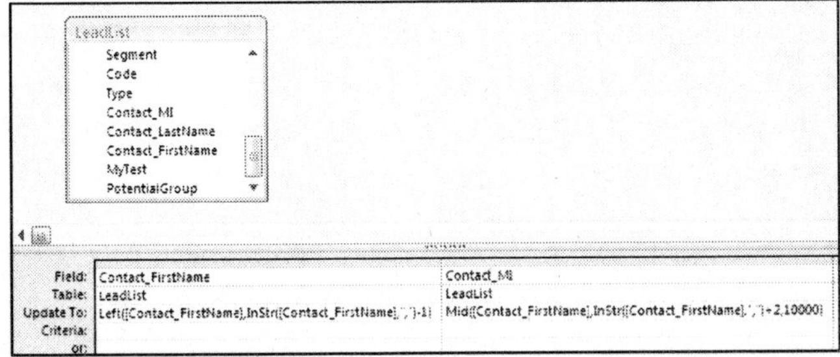

Figure 4-34: This query parses out the first name and the middle initial from the Contact_FirstName field.

ContactName	Contact_LastName	Contact_FirstName	Contact_MI
DINBY, IRNIST, I.	DINBY	IRNIST	I.
MCGEVIRN, HIGH, B.	MCGEVIRN	HIGH	B.
DATTCO, KATHY, R.	DATTCO	KATHY	R.
TAYIH, HANABAL, T.	TAYIH	HANABAL	T.
LIMIK, CHRASTEPHIR, O.	LIMIK	CHRASTEPHIR	O.
WALLEIGHBY, FRANK, S.	WALLEIGHBY	FRANK	S.
KRIMSAIK, PIRRY, D.	KRIMSAIK	PIRRY	D.
SANTEN, MACHEIL, S.	SANTEN	MACHEIL	S.
MSWUINIY, RACHERD, T.	MSWUINIY	RACHERD	T.
PHILEN, DALE, H.	PHILEN	DALE	H.
JPERTIN, HANK, G.	JPERTIN	HANK	G.
PITIRS, JEE, P.	PITIRS	JEE	P.
KIQJA, CANDY, D.	KIQJA	CANDY	D.
PERTIN, HANK, G.	PERTIN	HANK	G.
CHESIN, JENATHAN, G.	CHESIN	JENATHAN	G.

Figure 4-35: With two queries, you have successfully parsed the ContactName field into three separate fields.

Summary

Data transformation is the process of cleaning up your data. Before you can perform any kind of meaningful analysis on data in this state, it's important to go through a process of data cleanup. Although Access has several built-in functions and tools that enable you to transform data, most users find themselves exporting data to Excel in order to perform these tasks.

As this chapter shows, there is no need to take the extra effort of moving records to Excel to transform data. Access can easily perform various types of data cleanup to include removing duplicates, concatenating strings of text, filling in blank fields, parsing characters, replacing text, changing case, and augmenting data with your own text.

CHAPTER

5

Working with Calculations and Dates

The truth is that few organizations can analyze their raw data at face value. More often than not, some preliminary analysis with calculations and dates must be carried out before the big-picture analysis can be performed. Again, Excel is the preferred platform for working with calculations and dates. However, as you will learn in this chapter, Access provides a wide array of tools and built-in functions that make working with calculations and dates possible.

Using Calculations in Your Analysis

If you are an Excel user trying to familiarize yourself with Access, one of the questions you undoubtedly have is, "Where do the formulas go?" In Excel, you have the flexibility to enter a calculation via a formula directly into the dataset you are analyzing. You do not have this ability in Access. So the question is, where do you store calculations in Access?

As you have already learned, things work differently in Access. The natural structure of an Access database forces you to keep your data separate from your analysis. In this light, you will not be able to store a calculation (a formula) in your dataset. Now, it is true that you can store the calculated results as hard data, but using tables to store calculated results is problematic for several reasons:

- Stored calculations take up valuable storage space.
- Stored calculations require constant maintenance as the data in your table changes.
- Stored calculations generally tie your data to one analytical path.

Instead of storing the calculated results as hard data, it is a better practice to perform calculations at the precise moment when they are needed. This ensures the most current and accurate results and does not tie your data to one particular analysis.

Common Calculation Scenarios

In Access, calculations are performed by using expressions. An *expression* is a combination of values, operators, or functions that are evaluated to return a separate value to be used in a subsequent process. For example, 2+2 is an expression that returns the integer 4, which can be used in a subsequent analysis. Expressions can be used almost anywhere in Access to accomplish various tasks: in queries, forms, reports, data access pages, and even in tables to a certain degree. In this section, you will learn how to expand your analysis by building real-time calculations using expressions.

Using Constants in Calculations

Most calculations typically consist of hard-coded numbers or *constants*. A constant is a static value that does not change. For example, in the expression `[Price]*1.1`, `1.1` is a constant; the value of `1.1` will never change. Figure 5-1 demonstrates how a constant can be used in an expression within a query.

In this example, you are building a query that analyzes how the current price for each product compares to the same price with a 10 percent increase. The expression, entered under the alias Increase, multiplies the price field of each record with a constant value of `1.1`, calculating a price that is 10 percent over the original value in the Price field.

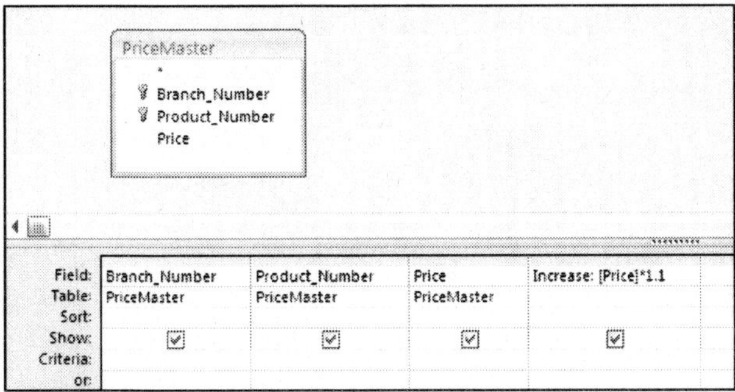

Figure 5-1: In this query, you are using a constant to calculate a 10 percent price increase.

Using Fields in Calculations

Not all of your calculations will require you to specify a constant. In fact, many of the mathematical operations you will carry out will be performed on data that already resides in fields within your dataset. You can perform calculations using any fields formatted as number or currency.

For example, in the query shown in Figure 5-2, you are not using any constants. Instead, your calculation will be executed using the values in each record of the dataset. This is similar to referencing cell values in an Excel formula.

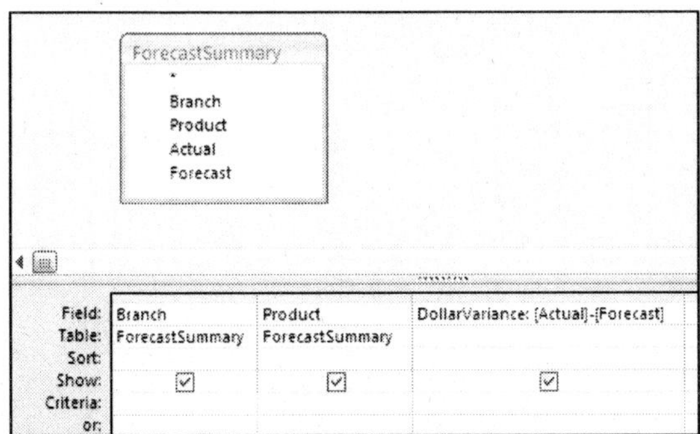

Figure 5-2: In this query, you are using two fields in a Dollar Variance calculation.

Using the Results of Aggregation in Calculations

Using the result of an aggregation as an expression in a calculation enables you to perform multiple analytical steps in one query. In the example in Figure 5-3, you are running an aggregate query. This query executes in the following order.

1. The query first groups your records by branch number.
2. The query calculates the count of invoices and the sum of revenue for each branch.
3. The query assigns the aliases you have defined respectively ("InvoiceCount" and "Rev").
4. The query then uses the aggregation results for each branch as expressions in your "AvgDollarPerInvoice" calculation.

Using the Results of One Calculation as an Expression in Another

Keep in mind that you are not limited to one calculation per query. In fact, you can use the results of one calculation as an expression in another calculation. Figure 5-4 illustrates this concept.

In this query, you are first calculating an adjusted forecast and then using the results of that calculation in another calculation that returns the variance of Actual versus Adjusted Forecast.

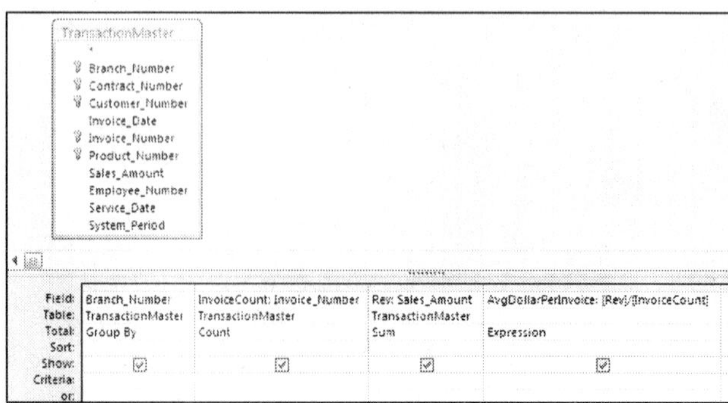

Figure 5-3: In this query, you are using the aggregation results for each branch number as expressions in your calculation.

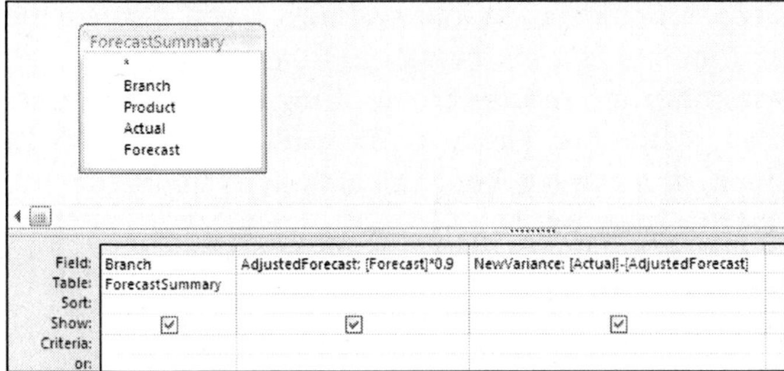

Figure 5-4: This query uses the results of one calculation as an expression in another.

Using a Calculation as an Argument in a Function

Look at the query in Figure 5-5. The calculation in this query returns a number with a fractional part. That is, it returns a number that contains a decimal point followed by many trailing digits. You would like to return a round number, however, making the resulting dataset easier to read.

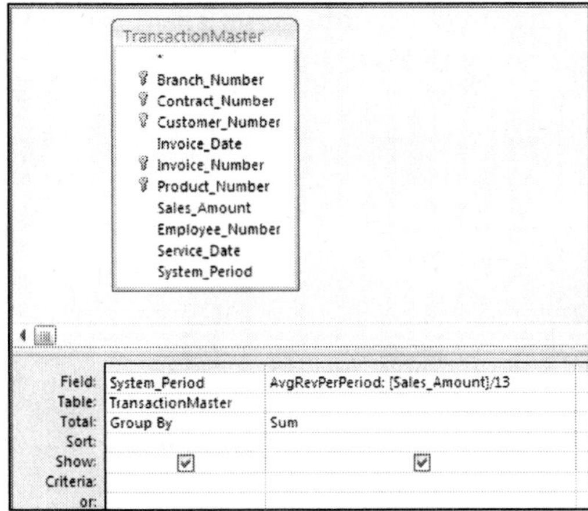

Figure 5-5: The results of this calculation will be difficult to read because they are all fractions that have many digits trailing a decimal point. Forcing the results into round numbers will make for easier reading.

To force the results of your calculation into an integer, you can use the `Int` function. The `Int` function is a mathematical function that removes the fractional part of a number and returns the resulting integer. This function takes one argument, a number. However, instead of hard coding a number into this function, you can use your calculation as the argument. Figure 5-6 demonstrates this concept.

NOTE **You can use calculations that result in a number value in any function where a number value is accepted as an argument.**

Using the Expression Builder to Construct Calculations

If you are not yet comfortable manually creating complex expressions with functions and calculations, Access provides the Expression Builder. The Expression Builder guides you through constructing an expression with a few clicks of the mouse. Avid Excel users may relate the Expression Builder to the Insert Function Wizard found in Excel. The idea is that you build your expression by simply selecting the necessary functions and data fields.

To activate the Expression Builder, right-click inside the cell that contains your expression and select Build, as shown in Figure 5-7.

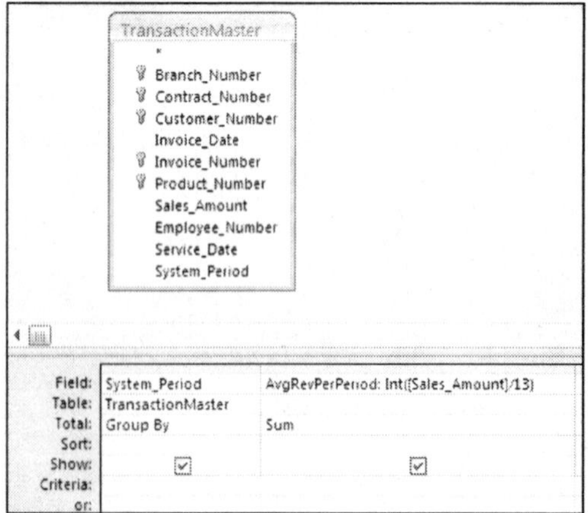

Figure 5-6: You can use your calculation as the argument in the `Int` function, allowing you to remove the fractional part the resulting data.

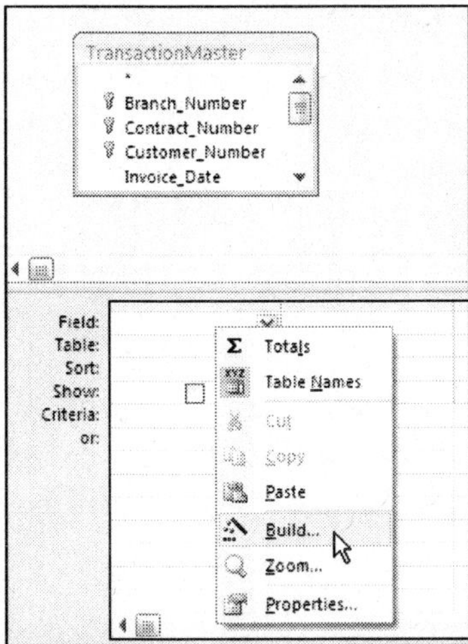

Figure 5-7: Activate the Expression Builder by right-clicking inside the Field row of the query grid and selecting Build.

NOTE **In fact, you can activate the Expression Builder by right-clicking anywhere you would write expressions, including: control properties in forms, control properties in reports, field properties in tables, as well as in the query design grid.**

As you can see in Figure 5-8, the Expression Builder has four panes to work in. The upper pane is where you enter the expression. The lower panes show the different objects available to you. In the lower left pane you can see the five main database objects: tables, queries, forms, reports, and functions.

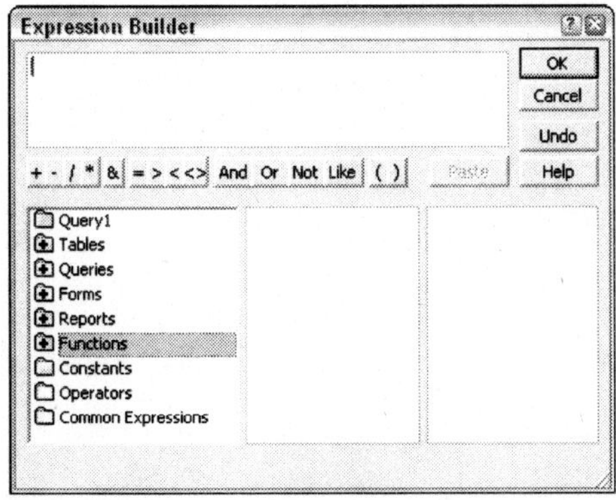

Figure 5-8: The Expression Builder displays all the database objects you can use in your expression.

Double-click any of the five main database objects to drill down to the next level of objects. By double-clicking the Functions object, for example, you will be able to drill into the Built-In Functions folder where you will see all the functions available to you in Access. Figure 5-9 shows the Expression Builder set to display all the available math functions.

The idea is that you double-click the function you need and Access will automatically enter the function in the upper pane of the Expression Builder. In the example shown in Figure 5-10, the selected function is the `Round` function. As you can see, the function is immediately placed in the upper pane of the Expression Builder and Access shows you the arguments needed to make the function work. In this case, you need a Number argument and a Precision argument.

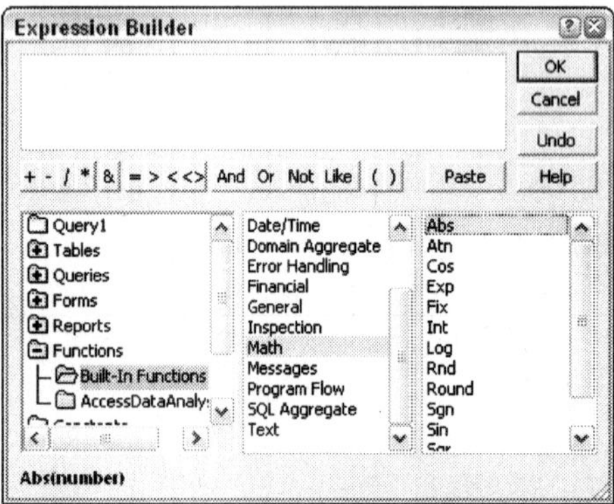

Figure 5-9: Similar to the Insert Function Wizard in Excel, the Expression Builder displays all the functions available to you.

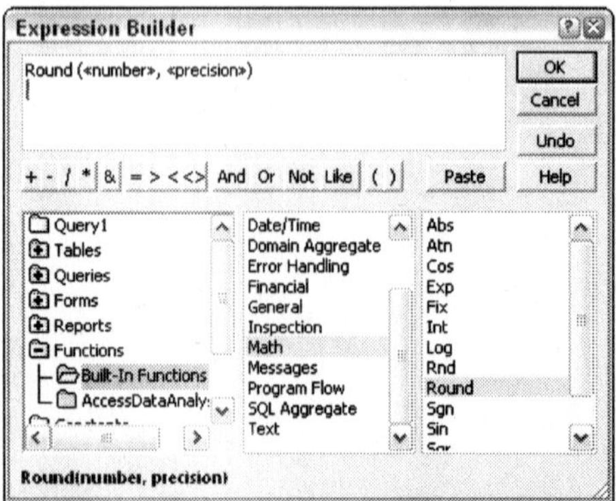

Figure 5-10: Access tells you which arguments are needed to make the function work.

If you don't know what an argument means, simply highlight the argument in question and then click the Help button. Access will activate a help window that provides an explanation of the function. As shown in Figure 5-11, for example, the `Round` function requires a number to be rounded and an optional Precision argument, which, in this case, indicates the number of decimal places that are used in the rounding operation.

As you can see in Figure 5-12, instead of using a hard-coded number in the `Round` function, an expression is used to return a dynamic value. This calculation will divide the sum of [TransactionMaster]![Sales_Amount] by 13. Since the Precision argument is optional, that argument is left off.

When you are satisfied with your newly created expression, click the OK button to insert it into the query grid. Figure 5-13 shows that the new expression has been added as a field. Note that the new field has a default alias of Expr1; you can rename this to something more meaningful.

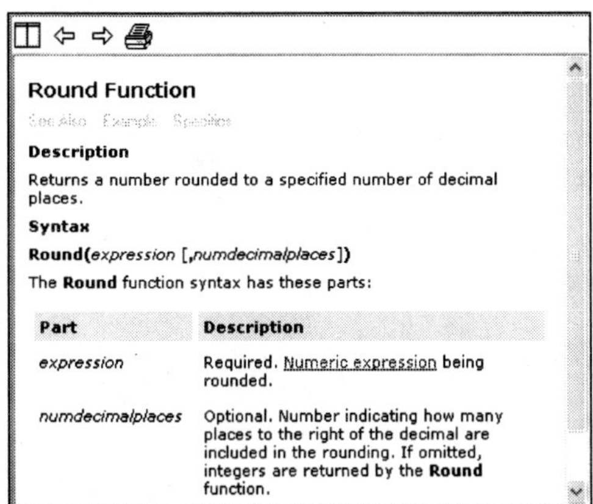

Figure 5-11: Help files are available to explain each function in detail.

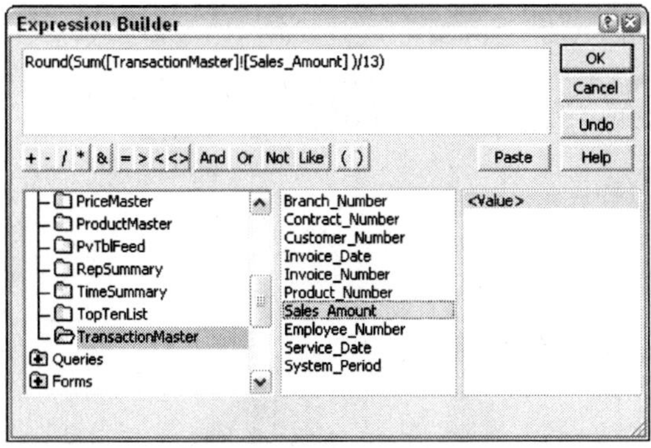

Figure 5-12: The function here will round the results of the calculation, ([TransactionMaster]![Sales_Amount])/13.

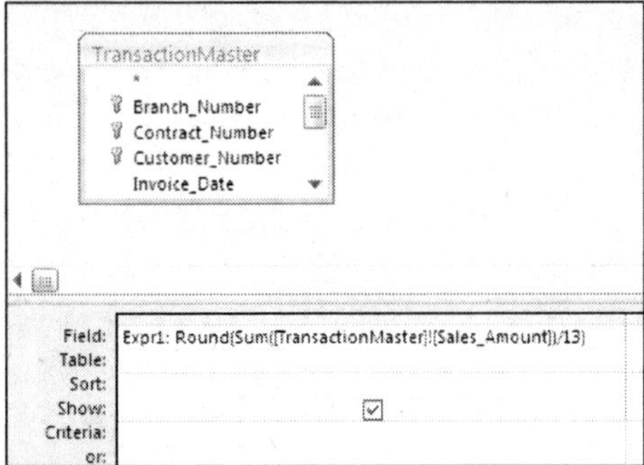

Figure 5-13: Your newly created expression has been added.

Common Calculation Errors

No matter what platform you are using to analyze your data, there is always the risk of errors when working with calculations. There is no magic function in Access that will help you prevent errors in your analysis. However, there are a few fundamental actions you can take to avoid some of the most common calculation errors.

Understanding the Order of Operator Precedence

You might remember from your algebra days that when working with a complex equation, executing multiple mathematical operations, the equation does not necessarily evaluate left to right. Some operations have precedence over others and therefore must occur first. The Access environment has similar rules regarding the order of operator precedence. When you are using expressions and calculations that involve several operations, each operation is evaluated and resolved in a predetermined order. It is important to know the order of operator precedence in Access. An expression that is incorrectly built may cause errors on your analysis.

The order of operations for Access is as follows:

1. Evaluate items in parentheses.
2. Perform exponentiation (^ calculates exponents).
3. Perform negation (- converts to negative).
4. Perform multiplication (* multiplies) and division (/ divides) at equal precedence.
5. Perform addition (+ adds) and subtraction (- subtracts) at equal precedence.

6. Evaluate string concatenation (&).
7. Evaluate comparison and pattern matching operators (>, <, =, <>, >=, <=, Like, Between, Is) at equal precedence.
8. Evaluate logical operators in the following order: Not, And, Or.

NOTE **Operations that are equal in precedence are performed from left to right.**

How can understanding the order of operations ensure that you avoid analytical errors? Consider this basic example. The correct answer to the calculation, `(20+30)*4`, is 200. However, if you leave off the parentheses (as in `20+30*4`), Access will perform the calculation like this: `30*4 = 120 + 20 = 140`. The order of operator precedence mandates that Access performs multiplication before addition. Therefore, entering `20+30*4` will give you the wrong answer. Because the order of operator precedence in Access mandates that all operations in parentheses be evaluated first, placing `20+30` inside parentheses ensures the correct answer.

Watching Out for Null Values

A *Null value* represents the absence of any value. When you see a data item in an Access table that is empty or has no information in it, it is considered Null.

The concept of a Null value causing errors in a calculation might initially seem strange to Excel power-users. In Excel, if there is a Null value within a column of numbers, the column can still be properly evaluated because Excel simply reads the Null value as zero. This is not the case in Access. If Access encounters a Null value, it does not assume that the Null value represents zero. Instead, it immediately returns a Null value as the answer. To illustrate this behavior, build the query shown in Figure 5-14.

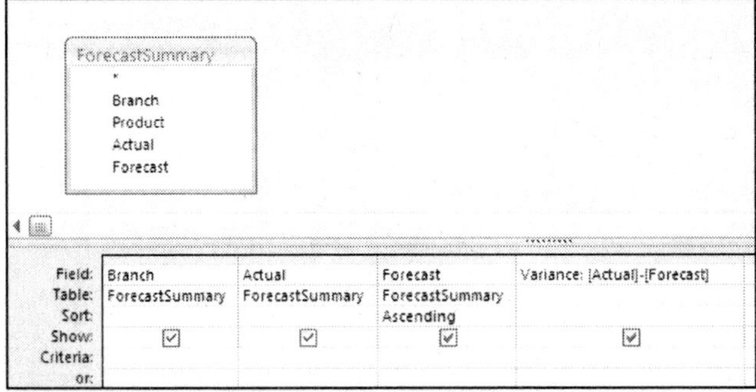

Figure 5-14: To demonstrate how Null values can cause calculation errors, build this query in Design view.

Run the query, and you will see the results shown in Figure 5-15. Notice that the Variance calculations for the first five records do not show the expected results; instead, they show Null values. This is because the forecast values for those records are Null values.

Looking at Figure 5-15, you can imagine how a Null calculation error can wreak havoc on your analysis, especially if you have an involved analytical process. Furthermore, Null calculation errors can be difficult to identify and fix. This is a good place to remind you that you should rarely use Null values in your tables. Instead, you should use a logical value that represents *no data* (for example, zero, NA, or Undefined).

That being said, you can avoid Null calculation errors by using the `Nz` function. The `Nz` function enables you to convert any Null value that is encountered to a value you specify.

Armed with this new information, you can adjust the query in Figure 5-14 to utilize the `Nz` function. Since the problem field is the Forecast field, you would pass the Forecast field through the `Nz` function. Figure 5-16 shows the adjusted query.

Branch	Actual	Forecast	Variance
701717	38,212		
101419	34,576		
101313	32,822		
806211	43,974		
806211	69,558		
806708	7,003	0	7003
305118	4,179	0	4179
601716	4,273	0	4273
806708	4,667	0	4667
202714	5,340	0	5340
308118	6,087	0	6087
101419	6,317	0	6317
602310	3,677	0	3677
402705	6,794	0	6794
490360	7,147	0	7147

Figure 5-15: As you can see, when any variable in your calculation is Null, the resulting answer is a Null value.

ABOUT THE NZ FUNCTION

`Nz(variant, valueifnull)`

The `Nz` function takes two arguments:

- `variant`: **The data you are working with.**
- `valueifnull`: **The value you want returned if the `variant` is Null.**

`NZ([MyNumberField],0)` **converts any Null value in** `MyNumberField` **to zero.**

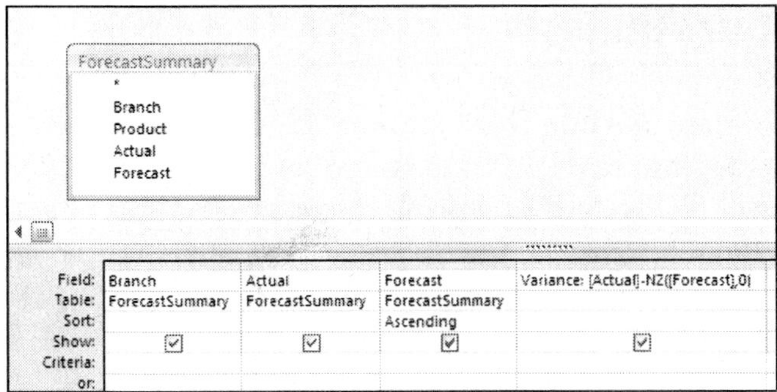

Figure 5-16: Pass the Forecast field through the `Nz` function to convert Null values to zero.

As you can see in Figure 5-17, the first five records now show a Variance value even though the values in the Forecast field are Null. Note that the `NZ` function did not physically place a zero in the Null values. The `NZ` function merely told access to treat the Nulls as zeros when calculating the Variance field.

Watching the Syntax in Your Expressions

Basic syntax mistakes in your calculation expressions can also lead to errors. Follow these basic guidelines to avoid slip-ups:

- If you are using fields in your calculations, enclose their names in square brackets ([ ]).
- Make sure you spell the names of the fields correctly.
- When assigning an alias to your calculated field, be sure you don't use a name that currently exists in the table(s) being calculated.
- Do not use illegal characters — period (.), exclamation mark (!), square brackets ([ ]) or an ampersand (&) — in your aliases.

Branch	Actual	Forecast	Variance
701717	38,212		38212
101419	34,576		34576
101313	32,822		32822
806211	43,974		43974
806211	69,558		69558
806708	7,003	0	7003
305118	4,179	0	4179
601716	4,273	0	4273
806708	4,667	0	4667
202714	5,340	0	5340
308118	6,087	0	6087
101419	6,317	0	6317
602310	3,677	0	3677
402705	6,794	0	6794
490360	7,147	0	7147

Figure 5-17: The first five records now show a Variance value.

Using Dates in Your Analysis

In Access, every possible date starting from January 1, 1900 is stored as a serial number. For example, January 1, 1900 is stored as 1; January 2, 1900 is stored as 2; and so on. This system of storing dates as serial numbers, commonly called the *1900 system,* is the default date system for all Microsoft Office applications. You can take advantage of this system to perform calculations with dates.

Simple Date Calculations

Figure 5-18 shows one of the simplest calculations you can perform on a date. In this query, you are adding 30 to each invoice date. This effectively returns the invoice date plus 30 days, giving you a new date.

WARNING **To be calculated correctly, dates must reside in a field that is formatted as a Date/Time field. If you enter a date into a Text field, the date will continue to look like a date, but Access will treat it like a string. The end result is that any calculation done on dates in this Text formatted field will fail. Ensure that all dates are stored in fields that are formatted as Date/Time.**

You can also calculate the number of days between two dates. The calculation in Figure 5-19, for example, essentially subtracts the serial number of one date from the serial number of another date, leaving you the number of days between the two dates.

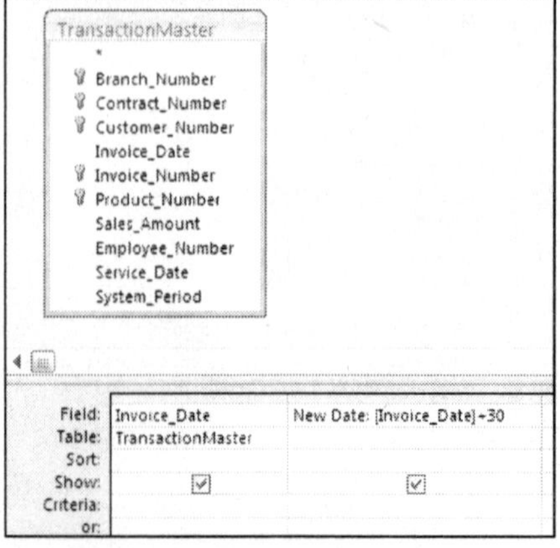

Figure 5-18: You are adding 30 to each invoice date, effectively creating a date that is equal to the invoice date plus 30 days.

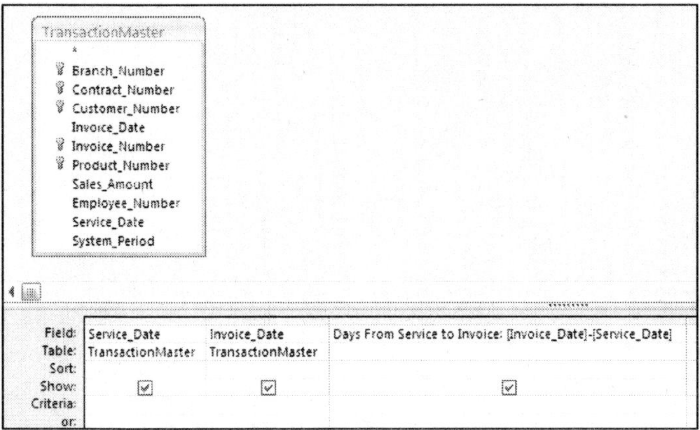

Figure 5-19: In this query, you are calculating the number of days between two dates.

Advanced Analysis Using Functions

As of Access 2007, 25 built-in Date/Time functions are available. Some of these are functions you will very rarely encounter, whereas you will use others routinely in your analyses. This section discusses a few of the basic Date/Time functions that will come in handy in your day-to-day analysis.

The Date Function

The `Date` function is a built-in Access function that returns the current system date — in other words, today's date. With this versatile function, you never have to hard-code today's date in your calculations. That is to say, you can create dynamic calculations that use the current system date as a variable, giving you a different result every day. In this section, you will look at some of the ways you can leverage the `Date` function to enhance your analysis.

Finding the Number of Days Between Today and a Past Date

Imagine that you have to calculate aged receivables. You would need to know the current date to determine how overdue the receivables are. Of course, you could type in the current date by hand, but that can be cumbersome and prone to error.

To demonstrate how to use the `Date` function, create the query shown in Figure 5-20.

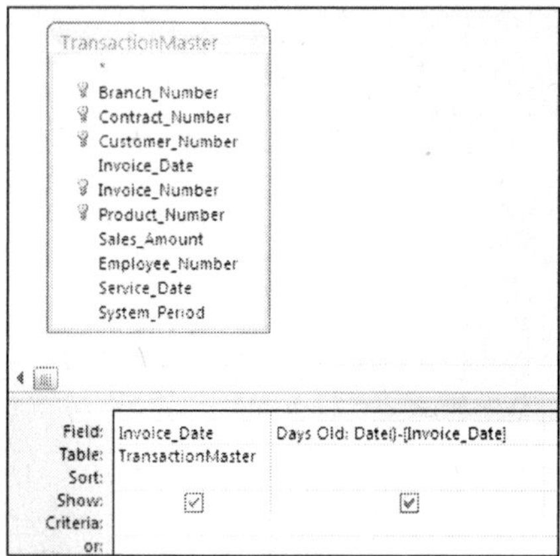

Figure 5-20: This query returns the number of days between today's date and each invoice date.

Using the Date Function in a Criteria Expression

You can use the `Date` function to filter out records by including it in a criteria expression. For example, the query shown in Figure 5-21 returns all records with an invoice date older than 90 days.

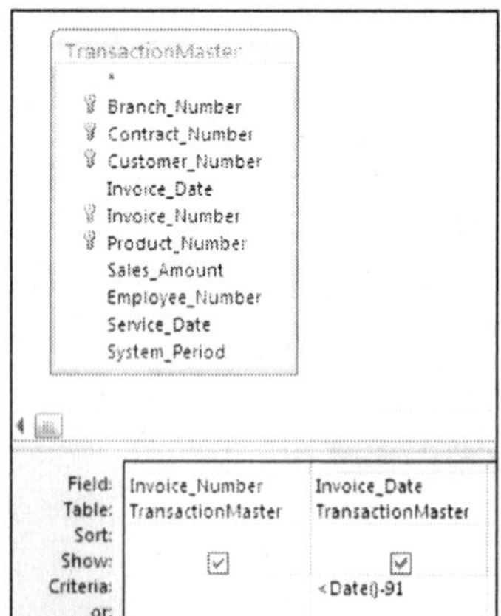

Figure 5-21: No matter what day it is today, this query returns all invoices older than 90 days.

Calculating an Age in Years Using the Date Function

Imagine that you have been asked to provide a list of employees along with the number of years they have been employed by the company. To accomplish this task, you will have to calculate the difference between today's date and each active employee's hire date.

The first step is to build the query shown in Figure 5-22.

When you look at the query results, shown in Figure 5-23, you will realize that the calculation results in the number of days between the two dates, not the number of years.

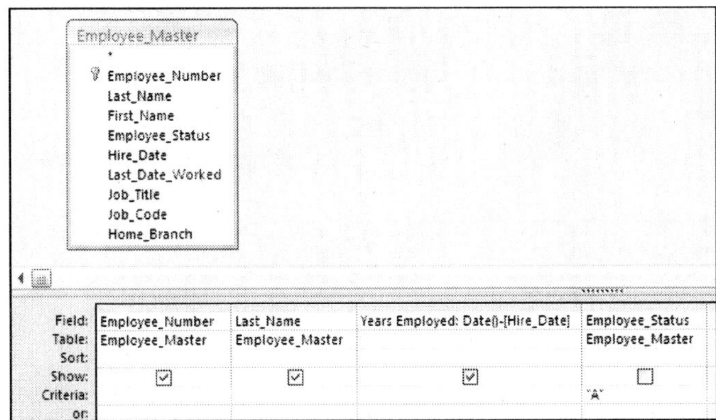

Figure 5-22: You are calculating the difference between today's date and each active employee's hire date.

Employee_Number	Last_Name	Years Employed
104	WIBB	4570
1044	BLECKMAN	5226
1054	STEMPFL	10694
106	CESTENGIAY	3835
113	TRIDIL	6565
1130	RIID	7535
1135	FERNEM	5850
1156	RACHERDS	6992
1245	HERPIR	4388
1336	RACHTIR	7510
1344	ZAMMIRMAN	3205
1416	CERMACHEIL	5877
142	CETE	2911
1435	HIGHIS	5200
145	ERSINEILT	2939

Figure 5-23: This dataset shows the number of days, not the number of years.

To fix this, switch back to Design View and divide your calculation by 365.25, which is the average number of days in a year when you account for leap years. Figure 5-24 demonstrates this change. Note that your original calculation is now wrapped in parentheses to avoid errors due to order of operator precedence.

A look at the results, shown in Figure 5-25, proves that you are now returning the number of years. All that is left to do is to strip away the fractional portion of the date using the `Int` function. Why the `Int` function? The `Int` function does not round the year up or down; it merely converts the number to a readable integer.

TIP **Want to actually round the number of years? You can simply wrap your date calculation in the** `Round` **function. The** `Round` **function is highlighted in Appendix A of this book.**

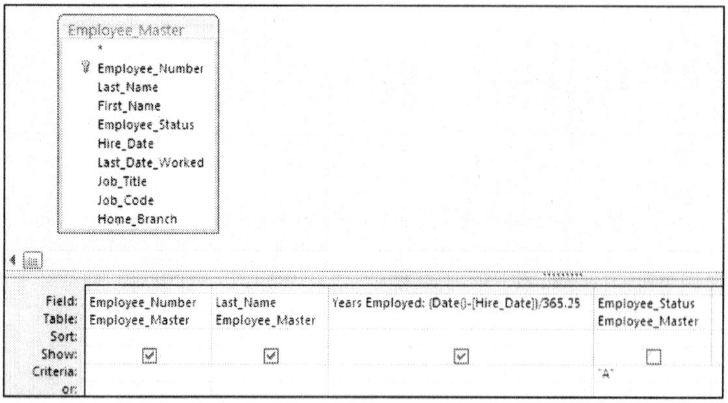

Employee_Master
*
Employee_Number
Last_Name
First_Name
Employee_Status
Hire_Date
Last_Date_Worked
Job_Title
Job_Code
Home_Branch

Field:	Employee_Number	Last_Name	Years Employed: (Date()-[Hire_Date])/365.25	Employee_Status
Table:	Employee_Master	Employee_Master		Employee_Master
Sort:				
Show:	☑	☑	☑	☐
Criteria:				"A"
or:				

Figure 5-24: Divide your original calculation by 365.25 to convert the answer to years.

Employee_Number	Last_Name	Years Employed
104	WIBB	12.5119780971937
1044	BLECKMAN	14.3080082135524
1054	STEMPFL	29.2785763175907
106	CESTENGIAY	10.4996577686516
113	TRIDIL	17.9739904175222
1130	RIID	20.6297056810404
1135	FERNEM	16.0164271047228
1156	RACHERDS	19.1430527036277
1245	HERPIR	12.0136892539357
1336	RACHTIR	20.5612594113621
1344	ZAMMIRMAN	8.77481177275839
1416	CERMACHEIL	16.0903490759754
142	CETE	7.96988364134155
1435	HIGHIS	14.2368240930869
145	ERSINEILT	8.04654346338125
1464	GRANTHEM	18.2778918548939

Figure 5-25: Your query is now returning years, but you will have to strip away the fractional portion of your answer.

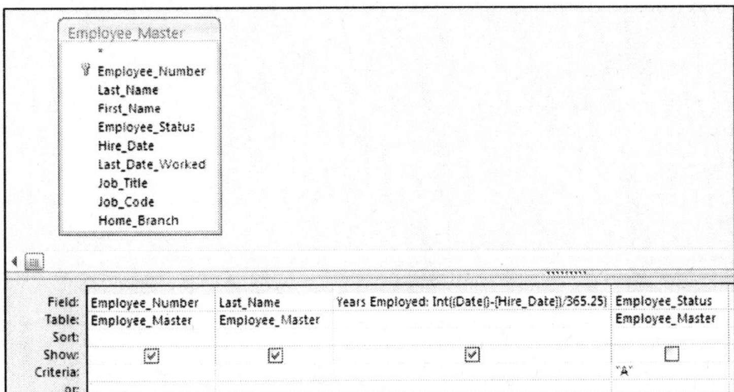

Figure 5-26: Running this query returns the number of years each employee has been with the company.

Wrapping your calculation in the `Int` function ensures that your answer will be a clean year without fractions (see Figure 5-26).

TIP **You can calculate a person's age using the same method. Simply replace the hire date with the date of birth.**

NOTE **Note that you will often have to wrap your date calculations inside of conversion functions. Conversion functions enable you to convert the results of your calcuation to numbers that are valid for a specific operation and achieve the correct analysis. A few examples of conversion functions are the `Int`, `Round`, and `Fix` functions. The `Int` and `Fix` functions convert a number to the nearest integer, removing the fractional portion of the number, whereas the `Round` function enables you to round a number to a specified number of decimal places.**

The Year, Month, Day, and Weekday Functions

The `Year`, `Month`, `Day`, and `Weekday` functions are used to return an integer that represents their respective parts of a date. All of these functions require a valid date as an argument. For example:

- `Year(#12/31/1997#)` returns 1997.
- `Month(#12/31/1997#)` returns 12.
- `Day(#12/31/1997#)` returns 31.
- `Weekday(#12/31/1997#)` returns 4.

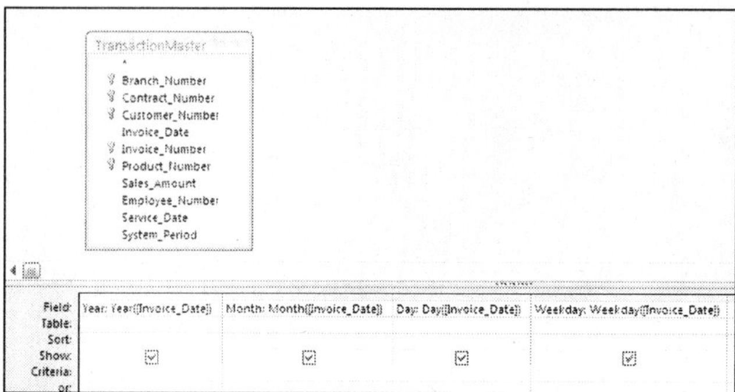

Figure 5-27: The `Year`, `Month`, `Day`, and `Weekday` functions enable you to parse out a part of a date.

NOTE **The `Weekday` function returns the day of the week from a date. In Access weekdays are numbered from 1 to 7 starting with Sunday. Therefore, if the `Weekday` function returns 4, then the day of the week represented is Wednesday.**

Figure 5-27 demonstrates how you would use these functions in a query environment.

TRICKS OF THE TRADE: AN EASY WAY TO QUERY ONLY WORKDAYS

Suppose that you have been asked to provide the total amount of revenue generated by each of your company's branches, but only on those dates that are company workdays. Workdays are defined as days that are not weekends or holidays.

The first thing you need to accomplish this task is a table that lists all the company holidays. Figure 5-28 shows that a Holidays table can be nothing more than one field listing all the dates that constitute a holiday.

Holidays
1/1/2004
1/19/2004
5/31/2004
7/5/2004
9/6/2004
11/25/2004
11/26/2004
12/23/2004
12/24/2004
12/31/2004
*

Figure 5-28: In this database, the HolidaysMaster table contains a column called Holidays that lists all the dates that are counted as company holidays.

After you have established a table that contains all the company holidays, it's time to build the query. Figure 5-29 demonstrates how to build a query that filters non-workdays.

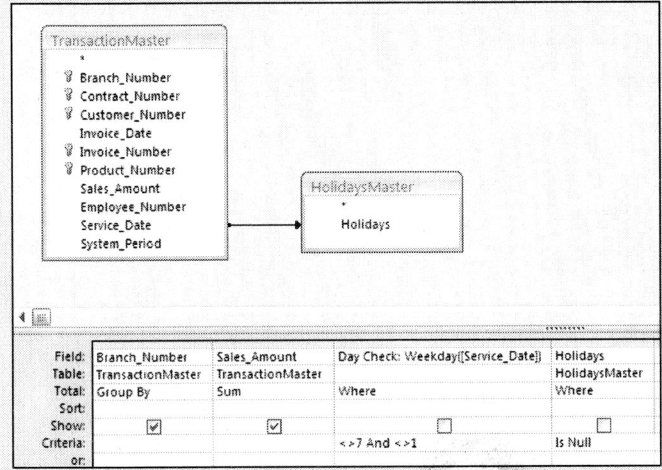

Figure 5-29: Using the HolidaysMaster table and a simple `Weekday` function, you can filter non-workdays.

Take a moment to analyze what is going on in Figure 5-29.

1. **You create a left join from TransactionMaster to HolidaysMaster to tell Access that you want all the records from TransactionMaster.**
2. **You then use the Is Null criteria under Holidays. This limits the TransactionMaster to only those dates that do not match any of the holidays listed in the HolidaysMaster.**
3. **You then create a field called Day Check where you are returning the weekday of every service date in the TransactionMaster.**
4. **You filter the newly created Day Check field to filter out those weekdays that represent Saturdays and Sundays (1 and 7).**

The DateAdd function

A common analysis for many organizations is to determine on which date a certain benchmark will be reached. For example, most businesses want to know what date will an invoice become 30 days past due. Furthermore, what date should a warning letter be sent to the customer? An easy way to perform these types of analyses is to use the `DateAdd` function. The `DateAdd` function returns a date to which a specified interval has been added.

ABOUT THE DATEADD FUNCTION

`DateAdd(interval, number, date)`

The `DateAdd` function returns a date to which a specified interval has been added. There are three required arguments in the `DateAdd` function.

- `interval` **(required): The interval of time you want to use. The intervals available are as follows:**
  - `"yyyy"`**: Year**
  - `"q"`**: Quarter**
  - `"m"`**: Month**
  - `"y"`**: Day of year**
  - `"d"`**: Day**
  - `"w"`**: Weekday**
  - `"ww"`**: Week**
  - `"h"`**: Hour**
  - `"n"`**: Minute**
  - `"s"`**: Second**
- `number` **(required): The number of intervals to add. A positive number returns a date in the future, whereas a negative number returns a date in the past.**
- `date` **(required): The date value with which you are working.**

For example:

- `DateAdd("ww",1,#11/30/2004#)` **returns 12/7/2004.**
- `DateAdd("m",2,#11/30/2004#)` **returns 1/30/2005.**
- `DateAdd("yyyy",-1,#11/30/2004#)` **returns 11/30/2003.**

The query shown in Figure 5-30 illustrates how the `DateAdd` function can be used in determining the exact date a specific benchmark is reached. You are creating two new fields with this query: Warning and Overdue. The `DateAdd` function used in the Warning field will return the date that is three weeks from the original invoice date. The `DateAdd` function used in the Overdue field will return the date that is one month from the original invoice date.

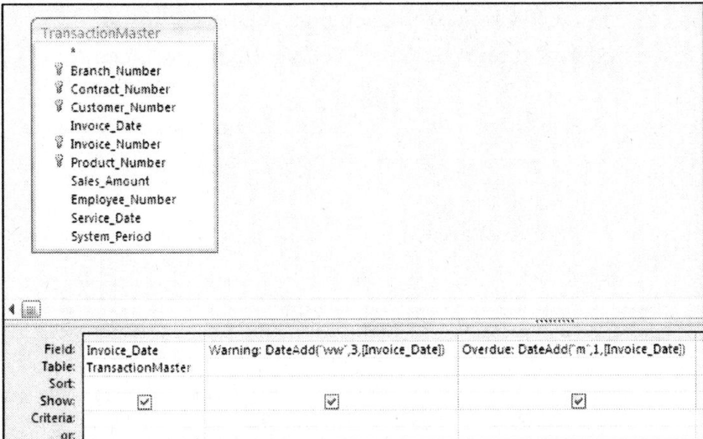

Figure 5-30: This query gives you the original invoice date, the date you should send a warning letter, and the date the invoice will be 30 days overdue.

Grouping Dates into Quarters

Why would you need to group your dates into quarters? Most databases store dates rather than quarter designations. Therefore, if you wanted to analyze data on a quarter-over-quarter basis, you would have to convert dates into quarters. Surprisingly, there is no `Date/Time` function that enables you to group dates into quarters. There is, however, the `Format` function.

The `Format` function belongs to the Text category of functions and allows you to convert a variant into a string based on formatting instructions. From the perspective of analyzing dates, there are several valid instructions you can pass to a `Format` function.

`Format(#01/31/2004#, "yyyy")` returns 2004.

`Format(#01/31/2004#, "yy")` returns 04.

`Format(#01/31/2004#, "q")` returns 1.

`Format(#01/31/2004#, "mmm")` returns Jan.

`Format(#01/31/2004#, "mm")` returns 01.

`Format(#01/31/2004#, "d")` returns 31.

`Format(#01/31/2004#, "w")` returns 7.

`Format(#01/31/2004#, "ww")` returns 5.

NOTE **Keep in mind that the value returned when passing a date through a `Format` function is a string that cannot be used in subsequent calculations.**

The query in Figure 5-31 shows how you would group all the service dates into quarters and then group the quarters to get a sum of revenue for each quarter.

If you want to get fancy, you can insert the `Format` function in a crosstab query, using Quarter as the column (see Figure 5-32).

As you can see in Figure 5-33, the resulting dataset is a clean look at revenue by product, by quarter.

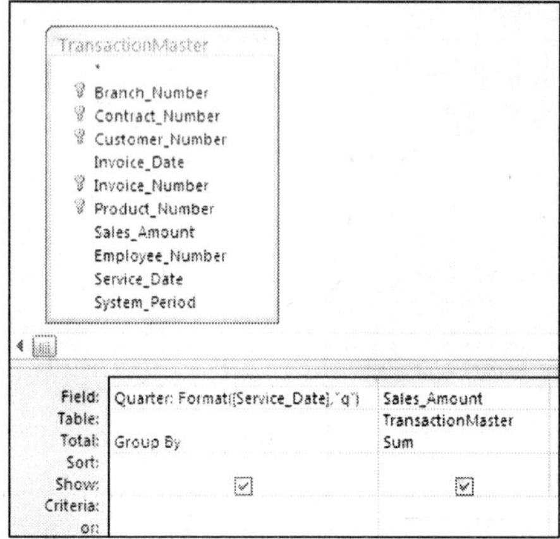

Figure 5-31: You can group dates into quarters by using the `Format` function.

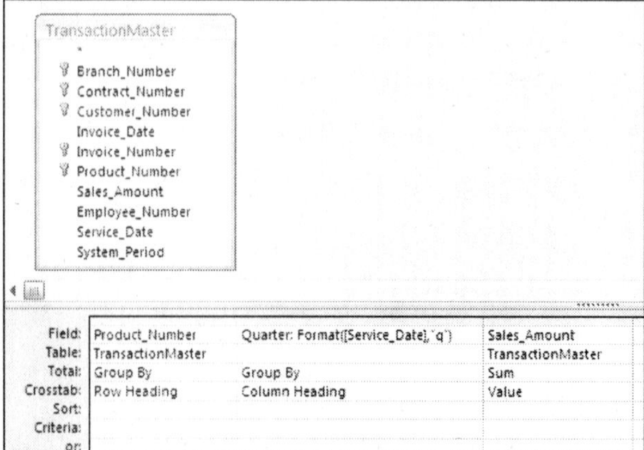

Figure 5-32: You can also use the `Format` function in a crosstab query.

Product_Number	1	2	3	4
16000	$575,148.34	$615,635.94	$607,250.40	$563,126.73
30300	$624,226.35	$685,701.43	$679,602.99	$638,267.25
70700	$545,062.66	$565,352.79	$551,256.32	$517,260.35
81150	$259,345.81	$295,265.31	$294,802.38	$289,182.27
87000	$294,056.23	$312,162.99	$300,570.77	$284,121.61
90830	$297,286.66	$324,844.67	$332,029.86	$322,629.36

Figure 5-33: You have successfully grouped your dates into quarters.

The DateSerial Function

The `DateSerial` function enables you to construct a date value by combining given year, month, and day components. This function is perfect for converting disparate strings that, together, represent a date, into an actual date.

The wonderful thing about the `DateSerial` function is that you can pass other date expressions as arguments. For example, pretend that the system date on your PC is August 1, 2005. For those of you who have been paying attention, this means that the `Date` function would return August 1, 2005. That being the case, the following expression would return August 1, 2005.

```
DateSerial ( Year(Date()) , Month(Date()) , Day(Date()) )
```

NOTE `Year(Date())` **returns the current year,** `Month(Date())` **returns the current month, and** `Day(Date())` **returns the current day.**

ABOUT THE DATESERIAL FUNCTION

`DateSerial(Year, Month, Day)`

The `DateSerial` **function has three arguments:**

- `Year` **(required): Any number or numeric expression from 100 to 9999.**
- `Month` **(required): Any number or numeric expression.**
- `Day` **(required): Any number or numeric expression.**

For example, `DateSerial(2004, 4, 3)` **returns April 3, 2004.**

So how is this helpful? Well, now you can put a few twists on this by performing calculations on the expressions within the `DateSerial` function. Consider some of the possibilities:

- Get the first day of last month by subtracting `1` from the current month and using `1` as the `Day` argument.

```
DateSerial(Year(Date()), Month(Date()) - 1, 1)
```

- Get the first day of next month by adding `1` to the current month and using `1` as the `Day` argument.

```
DateSerial(Year(Date()), Month(Date()) + 1, 1)
```

- Get the last day of this month by using `0` as the `Day` argument.

```
DateSerial(Year(Date()), Month(Date()), 0)
```

- Get the last day of next month by adding `1` to the current month and using `0` as the `Day` argument.

```
DateSerial(Year(Date()), Month(Date()) +1, 0)
```

TIP **Passing a `0` to the `Day` argument will automatically get you the last day of the month specified in the `DateSerial` function.**

Summary

Not many analysts know that Access has the ability to perform calculations. In fact, the most common question asked about Access is, "Where do the formulas go?" The reality is that Access provides a wide array of tools and built-in functions that make performing calculations possible.

The first thing to remember is that calculations are typically not stored in Access tables as formulas are stored in Excel. There are several reasons for this:

- Stored calculations take up valuable storage space.
- Stored calculations require constant maintenance as the data in your table changes.
- Stored calculations generally tie your data to one analytical path.

Instead of storing the calculated results as hard data, calculations in Access are typically performed in real time with the use of various types of queries.

In addition to performing mathematical calculations, Access has the ability to perform calculations with dates. This is because Access stores every possible date starting from January 1, 1900, as a serial number. You can take advantage of this system to perform queries using date calculations. For example, you can find all invoices over 90 days old, you can calculate the seniority of each employee, you can calculate the due date of an order, and the list goes on.

CHAPTER

6

Performing Conditional Analysis

Up until now, your analyses have been straightforward. You build a query, you add some criteria, you add a calculation, you save the query, then you run the query whenever you need to. What happens, however, if the criteria that govern your analysis change frequently, or if your analytical processes depend on certain conditions being met? In these situations, you would use a *conditional analysis*, an analysis whose outcome depends on a pre-defined set of conditions. Barring VBA code, there are several tools and functions that enable you to build conditional analyses; some of these are parameter queries, the `IIf` function, and the `Switch` function. In this chapter, you learn how these tools and functions can help you save time, organize your analytical processes, and enhance your analysis.

Using Parameter Queries

You will find that when building your analytical processes, it will often be difficult to anticipate every single combination of criteria that may be needed. This is where parameter queries can help.

A *parameter query* is an interactive query that prompts you for criteria before the query is run. A parameter query is useful when you need to ask a query different questions using different criteria each time it is run. To get a firm understanding of how a parameter query can help you, build the query in Figure 6-1. With this query, you want to see the total revenue for each branch during the 200405 system period.

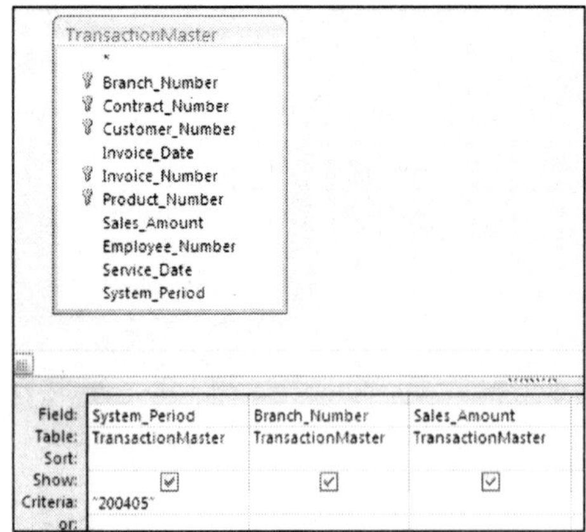

Figure 6-1: This query has a hard-coded criterion for system period.

Although this query will give you what you need, the problem is that the criterion for system period is hard-coded as 200405. That means if you want to analyze revenue for a different period, you essentially have to rebuild the query. Using a parameter query enables you to create a conditional analysis; that is, an analysis based on variables you specify each time you run the query. To create a parameter query, simply replace the hard-coded criteria with text that you have enclosed in square brackets ([ ]), as shown in Figure 6-2.

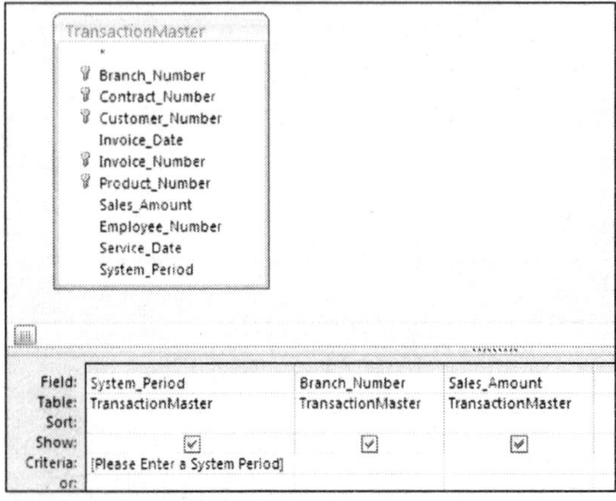

Figure 6-2: To create a parameter query, replace the hard-coded criteria with text enclosed in square brackets ([ ]).

Running a parameter query forces the Enter Parameter Value dialog box to open and ask for a variable. Note that the text you typed inside the brackets of your parameter appears in the dialog box. At this point, you would simply enter your parameter, as shown in Figure 6-3.

How Parameter Queries Work

When you run a parameter query, Access attempts to convert any text to a literal string by wrapping the text in quotes. However, if you place square brackets ([ ]) around the text, Access thinks that it is a variable and tries to bind some value to the variable using the following series of tests:

1. Access checks to see if the variable is a field name. If Access identifies the variable as a field name, that field is used in the expression.
2. If the variable is not a field name, Access checks to see if the variable is a calculated field. If Access determines the expression is indeed a calculated field, it simply carries out the mathematical operation.
3. If the variable is not a calculated field, Access checks to see if the variable is referencing an object such as a control on an open form or open report.
4. If all else fails, the only remaining option is to ask the user what the variable is, so Access displays the Enter Parameter Value dialog box, showing the text you entered in the Criteria row.

Ground Rules of Parameter Queries

As with all of the other functionality in Access, parameter queries come with their own set of ground rules that you should follow in order to use them properly.

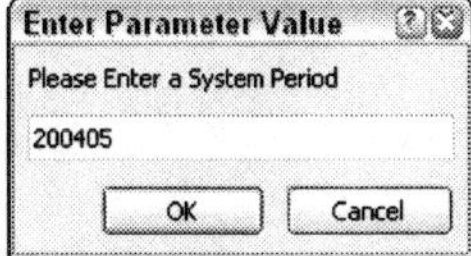

Figure 6-3: Enter your criteria in the Enter Parameter Value dialog box and click OK.

- You must place square brackets ([ ]) around your parameter. If you do not, Access will automatically convert your text into a literal string.
- You cannot use the name of a field as a parameter. If you do, Access will simply replace your parameter with the current value of the field.
- You cannot use a period (.), an exclamation mark (!), square brackets ([]), or an ampersand (&) in your parameter's prompt text.
- You must limit the number of characters in your parameter's prompt text. Entering parameter prompt text that is too long may result in your prompt being cut off in the Enter Parameter Value dialog box. Moreover, you should make your prompts as clear and concise as possible.

TIP **If you really want to use a field name in your parameter's prompt, you can follow the field name with other characters. For example, instead of using** `[System_Period]`**, you could use** `[System_Period: ?]`**. As you read this, keep in mind that there is nothing magic about the colon (:) or the question mark (?). Any character will do. The idea is to allow Access to differentiate between your parameter and the field name while matching the original field name as closely as possible.**

Working with Parameter Queries

The example shown in Figure 6-2 uses a parameter to define a single criterion. Although this is the most common way to use a parameter in a query, there are many ways to exploit this functionality. In fact, it is safe to say that the more innovative you get with your parameter queries, the more elegant and advanced your impromptu analysis will be. This section covers some of the different ways you can use parameters in your queries.

Working with Multiple Parameter Conditions

You are not in any way limited in the number of parameters you can use in your query. Figure 6-4 demonstrates how you can utilize more than one parameter in a query. When you run this query, you will be prompted for both a system period and a branch number, enabling you to dynamically filter on two data points without ever having to rewrite your query.

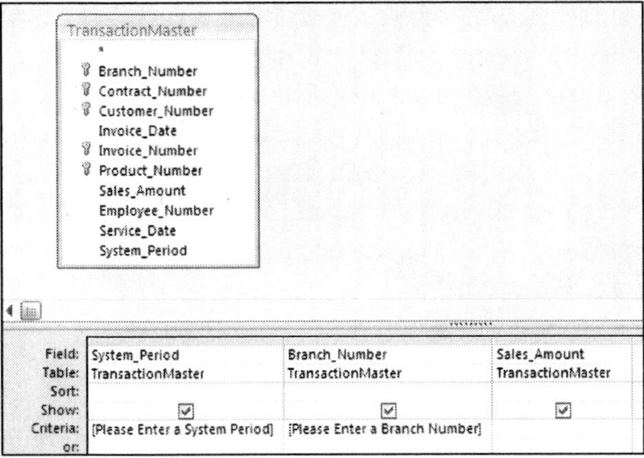

Figure 6-4: This query asks you to enter a system period and then a branch number.

Combining Parameters with Operators

You can combine parameter prompts with any operator you would normally use in a query. Using parameters in conjunction with standard operators enables you to dynamically expand or contract the filters in your analysis without rebuilding your query. To demonstrate how this works, build the query shown in Figure 6-5.

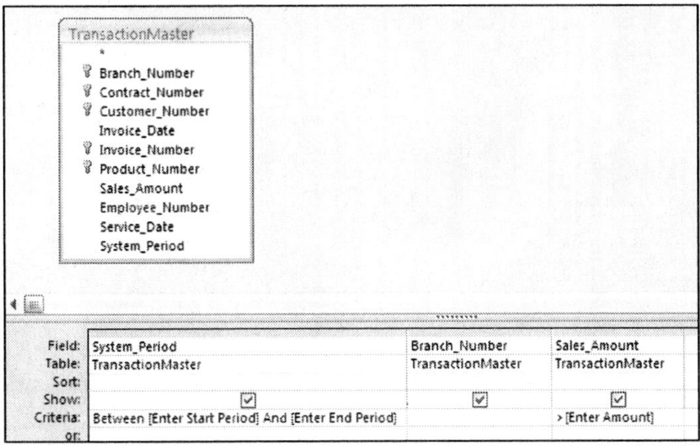

Figure 6-5: This query combines standard operators with parameters in order to limit the results.

This query uses the `BETWEEN...AND` operator and the > (greater than) operator to limit the results of the query based on the user defined parameters. Since there are three parameter prompts built into this query, you will be prompted for inputs three times: once for a starting period, once for an ending period, and once for a dollar amount. The number of records returned will depend on the parameters you input. For example, if you input 200401 as the starting period, 200403 as the ending period, and 500 as the dollar amount, you will get 175 records.

Combining Parameters with Wildcards

One of the problems with a parameter query is that if the parameter is ignored when the query is run, the query will return no records. One way to get around this problem is to combine your parameter with a wildcard so that if the parameter is indeed ignored, all records will be returned. To demonstrate how you can use a wildcard with a parameter, build the query shown in Figure 6-6. When you run this query, it will prompt you for a branch number. Because you are using the wildcard, you have the option of filtering out a single branch by entering a branch number into the parameter, or you can ignore the parameter to return all records.

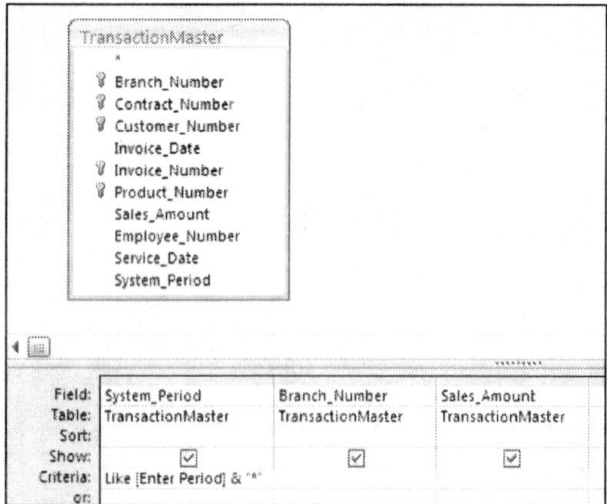

Figure 6-6: If the parameter in this query is ignored, the query returns all records thanks to the wildcard (*).

TIP **Using the wildcard with a parameter also enables users to enter in a partial parameter and still get results. Suppose, for example, that the criteria in your parameter query is**

```
Like [Enter Lastname] & "*"
```

Entering "A" as the parameter would return all last names that start with the letter *A*.

Or, suppose the criteria in your parameter query is

```
Like "*" & [Enter Lastname] & "*"
```

Entering "A" would return all last names that contain the letter *A*.

Using Parameters as Calculation Variables

You are not limited to using parameters as criteria for a query; you can use parameters anywhere you use a variable. In fact, a particularly useful way to use parameters is in calculations. For example, the query in Figure 6-7 enables you to analyze how a price increase will affect current prices based on the percent increase you enter. When you run this query, you will be asked to enter a percentage by which you want to increase your prices. When you pass your percentage, the parameter query uses it as a variable in the calculation.

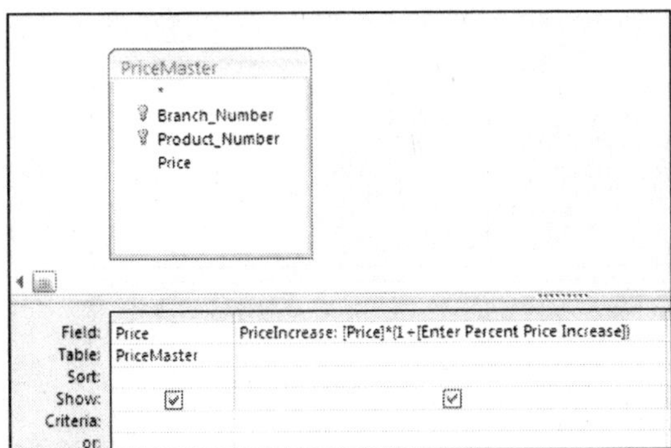

Figure 6-7: You can use parameters in calculations, enabling you to change the calculation variables each time you run the query.

Using Parameters as Function Arguments

You can also use parameters as arguments within functions. Figure 6-8 demonstrates the use of the `DateDiff` function using parameters instead of hard-coded dates. When this query is run, you will be prompted for a start date and an end date. Those dates will then be used as arguments in the `DateDiff` functions. Again, this enables you to specify new dates each time you run the query without ever having to rebuild the query.

WARNING **This will only work if the nature of the data you enter as your parameter fits into the function argument. For example, if you are using a parameter in a `DateDiff` function, the variable you assign that parameter must be a Date or the function won't work.**

NOTE **You will notice that when you run the query in Figure 6-8, you will only have to enter the Start date and the End date one time although they are both used in two places in the query. This is because when you assign a variable to a parameter, that assignment persists to every future instance of that parameter.**

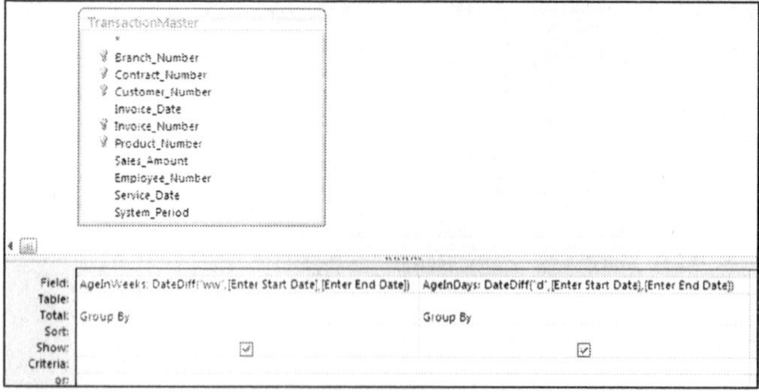

Figure 6-8: You can use parameters as arguments in functions instead of hard-coded values.

TIP **The `Instr` function searches for a specified string in another string and returns its position number.**

NOTE **This parameter query will work even without the commas separating each variable you enter. Commas are a cosmetic addition to make it easier to read the variables.**

TRICKS OF THE TRADE: CREATING A PARAMETER PROMPT THAT ACCEPTS MULTIPLE ENTRIES

The parameter query in Figure 6-9 enables you to dynamically filter results by a variable period that you specify within the parameter. However, this query does not enable you to see results for more than one period at a time.

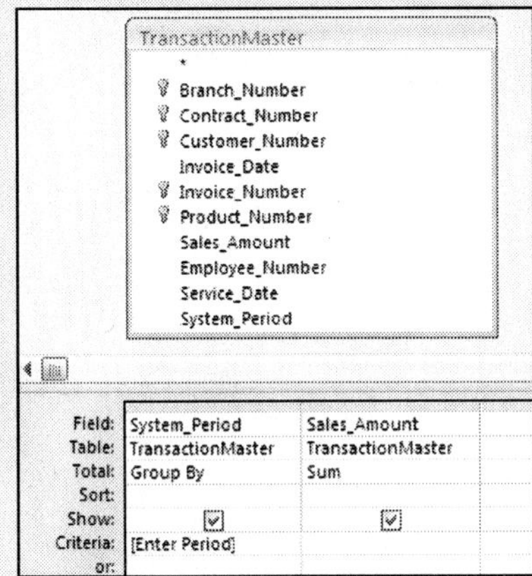

Figure 6-9: This query enables you to filter only one period at a time.

You could use more than one parameter, as shown in Figure 6-10. Unlike the query in Figure 6-9, this query enables you to include more than one period in your query results. However, you would still be limited to the number of parameters built into the query (in this case, three).

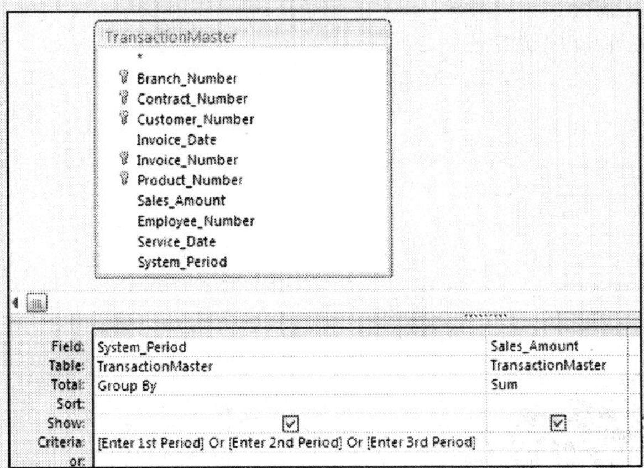

Figure 6-10: This query enables you to filter by three periods at a time instead of one. But what if you need to filter more than three periods?

(continued)

TRICKS OF THE TRADE: CREATING A PARAMETER PROMPT THAT ACCEPTS MULTIPLE ENTRIES *(Continued)*

So how do you allow for any number of parameter entries? The answer is relatively easy. You create a parameter that is passed through an `Instr` ("in string") function to test for a position number. The query shown in Figure 6-11 demonstrates how to do this.

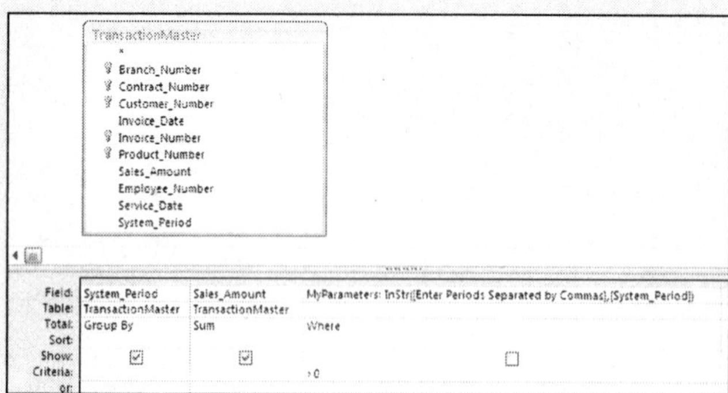

Figure 6-11: This parameter query allows for multiple entries in a parameter.

Notice that the parameter is not being used as criteria for the System_Period field. Instead, it is being used in an `Instr` function to test for the position number of the variable you enter into the parameter prompt, as follows:

```
InStr([Enter Periods separated by commas],[System_Period])
```

If the `Instr` function finds your variable, it returns a position number; if not, it returns 0. Therefore, you only want records that returned a position number greater than zero (hence, the criteria for the parameter).

When you run this query, Access will display the standard Enter Parameter Value dialog box (see Figure 6-12). You can then type in as many variables as you want.

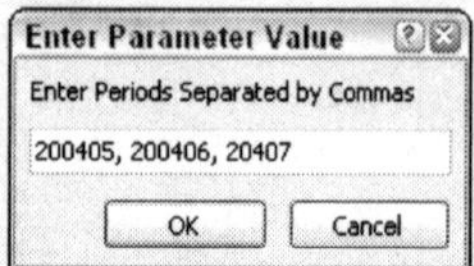

Figure 6-12: Simply type in as many parameters you want.

Using Conditional Functions

Parameter queries are not the only tools in Access that allow for conditional analysis. Access also has built-in functions that facilitate value comparisons, data validation, and conditional evaluation. Two of these functions are the `IIf` function and the `Switch` function. These conditional functions (also called program flow functions) are designed to test for conditions and provide different outcomes based on the results of those tests. In this section you learn how to control the flow of your analysis by utilizing the `IIf` and `Switch` functions.

The IIf Function

The `IIf` (immediate if) function replicates the functionality of an `IF` statement for a single operation. The `IIf` function evaluates a specific condition and returns a result based on a `True` or `False` determination.

TIP **Think of the commas in an `IIf` function as `THEN` and `ELSE` statements. Consider the following `IIf` function, for instance:**

```
IIf(Babies = 2 , "Twins", "Not Twins")
```

This function translates to: If Babies equals 2, then Twins, else Not Twins.

Using IIf to Avoid Mathematical Errors

To demonstrate a simple problem where the `IIf` function comes in handy, build the query shown in Figure 6-13.

ABOUT THE IIF FUNCTION

`IIf(Expression, TrueAnswer, FalseAnswer)`

To use the `IIf` function, you must provide three required arguments: the expression to be evaluated, a value to be returned if the expression is `True`, and a value to be returned if the expression is `False`.

- `Expression` **(required): The expression you want to evaluate.**
- `TrueAnswer` **(required): The value to return if the expression is `True`.**
- `FalseAnswer` **(required): The value to return if the expression is `False`.**

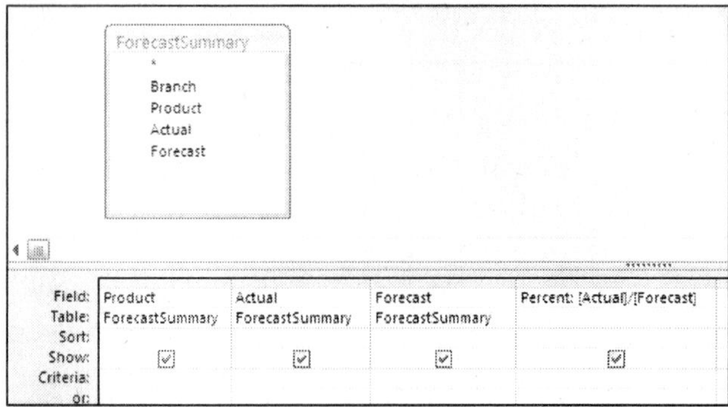

Figure 6-13: This query performs a calculation on the Actual and the Forecast fields to calculate a percent to forecast.

When you run the query, you will notice that not all the results are clean. As you can see in Figure 6-14, you are getting some errors due to division by zero. That is to say, you are dividing actual revenues by forecasts that are 0.

Although this seems like a fairly benign issue, in a more complex, multi-layered analytical process, these errors could compromise the integrity of your data analysis. To avoid these errors, you can perform a conditional analysis on your dataset using the `IIf` function, evaluating the Forecast field for each record before performing the calculation. If the forecast is 0, you will bypass the calculation and simply return a value of 0. If the forecast is not 0, you will perform the calculation to get the correct value. The `IIf` function would look like this:

```
IIf([Forecast]=0,0,[Actual]/[Forecast])
```

Product	Actual	Forecast	Percent
90830	171	0	#Error
90830	520	658	79.03%
90830	706	727	97.11%
90830	1,025	1,206	84.99%
90830	1,064	1,400	76.00%
90830	1,195	0	#Error
90830	1,370	0	#Error
90830	1,463	0	#Error
90830	1,483	1,786	83.03%
90830	1,522	1,951	78.01%
90830	1,525	0	#Error
81150	2,207	0	#Error
90830	2,487	3,148	79.00%
87000	2,558	3,238	79.00%
70700	2,580	2,899	89.00%
87000	2,701	3,141	85.99%
70700	3,022	3,825	79.01%
90830	3,296	0	#Error

Figure 6-14: The errors shown in the results are due to the fact that some revenues are being divided by zeros.

Figure 6-15 demonstrates how this `IIf` function is put into action. As you can see in Figure 6-16, the errors have been avoided.

Using IIf to Save Time

You can also use the `IIf` function to save steps in your analytical processes and, ultimately, save time. For example, imagine that you need to tag customers in a lead list as either large-sized customers or small-sized customers, based on their dollar potential. You decide that you will update the MyTest field in your dataset with "LARGE" or "SMALL" based on the revenue potential of the customer.

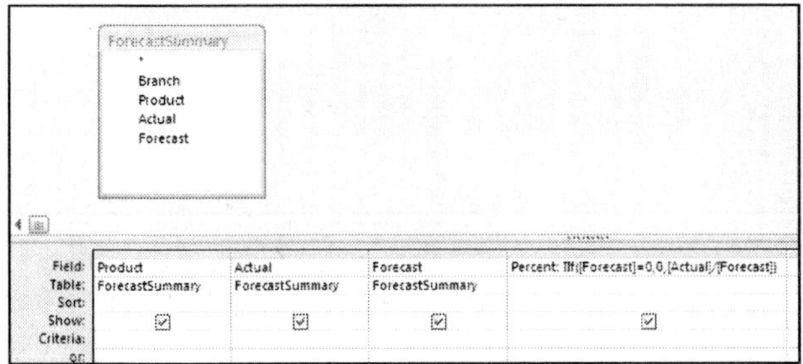

Figure 6-15: This `IIf` function enables you to test for forecasts with a value of 0 and bypass them when performing your calculation.

Product	Actual	Forecast	Percent
90830	171	0	0.00%
90830	520	658	79.03%
90830	706	727	97.11%
90830	1,025	1,206	84.99%
90830	1,064	1,400	76.00%
90830	1,195	0	0.00%
90830	1,370	0	0.00%
90830	1,463	0	0.00%
90830	1,483	1,786	83.03%
90830	1,522	1,951	78.01%
90830	1,525	0	0.00%
81150	2,207	0	0.00%
90830	2,487	3,148	79.00%
87000	2,558	3,238	79.00%
70700	2,580	2,899	89.00%
87000	2,701	3,141	85.99%
70700	3,022	3,825	79.01%
90830	3,296	0	0.00%

Figure 6-16: The `IIf` function helps you avoid the division by zero errors.

Without the `IIf` function, you would have to run the two Update queries shown in Figures 6-17 and 6-18 to accomplish this task.

Will the queries in Figures 6-17 and 6-18 do the job? Yes. However, you could accomplish the same task with one query using the `IIf` function.

The update query shown in Figure 6-19 illustrates how you can use an `IIf` function as the update expression.

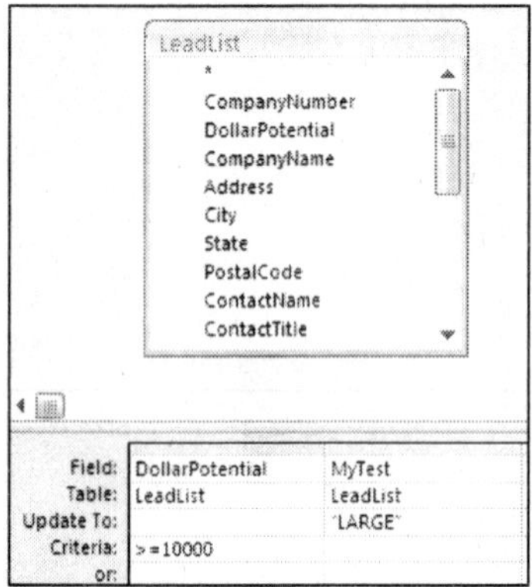

Figure 6-17: This query updates the MyTest field to tag all customers that have a revenue potential at or above 10,000 dollars with the word "LARGE".

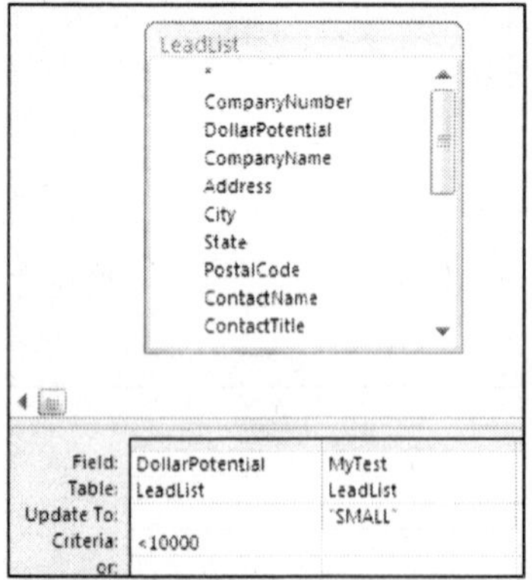

Figure 6-18: This query updates the MyTest field to tag all customers that have a revenue potential less than 10,000 dollars with the word "SMALL".

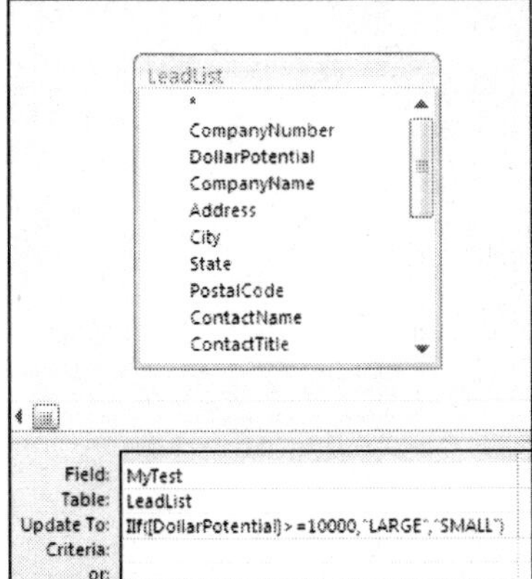

Figure 6-19: You can accomplish the same task in one query using the IIf function.

Take a moment and look at the `IIf` function being used as the update expression.

```
IIf([DollarPotential]>=10000,"LARGE","SMALL")
```

This function tells Access to evaluate the DollarPotential field of each record. If the DollarPotential field is greater than or equal to 10,000, use "LARGE" as the update value. If not, use "SMALL".

TIP **You can use conditional operators (AND, OR, BETWEEN) within your `IIf` functions to add layers to your condition expression. For example, the following function tests for a branch number and a hire date to get a `True` or a `False` value.**

```
IIf([Home_Branch] = '920681' And [Hire_Date] > #1/1/1985# ,"True","False")
```

Nesting IIf Functions for Multiple Conditions

Sometimes the condition you need to test for is too complex to be handled by a basic `IF...THEN...ELSE` structure. In such cases, you can use nested `IIf` functions — that is, `IIf` functions that are embedded in other `IIf` functions. Consider the following example:

```
IIf([VALUE]>100,"A",IIf([VALUE]<100,"C","B"))
```

This function verifies whether VALUE is greater than 100. *If* it is, *then* "A" is returned; if not (*else*), a second `IIf` function is triggered. The second `IIf` function verifies whether VALUE is less than 100. *If* yes, *then* "C" is returned; if not (*else*), "B" is returned.

The idea here is that because an `IIf` function results in a `True` or `False` answer, you can expand your condition by setting the "`False`" expression to another `IIf` function instead of to a hard-coded value. This triggers another evaluation. There is no limit to the number of nested `IIf` functions you can use.

Using IIf Functions to Create Crosstab Analyses

Many seasoned analysts use the `IIf` function to create custom crosstab analyses in lieu of using a crosstab query. Among the many advantages of creating crosstab analyses without a crosstab query is the ability to categorize and group otherwise unrelated data items.

In the example shown in Figure 6-20, you are returning the sum of sales amount for two groups of employees: those with a hire date before January 1, 2004 and those with a hire date after January 1, 2004. Categorizations this specific would not be possible with a crosstab query.

The result, shown in Figure 6-21, is every bit as clean and user-friendly as the results would be from a crosstab query.

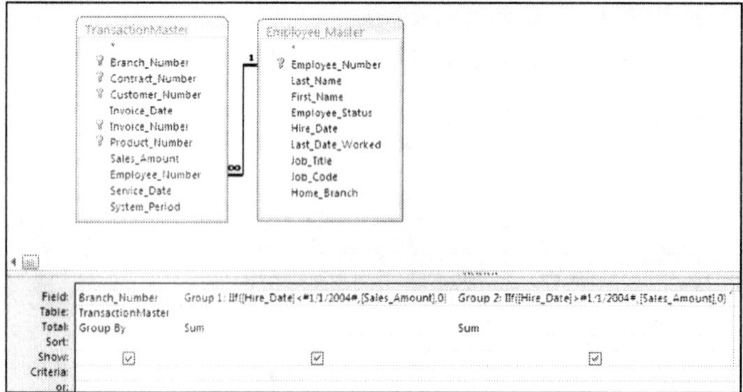

Figure 6-20: This query demonstrates how to create a crosstab analysis without using a crosstab query.

Branch_Number	Group 1	Group 2
101313	$403,589.43	$41,041.45
101419	$124,151.92	$445.23
102516	$63,227.89	$0.00
103516	$84,783.80	$16,880.48
173901	$81,848.30	$25,367.60
201605	$60,579.76	$9,237.84
201709	$87,774.28	$9,078.73
201714	$284,268.19	$4,445.38
201717	$450,524.08	$0.00
202600	$151,337.96	$0.00
202605	$262,201.44	$80,335.26
202714	$83,176.87	$29,897.72
208605	$64,357.22	$0.00
301301	$133,469.84	$23,765.20
301316	$302,425.79	$95,320.43

Figure 6-21: The resulting dataset gives you a clean crosstab-style view of your data.

Another advantage of creating crosstab analyses without a crosstab query is the ability to include more than one calculation in your crosstab report. For example, Figure 6-22 illustrates a query where the number of transactions is being returned in addition to the sum of sales amount. Again, this would not be possible with a crosstab query.

As you can see in Figure 6-23, the resulting dataset provides a great deal of information in an easy-to-read format.

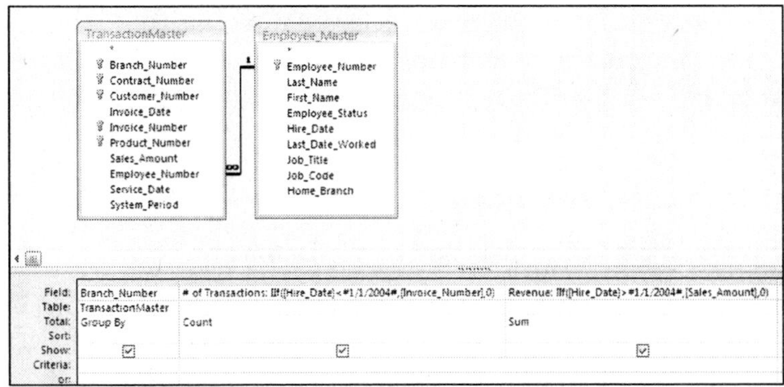

Figure 6-22: Creating crosstab-style reports using the `IIf` function enables you to calculate more than one value.

Branch_Number	# of Transactions	Revenue
101313	3650	$41,041.45
101419	758	$445.23
102516	381	$0.00
103516	623	$16,880.48
173901	622	$25,367.60
201605	469	$9,237.84
201709	485	$9,078.73
201714	1716	$4,445.38
201717	2709	$0.00
202600	1028	$0.00
202605	2153	$80,335.26
202714	678	$29,897.72
208605	441	$0.00
301301	985	$23,765.20
301316	3061	$95,320.43
301505	661	$0.00

Figure 6-23: This analysis would be impossible to create in a crosstab query, where multiple calculations are not allowed.

The Switch Function

The `Switch` function enables you to evaluate a list of expressions and return the value associated with the expression determined to be `True`. To use the `Switch` function, you must provide a minimum of one expression and one value.

The power of the `Switch` function comes in evaluating multiple expressions at one time and determining which one is `True`. To evaluate multiple expressions, simply add another `Expression` and `Value` to the function, as follows:

```
Switch(Expression1, Value1, Expression2, Value2, Expression3, Value3)
```

When executed, this `Switch` function evaluates each expression in turn. If an expression evaluates to `True`, the value that follows that expression is returned. If more than one expression is `True`, the value for the first `True` expression is returned (the others are ignored). Keep in mind that there is no limit to the number of expressions you can evaluate with a `Switch` function.

ABOUT THE SWITCH FUNCTION

```
Switch(Expression, Value)
```

- `Expression` **(required): The expression you want to evaluate.**
- `Value` **(required): The value to return if the expression is True.**

WARNING **If none of the expressions in your `Switch` function evaluate as `True`, the function will return a `Null` value. For example, the following function evaluates `Count` and returns a value based on it.**

```
Switch([Count] < 10, "Low", [Count] > 15, "High")
```

The problem with this function is that if `Count` comes in between 10 and 15, you will get a `Null` value because none of the expressions include those numbers. This may indirectly cause errors in other parts of your analysis.

To avoid this scenario, you can add a catch-all expression and provide a value to return if none of your exppresions are determined to be `True`.

```
Switch([Count] < 10, "Low", [Count] > 15, "High", True, "Middle")
```

Adding `True` as the last expression forces the value `"Middle"` to be returned instead of a `Null` value if none of the other expressions evaluate as `True`.

Comparing the IIf and Switch Functions

Although the `IIf` function is a versatile tool that can handle most conditional analysis, the fact is that the `IIf` function has a fixed number of arguments that limits it to a basic `IF...THEN...ELSE` structure. This limitation makes it difficult to evaluate complex conditions without using nested `IIf` functions. Although there is nothing wrong with nesting `IIf` functions, there are analyses where the numbers of conditions that need to be evaluated make building a nested `IIf` impractical at best.

To illustrate this point, consider this scenario. It is common practice to classify customers into groups based on annual revenue, or how much they spend with your company. Imagine that your organization has a policy of classifying customers into four groups: A, B, C, and D (see Table 6-1).

You have been asked to classify the customers in the TransactionMaster table, based on each customer's sales transactions. You can actually do this using either the `IIf` function or the `Switch` function.

Table 6-1: Customer Classifications

ANNUAL REVENUE	CUSTOMER CLASSIFICATION
>= $10,000	A
>=5,000 but < $10,000	B
>=$1,000 but < $5,000	C
<$1,000	D

The problem with using the `IIf` function is that this situation calls for some hefty nesting. That is, you will have to use `IIf` expressions within other `IIf` expressions to handle the easy layer of possible conditions. Here is how the expression would look if you opted to use the `IIf` function.

```
IIf([REV]>=10000,"A",IIf([REV]>=5000 And [REV]<10000,"B",
IIf([REV]>1000 And [REV]<5000,"C","D")))
```

As you can see, not only is it difficult to determine what is going on here, but this is so convoluted, the chances of making a syntax or logic error are high.

In contrast to the preceding nested `IIf` function, the following `Switch` function is rather straightforward:

```
Switch([REV]<1000,"D",[REV]<5000,"C",[REV]<10000,"B",True,"A")
```

This function tells Access that if `REV` is less than `1000`, then return a value of `"D"`. If `REV` is less than `5000`, then return a value of `"C"`. If `REV` is less than `10000`, then return `"B"`. If all else fails, use `"A"`. Figure 6-24 demonstrates how you would use this function in a query.

NOTE **You may shrewdly notice that those records that are less than 1000 will also be less than 10000. So why don't all the records get tagged with a value of "B"? Remember that the `Switch` function evaluates your expressions from left to right and only returns the value of the first expression that evaluates to `True`.**

In this light, you will want to sort the expressions in your `Switch` function accordingly, using an order that is conducive to the logic of your analysis.

When you run the query, you will see the resulting dataset shown in Figure 6-25.

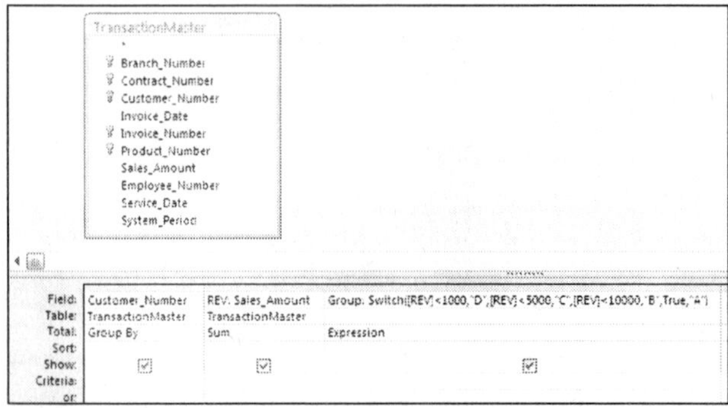

Figure 6-24: Using the `Switch` function is sometimes more practical than using nested `IIf` functions. This query will classify customers by how much they spend.

Customer_Number	REV	Group
2801341	$1,457.67	C
2801368	$15,998.08	A
2801486	$1,008.05	C
2801716	$2,993.50	C
2801733	$3,757.54	C
2802129	$819.14	D
2803311	$539.87	D
2803937	$145.02	D
2804369	$1,009.16	C
2804690	$905.66	D
2805204	$1,279.33	C
2805260	$7,741.25	B
2805391	$9,617.16	B
2805406	$675.30	D
2805499	$448.51	D

Figure 6-25: Each customer is conditionally tagged with a group designation based on annual revenue.

Summary

You will often need to perform analyses where specifications and circumstances for the analysis are variable. That is, the parameters and conditions for the analysis change each time you run it. In such cases, you will need to perform a *conditional analysis* — an analysis whose outcome depends on a pre-defined set of conditions. Access has several built-in tools that enable conditional analyses; some of these are parameter queries, the `IIf` function, and the `Switch` function.

A *parameter query* is an interactive query that prompts you for criteria before the query is run. This type of query is often used when different criteria needs to be passed each time it is run. Running a parameter query forces the Enter Parameter Value dialog box to open and you simply enter your parameter.

Parameter queries are not the only tools in Access that allow for conditional analysis. Access also has built-in functions that facilitate value comparisons, data validation, and conditional evaluation. These conditional functions (also called program flow functions) are designed to test for conditions and provide different outcomes based on the results of those tests. Two of these functions are the `IIf` function and the `Switch` function.

The `IIf` (immediate if) function replicates the functionality of the Excel `IF` function, evaluating a specific condition as `True` or `False`. The `IIf` function saves steps in your analytical processes and, ultimately, saves time. The `Switch` function enables you to evaluate a list of expressions and return the value associated with the expression determined to be

True. The power of the Switch function comes in evaluating multiple expressions at one time and determining which one is True.

Leveraging and employing conditional analysis is not only easy, but it helps save you time, organizes your analytical processes, and ultimately enhances your analysis.

Basic Analysis Techniques

CHAPTER

7

Understanding and Using SQL

SQL (Structured Query Language), commonly pronounced *sequel*, is the language relational database management systems such as Access use to perform their various tasks. To tell Access to perform any kind of query, you must convey your instructions in SQL. Don't panic; the truth is that you have already been building and using SQL statements without knowing it.

In this chapter, you will discover the role that SQL plays in your dealings with Access and learn how to understand the SQL statements generated when building queries. You will also explore some of the advanced actions you can take with SQL statements, enabling you to accomplish actions that go beyond the Access user interface. The basics you learn here will lay the foundation for your ability to perform the advanced techniques you will encounter in subsequent chapters.

Understanding Basic SQL

A major reason your exposure to SQL is limited is that Access is more user-friendly than most people give it credit for being. The fact is that Access performs a majority of its actions in user-friendly environments that hide the real grunt work that goes on behind the scenes.

For a demonstration of this, build in Design view the query you see in Figure 7-1. In this relatively simple query, you are asking for the sum of revenue by branch and system period.

Next, go up to the Design tab on the application ribbon and select View → SQL View. Access switches from Design view to the view you see in Figure 7-2.

As you can see in Figure 7-2, while you were busy designing your query in Design view, Access was diligently creating the SQL statement that will allow the query to run. This example shows that with the user-friendly interface provided by Access, you don't necessarily need to know the SQL behind each query. The question now becomes: if you can run queries just fine without knowing SQL, why bother to learn it?

Admittedly, the convenient query interface provided by Access does make it a bit tempting to go through life not really understanding SQL. However, if you want to harness the real power of data analysis with Access, it is important to understand the fundamentals of SQL. In this chapter, you will get a solid understanding of SQL as well as insights into some techniques that leverage it to enhance your data analysis.

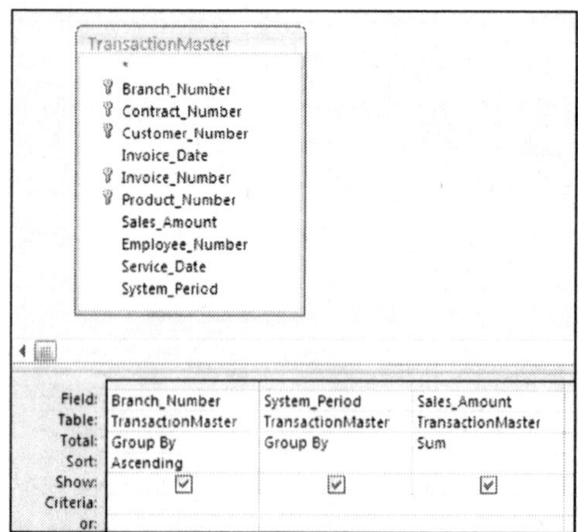

Figure 7-1: Build this relatively simple query in Design view.

```
SELECT TransactionMaster.Branch_Number, TransactionMaster.System_Period, Sum(TransactionMaster.Sales_Amount) AS SumOfSales_Amount
FROM TransactionMaster
GROUP BY TransactionMaster.Branch_Number, TransactionMaster.System_Period
ORDER BY TransactionMaster.Branch_Number;
```

Figure 7-2: You can get to SQL view by selecting View → SQL View.

The SELECT Statement

The SELECT statement, the cornerstone of SQL, enables you to retrieve records from a dataset. The basic syntax of a SELECT statement is:

```
SELECT column_name(s)
FROM table_name
```

The SELECT statement is most often used with a FROM clause. The FROM clause identifies the table or tables that make up the source for the data.

Try this: Start a new query in Design view. Close the Show Table dialog box (if it is open), go up to the Design tab on the application ribbon, and select View → SQL View. In the SQL view, type in the SELECT statement shown in Figure 7-3, and then run the query by selecting Run in the Design tab of the ribbon.

Congratulations! You have just written your first query manually.

NOTE You may notice that the SQL statement automatically created by Access in Figure 7-2 has a semicolon at the end of it. This semicolon is not required for Access to run the query. The semicolon is a standard way to end a SQL statement and is required by some database programs. However, it is not necessary to end your SQL statements with a semicolon in Access, as Access will automatically add it when the query compiles.

Selecting Specific Columns

You can retrieve specific columns from your dataset by explicitly defining the columns in your SELECT statement, as follows:

```
SELECT Employee_Number, Last_Name, First_Name
FROM Employee_Master
```

```
SELECT Employee_Number
FROM Employee_Master
```

Figure 7-3: A basic SELECT statement in SQL view.

WARNING **Any column in your database that has a name which includes spaces or a non-alphanumeric character must be enclosed within brackets ([ ]) in your SQL statement. For example, the SQL statement selecting data from a column called Last Name would look like this:** `SELECT [Last Name] FROM EmployeeTable`.

Selecting All Columns

Using the wildcard (*) enables you to select all columns from a dataset without having to define every column explicitly:

```
SELECT *
FROM Employee_Master
```

The WHERE Clause

You can use the `WHERE` clause in a `SELECT` statement to filter your dataset and conditionally select specific records. The `WHERE` clause is always used in combination with an operator such as: = (equal), <> (not equal), > (greater than), < (less than), >= (greater than or equal to), <= (less than or equal to), BETWEEN (within general range).

The following SQL statement retrieves only those employees whose last name is Jehnsen:

```
SELECT Employee_Number, Last_Name, First_Name
FROM Employee_Master
WHERE Last_Name = "JEHNSEN"
```

And this SQL statement retrieves only those employees whose hire date is later than May 16, 2004:

```
SELECT Employee_Number, Last_Name, First_Name
FROM Employee_Master
WHERE Hire_Date > #5/16/2004#
```

NOTE **Note in the preceding two examples that the word Jehnsen is wrapped in quotes ("Jehnsen") and the date 5/16/2004 is wrapped in the number signs (#5/16/2004#). When referring to a text value in a SQL statement, you must place quotes around the value, whereas refering to a date requires the number signs be used.**

Making Sense of Joins

You will often need to build queries that require two or more related tables be joined to achieve the desired results. For example, you may want to join an employee table to a transaction table in order create a report that contains both transaction details and information on the employees who logged those transactions. The type of join used will determine the records that will be output.

Inner Joins

An *inner join* operation tells Access to select only those records from both tables that have matching values. Records with values in the joined field that do not appear in both tables are omitted from the query results. Figure 7-4 represents the inner join operation visually.

The following SQL statement selects only those records where the employee numbers in the Employee_Number field are in both the Employee_Master table and the TransactionMaster table.

```
SELECT Employee_Master.Last_Name, TransactionMaster.Sales_Amount
FROM Employee_Master INNER JOIN TransactionMaster
ON Employee_Master.Employee_Number = TransactionMaster.Employee_Number
```

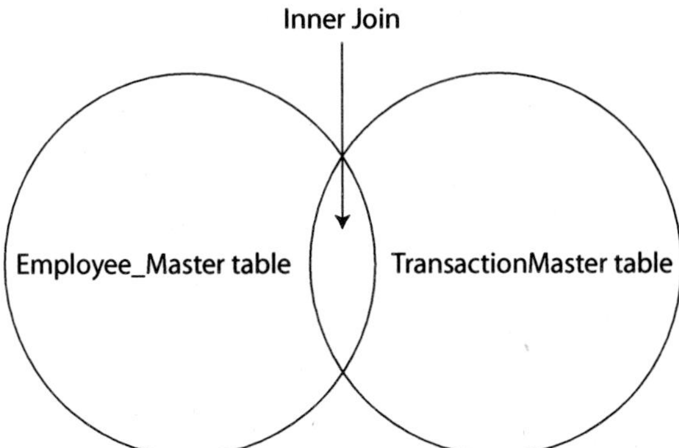

Figure 7-4: An inner join operation selects only the records that have matching values in both tables. The arrows point to the records that will be included in the results.

Outer Joins

An *outer join* operation tells Access to select all the records from one table and only the records from a second table with matching values in the joined field. There are two types of outer joins: left joins and right joins.

A *left join* operation (sometimes called an *outer left join*) tells Access to select all the records from the first table regardless of matching *and* only those records from the second table that have matching values in the joined field. Figure 7-5 represents the left join operation visually.

This SQL statement selects all records from the Employee_Master table and only those records in the TransactionMaster table that have employee numbers that exist in the Employee_Master table.

```
SELECT Employee_Master.Last_Name, TransactionMaster.Sales_Amount
FROM Employee_Master LEFT JOIN TransactionMaster ON
Employee_Master.Employee_Number = TransactionMaster.Employee_Number
```

A *right join* operation (sometimes called an *outer right join*) tells Access to select all the records from the second table regardless of matching, *and* only those records from the first table that have matching values in the joined field (see Figure 7-6).

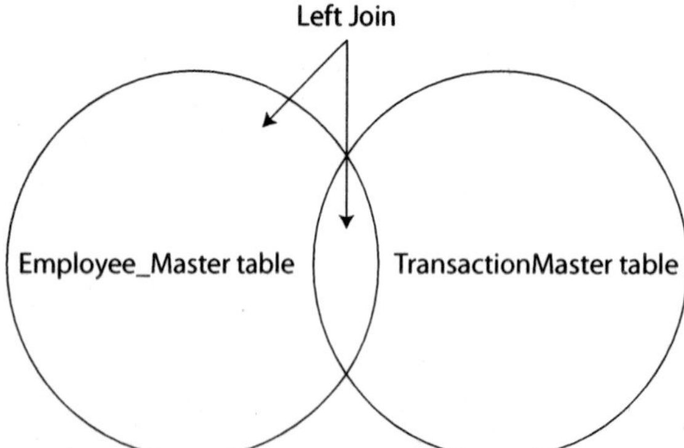

Figure 7-5: A left join operation will select all records from the first table and only those records from the second table that have matching values in both tables. The arrows point to the records that will be included in the results.

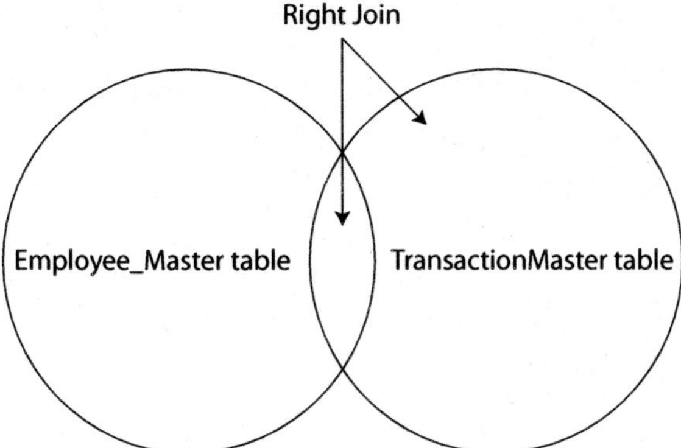

Figure 7-6: A right join operation selects all records from the second table and only those records from the first table that have matching values in both tables. The arrows point to the records that will be included in the results.

This SQL statement selects all records from the TransactionMaster table and only those records in the Employee_Master table that have employee numbers that exist in the TransactionMaster table.

```
SELECT Employee_Master.Last_Name, TransactionMaster.Sales_Amount
FROM Employee_Master RIGHT JOIN TransactionMaster ON
Employee_Master.Employee_Number = TransactionMaster.Employee_Number
```

TIP **Notice that in the preceding join statements, table names are listed before each column name separated by a dot (for example, Employee_Master.Last_Name). When you are building a SQL statement for a query that utilizes multiple tables, it is generally good practice to refer to the table names as well as field names in order to avoid confusion and errors. Access does this for all queries automatically.**

Getting Fancy with Advanced SQL Statements

You will soon realize that the SQL language itself is a quite versatile, enabling you to go far beyond basic `SELECT`, `FROM`, `WHERE` statements. In this section, you explore some of the advanced actions you can accomplish with SQL.

Expanding Your Search with the Like Operator

By itself the `Like` operator is no different than the equal (=) operator. For example, these two SQL statements will return the same number of records:

```
SELECT Employee_Number, Job_Title
FROM Employee_Master
WHERE Job_Title="TEAMLEAD 1"

SELECT Employee_Number, Job_Title
FROM Employee_Master
WHERE Job_Title Like"TEAMLEAD 1"
```

The Like operator is typically used with wildcard characters to expand the scope of your search to include any record that matches a pattern. The wildcard characters that are valid in Access are as follows:

- *: The asterisk represents any number and type characters.
- ?: The question mark represents any single character.
- #: The pound or hash symbol represents any single digit.
- []: The brackets enable you to pass a single character or an array of characters to the Like operator. Any values matching the character values within the brackets will be included in the results.
- [!]: The brackets with an embedded exclamation point allow you to pass a single character or an array of characters to the Like operator. Any values matching the character values following the exclamation point will be excluded from the results.

Listed in Table 7-1 are some example SQL statements that use the `Like` operator to select different records from the same table column.

Table 7-1: Selection Methods using the `Like` Operator

WILDCARD CHARACTER(S) USED	SQL STATEMENT EXAMPLE	RESULT
*	SELECT Field1 FROM Table1 WHERE Field1 Like "A*"	Selects all records where Field1 starts with the letter A
*	SELECT Field1 FROM Table1 WHERE Field1 Like "*A*"	Selects all records where Field1 includes the letter A

Table 7-1: *(continued)*

WILDCARD CHARACTER(S) USED	SQL STATEMENT EXAMPLE	RESULT
?	`SELECT Field1 FROM Table1 WHERE Field1 Like "???"`	Selects all records where the length of Field1 is three characters long
?	`SELECT Field1 FROM Table1 WHERE Field1 Like "B??"`	Selects all records where Field1 is a three-letter word that starts with B
#	`SELECT Field1 FROM Table1 WHERE Field1 Like "###"`	Selects all records where Field1 is a number that is exactly three digits long
#	`SELECT Field1 FROM Table1 WHERE Field1 Like "A#A"`	Selects all records where the value in Field1 is a three-character value that starts with A, contains one digit, and ends with A
#, *	`SELECT Field1 FROM Table1 WHERE Field1 Like "A#*"`	Selects all records where Field1 begins with A and any digit
[], *	`SELECT Field1 FROM Table1 WHERE Field1 Like "*[$%!*/]*"`	Selects all records where Field1 includes any one of the special characters shown in the SQL statement
[!], *	`SELECT Field1 FROM Table1 WHERE Field1 Like "*[!a-z]*"`	Selects all records where the value of Field1 is *not* a text value, but a number value
[!], *	`SELECT Field1 FROM Table1 WHERE Field1 Like "*[!0-9]*"`	Selects all records where the value of Field1 is *not* a number value, but a text value

Selecting Unique Values and Rows without Grouping

The `DISTINCT` predicate enables you to retrieve only unique values from the selected fields in your dataset. For example, the following SQL statement selects only unique job titles from the Employee_Master table, resulting in six records:

```
SELECT DISTINCT Job_Title
FROM Employee_Master
```

If your SQL statement selects more than one field, the combination of values from all fields must be unique for a given record to be included in the results.

Using SELECT DISTINCT is different from using GROUP BY or an aggregate query. There is no grouping going on here; Access is simply running through the records and retrieving the unique values. To see how GROUP BY compares to SELECT DISTINCT, read the following sections.

If you require that the entire row be unique, you could us the DISTINCTROW predicate. The DISTINCTROW predicate enables you to retrieve only those records for which the entire row is unique. That is to say, the combination of all values in the selected fields does not match any other record in the returned dataset. You would use the DISTINCTROW predicate just as you would in a SELECT DISTINCT clause.

```
SELECT DISTINCTROW Job_Title
FROM Employee_Master
```

Grouping and Aggregating with the GROUP BY Clause

The GROUP BY clause makes is possible to aggregate records in your dataset by column values. When you create an aggregate query in Design view, you are essentially using the GROUP BY clause. The following SQL statement groups the Home_Branch field and gives you the count of employees in every branch.

```
SELECT Home_Branch, Count(Employee_Number)
FROM Employee_Master
GROUP BY Home_Branch
```

The HAVING Clause

When you are using the GROUP BY clause, you cannot specify criteria using the WHERE clause. Instead, you will need to use the HAVING clause. The following SQL statement groups the Home_Branch field and only gives you the count of employees in branch 601306:

```
SELECT Home_Branch, Count(Employee_Number)
FROM Employee_Master
GROUP BY Home_Branch
HAVING Home_Branch = "601306"
```

Setting Sort Order with the ORDER BY Clause

The ORDER BY clause enables you to sort data by a specified field. The default sort order is ascending; therefore, sorting your fields in ascending order requires no explicit instruction. The following SQL statement sorts the resulting records by Last_Name ascending, then First_Name ascending:

```
SELECT Employee_Number, Last_Name, First_Name
FROM Employee_Master
ORDER BY Last_Name, First_Name
```

To sort in descending order, you must use the DESC reserved word after each column you want sorted in descending order. The following SQL statement will sort the resulting records in by Last_Name descending, then First_Name ascending:

```
SELECT Employee_Number, Last_Name, First_Name
FROM Employee_Master
ORDER BY Last_Name DESC, First_Name
```

Creating Aliases with the AS Clause

The AS clause enables you to assign aliases to your columns and tables. There are generally two reasons you would want to use aliases: either you want to make column or table names shorter and easier to read, or you are working with multiple instances of the same table and you need a way to refer to one instance or the other.

Creating a Column Alias

The following SQL statement groups the Home_Branch field and gives you the count of employees in every branch. In addition, the alias MyCount has been given to the column containing the count of Employee Number by including the AS clause.

```
SELECT Home_Branch, Count(Employee_Number)AS MyCount
FROM Employee_Master
GROUP BY Home_Branch
```

Creating a Table Alias

This SQL statement gives the `Employee_Master` the alias `MyTable`.

```
SELECT Home_Branch, Count(Employee_Number)
FROM Employee_Master AS MyTable
GROUP BY Home_Branch
```

SELECT TOP and SELECT TOP PERCENT

When you run a `SELECT` query, you are retrieving all records that meet your definitions and criteria. When you run the `SELECT TOP` statement, or a top values query, you are telling Access to filter your returned dataset to show only a specific number of records.

Top Values Queries Explained

To get a clear understanding of what the `SELECT TOP` statement does, build the aggregate query shown in Figure 7-7.

Right-click the grey area above the white query grid and then select Properties. This activates the Property Sheet dialog box shown in Figure 7-8. In the Property Sheet dialog box, change the Top Values property to 25.

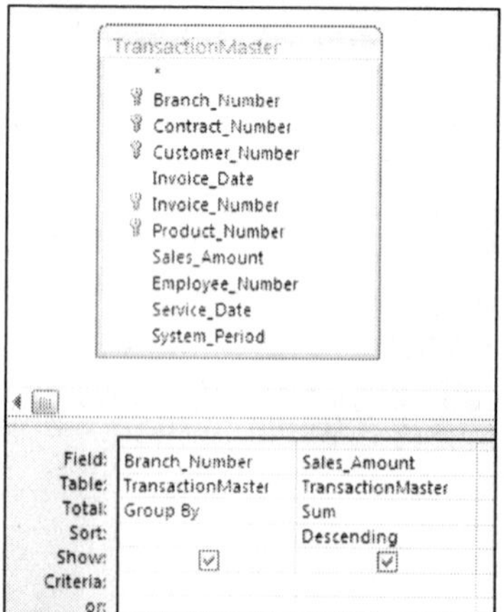

Figure 7-7: Build this aggregate query in Design view. Take note that the query is sorted descending on the Sum of Sales_Amount.

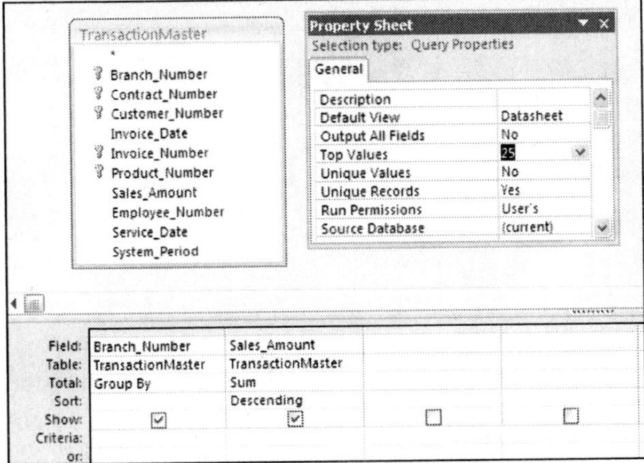

Figure 7-8: Change the Top Values property to 25.

As you can see in Figure 7-9, after you run this query, only the branches that fall into the top 25 by sum of sales amount are returned. If you want the bottom 25 branches, simply change the sort order of the sum of sales amount to ascending.

Branch_Number	SumOfSales_Amount
701715	$484,817.65
501717	$452,318.39
201717	$450,524.08
101313	$444,630.88
701309	$417,157.87
301316	$397,746.22
601306	$374,888.86
202605	$342,536.70
801211	$335,110.37
803717	$333,577.98
503405	$330,179.80
804211	$307,115.74
701407	$293,297.07
201714	$288,713.58
302301	$251,174.69
701717	$237,453.85
806211	$231,354.67
401612	$229,226.64
940381	$224,347.84
590140	$223,931.16
501619	$208,664.73
301619	$191,276.35
702309	$190,862.80
801607	$186,937.48
601716	$168,872.59

Figure 7-9: Running the query gives you the top 25 branches by sum of sales amount.

SELECT TOP

The SELECT TOP statement is easy to spot. This is the same query used to run the results in Figure 7-9.

```
SELECT TOP 25 Branch_Number, Sum(Sales_Amount) AS SumOfSales_Amount
FROM TransactionMaster
GROUP BY Branch_Number
ORDER BY Sum(Sales_Amount) DESC
```

Bear in mind that you don't have to be working with totals or currency to use a top values query. In the following SQL statement, you are returning the 25 employees that have the earliest hire date in the company, effectively producing a seniority report:

```
SELECT TOP 25 Employee_Number, Last_Name, First_Name, Hire_Date
FROM Employee_Master
ORDER BY Hire_Date ASC
```

SELECT TOP PERCENT

The SELECT TOP PERCENT statement works in exactly the same way as SELECT TOP except the records returned in a SELECT TOP PERCENT statement represent the *Nth* percent of total records rather than the *Nth* number of records. For example, the following SQL statement will return the top 25 percent of records by sum of sales amount:

```
SELECT TOP 25 PERCENT Branch_Number, Sum(Sales_Amount) ↵
AS SumOfSales_Amount
FROM TransactionMaster
GROUP BY Branch_Number
ORDER BY Sum(Sales_Amount) DESC
```

NOTE **Keep in mind that** SELECT TOP PERCENT **statements only give you the top or bottom percent of the total number of records in the returned dataset, not the percent of the total value in your records. For example, the preceding SQL statement does not give you only those records that make up 25 percent of the total value of Sales_Amount. It will only give you the top 25 percent of records in the returned dataset.**

Performing Action Queries via SQL Statements

You may not have thought about it before, but when you build an action query, you are building a SQL statement that is specific to that action. These SQL statements make it possible for you to go beyond just selecting records.

Make-Table Queries Translated

Make-table queries use the `SELECT...INTO` statement to make a hard-coded table that contains the results of your query. The following example first selects employee number, last name, and first name, and then creates a new table called Employees:

```
SELECT Employee_Number,Last_Name,First_Name INTO Employees
FROM Employee_Master;
```

Append Queries Translated

Append queries use the `INSERT INTO` statement to insert new rows into a specified table. The following example inserts new rows into the Employee_Master table from the Employees table:

```
INSERT INTO Employee_Master (Employee_Number, Last_Name, First_Name)
SELECT Employees.Employee_Number, Employees.Last_Name, ⮐
Employees.First_Name
FROM Employees
```

Update Queries Translated

Update queries use the `UPDATE` statement in conjunction with `SET` in order to modify the data in a dataset. This example updates the Price field in the PriceMaster table to increase prices by 10 percent.

```
UPDATE PriceMaster SET Price = [Price]*1.1
```

Delete Queries Translated

Delete queries use the DELETE statement to delete rows in a dataset. In the example here, you are deleting all rows from the Employee_Master table that have no values in the Employee_Status field.

```
DELETE *
FROM Employee_Master
WHERE Employee_Status Is Null
```

Creating Crosstabs with the TRANSFORM Statement

The TRANSFORM statement enables the creation of a Crosstab dataset that displays data in a compact view. The TRANSFORM statement requires three main components to work:

- The field to be aggregated
- The SELECT statement that determines the row content for the crosstab
- The field that will make up the column of the crosstab (the pivot field)

The syntax is as follows:

```
TRANSFORM Aggregated_Field
SELECT Field1, Field2 FROM Table1 GROUP BY Select Field1, Field2
PIVOT Pivot_Field
```

For example, the following statement creates a crosstab that shows region and market on the rows and products on the columns, with revenue in the center of the crosstab.

```
TRANSFORM Sum(Revenue) AS SumOfRevenue
SELECT Region, Market
FROM PvTblFeed
GROUP BY Region, Market
PIVOT Product_Description
```

Using SQL Specific Queries

SQL specific queries are essentially action queries that cannot be run through the Access query grid. These queries must be run either in SQL view or via code (macro or VBA). There are several types of SQL specific queries, each performing a specific action. This section introduces you to a few of these queries, focusing on those that can be used in Access to shape and configure data tables.

Merging Datasets with the UNION Operator

The `UNION` operator is used to merge two compatible SQL statements to produce one read-only dataset. For example, the following `Select` statement produces a dataset (Figure 7-10) that shows revenue by employee for each branch.

```
SELECT Branch_Number, Employee_Number, Revenue AS REV
FROM MainSummary
```

A second `Select` statement produces a separate dataset (Figure 7-11) that shows total revenue by branch.

```
SELECT Branch_Number, "Branch Total" AS Employee, Sum(Revenue) AS REV
FROM MainSummary
GROUP BY Branch_Number
```

Branch_Number	Employee_Number	REV
173901	160367	$21,626.22
173901	164234	$3,339.80
173901	4432	$33,136.05
173901	5366	$26,604.17
173901	55324	$20,012.57
173901	60405	$401.57
173901	6446	$1,693.94
201605	160512	$7,378.91
201605	164264	$3,812.67
201605	164465	$4,801.11
201605	164466	$624.06
201605	2522	$6,168.00
201605	52361	$18,559.19
201605	5445	$817.03
201605	64006	$27,656.63
201709	1135	$1,477.21
201709	160126	$5,164.42
201709	160254	$1,428.72
201709	164065	$896.10

Figure 7-10: This dataset shows revenue by employee and branch.

Branch_Number	Employee	REV
101313	Branch Total	$444,630.88
101419	Branch Total	$124,597.15
102516	Branch Total	$63,227.89
103516	Branch Total	$101,664.28
173901	Branch Total	$107,215.90
201605	Branch Total	$69,817.60
201709	Branch Total	$96,853.01
201714	Branch Total	$288,713.58
201717	Branch Total	$450,524.08
202600	Branch Total	$151,337.96
202605	Branch Total	$342,536.70
202714	Branch Total	$113,074.59
208605	Branch Total	$64,357.22
301301	Branch Total	$157,235.04

Figure 7-11: This dataset shows total revenue by branch.

The idea is to bring these two datasets together to create an analysis that will show detail and totals all in one table. The `UNION` operator is ideal for this type of work, merging the results of the two `Select` statements. To use the `UNION` operator, simply start a new query in SQL view and enter the following syntax:

```
SELECT Branch_Number, Employee_Number, Revenue AS REV
FROM MainSummary
UNION
SELECT Branch_Number, "Branch Total" AS Employee, Sum(Revenue) AS REV
FROM MainSummary
GROUP BY Branch_Number
```

As you can see, the preceding statement is nothing more than the two SQL statements brought together with a `Union` operator. When the two are merged (Figure 7-12), the result is a dataset that shows both details and totals in one table!

Branch_Number	Employee_Number	REV
173901	160367	$21,626.22
173901	164234	$3,339.80
173901	4432	$33,136.05
173901	5366	$26,604.17
173901	55324	$20,012.57
173901	60405	$401.57
173901	6446	$1,693.94
173901	Branch Total	$107,215.90
201605	160512	$7,378.91
201605	164264	$3,812.67
201605	164465	$4,801.11
201605	164466	$624.06
201605	2522	$6,168.00
201605	52361	$18,559.19
201605	5445	$817.03
201605	64006	$27,656.63
201605	Branch Total	$69,817.60

Figure 7-12: The two datasets have now been combined to create a report that provides summary and detail data.

NOTE **When a union query is run, Access matches the columns from both datasets by their position in the SELECT statement. That means two things: your SELECT statements must have the same number of columns, and the columns in both statements should, in most cases, be in the same order.**

Creating a Table with the CREATE TABLE Statement

Often in your analytical processes, you will need to create a temporary table in order to group, manipulate, or simply hold data. The CREATE TABLE statement allows you to do just that with one SQL specific query.

Unlike a make-table query, the CREATE TABLE statement is designed to create only the structure or schema of a table. No records are ever returned with a CREATE TABLE statement. This statement allows you to strategically create an empty table at any point in your analytical process.

The basic syntax for a CREATE TABLE statement is as follows:

```
CREATE TABLE TableName
(<Field1Name> Type(<Field Size>), <Field2Name> Type(<Field Size>))
```

To use the CREATE TABLE statement, simply start a new query in SQL view and define the structure for your table.

In the following example, a new table called TempLog is created with three fields. The first field is a Text field that can accept 50 characters, the second field is a Text field that can accept 150 characters, and the third field is a Date field.

```
CREATE TABLE TempLog
([User] Text(50), [Description] Text, [LogDate] Date)
```

NOTE **You will notice that in the preceding example, no field size is specified for the second text column. If the field size is omitted, Access will use the default field size specified for the database.**

Manipulating Columns with the ALTER TABLE Statement

The ALTER TABLE statement provides some additional methods of altering the structure of a table behind the scenes. There are several clauses you can use with the ALTER TABLE statement, three of which are quite useful in Access data analysis: ADD, ALTER COLUMN, and DROP COLUMN.

NOTE **The ALTER TABLE statement along with its various clauses is used much less frequently than the SQL statements mentioned earlier in this chapter. However, the ALTER TABLE statement comes in handy when your analytical processes require you to change the structure of tables on-the-fly, helping you avoid any manual manipulations that may have to be done.**

It should be noted that there is no way to undo any actions performed using an ALTER TABLE statement. This fact obviously calls for some caution when using these statements.

Adding a Column with the ADD Clause

As the name implies, the ADD clause enables you to add a column to an existing table. The basic syntax is as follows:

```
ALTER TABLE <TableName>
ADD <ColumnName> Type(<Field Size>)
```

To use the ADD statement, simply start a new query in SQL view and define the structure for your new column. For example, running the example statement shown here will create a new column called SupervisorPhone to be added to a table called TempLog:

```
ALTER TABLE TempLog
ADD SupervisorPhone Text(10)
```

Altering a Column with the ALTER COLUMN Clause

When using the ALTER COLUMN clause, you specify an existing column in an existing table to edit. This clause is used primarily to change the data type and field size of a given column. The basic syntax is as follows:

```
ALTER TABLE <TableName>
ALTER COLUMN <ColumnName> Type(<Field Size>)
```

To use the ALTER COLUMN statement, simply start a new query in SQL view and define changes for the column in question. For example, the example statement shown here will change the field size of the SupervisorPhone field.

```
ALTER TABLE TempLog
ALTER COLUMN SupervisorPhone Text(13)
```

Deleting a Column with the DROP COLUMN Clause

The `DROP COLUMN` clause enables you to delete a given column from an existing table. The basic syntax is as follows:

```
ALTER TABLE <TableName>
DROP COLUMN <ColumnName>
```

To use the `DROP COLUMN` statement, simply start a new query in SQL view and define the structure for your new column. For example, running the example statement shown here will delete the column called SupervisorPhone from the TempLog table:

```
ALTER TABLE TempLog
DROP COLUMN SupervisorPhone
```

Summary

SQL (Structured Query Language) is the language that relational database management systems such as Access use to perform their various tasks. With SQL, you can perform many of the queries you perform through the Access front end, along with some tasks that go beyond the user interface.

You can build your queries with SQL statements by working in SQL view. You can get to SQL view by starting a new query and then selecting View → SQL View in the Design tab.

When in SQL view, you can create SQL statements that select, filter, delete, or update data, and even create or alter table structures. Knowing the basics of SQL will give you the solid foundation you need to perform the more advanced querying techniques in Access.

CHAPTER

8

Subqueries and Domain Aggregate Functions

Often, you will carry out your analyses in layers, each layer of analysis using or building on the previous layer. This practice of building layers into analytical processes is actually very common. For example, when you build a query using another query as the data source, you are layering your analysis. When you build a query based on a temporary table created by a make-table query, you are also layering your analysis.

All of these conventional methods of layering analyses have two things in common. First, they all add a step to your analytical processes. Every query that has to be run in order to feed another query, or every temporary table that has to be created in order to advance your analysis, adds yet another task that must be completed before you get your final results. Second, they all require the creation of temporary tables or transitory queries, inundating your database with table and query objects that lead to a confusing analytical process as well as a database that bloats easily. This is where subqueries and domain aggregate functions can help.

Subqueries and domain aggregate functions enable you to build layers into your analysis within one query, eliminating the need for temporary tables or transitory queries. Sounds useful right? So why is that you haven't heard about these before? The primary reason is that using the conventional methods mentioned before is easy enough that most analysts don't bother looking for more options. The other reason is that both subqueries and domain aggregate functions require an understanding of SQL (Structured Query Language). Most Access users don't have the time or inclination to learn SQL.

Now that you have covered the fundamentals of SQL in Chapter 7, you are ready to leverage both subqueries and domain aggregate functions to streamline your analytical processes, as well as expand and enhance your analysis.

Enhancing Your Analysis with Subqueries

Subqueries (sometimes referred to as *subselect queries*) are select queries that are nested within other queries. The primary purpose of a subquery is to enable you to use the results of one query within the execution of another. With subqueries, you can answer a multiple-part question, specify criteria for further selection, or define new fields to be used in your analysis.

The query shown in Figure 8-1 demonstrates how a subquery is used in the design grid. As you look at this, remember that this is one example of how a subquery can be used. Subqueries are not limited to being used as criteria.

If you were to build the query in Figure 8-1 and switch to SQL view, you would see the following SQL statement. Can you pick out the subquery? Look for the second `SELECT` statement.

```
SELECT Employee_Number, Last_Name, Home_Branch
FROM Employee_Master
WHERE Home_Branch IN
     (SELECT [Branch_Number]FROM[LocationMaster]WHERE[Market]="DALLAS")
```

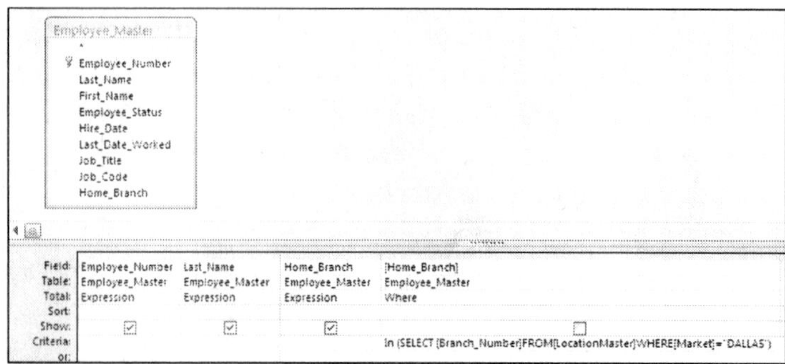

Figure 8-1: To use a subquery in the Query Design view, simply enter the SQL statement.

NOTE **Subqueries must always be enclosed in parentheses.**

The idea behind a subquery is that the subquery is executed first, and the results are used in the outer query (the query in which the subquery is embedded) as a criterion, an expression, a parameter, and so on. In the example shown in Figure 8-1, the subquery first returns a list of branches that belong to the Dallas market. Then the outer query uses that list as criteria to filter out any employee who does not belong to the Dallas market.

Why Use Subqueries?

Subqueries often run more slowly than a standard query using a join. This is because subqueries either are executed against an entire dataset or are evaluated multiple times per row processed by the outer query. This makes them slow to execute especially if you have a large dataset. So why use them?

Many analyses require multiple step processes that use temporary tables or transitory queries. Although there is nothing inherently wrong with temporary tables and queries, an excess amount of them in your analytical processes could lead to a confusing analytical process as well as a database that bloats easily.

Even though using subqueries comes with a performance hit, it may be an acceptable trade for streamlined procedures and optimized analytical processes. You will even find that as you become more comfortable with writing your own SQL statements, you will use subqueries on-the-fly to actually *save* time.

Subquery Ground Rules

You should be aware of the following rules and restrictions when using subqueries:

- Your subquery must have at least one `SELECT` statement and a `FROM` clause in its SQL string.
- You must enclose your subquery in parentheses.
- Theoretically, you can nest up to 31 subqueries within a query. This number, however, is based on your system's available memory and the complexity of your subqueries.
- You can use a subquery as an expression as long as it returns a single value.

- You can use the ORDER BY clause in a subquery only if the subquery is a SELECT TOP or SELECT TOP PERCENT statement.
- You cannot use the DISTINCT keyword in a subquery that includes the GROUP BY clause.
- You must implement table aliases in queries in which a table is used in both the outer query and the subquery.

Creating Subqueries without Typing SQL Statements

You may have the tendency to shy away from subqueries because you may feel uncomfortable with writing your own SQL statements. Indeed, many of the SQL statements necessary to perform the smallest analysis can seem daunting.

Imagine, for example, that you have been asked to provide the number of employees that have a time in service greater than the average time in service for all employees in the company. Sounds like a relatively simple analysis, and it *is* simple when you use a subquery. But where do you start? Well, you could just write a SQL statement into the SQL view of a query and run it. But the truth is that not many Access users create SQL statements from scratch. The smart ones utilize the built-in functionalities of Access to save time and headaches. The trick is to split the analysis into manageable pieces.

In this scenario, the first step is to find the average time in service for all employees in the company. To do this, create the query shown in Figure 8-2.

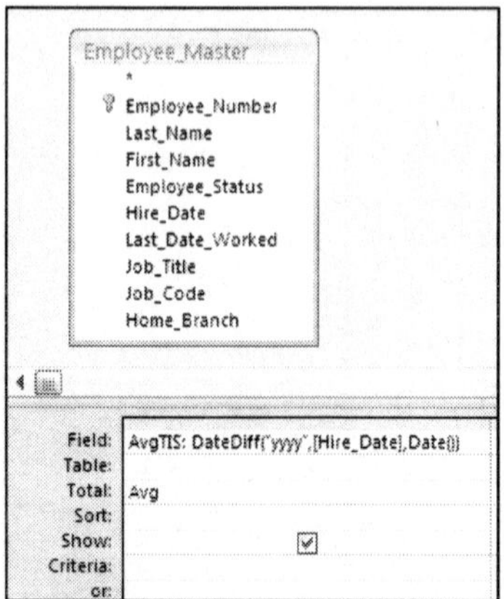

Figure 8-2: Create a query to find the average time in service for all employees.

Next, switch to SQL view, shown in Figure 8-3, and copy the SQL statement.

The next step is to create a query that will count the number of employees by time in service, as shown in Figure 8-4.

Right-click in the Criteria row under the TIS field and select Zoom. This opens the Zoom dialog box shown in Figure 8-5. This dialog box enables you to work with text that is too long to be easily seen at one time in the query grid. With the Zoom dialog box open, paste the SQL statement you copied previously into to the white input area.

NOTE **Remember that subqueries must be enclosed in parentheses, so you will want to enter parentheses around the SQL statement you just pasted. You will also need to make sure you delete all carriage returns that were put in automatically by Access.**

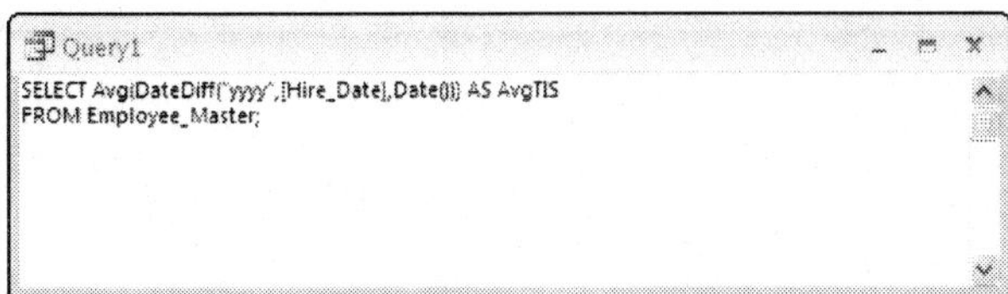

Figure 8-3: Switch to SQL view and copy the SQL statement.

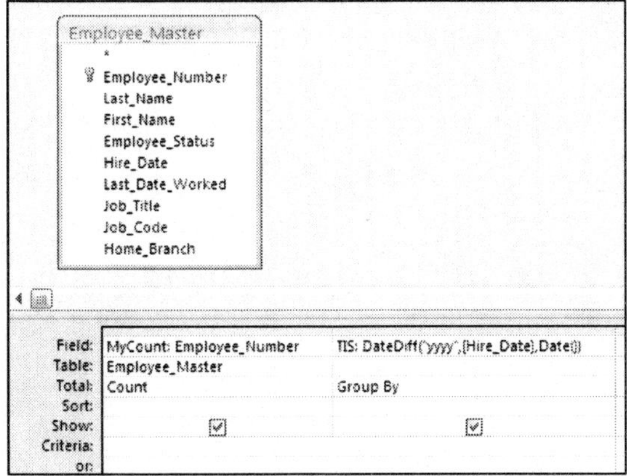

Figure 8-4: Create a query to count the number of employees by time in service.

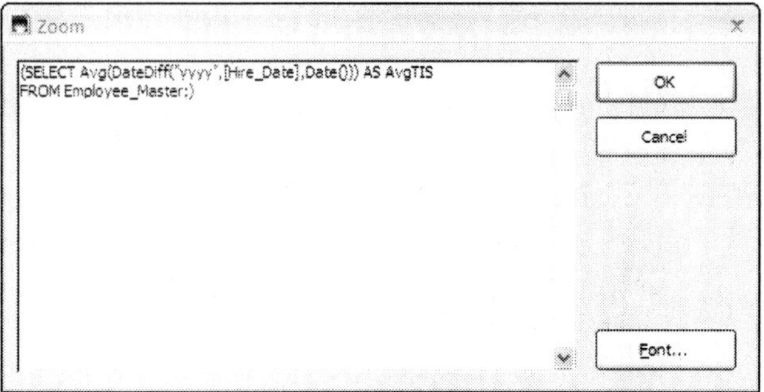

Figure 8-5: Paste the first SQL statement you copied into the Criteria row of the TIS field.

Finish off the query by entering a greater than (>) sign in front of your subquery and change the aggregate function of the TIS row to a `WHERE` clause. At this point your query should look like the one shown in Figure 8-6.

Now if you go to the SQL view of the query shown in Figure 8-6, you will see the following SQL statement:

```
SELECT Count(Employee_Master.Employee_Number) AS MyCount
FROM Employee_Master
WHERE (((DateDiff("yyyy",[Hire_Date],Date()))
     >(SELECT Avg(DateDiff("yyyy",[Hire_Date],Date())) AS AvgTIS
     FROM Employee_Master;)));
```

The beauty is that you did not have to type all this syntax. You simply used your knowledge of Access to piece together the necessary actions that needed to be taken in order to get to the answer. As you become more familiar with SQL, you will find that you will be able to create subqueries manually without problems.

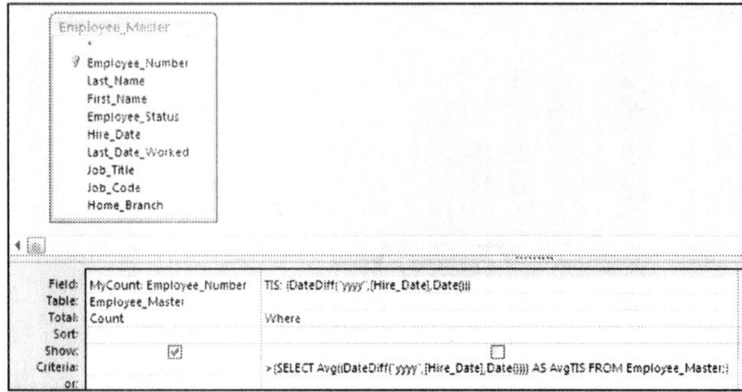

Figure 8-6: Running this query will tell you there are 228 employees that have a time in service greater than the company average.

Using IN and NOT IN with Subqueries

The IN and NOT IN operators enable you to run two queries in one. The idea is that the subquery executes first, and then the resulting dataset will be used by the outer query to filter the final output.

The example SQL statement demonstrated here will first run a subquery that will select all customers that belong to branch number 101419 *and* that are based in MI (Michigan). The outer query will then use the resulting dataset as a criterion to return the sum of sales amount for only those customers that match the customer numbers returned in the subquery.

```
SELECT System_Period, Sum(Sales_Amount) AS Revenue
FROM TransactionMaster
WHERE Customer_Number IN
(SELECT [Customer_Number] FROM [CustomerMaster] WHERE [Branch_Num] =⮐
"101419" AND [State] = "MI")
GROUP BY System_Period
```

You would use NOT IN to go the opposite way and return the sum of sales amount for those customers that do not match the customer numbers returned in the subquery.

TIP **You can find the examples in this section in the sample database for this book, located at** www.wiley.com**.**

Using Subqueries with Comparison Operators

As its name implies, a comparison operator (such as =, <, >, <=, >=, <>) compares two items and returns True or False. When you use a subquery with a comparison operator, you are asking Access to compare the resulting dataset of your outer query to that of the subquery.

For example, to analyze the employees that have an annual revenue less than the average annual revenue of all employees in the company, you can use the following SQL statement:

```
SELECT Branch_Number, Employee_Number, Revenue
FROM MainSummary
WHERE Revenue
     <(SELECT Avg(Revenue)FROM MainSummary)
```

The subquery runs first, giving you the average revenue of all employees. This is a single value that Access then uses to compare the outer query's resulting dataset. In other words, the annual revenue for each employee is compared to the company average. If an employee's annual revenue is less than the company average, it is included in the final output; otherwise, it is excluded.

NOTE **A subquery that is used with a comparison operator must return a single value.**

Using Subqueries as Expressions

In every example so far you have used subqueries in conjunction with the `WHERE` clause, effectively using the results of a subquery as criterion for your outer query. However, you can also use a subquery as an expression, as long as the subquery returns a single value. The query shown in Figure 8-7 demonstrates how you can use a subquery as an expression in a calculation.

This example uses a subquery to get the average revenue per employee for the entire company; that subquery returns a single value. You are then using that value in a calculation to determine the variance between each employee's annual revenue and the average revenue for the company. Figure 8-8 shows the output of this query.

MainSummary
*
Branch_Number
Employee_Number
Revenue

Field:	Employee_Number	Annual Rev: Revenue	Variance from Company Avg: [Annual Rev]-(SELECT Avg(Revenue)FROM MainSummary)
Table:	MainSummary	MainSummary	
Total:	Group By	Sum	Expression
Sort:			
Show:	☑	☑	☑
Criteria:			
or:			

Figure 8-7: You are using a subquery as an expression in a calculation.

Employee_Number	Annual Rev	Variance from Company Avg
104	$9,023.50	($6,985.70)
1044	$447.33	($15,561.86)
1050	$179.74	($15,829.4592)
1054	$54,147.73	$38,138.53
106	$38,013.36	$22,004.17
113	$963.06	($15,046.14)
1130	$67,961.15	$51,951.95
1135	$1,477.21	($14,531.98)
1156	$192.07	($15,817.13)
1245	$38,189.81	$22,180.61
1336	$75,489.77	$59,480.57
1344	$12,242.75	($3,766.44)
1416	$1,120.57	($14,888.63)
142	$1,622.30	($14,386.90)
1435	$43,118.02	$27,108.83

Figure 8-8: Your query result.

Using Correlated Subqueries

A *correlated subquery* is essentially a subquery that refers back to a column that is in the outer query. What makes correlated subqueries unique is that although standard subqueries are evaluated one time to get a result, a correlated subquery has to be evaluated multiple times — once for each row processed by the outer query. To illustrate this point, consider the following two SQL statements.

Uncorrelated Subqueries

This first SQL statement uses an uncorrelated subquery. How can you tell? The subquery is not referencing any column in the outer query. This subquery will be evaluated one time to give you the average revenue for the entire dataset.

```
SELECT MainSummary.Branch_Number,
     (SELECT Avg(Revenue)FROM MainSummary)
     FROM MainSummary
```

Correlated Subqueries

This second SQL statement is using a correlated subquery. The subquery is reaching back into the outer query and referencing the Branch_Number column, effectively forcing the subquery to be evaluated for every row that is processed by the outer query. The end result of this query is a dataset that shows the average revenue for every branch in the company.

```
SELECT MainSummary.Branch_Number,
     (SELECT Avg(Revenue)FROM MainSummary AS M2
     WHERE M2.Branch_Number = MainSummary.Branch_Number) AS AvgByBranch
FROM MainSummary
GROUP BY MainSummary.Branch_Number
```

TIP **Try to give your tables alias names that make sense. For example, if both your outer query and subquery are using the MainSummary table, you could give the table an alias of M1 in your outer query, while naming the same table M2 in your subquery. This would give you an easy visual indication of which table you are refering to.**

USING ALIASES WITH CORRELATED SUBQUERIES

Note that in the correlated subquery, you are using the `AS` clause to establish a table alias of M2. The reason for this is that the subquery and the outer query are both utilizing the same table. By giving one of the tables an alias, you allow Access to distinguish exactly which table you are referring to in your SQL statement. Although the alias in this SQL statement is assigned to the subquery, you can just as easily assign an alias to the table in the outer query.

Note that the character M2 holds no significance. In fact, you can use any text string you like, as long as the alias and the table name combined do not exceed 255 characters.

To assign an alias to a table in Design view, simply right-click on the field list and select Properties, as shown in Figure 8-9.

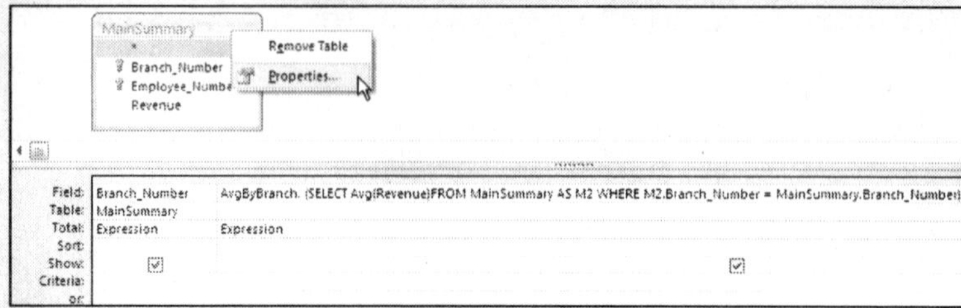

Figure 8-9: Right-click the field list and select Properties.

Next, edit the Alias property to the one you would like to use (see Figure 8-10). You will know that it took effect when the name on the Field List changes to your new alias.

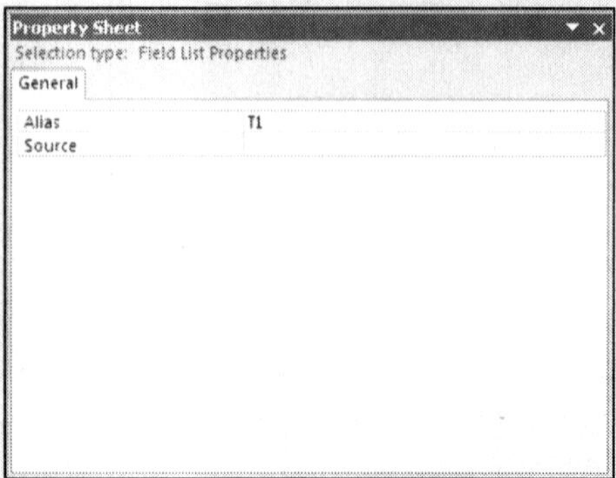

Figure 8-10: Enter the table alias into the Alias property.

Using a Correlated Subquery as an Expression

You can use a correlated subquery to peel back different layers from your data. The example shown in Figure 8-8 uses an uncorrelated subquery to determine the variance between each employee's annual revenue and the average revenue for the company.

Adding a correlation for each branch number enables you to determine the variance between each employee's annual revenue and the average revenue for that employee's branch.

```
SELECT M1.Employee_Number, Sum(M1.Revenue) AS YrRevenue, [YrRevenue]-
     (SELECT Avg(Revenue) FROM MainSummary AS M2
     WHERE M2.Branch_Number = M1.Branch_Number)
AS Variance
FROM MainSummary AS M1
GROUP BY M1.Branch_Number, M1.Employee_Number
```

Using Subqueries within Action Queries

Action queries can be fitted with subqueries just as easily as select queries can. Here are a few examples of how you would use a subquery in an action query.

A Subquery in a Make-Table Query

This example illustrates how to use a subquery within a make-table query.

```
SELECT E1.Employee_Number, E1.Last_Name, E1.First_Name
INTO OldSchoolEmployees
FROM Employee_Master as E1
WHERE E1.Employee_Number IN
     (SELECT E2.Employee_Number
     FROM Employee_Master AS E2
     WHERE E2.Hire_Date <#1/1/1995#)
```

A Subquery in an Append Query

This example uses a subquery within an append query.

```
INSERT INTO CustomerMaster ( Customer_Number, Customer_Name, State )
SELECT CompanyNumber,CompanyName,State
FROM LeadList
WHERE CompanyNumber Not IN
     (SELECT Customer_Number from CustomerMaster)
```

A Subquery in an Update Query

This example uses a subquery in an update query.

```
UPDATE PriceMaster SET Price = [Price]*1.1
WHERE Branch_Number IN
     (SELECT Branch_Number from LocationMaster WHERE Region = "South")
```

A Subquery in a Delete Query

This example uses a subquery in a delete query.

```
DELETE CompanyNumber
FROM LeadList
WHERE CompanyNumber IN
     (SELECT Customer_Number from CustomerMaster)
```

TRICKS OF THE TRADE: GETTING THE SECOND QUARTILE OF A DATASET WITH ONE QUERY

You can easily pull out the second quartile of a dataset by using a top values subquery.

1. **The first step is to create a top values query that returns the top 25 percent of your dataset. Again, you can specify that a query is a top values query by right-clicking the grey area above the white query grid and selecting Properties. When in the Property Sheet dialog box, adjust the Top Values property to return the top *n*th value you need as demonstrated in Figure 8-11. For this example, use 25%.**

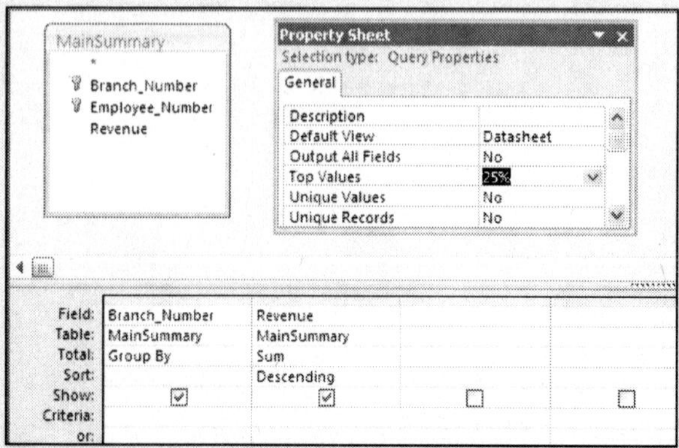

Figure 8-11: Create a query that returns the top 25 percent of your dataset.

2. **Next, switch to SQL view, shown in Figure 8-12, and copy the SQL string.**

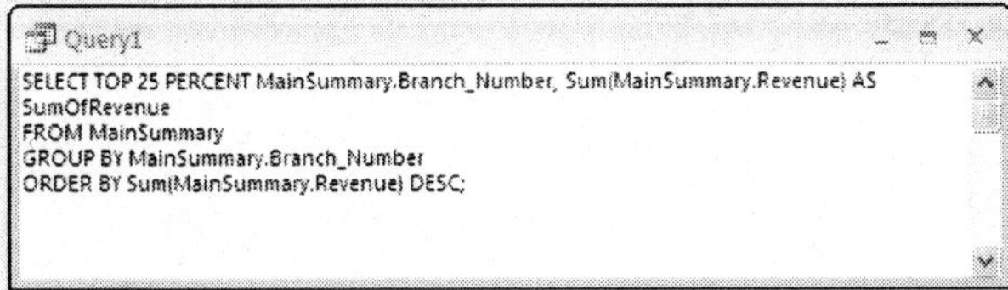

Figure 8-12: Copy the SQL statement that makes up the query.

3. **Switch back to Design view. The idea is to paste the SQL statement you just copied into the Criteria row of the Branch_Number field. To do this, right-click inside the Criteria row of the Branch_Number field and select Zoom. Then paste the SQL statement inside the Zoom dialog box, as shown in Figure 8-13.**

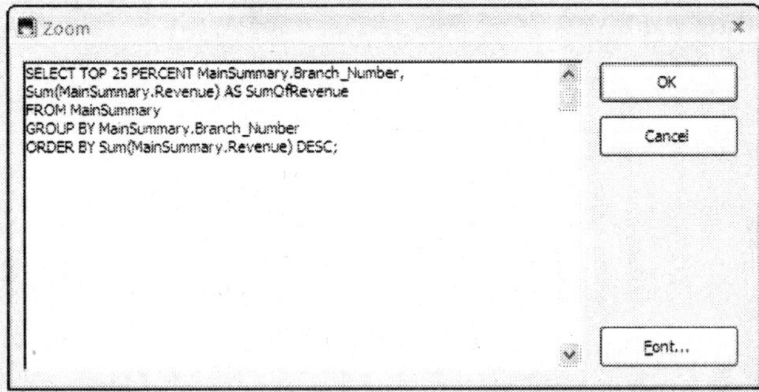

Figure 8-13: Paste the SQL statement into the Criteria row of Branch_Number.

4. **This next part is a little tricky. You will need to perform the following edits on the SQL statement in order to make it work for this situation:**
   a. **Because this subquery is a criteria for the Branch_Number field, you only need to select Branch_Number in the SQL statement; therefore, you can remove the line `Sum(MainSummary.Revenue) AS SumOfRevenue`.**
   b. **Remove the comma at the end of the first line.**
   c. **Delete all carriage returns**
   d. **Place parentheses around the subquery and put the `NOT IN` operator in front of it all.**

(continued)

TRICKS OF THE TRADE: GETTING THE SECOND QUARTILE OF A DATASET WITH ONE QUERY *(Continued)*

At this point, your Zoom dialog box should look like the one shown in Figure 8-14.

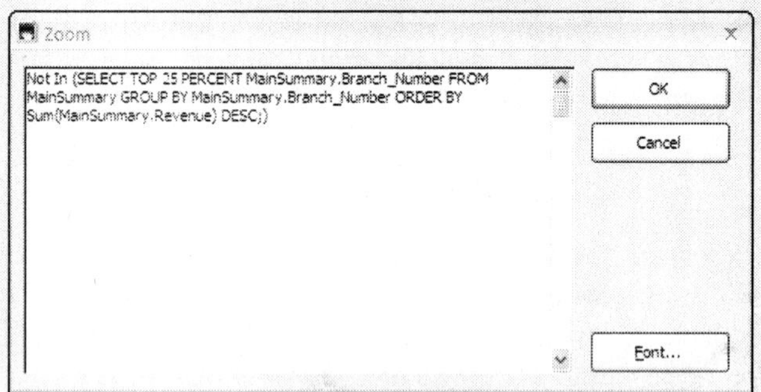

Figure 8-14: After some cleanup, your query is ready to run.

There you have it. Running this query returns the second quartile in the dataset. To get the third quartile, simply replace `TOP 25 PERCENT` **in the subquery with** `TOP 50 PERCENT`**; to get the fourth quartile, use** `TOP 75 PERCENT`.

NOTE **Be sure to check this book's sample file to get a few more examples that highlight how subqueries can help you find solutions to common analytical needs.**

Domain Aggregate Functions

Domain aggregate functions enable you to extract and aggregate statistical information from an entire dataset (a domain). These functions differ from aggregate queries in that an aggregate query groups data before evaluating the values, whereas a domain aggregate function evaluates the values for the entire dataset; thus, a domain aggregate function will never return more than one value. To get a clear understanding of the difference between an aggregate query and a domain aggregate function, build the query shown in Figure 8-15.

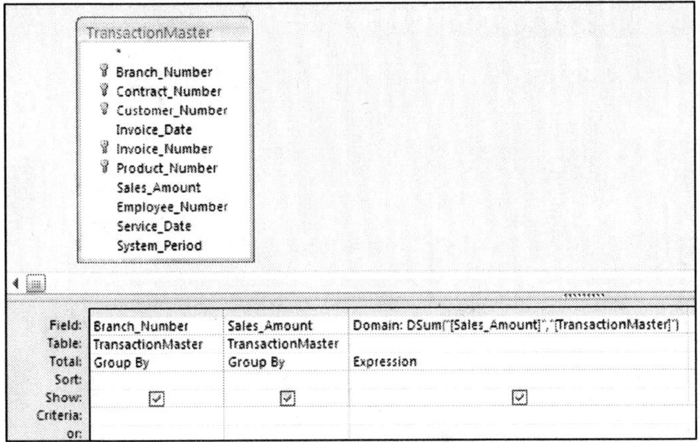

Figure 8-15: This query shows you the difference between an aggregate query and a domain aggregate function.

Run the query to get the results you see in Figure 8-16. You will notice that the SumOfSales_Amount column contains a different total for each branch number, whereas the Domain column (the domain aggregate function) contains only one total (for the entire dataset).

NOTE **Although the examples in this chapter show domain aggregate functions used in query expressions, keep in mind that you can use these functions in macros, modules, or the calculated controls of forms and reports.**

Branch_Number	Sales_Amount	Domain
101313	$92.90	10774189.4594
101313	$123.68	10774189.4594
101313	$135.17	10774189.4594
101313	$171.66	10774189.4594
101313	$198.92	10774189.4594
101419	$98.73	10774189.4594
101419	$121.82	10774189.4594
101419	$134.54	10774189.4594
101419	$166.23	10774189.4594
101419	$169.58	10774189.4594
101419	$445.23	10774189.4594
102516	$122.85	10774189.4594
102516	$151.74	10774189.4594
102516	$184.06	10774189.4594
102516	$190.21	10774189.4594

Figure 8-16: You can clearly see the difference between an aggregate query and a domain aggregate function.

THE ANATOMY OF DOMAIN AGGREGATE FUNCTIONS

There are 12 different domain aggregate functions, but they all have the same anatomy:

```
FunctionName("[Field Name]","[Dataset Name]",
"[Criteria]")
```

- `FunctionName`: **This is the name of the domain aggregate function you are using.**
- `Field Name` **(required): This expression identifies the field containing the data with which you are working.**
- `Dataset Name` **(required): This expression identifies the table or query you are working with; also known as the domain.**
- `Criteria` **(optional): This expression is used to restrict the range of data on which the domain aggregate function is performed. If no criteria are specified, the domain aggregate function is performed against the entire dataset.**

NOTE **You cannot use a parameter query with a domain aggregate function.**

Understanding the Different Domain Aggregate Functions

There are 12 different domain aggregate functions in Access; each one performs a different operation. In this section, you will take a moment to review the purpose and utility of each function.

DSum

The `DSum` function returns the total sum value of a specified field in the domain. For example, `DSum("[Sales_Amount]", "[TransactionMaster]")` returns the total sum of sales amount in the TransactionMaster table.

DAvg

The `DAvg` function returns the average value of a specified field in the domain. For example, `DAvg("[Sales_Amount]", "[TransactionMaster]")` returns the average sales amount in the TransactionMaster table.

DCount

The `DCount` function returns the total number of records in the domain. `DCount("*", "[TransactionMaster]")`, for example, returns the total number of records in the TransactionMaster table.

DLookup

The `DLookup` function returns the first value of a specified field that matches the criteria you define within the `DLookup` function. If you don't supply any criteria, the `DLookup` function returns a random value in the domain. For example, `DLookUp("[Last_Name]","[Employee_Master]", "[Employee_Number]='42620' ")` returns the value in the Last_Name field of the record where the Employee_Number is '42620'.

NOTE `DLookup` **functions are particularly useful when you need to retrieve a value from an outside dataset.**

DMin and DMax

The `DMin` and `DMax` functions return the minimum and maximum values in the domain, respectively. `DMin("[Sales_Amount]", "[Transaction Master]")` would return the lowest sales amount in the TransactionMaster table, whereas `DMax("[Sales_Amount]", "[TransactionMaster]")` would return the highest sales amount.

DFirst and DLast

The `DFirst` and `DLast` functions return the first and last values in the domain, respectively. `DFirst("[Sales_Amount]", "[Transaction Master]")` returns the first sales amount in the TransactionMaster table, whereas `DLast("[Sales_Amount]", "[TransactionMaster]")` returns the last.

DStDev, DStDevP, DVar, and DvarP

You can use the `DStDev` and `DStDevP` functions to return the standard deviation across a population sample and a population, respectively. Similarly, the `DVar` and the `DVarP` functions return the variance across a population sample and a population, respectively. `DStDev("[Sales_Amount]", "[TransactionMaster]")` returns the standard deviation of all sales amounts in the TransactionMaster table. `DVar ("[Sales_Amount]", "[TransactionMaster]")` returns the variance of all sales amounts in the TransactionMaster table.

Examining the Syntax of Domain Aggregate Functions

Domain aggregate functions are unique in that the syntax required to make them work actually varies depending on the scenario. This has led to some very frustrated users who have given up on domain aggregate functions altogether. This section describes some general guidelines that will help you in building your domain aggregate functions.

Using No Criteria

In this example, you are summing the values in the Sales_Amount field from the TransactionMaster table (domain). Your field names and dataset names must always be wrapped in quotes.

```
DSum("[Sales_Amount]","[TransactionMaster]")
```

Also, note the use of brackets. Although not always required, it is best practice to use brackets when identifying a field, a table, or a query.

Using Text Criteria

In this example, you are summing the values in the Sales_Amount field from the TransactionMaster table (domain) where the value in the System_Period field is 200405. Note that the System_Period field is formatted as text. When specifying criteria that is textual or a string, your criterion must be wrapped in single quotes. In addition, your entire criteria expression must be wrapped in double quotes.

```
DSum("[Sales_Amount]", "[TransactionMaster]", "[System_Period] = '200405' ")
```

TIP **You can use any valid `WHERE` clause in the criteria expression of your domain aggregate functions. This adds a level of functionality to domain aggregate functions, as they can support the use of multiple columns and logical operators such as `AND`, `OR`, `NOT`, and so on. For example:**

```
DSum("[Field1]", "[Table]", "[Field2] = 'A' OR [Field2] = 'B' AND [Field3] = 2")
```

If you are referencing a control inside of a form or report, the syntax changes a bit:

```
DSum("[Sales_Amount]", "[TransactionMaster]", "[System_Period] = ⮐
' " & [MyTextControl] & " ' " )
```

Note that you are using single quotes to convert the control's value to a string. In other words, if the value of the form control is 200405, then `"[System_Period] = ' " & [MyTextControl] & " ' "` is essentially translated to read `"[System_Period] = '200405' "`.

Using Number Criteria

In this example, you are summing the values in the Sales_Amount field from the TransactionMaster table (domain) where the value in the Sales_Amount field is greater than 500. Note that you are not using the single quotes since the Sales_Amount field is an actual number field.

```
DSum("[Sales_Amount]", "[TransactionMaster]", "[Sales_Amount] > 500 ")
```

If you are referencing a control inside of a form or report, the syntax changes a bit:

```
DSum("[Sales_Amount]", "[TransactionMaster]", "[Sales_Amount] >" ⮐
[MyNumericControl])
```

Using Date Criteria

In this example, you are summing the values in the Sales_Amount field from the TransactionMaster table (domain) where the value in the Service_Date field is 01/05/2004.

```
DSum("[Sales_Amount]", "[TransactionMaster]", "[Service_Date] = #01/05/04# ")
```

If you are referencing a control inside of a form or report, the syntax changes a bit:

```
DSum("[Sales_Amount]", "[TransactionMaster]", "[Service_Date] = ⮐
#" & [MydateControl] & "#")
```

Note that you are using number signs to convert the control's value to a date. In other words, if the value of the form control is `01/05/2004`, then `"[Service_Date] = #" & [MydateControl] & "#"` is essentially translated to read `"[Service_Date] = #01/05/2004# "`.

Using Domain Aggregate Functions

Like subqueries, domain aggregate functions are not very efficient when it comes to performing large-scale analyses and crunching very large datasets. These functions are better suited for use in specialty analyses with smaller subsets of data. Indeed, you will most often find domain aggregate functions in environments where the dataset being evaluated is predictable and controlled (form example, functions, forms, and reports). This is not to say, however, that domain aggregate functions don't have their place in your day-to-day data analysis. This section explains how you can use domain aggregate functions to accomplish some common tasks.

Calculating the Percent of Total

The query shown in Figure 8-17 returns products by group and the sum of sales amount for each product. This is a worthwhile analysis, but you could easily enhance it by adding a column that would give you the percent of total revenue for each product.

To get the percent of the total dollar value that each product makes up, you naturally would have to know the total dollar value of the entire dataset. This is where a `DSum` function can come in handy. The following `DSum` function returns the total value of the dataset:

```
DSum("[Sales_Amount]","[TransactionMaster]")
```

Now you can use this function as an expression in the calculation that returns the *percent of total* for each product group. Figure 8-18 demonstrates how.

Product_Description	SumOfSales_Amount
Cleaning & Housekeeping Services	$1,138,595.78
Facility Maintenance and Repair	$2,361,161.41
Fleet Maintenance	$2,627,798.02
Green Plants and Foliage Care	$1,276,790.55
Landscaping/Grounds Care	$1,190,911.60
Predictive Maintenance/Preventative Maintenance	$2,178,932.11

Figure 8-17: You want to add a column that shows the percent of total revenue for each product.

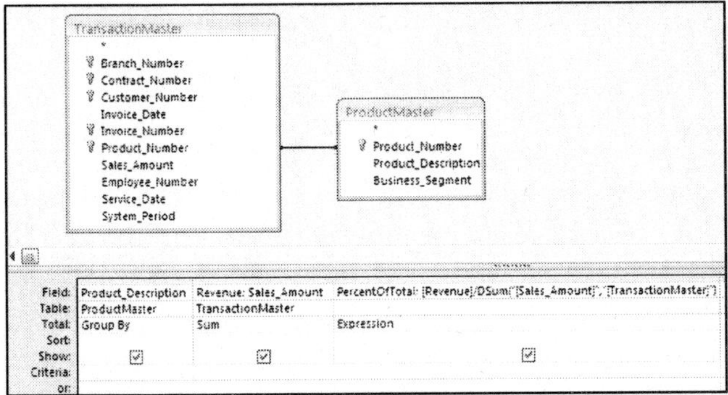

Figure 8-18: Use a `DSum` function as an expression in a calculation to get "Percent of Total".

The result, shown in Figure 8-19, proves that this is a quick and easy way to get both total by group and percent of total with one query.

Creating a Running Count

The query in Figure 8-20 uses a `DCount` function as an expression to return the number of invoices processed on each specific invoice day.

Product_Description	Revenue	PercentOfTotal
Cleaning & Housekeeping Services	$1,138,595.78	10.6%
Facility Maintenance and Repair	$2,361,161.41	21.9%
Fleet Maintenance	$2,627,798.02	24.4%
Green Plants and Foliage Care	$1,276,790.55	11.9%
Landscaping/Grounds Care	$1,190,911.60	11.1%
Predictive Maintenance/Preventative Maintenance	$2,178,932.11	20.2%

Figure 8-19: You retrieved both total by group and percent of total with one query.

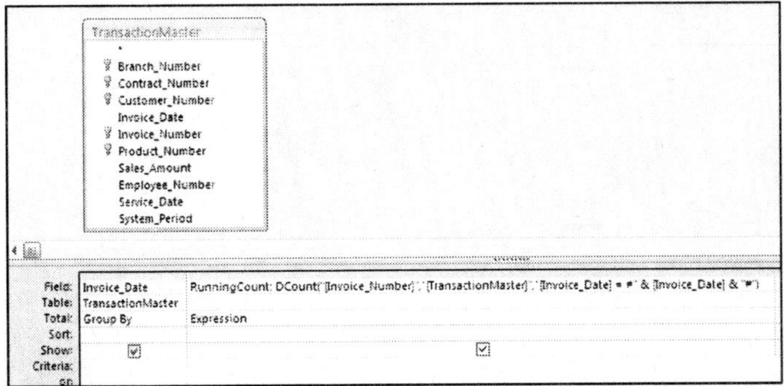

Figure 8-20: This query returns all invoice dates and the number of invoices processed on each date.

Take a moment to analyze what this `DCount` function is doing.

```
DCount("[Invoice_Number]","[TransactionMaster]","[Invoice_Date] =
#" & [Invoice_Date] & "#")
```

This `DCount` function gets the count of invoices where the invoice date equals (=) each invoice date returned by the query. So, in context of the query shown in Figure 8-20, the resulting dataset shows each invoice date and its own count of invoices.

What would happen if you were to alter the `DCount` function to tell it to return the count of invoices where the invoice date equals or is earlier than (<=) each invoice date returned by the query, as follows?

```
DCount("[Invoice_Number]","[TransactionMaster]","[Invoice_Date] <=
#" & [Invoice_Date] & "#")
```

The `DCount` function would return the count of invoices for each date *and* the count of invoices for any earlier date, thereby giving you a running count.

To put this into action, simply replace the = operator in the `DCount` function with the <= operator, as shown in Figure 8-21.

Figure 8-22 shows the resulting running count.

TIP **You can achieve a running sum instead of a running count by using the** `DSum` **function.**

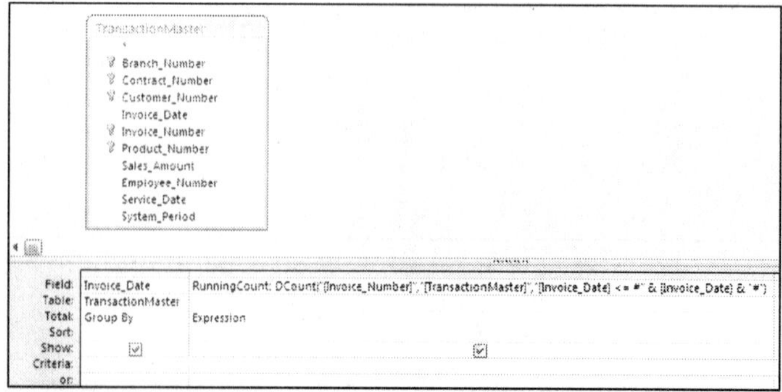

Figure 8-21: Use the <= operator in your `DCount` function to return the count of invoice dates that equals or is less than the date returned by the query.

Invoice_Date	RunningCount
1/5/2004	8
1/6/2004	195
1/7/2004	406
1/8/2004	623
1/9/2004	884
1/12/2004	1120
1/13/2004	1344
1/14/2004	1540
1/15/2004	1802
1/16/2004	1996
1/19/2004	2237
1/20/2004	2356
1/21/2004	2521
1/22/2004	2694
1/23/2004	2912

Figure 8-22: You now have a running count in your analysis.

Using a Value from the Previous Record

The query in Figure 8-23 uses a `DLookup` function to return the revenue value from the previous record. This value is placed into a new column called Yesterday.

This method is similar to the one used when creating a running sum in that it revolves around manipulating a comparison operator in order to change the meaning of the domain aggregate function. In this case, the `DLookup` searches for the revenue value where the invoice date is equal to each invoice date returned by the query minus one (`-1`). If you subtract one from a date, you get yesterday's date!

```
DLookUp("[Revenue]","[TimeSummary]","[Invoice_Date] = ⮐
#" & [Invoice_Date]-1 & "#")
```

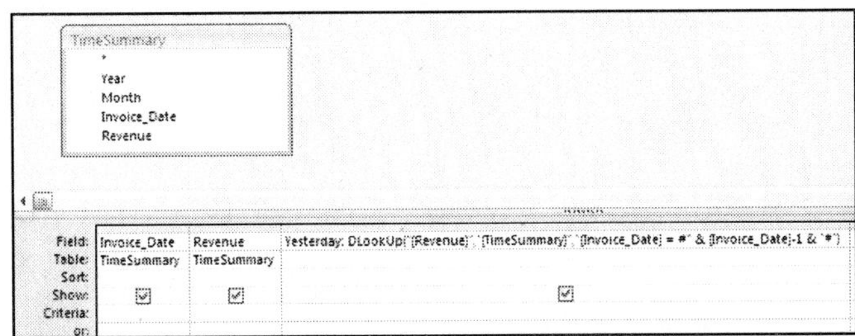

Figure 8-23: This query uses a `DLookup` to refer to the previous revenue value.

TIP **If you add 1 you will get the next record in the sequence. However, this trick will not work with textual fields. This only works with date and numeric fields. If you are working with a table that does not contain any numeric or date fields, create an autonumber field. This will give you a unique numeric identifier that you can use.**

Running the query in Figure 8-23 yields the results shown in Figure 8-24.

You can enhance this analysis by adding a calculated field that gives you the dollar variance between today and yesterday. Create a new column and enter **[Revenue]-NZ([Yesterday],0)**, as shown in Figure 8-25. Note that the Yesterday field is wrapped in an `NZ` function in order to avoid errors caused by null fields.

Figure 8-26 shows the result.

Invoice_Date	Revenue	Yesterday
1/5/2004	$1,218.87	
1/6/2004	$29,280.65	1218.8734
1/7/2004	$34,418.48	29280.6534
1/8/2004	$34,437.67	34418.4828
1/9/2004	$41,319.75	34437.6745
1/12/2004	$37,923.82	
1/13/2004	$37,900.75	37923.8214
1/14/2004	$33,318.55	37900.7498
1/15/2004	$44,478.61	33318.5515
1/16/2004	$31,350.05	44478.6144
1/19/2004	$39,003.20	
1/20/2004	$19,304.81	39003.2
1/21/2004	$27,029.77	19304.8096
1/22/2004	$30,825.20	27029.7725
1/23/2004	$35,443.71	30825.1963
1/26/2004	$31,398.60	
1/27/2004	$29,787.17	31398.5956

Figure 8-24: You can take this functionality a step further and perform a calculation on the Yesterday field.

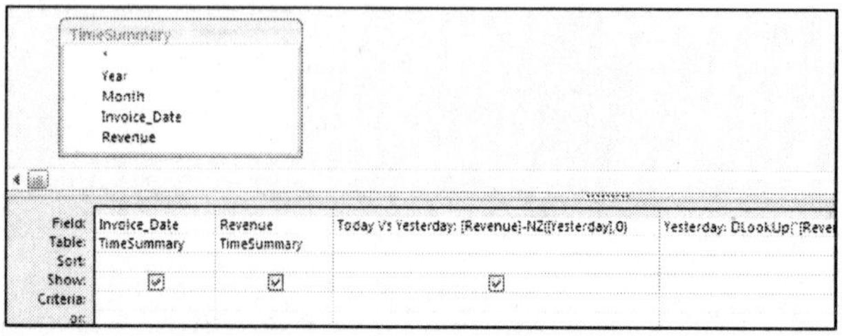

TimeSummary: *, Year, Month, Invoice_Date, Revenue

Field:	Invoice_Date	Revenue	Today Vs Yesterday: [Revenue]-NZ([Yesterday],0)	Yesterday: DLookUp("[Reve
Table:	TimeSummary	TimeSummary		
Sort:				
Show:	☑	☑	☑	
Criteria:				
or:				

Figure 8-25: Enhance your analysis by adding a variance between today and yesterday.

Invoice_Date	Revenue	Today Vs Yesterday	Yesterday
1/5/2004	$1,218.87	$1,218.87	
1/6/2004	$29,280.65	$28,061.78	1218.8734
1/7/2004	$34,418.48	$5,137.83	29280.6534
1/8/2004	$34,437.67	$19.19	34418.4828
1/9/2004	$41,319.75	$6,882.07	34437.6745
1/12/2004	$37,923.82	$37,923.82	
1/13/2004	$37,900.75	($23.07)	37923.8214
1/14/2004	$33,318.55	($4,582.20)	37900.7498
1/15/2004	$44,478.61	$11,160.06	33318.5515
1/16/2004	$31,350.05	($13,128.57)	44478.6144
1/19/2004	$39,003.20	$39,003.20	
1/20/2004	$19,304.81	($19,698.39)	39003.2
1/21/2004	$27,029.77	$7,724.96	19304.8096
1/22/2004	$30,825.20	$3,795.42	27029.7725
1/23/2004	$35,443.71	$4,618.51	30825.1963
1/26/2004	$31,398.60	$31,398.60	
1/27/2004	$29,787.17	($1,611.43)	31398.5956

Figure 8-26: Another task made possible by domain aggregate functions.

Summary

Subqueries and domain aggregate functions enable you to build layers into your analysis within one query, eliminating the need for temporary tables or transitory queries. You can leverage both subqueries and domain aggregate functions to streamline your analytical processes, as well as expand and enhance your analysis.

Subqueries are select queries that are nested within other queries, enabling you to use the results of one query within the execution of another. The idea behind a subquery is that the subquery is executed first, and the results are used in the outer query (the query in which the subquery is embedded) as a criterion, an expression, a parameter, and so on. Although subqueries often run more slowly than a standard query using a join, there are situations where the performance hit may be an acceptable trade-off for streamlined procedures and optimized analytical processes.

Domain aggregate functions enable you to extract and aggregate statistical information from an entire dataset (a domain). Unlike aggregate queries where the data is grouped before evaluation, a domain aggregate function evaluates the values for the entire dataset. There are 12 different domain aggregate functions: `DSum`, `DAvg`, `DCount`, `DLookup`, `DMin`, `DMax`, `DFirst`, `DLast`, `DStDev`, `DStDevP`, `DVar`, and `DVarP`. Domain aggregate functions are ideal for specialty analyses such as calculating the percent of a total, creating a running count, creating a running sum, or using values from previous records.

CHAPTER

9

Running Descriptive Statistics in Access

Descriptive statistics enable you to present large amounts of data in quantitative summaries that are simple to understand. When you total data, count data, and average data, you are producing descriptive statistics. It is important to note that descriptive statistics are used only to profile a dataset and enable comparisons that can be used in other analyses. This is different from *inferential statistics*, where you infer conclusions that extend beyond the scope of the data. To help solidify the difference between descriptive and inferential statistics, consider a customer survey. Descriptive statistics summarize the survey results for all customers and describe the data in understandable metrics, whereas inferential statistics infer conclusions such as customer loyalty based on the observed differences between groups of customers.

When it comes to inferential statistics, Excel is better suited to handle these types of analyses than Access. Why? First, Excel comes with a plethora of built-in functions and tools that make it easy to perform inferential statistics; tools that Access simply does not have. Secondarily, inferential statistics is usually performed on small subsets of data that can be analyzed and presented by Excel. Running *descriptive statistics*, on the other hand, is quite useful in Access. In fact, running descriptive statistics in Access versus Excel is often the smartest option due to the structure and volume of the dataset.

TIP **The examples shown in this chapter can all be found in the sample database for this book. The sample database for this book can be found at** `www.wiley.com`.

Basic Descriptive Statistics

This section discusses some of the basic tasks you can perform by using descriptive statistics, including

- Running descriptive statistics with aggregate queries
- Ranking records in a dataset
- Determining the mode and median of a dataset
- Creating random samplings from a dataset

Running Descriptive Statistics with Aggregate Queries

At this point in the book, you have run many Access queries, some of which have been aggregate queries. Little did you know that when you ran those aggregate queries, you were actually creating descriptive statistics. It's true. The simplest descriptive statistics can be generated using an aggregate query. To demonstrate this point, build the query shown in Figure 9-1.

Similar to the descriptive statistics functionality found in Excel, the result of this query, shown in Figure 9-2, provides key statistical metrics for the entire dataset.

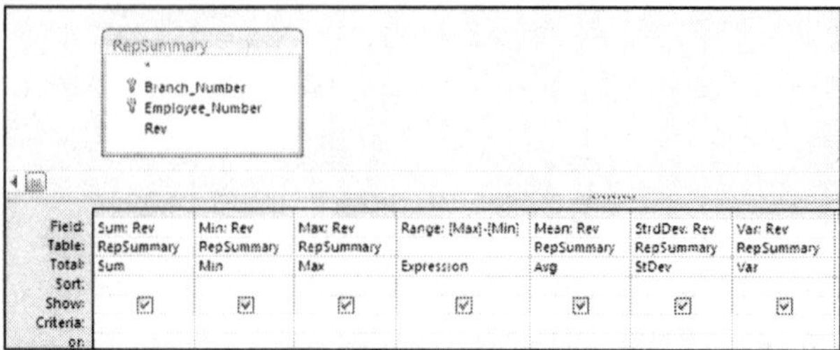

Figure 9-1: Running this aggregate query will provide a useful set of descriptive statistics.

Sum	Min	Max	Range	Mean	StrdDev	Var
$10,774,159	$86	$137,707	$137,621	$16,009	$21,059	$443,484,375

Figure 9-2: Key statistical metrics for the entire dataset.

You can easily add layers to your descriptive statistics. In Figure 9-3, you are adding the Branch_Number field to your query. This will give you key statistical metrics for each branch.

As you can see in Figure 9-4, you can now compare the descriptive statistics across branches to measure how they perform against each other.

Determining Rank, Mode, and Median

Ranking the records in your dataset, getting the mode of a dataset, and getting the median of a dataset are all tasks which a data analyst will need to perform from time to time. Unfortunately, Access does not provide built-in functionality to perform these tasks easily. This means you will have to come up with a way to carry out these descriptive statistics. In this section, you will learn some of the techniques you can use to determine rank, mode, and median.

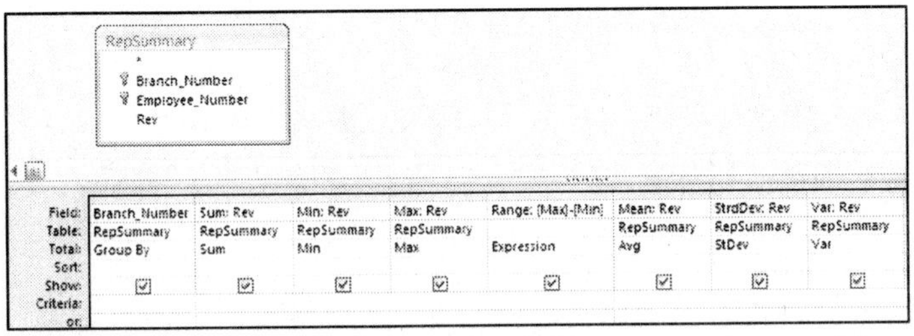

RepSummary
*
Branch_Number
Employee_Number
Rev

Field:	Branch_Number	Sum: Rev	Min: Rev	Max: Rev	Range: [Max]-[Min]	Mean: Rev	StrdDev: Rev	Var: Rev
Table:	RepSummary	RepSummary	RepSummary	RepSummary		RepSummary	RepSummary	RepSummary
Total:	Group By	Sum	Min	Max	Expression	Avg	StDev	Var
Sort:								
Show:	☑	☑	☑	☑	☑	☑	☑	☑
Criteria:								
or:								

Figure 9-3: Add the Branch_Number field to your query to add another dimension to your analysis.

Branch_Number	Sum	Min	Max	Range	Mean	StrdDev	Var
101313	$444,631	$124	$78,824	$78,700	$22,232	$29,111	$847,454,523
101419	$124,597	$99	$46,645	$46,546	$20,766	$19,027	$362,039,701
102516	$63.228	$678	$36,387	$35,709	$21,076	$18,390	$338,192,979
103516	$101,664	$151	$31,428	$31,277	$6,778	$9,338	$87,200,336
173901	$107,216	$402	$33,136	$32,734	$13,402	$13,371	$178,773,758
201605	$69,818	$624	$27,657	$27,033	$8,727	$9,496	$90,165,337
201709	$96,853	$184	$42,778	$42,593	$6,918	$12,375	$153,131,218
201714	$288,714	$145	$57,803	$57,658	$12,553	$15,901	$252,833,070
201717	$450,524	$169	$61,521	$61,352	$34,656	$25,160	$633,007,891
202600	$151,338	$277	$58,473	$58,196	$18,917	$25,557	$653,147,704
202605	$342,537	$147	$62,042	$61,895	$16,311	$17,878	$319,637,725
202714	$113,075	$546	$48,963	$48,417	$16,154	$17,503	$306,365,820
208605	$64,357	$439	$45,740	$45,301	$16,089	$20,721	$429,353,387
301301	$157,235	$134	$48,733	$48,599	$12,095	$17,042	$290,427,891
301316	$397,746	$99	$77,452	$77,354	$12,053	$17,227	$296,779,598

Figure 9-4: You have a summary view of the descriptive statistics for each branch.

Ranking the Records in Your Dataset

You will undoubtedly encounter scenarios where you will have to rank the records in your dataset based on a specific metric such as revenue. A record's rank is not only useful in presenting data, but it is also a key variable when calculating advanced descriptive statistics such as median, percentile, and quartile.

The easiest way to determine a record's ranking within a dataset is by using a correlated subquery. The query shown in Figure 9-5 demonstrates how a rank is created using a subquery.

Take a moment to examine the subquery that generates the rank.

```
(SELECT Count(*)FROM RepSummary AS M1 WHERE [Rev]>[RepSummary].[Rev])+1
```

This correlated subquery returns the total count of records from the M1 table (this is the RepSummary table with an alias of M1), where the Rev field in the M1 table is greater than the Rev field in the RepSummary table. The value returned by the subquery is then increased by one. Why increase the value by one? If you don't, the record with the highest value will return 0 because zero records are greater than the record with the highest value. The result would be that your ranking starts with 0 instead of 1. Adding one effectively ensures that your ranking starts with 1.

NOTE **Because this is a correlated subquery, this subquery is evaluated for every record in your dataset, thereby giving you a different rank value for each record. Correlated subqueries are covered in detail in Chapter 8.**

Figure 9-6 shows the result.

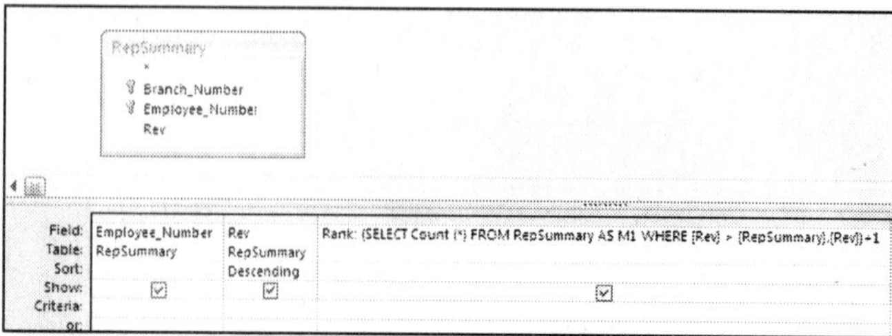

Figure 9-5: This query ranks employees by revenue.

Employee_Number	Rank	Rev
64621	1	$137,707.14
4136	2	$111,681.81
5060	3	$106,299.32
56422	4	$102,239.87
56405	5	$83,525.72
160034	6	$78,823.82
60425	7	$77,452.50
3466	8	$76,789.52
52635	9	$76,684.54
52404	10	$76,532.26
3660	11	$75,690.33
1336	12	$75,489.77
56416	13	$75,358.76
55144	14	$74,653.99
60224	15	$71,427.33

Figure 9-6: You have created a Rank column for your dataset.

TIP **This technique is also useful when you want to create an autonumber field within a query.**

Getting the Mode of a Dataset

The *mode* of a dataset is the number that appears the most often in a set of numbers. For example, the mode for 4, 5, 5, 6, 7, 5, 3, 4 is 5.

Unlike Excel, Access does not have a built-in `Mode` function, so you will have to create your own method of determining the mode of a dataset. Although there are various ways to get the mode of a dataset, one of the easiest is to use a query to count the occurrences of a certain data item, and then filter for the highest count. To demonstrate this method, build the query shown in Figure 9-7.

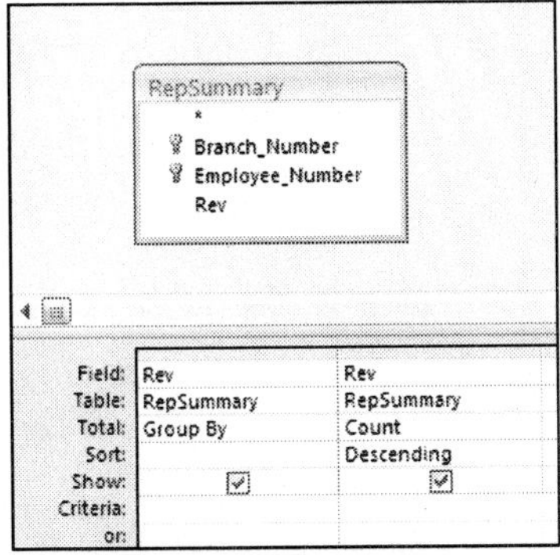

Figure 9-7: This query groups by the Rev field and then counts the occurrences of each number in the Rev field. The query is sorted in descending order by Rev.

The results, shown in Figure 9-8, do not seem very helpful, but if you turn this into a top values query, returning only the top 1 record, you would effectively get the mode.

Change the Top Values property to 1, as shown in Figure 9-9, and you will get the record with the highest count.

As you can see in Figure 9-10, you now have only one Rev figure — the one that occurs the most often. This is your mode.

Rev	CountOfRev
$158.60	4
$145.02	3
$154.55	3
$185.27	3
$245.78	3
$151.03	3
$122.89	3
$309.11	3
$254.34	2
$650.24	2
$168.82	2
$525.00	2
$179.99	2
$654.26	2
$401.57	2

Figure 9-8: Almost there. Turn this into a top values query and you'll have your mode.

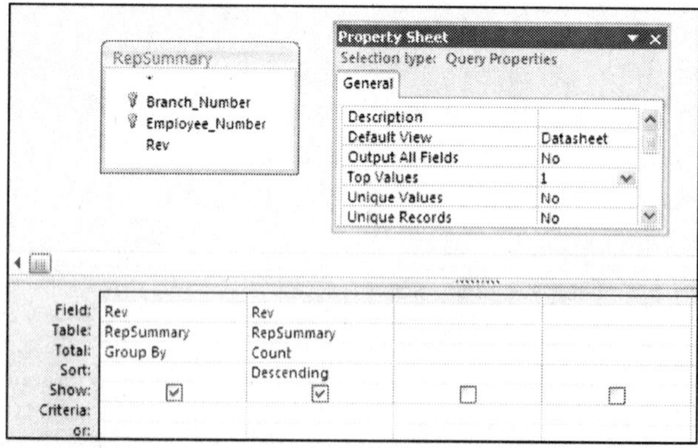

Figure 9-9: Set the Top Values property to 1.

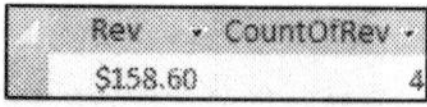

Rev	CountOfRev
$158.60	4

Figure 9-10: This is your mode.

NOTE **Keep in mind that in the event of a tie, a top values query will show all records. This will effectively give you more than one mode. You will have to make a manual determination which mode to use.**

Getting the Median of a Dataset

The *median* of a dataset is the number that is the middle number in the dataset. In other words, half of the numbers have values that are greater than the median, and half have values that are less than the median. For example, the median number in 3, 4, 5, 6, 7, 8, 9 is 6 because 6 is the middle number of the dataset.

TIP **Why can't you just calculate an average and be done with it? Sometimes, calculating an average on a dataset that contains outliers can dramatically skew your analysis. For example, if you were to calculate an average on the numbers, 32, 34, 35, 37, and 89, you would get an answer of 45.4. The problem is that 45.4 does not accurately represent the central tendency of this sampling of numbers. Using median on this sample makes more sense. The median in this case would be 35, which is more representative of what's going on in this data.**

Access does not have a built-in `Median` function, so you will have to create your own method of determining the median of a dataset. An easy way to get the median is to build a query in two steps. The first step is to create a query that sorts and ranks your records. The query shown in Figure 9-11 sorts and ranks the records in the RepSummary table.

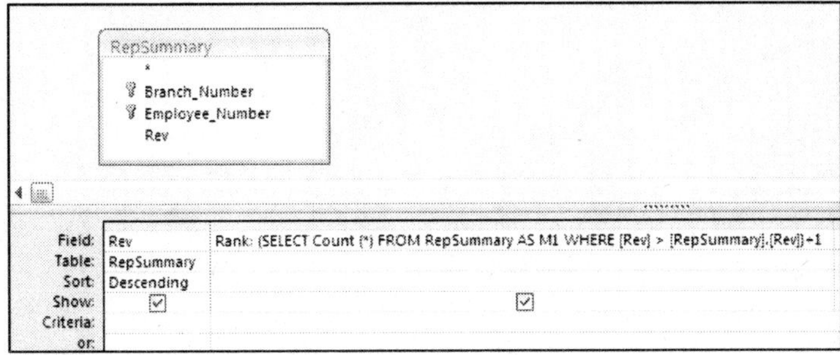

Figure 9-11: The first step in finding the median of a dataset is to assign a rank to each record.

The next step is to identify the median record in your dataset by counting the total number of records in the dataset and then dividing that number by two. Figure 9-12 shows the subquery that will return a middle value for the dataset. Note that the value is wrapped in an `Int` function to strip out the fractional portion of the number.

As you can see in Figure 9-13, the middle value is 336. You can go down to record 336 to see the median.

If you want to return only the median value, simply use the subquery as a criterion for the Rank field, as shown in Figure 9-14.

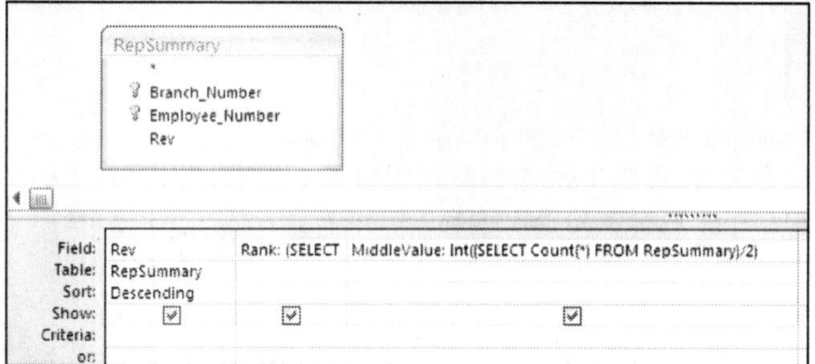

Figure 9-12: The Middle Value subquery counts all the records in the dataset and then divides that number by 2.

Rev	Rank	MiddleValue
$137,707.14	1	336
$111,681.81	2	336
$106,299.32	3	336
$102,239.87	4	336
$83,525.72	5	336
$78,823.82	6	336
$77,452.50	7	336
$76,789.52	8	336
$76,684.54	9	336
$76,532.26	10	336
$75,690.33	11	336
$75,489.77	12	336
$75,358.76	13	336
$74,653.99	14	336
$71,427.33	15	336

Figure 9-13: Go down to record 336 to get the median value of the dataset.

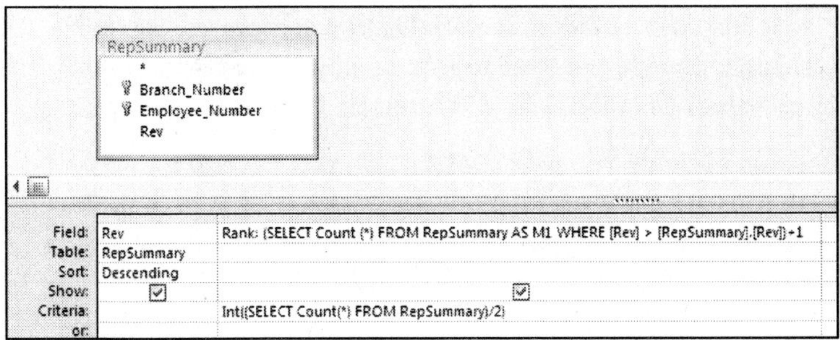

Figure 9-14: Using the subquery as a criterion for the Rank field ensures that only the median value is returned.

Pulling a Random Sampling from Your Dataset

Although the creation of a random sample of data does not necessarily fall into the category of descriptive statistics, a random sampling is often the basis for statistical analysis.

There are many ways to create a random sampling of data in Access, but one of the easiest is to use the `Rnd` function within a top values query. The `Rnd` function returns a random number based on an initial value. The idea is to build an expression that applies the `Rnd` function to a field that contains numbers, and then limit the records returned by setting the Top Values property of the query.

To demonstrate this method, start a query in Design view on the TransactionMaster table. Create a Random ID field, as shown in Figure 9-15, and then sort the field (either ascending or descending will work).

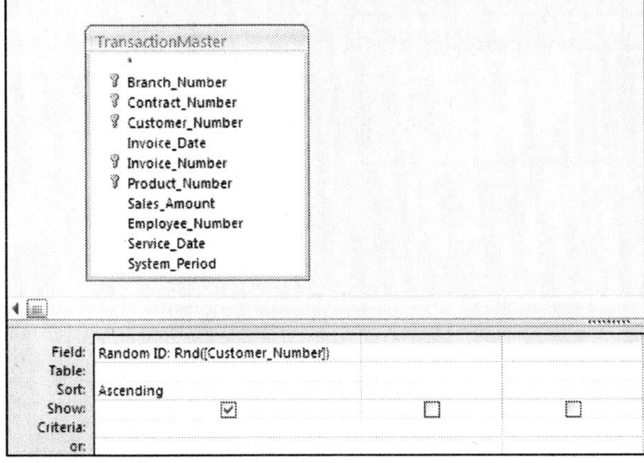

Figure 9-15: Start by creating a Random ID field using the `Rnd` function with the Customer_Number field.

NOTE **The** Rnd **function does not work with fields that contain text or Null values. Strangely enough, though, the** Rnd **function will work with fields that contain all numerical values even if the field is formatted as a Text type field.**

If your table is made up of fields that only contain text, you can add an Autonumber field to use with the Rnd **function. Another option is to pass the field containing text through the** Len **function, and then use that expression in your** Rnd **function. For example:** Rnd(Len([Mytext])).

Next, change the Top Values property of the query to the number of random records you want returned. The scenario shown in Figure 9-16 limits this dataset to 1,000 records.

The last step is to set the Show row for the Random ID field to False and add the fields you will want to see in your dataset. Run the query and you will have a completely random sampling of data. See Figure 9-17 for the results.

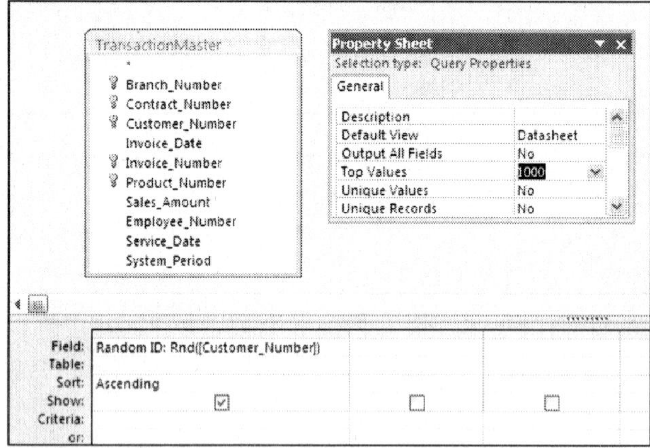

Figure 9-16: Limit the number of records returned by setting the Top Values property of the query.

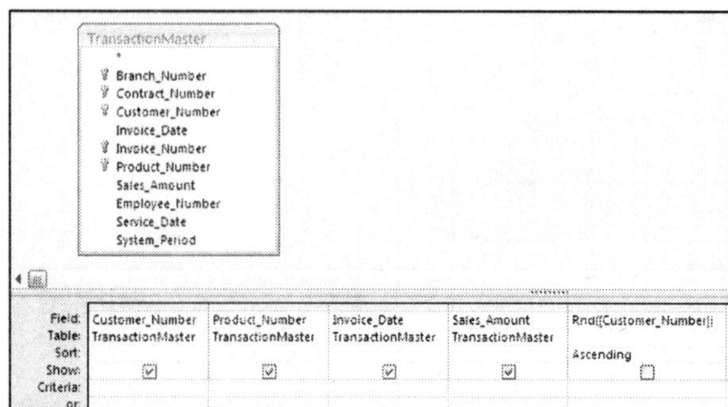

Figure 9-17: Running this query will produce a sample 1,000 random records.

WARNING **Re-running the query, switching the view state, or sorting the dataset, will result in a different set of random records. If you want to perform extensive analysis on an estabished set of random records that will not change, you will need to run this query as a make-table query in order to create a hard table.**

Advanced Descriptive Statistics

You will find that when working with descriptive statistics, a little knowledge goes a long way. Indeed, basic statistical analyses often times leads to more advanced statistical analyses. In this section you will build on the fundamentals you have just learned to create advanced descriptive statistics.

Calculating Percentile Ranking

A *percentile rank* indicates the standing of a particular score relative to the normal group standard. Percentiles are most notably used in determining performance on standardized tests. If a child scores in the 90th percentile on a standardized test, this means that his score is higher than 90 percent of the other children taking the test. Another way to look at it is to say that his score is in the top 10 percent of all the children taking the test. Percentiles are often used in data analysis as a method of measuring a subject's performance in relation to the group as a whole — for example, determining the percentile ranking for each employee based on annual revenue.

Calculating a percentile ranking for a dataset is simply a mathematical operation. The formula for a percentile rank is `(Record Count-Rank)/Record Count`. The trick is to getting all the variables needed for this mathematical operation.

To start, build the query you see in Figure 9-18. This query ranks each employee by annual revenue. Be sure to give your new field an alias of Rank.

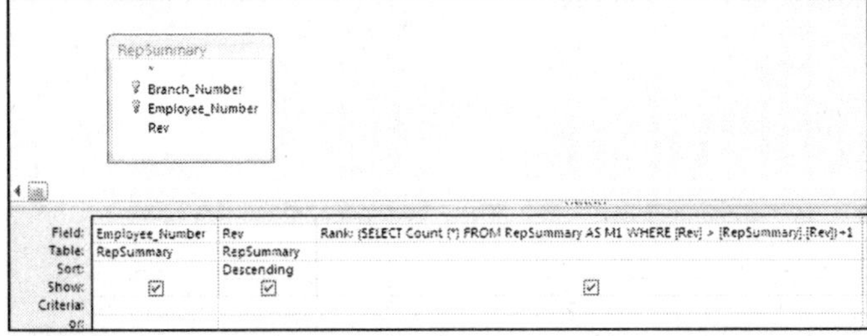

Figure 9-18: Start with a query that ranks employees by revenue.

Next, add a field that counts all the records in your dataset. As you can see in Figure 9-19, you are using a subquery to do this. Be sure to give your new field an alias of RCount.

Finally, create a calculated field with the expression `(RCount-Rank)/RCount`. At this point, your query should look like the one shown in Figure 9-20.

Running the query will give you the results shown in Figure 9-21.

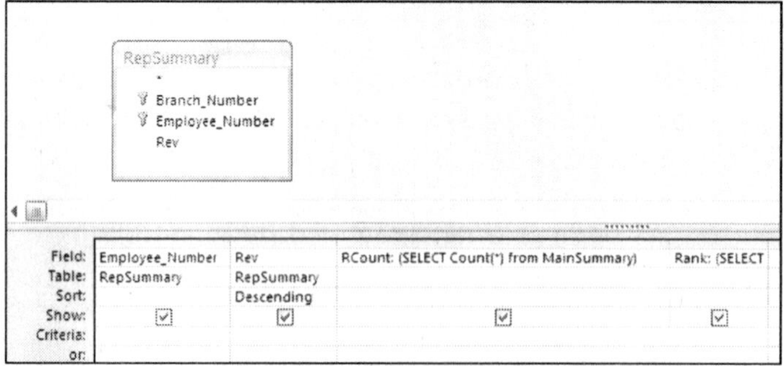

Figure 9-19: Add a field that returns a total dataset count.

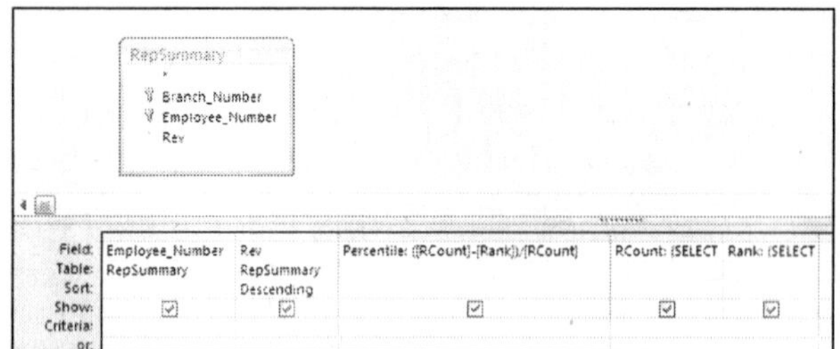

Figure 9-20: The final step is to create a calculated field that will give you the percentile rank for each record.

Employee_Number	Rank	Percentile	Rev	RCount
64621	1	99.85%	$137,707.14	673
4136	2	99.70%	$111,681.81	673
5060	3	99.55%	$106,299.32	673
56422	4	99.41%	$102,239.87	673
56405	5	99.26%	$83,525.72	673
160034	6	99.11%	$78,823.82	673
60425	7	98.96%	$77,452.50	673
3466	8	98.81%	$76,789.52	673
52635	9	98.66%	$76,684.54	673
52404	10	98.51%	$76,532.26	673
3660	11	98.37%	$75,690.33	673
1336	12	98.22%	$75,489.77	673
56416	13	98.07%	$75,358.76	673
55144	14	97.92%	$74,653.99	673
60224	15	97.77%	$71,427.33	673

Figure 9-21: You've successfully calculated the percentile rank for each employee.

Again, the resulting dataset enables you to measure each employee's performance in relation to the group as a whole. For example, the employee that is ranked 6th in the dataset is the 99th percentile, meaning that this employee earned more revenue than 99 percent of other employees.

Determining the Quartile Standing of a Record

A *quartile* is a statistical division of a dataset into four equal groups, with each group making up 25 percent of the dataset. The top 25 percent of a collection is considered to be the first quartile, whereas the bottom 25 percent is considered the fourth quartile. Quartile standings typically are used for the purposes of separating data into logical groupings that can be compared and analyzed individually. For example, if you want to establish a minimum performance standard around monthly revenue, you could set the minimum to equal the average revenue for employees in the second quartile. This ensures you have a minimum performance standard that at least 50 percent of your employees have historically achieved or exceeded.

Establishing the quartile for each record in a dataset does not involve a mathematical operation; rather, it is a question of comparison. The idea is to compare each record's rank value to the quartile benchmarks for the dataset. What are quartile benchmarks? Imagine that your dataset contains 100 records. Dividing 100 by 4 would give you the first quartile benchmark (25). This means that any record with a rank of 25 or less is in the first quartile. To get the second quartile benchmark, you would calculate `100/4*2`. To get the third, you would calculate `100/4*3` and so on.

Given that information, you know right away that you will need to rank the records in your dataset and count the records in your dataset. Start by building the query shown in Figure 9-22. Build the Rank field the same way you did in Figure 9-18. Build the RCount field the same way you did in Figure 9-19.

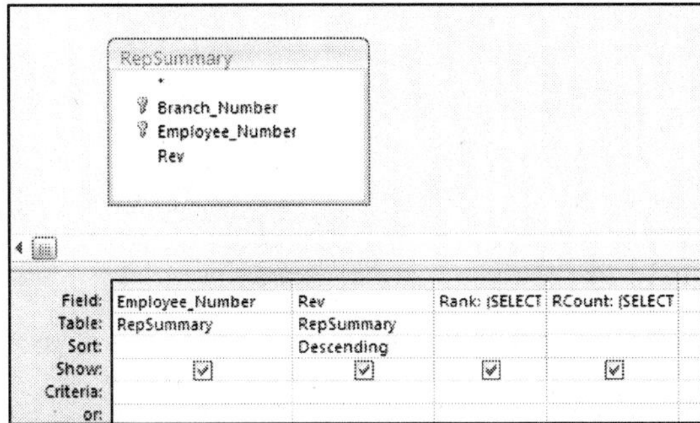

Figure 9-22: Start by creating a field named Rank that ranks each employee by revenue and a field named RCount that counts the total records in the dataset.

When you have created the Rank and RCount fields in your query, you can use these fields in a `Switch` function that will tag each record with the appropriate quartile standing. Take a moment and look at the `Switch` function you will be using.

```
Switch([Rank]<=[RCount]/4*1,"1st",[Rank]<=[RCount]/4*2,"2nd",
[Rank]<= [RCount]/4*3,"3rd",True,"4th")
```

This `Switch` function is going through four conditions, comparing each record's rank value to the quartile benchmarks for the dataset.

NOTE **For more information on the** `Switch` **function, see Chapter 6.**

Figure 9-23 demonstrates how this `Switch` function fits into the query. Note that you are using an alias of Quartile here.

As you can see in Figure 9-24, you can sort the resulting dataset on any field without compromising your quartile standing tags.

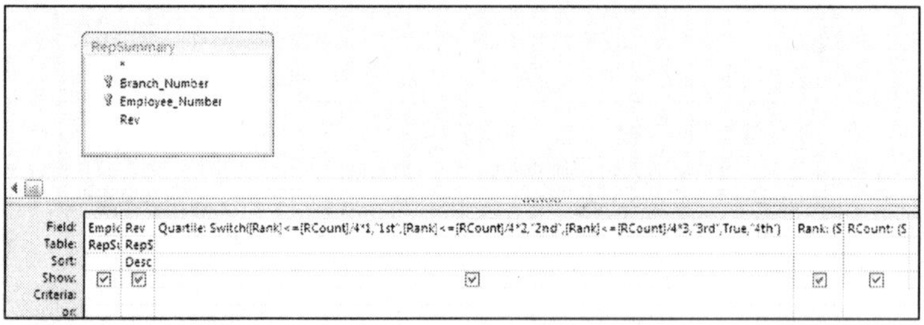

RepSummary
*
Branch_Number
Employee_Number
Rev

Field:	Emplc	Rev	Quartile: Switch([Rank]<=[RCount]/4*1,"1st",[Rank]<=[RCount]/4*2,"2nd",[Rank]<=[RCount]/4*3,"3rd",True,"4th")	Rank: (S	RCount: (S
Table:	RepSu	RepS			
Sort:		Desc			
Show:	☑	☑	☑	☑	☑
Criteria:					
or:					

Figure 9-23: Create the quartile tags using the `Switch` function.

Employee_Number	Rev	Rank	Quartile	RCount
104	$9,023.50	294	2nd	673
1044	$447.33	520	4th	673
1050	$179.74	614	4th	673
1054	$54,147.73	55	1st	673
106	$38,013.36	105	1st	673
113	$963.06	458	3rd	673
1130	$67,961.15	18	1st	673
1135	$1,477.21	429	3rd	673
1156	$192.07	602	4th	673
1245	$38,189.81	103	1st	673
1336	$75,489.77	12	1st	673
1344	$12,242.75	268	2nd	673
1416	$1,120.57	445	3rd	673
142	$1,622.30	421	3rd	673
1435	$43,118.02	89	1st	673

Figure 9-24: Your final dataset can be sorted any way without the danger of losing your quartile tags.

Creating a Frequency Distribution

A *frequency distribution* is a special kind of analysis that categorizes data based on the count of occurrences where a variable assumes a specified value attribute. Figure 9-25 illustrates a frequency distribution created by using the `Partition` function.

Employees	Dollars
158	: 499
183	500: 5499
49	5500: 10499
43	10500: 15499
31	15500: 20499
34	20500: 25499
36	25500: 30499
22	30500: 35499
23	35500: 40499
13	40500: 45499
19	45500: 50499
15	50500: 55499
17	55500: 60499
10	60500: 65499
5	65500: 70499
4	70500: 75499
6	75500: 80499

Figure 9-25: This frequency distribution is created by using the `Partition` function.

ABOUT THE PARTITION FUNCTION

`Partition(Number, Range Start, Range Stop, Interval)`

The `Partition` function identifies the range that a specific number falls into, indicating where the number occurs in a calculated series of ranges. The `Partition` function requires the following four arguments:

- `Number` **(required): The number you are evaluating. In a query environment, you typically use the name of a field to specify that you are evaluating all the row values of that field.**
- `Range Start` **(required): A whole number that is to be the start of the overall range of numbers. Note that this number cannot be less than zero.**
- `Range Stop` **(required): A whole number that is to be the end of the overall range of numbers. Note that this number cannot be equal to or less than the** `Range Start`**.**
- `Interval` **(required): A whole number that is to be the span of each range in the series from** `Range Start` **to** `Range Stop`**. Note that this number cannot be less than one.**

With this frequency distribution, you are clustering employees by the range of revenue dollars they fall in. For example, 183 employees fall into the 500: 5999 grouping, meaning that 183 employees earn between 500 and 5,999 revenue dollars per employee. Although there are several ways to get the results you see here, the easiest way to build a frequency distribution is to use the `Partition` function.

To create the frequency distribution you saw in Figure 9-25, build the query shown in Figure 9-26. As you can see in this query, you are using a `Partition` function to specify that you want you evaluate the Revenue field, start the series range at 500, end the series range at 100,000, and set the range intervals to 5,000.

You can also create a frequency distribution by group by adding a Group By field to your query. Figure 9-27 demonstrates this by adding the Branch_Number field.

The result is a dataset that contains a separate frequency distribution for each branch, detailing the count of employees in each revenue distribution range. See Figure 9-28.

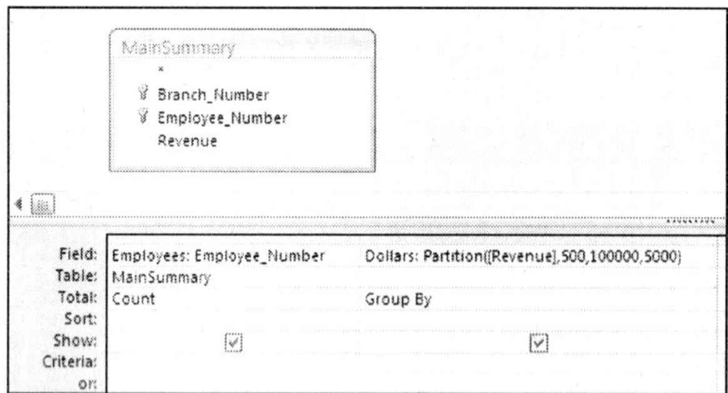

Figure 9-26: This simple query creates the frequency distribution you see in Figure 9-25.

MainSummary
*
Branch_Number
Employee_Number
Revenue

Field:	Branch_Number	Employees: Employee_Number	Dollars: Partition([Revenue],500,100000,5000)
Table:	MainSummary	MainSummary	
Total:	Group By	Count	Group By
Sort:			
Show:	☑	☑	☑
Criteria:			
or:			

Figure 9-27: This query will create a separate frequency distribution for each branch number in your dataset.

Branch_Number	Employees	Dollars
101313	3	: 499
101313	7	500: 5499
101313	2	5500: 10499
101313	1	15500: 20499
101313	1	20500: 25499
101313	1	25500: 30499
101313	1	45500: 50499
101313	1	60500: 65499
101313	1	70500: 75499
101313	2	75500: 80499
101419	2	: 499
101419	1	10500: 15499
101419	1	25500: 30499
101419	1	30500: 35499
101419	1	45500: 50499
102516	1	500: 5499
102516	1	25500: 30499
102516	1	35500: 40499
103516	4	: 499
103516	6	500: 5499
103516	1	5500: 10499
103516	1	10500: 15499
103516	2	15500: 20499
103516	1	30500: 35499

Figure 9-28: You have successfully created multiple frequency distributions with one query.

TRICKS OF THE TRADE: CREATING A HISTOGRAM CHART IN ACCESS

A *histogram chart* is a graphic representation of a frequency distribution. You can use these types of charts to easily pick out anomalies in a data collection.

Start your histogram chart by building the query shown in Figure 9-29.

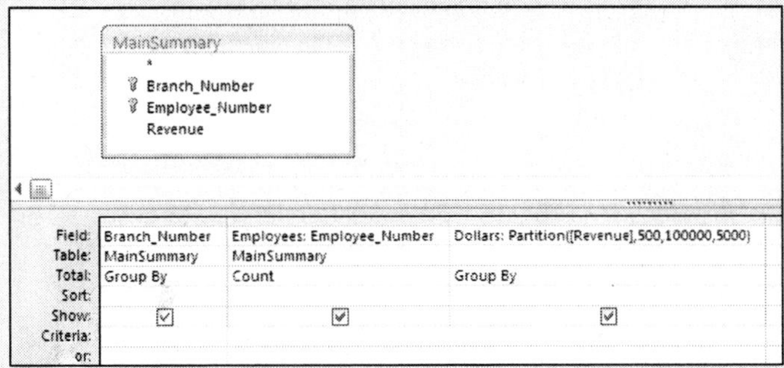

Figure 9-29: Build a query using the `Partition` function to create a frequency distribution.

Run the query to display the results of the frequency distribution operation (be sure to run the query). After you run the query, select View → PivotChart View as shown in Figure 9-30.

(continued)

TRICKS OF THE TRADE: CREATING A HISTOGRAM CHART IN ACCESS *(Continued)*

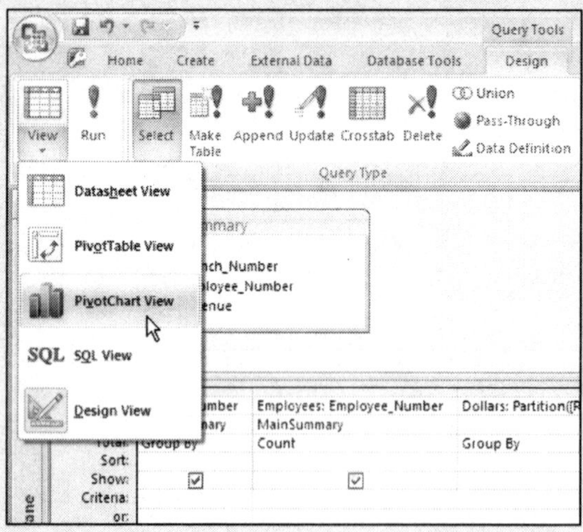

Figure 9-30: Switch to the PivotChart view.

Within a few seconds, Access will run your query and return the results in chart form. The result will be a histogram similar to the one illustrated here in Figure 9-31.

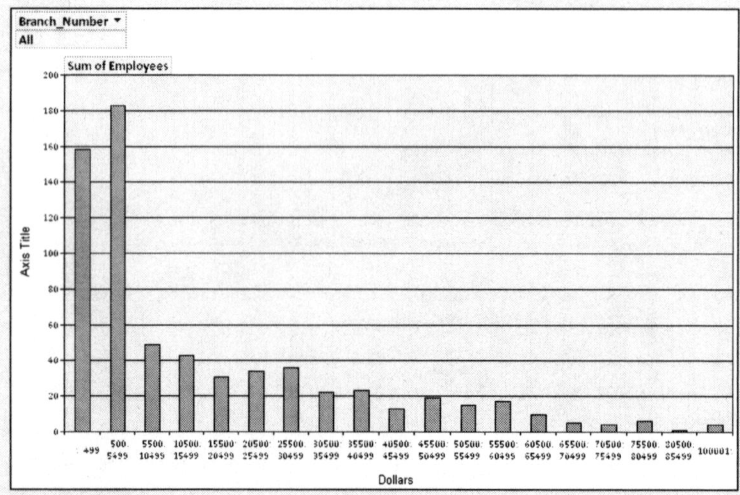

Figure 9-31: Your histogram chart is complete!

As if that isn't impressive enough, remember you have given yourself the ability to filter by branch number. To filter one branch, click the drop-down arrow next to the Branch_Number field, shown in Figure 9-32, and clear the All check box.

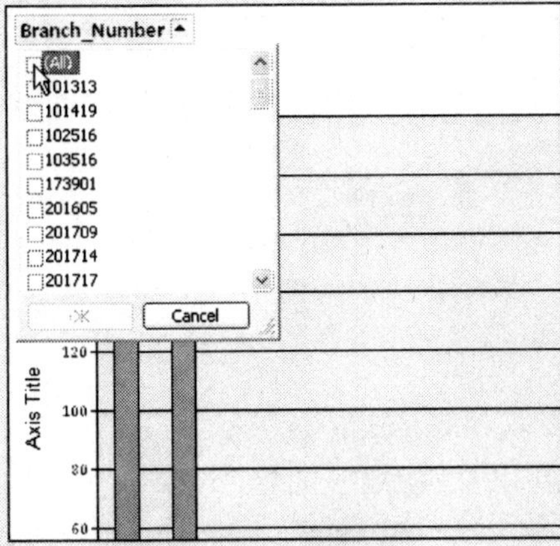

Figure 9-32: To filter by branch, click the drop-down arrow next to the Branch_Number field.

Select the check box for the branch you want to show, and then click OK. The PivotChart in Figure 9-33 presents the histogram chart for branch 301316.

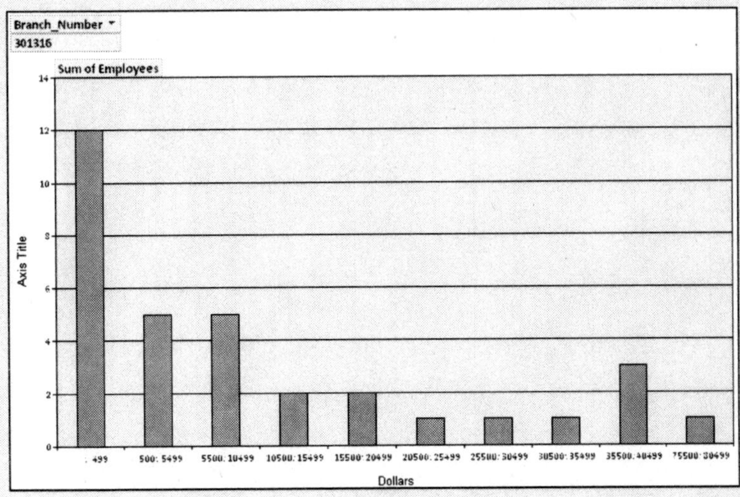

Figure 9-33: You have filtered all branches, showing only branch 301316.

Summary

Descriptive statistics enable you to profile a dataset and create comparisons that can be used in other analyses. With descriptive statistics, you can present large amounts of data in quantitative summaries that are meaningful, yet simple to understand. Although many users turn to Excel to perform statistical operations, running descriptive statistics in Access is often the smartest option due to the structure and volume of the data that is to be analyzed.

The simplest descriptive statistics can be generated using aggregate queries (sum, average, min, max, and so on), whereas more advanced descriptive analyses can be performed by leveraging the power of subqueries and domain aggregate functions. Indeed, using the tools and techniques you have learned thus far, you can create a wide array of descriptive analyses, from determining rank, mode, and median to creating a frequency distribution.

CHAPTER

10

Analyzing Data with Pivot Tables and Pivot Charts

A pivot table is one of the most robust analytical tools found in Excel. With a pivot table, you can group, summarize, and perform a wide variety of calculations in a fraction of the time it takes by hand. The most impressive functionality of a pivot table is the ability to interactively change its content, shape data, and alter its overall utility. You can drag and drop fields, dynamically change your perspective, recalculate totals to fit the current view, and interactively drill down to the detail records.

If pivot tables are your passion and the reason you use Excel, then let me share a secret with you — you have the power of pivot tables at your fingertips in your Access database. Access comes with its own version of the pivot table, enabling you to customize your analysis on the fly without rewriting your queries or turning to code.

In this chapter, you will discover that you can apply your knowledge of Excel pivot tables to Access, creating both pivot table and pivot chart analyses. You will learn how to leverage these powerful tools to change the way you analyze your Access data and the way you create your Excel exports.

TIP **This chapter focuses on using the power of pivot tables and pivot charts in Access. We assume that you are familiar with both the mechanics and the benefits of using pivot tables and pivot charts in Excel. If you are new to pivot tables altogether, consider picking up: *Pivot Table Data Crunching for Microsoft Office Excel 2007 (Business Solutions)*, ISBN: 0-7897-3601-2.**

Pivot Tables in Access?

For years, pivot tables could only be found in Excel. The closest equivalent to this functionality in pre-2000 versions of Access was the traditional crosstab query, which didn't come close to the analytical power of pivot tables. The first attempts at an Access-style pivot table came with Access 2000, where users had the ability to embed an Excel pivot table report inside of a form. Unfortunately, this feature was a bit clunky and left users with an interface that felt clumsy at best. However, Access 2000 also introduced a promising new technology in the form of Office Web Components. Office Web Components enabled users to create interactive web pages with functionality normally found only in Excel. One of these components was the PivotTable Component. Although this component did expose pivot table functionality to Access, the fact that it was limited for use only on Data Access Pages (ASP- and HTML-based web pages), made it an impractical tool for day-to-day data analysis.

With the release of Office XP, Microsoft gave Access users the ability to use the PivotTable and PivotChart components in both the query and form environments. This finally allowed for practical data analysis using pivot tables in Access. Alas, this functionality remained relatively untouched by many users, as it was difficult to find in previous versions.

In Access 2007, the PivotTable and PivotChart components still exist and have been brought to the forefront. So the only question for you is, why should you get excited about using pivot tables in Access?

From a data analysis point of view, pivot tables and pivot charts are some of the most powerful data-crunching tools found in Access today. Consider these capabilities:

- You can create multi-dimensional analyses that far surpass the limitations of traditional crosstab queries.
- You can interactively change your analysis without re-writing your query.

- You can dynamically sort, filter, group, and add custom calculations with a few clicks of the mouse.
- You have drill-down capabilities that enable you to collapse and expand analytical details without writing code.
- You can perform more of your analysis in Access instead of spending time exporting raw data back and forth to Excel.

The Anatomy of a Pivot Table

Figure 10-1 shows an empty pivot table. As you can see, a pivot table is comprised of four areas. Because how you choose to utilize these areas defines both the utility and the appearance of your pivot table, it's important to understand the functionality of each area.

The Totals and Detail Area

The totals and detail area, highlighted in Figure 10-2, is the area that calculates and supplies the details for your report. You can recognize this area by the phrase Drop Totals or Detail Fields Here. This area tends to be confusing for first-time users because it has a dual role. First, it displays aggregate totals such as Sum of Revenue, Count of Units, and Average of Price. Second, it stores detailed row data that is exposed upon expansion of Row and Column fields.

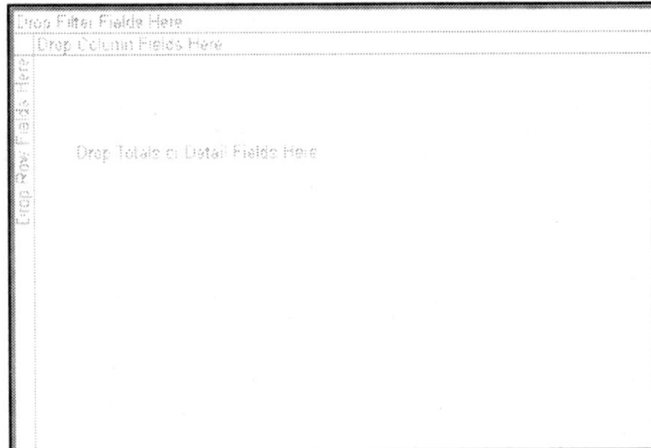

Figure 10-1: An empty pivot table in Access.

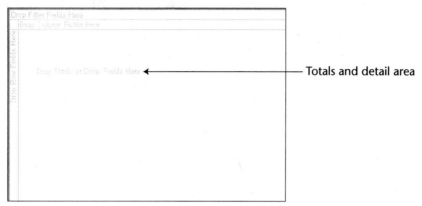

Figure 10-2: The totals and detail area calculates fields and stores record details.

The Row Area

The row area, highlighted in Figure 10-3, provides the headings down the left side of the pivot table. You can recognize this area by the phrase Drop Row Fields Here. Dropping a field into the row area displays each unique value in that field down the left side of the pivot table. In this area, you drop data fields of items you want to group and categorize — for example, locations, customer names, and products.

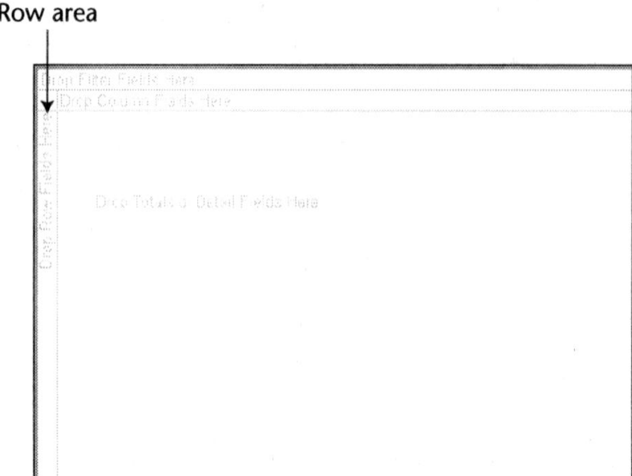

Figure 10-3: The row area displays values down the left side of the pivot table.

The Column Area

The column area, highlighted in Figure 10-4, provides the headings that span across the top of the pivot table. You can recognize this area by the phrase Drop Column Fields Here. Dropping a field into the column area will display each unique value in the field in a column-oriented perspective. The column area is ideal for showing trending over time. Examples of fields you can drop here include Months, Periods, and Years.

The Filter Area

The filter area, highlighted in Figure 10-5, allows for dynamic filtering of your pivot table based on a value in a field. You can recognize this area by the phrase Drop Filter Fields Here. The fields you drop here include items you would want to isolate and focus on, such as locations, employee names, and products.

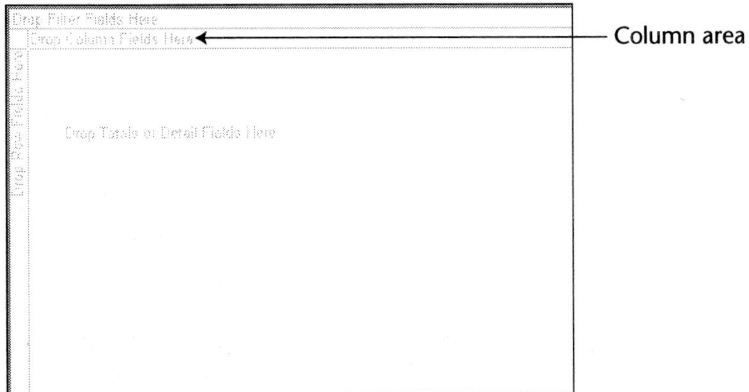

Figure 10-4: The column area displays values across the top of the pivot table.

Figure 10-5: The filter area allows you to filter your pivot table.

Creating a Basic Pivot Table

Start by building the query you see in Figure 10-6, and then go up to the Design tab and select View → PivotTable View.

At this point, you will see an empty pivot table, shown in Figure 10-7, and a list of fields that are in your dataset.

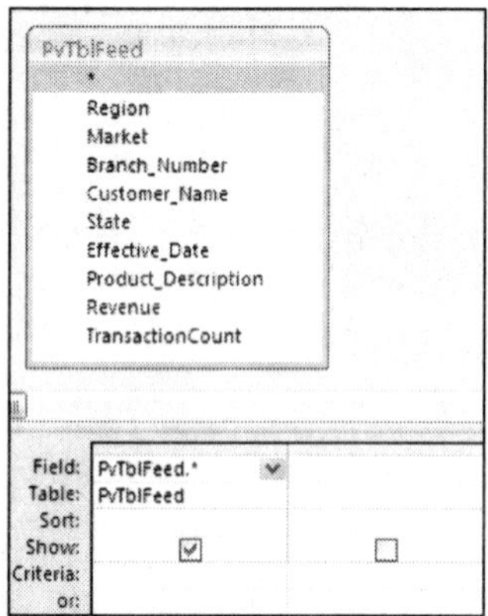

Figure 10-6: Build your query and then switch to PivotTable view.

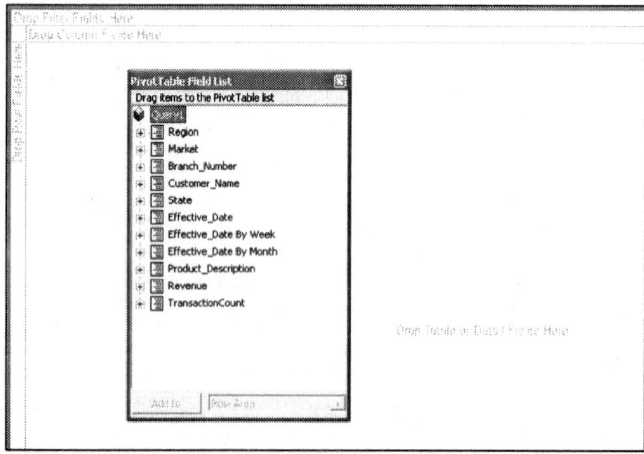

Figure 10-7: You will use the field list to build your pivot table.

The idea is to drag the fields you need into the pivot table's drop areas. How do you know which field goes where? This depends on two things: what are you measuring, and how do you want it presented. The answer to the first question will tell you which fields in your data source you will need to work with, and the answer to the second question will tell you where to place the fields. For example, if you want to measure the amount of revenue by region, you automatically know that you will need to work with the Revenue field and the Region field. In addition, you want regions to go down the left side of the report and revenues to be calculated for each region. Therefore, you know that the Region field will go into the row area while the Revenue field will go into the detail area.

Now that you know what you need, start by selecting the Region field from your field list and drag it to the row area as shown in Figure 10-8.

TIP **If you accidently close out your PivotTable Field List, simply right-click inside the pivot table and select Field List to reactivate it.**

Next, select the Revenue field, then select Data Area from the drop-down box at the bottom of the PivotTable field list as shown in Figure 10-9. Click the Add To button.

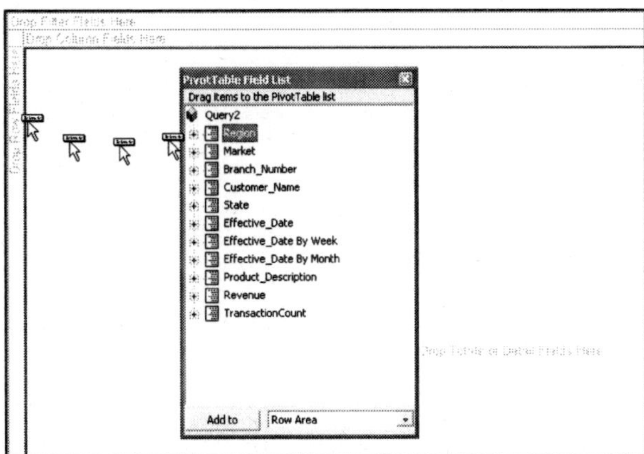

Figure 10-8: Drag the Region field to the row area of the pivot table.

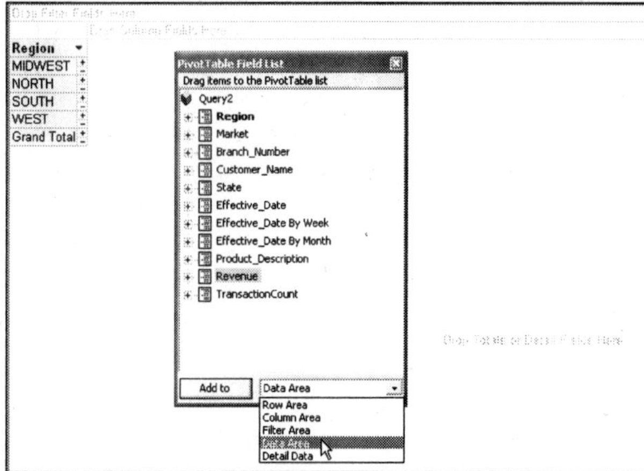

Figure 10-9: Add the Revenue field using the field list drop-down.

NOTE **Why not just drag the Revenue field to the detail area? The reason is that the Pivot Table Web Component requires that you view detail data before you add totals. So if you simply drag the Revenue field to the data area, the pivot table will not display the sum total of your revenue; instead it would display the detailed revenue for each record in your dataset. Keep in mind that in order to use the method shown in Figure 10-9, the field you are adding must be a numeric or currency field.**

At this point, your pivot table should look like the one shown in Figure 10-10.

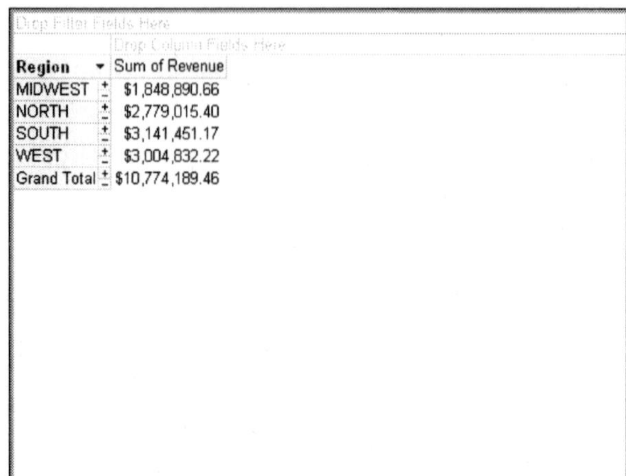

Region	Sum of Revenue
MIDWEST	$1,848,890.66
NORTH	$2,779,015.40
SOUTH	$3,141,451.17
WEST	$3,004,832.22
Grand Total	$10,774,189.46

Figure 10-10: You have created your first pivot table report!

You can add some dimension to this report by dragging the Product-Description field to the column area. As you can see in Figure 10-11, with this you now have a cross tabular view of revenue by region and product.

Now add the Market field to the row area and drag the Region field to the filter area (the area that reads Drop Filter Fields Here). Your pivot table should look like the one shown in Figure 10-12. With just a few mouse clicks, you not only have a totally new perspective on the same data, but you can now filter by region.

Drop Filter Fields Here

	Product_Description		
	Cleaning & Housekeeping Services	Facility Maintenance and Repair	Fleet Maintenance
Region	Sum of Revenue	Sum of Revenue	Sum of Revenue
MIDWEST	$174,518.08	$463,078.85	$448,800.61
NORTH	$534,284.19	$606,748.65	$610,791.49
SOUTH	$283,170.17	$846,508.06	$1,046,229.86
WEST	$146,623.34	$444,825.85	$521,976.06
Grand Total	$1,138,595.78	$2,361,161.41	$2,627,798.02

Figure 10-11: Drag the ProductDescription field to the column area of the pivot table.

Region
All

	Product_Description		
	Cleaning & Housekeeping Services	Facility Maintenance and Repair	Fleet Maintenance
Market	Sum of Revenue	Sum of Revenue	Sum of Revenue
BUFFALO	$66,844.23	$69,568.80	$86,461.34
CALIFORNIA	$37,401.55	$281,203.86	$337,224.62
CANADA		$294,258.33	$273,175.05
CHARLOTTE	$170,341.83	$223,346.86	$245,119.74
DALLAS	$18,807.34	$136,844.19	$156,152.05
DENVER	$12,563.96	$160,325.12	$170,188.42
FLORIDA	$20,448.86	$410,039.45	$556,003.84
KANSASCITY	$65,439.45	$132,119.42	$133,170.10
MICHIGAN	$243,451.28	$65,079.56	$66,408.19
NEWORLEANS	$73,572.13	$76,277.55	$88,954.24
NEWYORK	$223,988.68	$177,841.95	$184,746.91
PHOENIX	$96,685.78	$125,522.50	$150,788.58
SEATTLE	$12,536.02	$38,099.49	$33,962.86
TULSA	$96,514.67	$170,634.31	$145,442.10
Grand Total	$1,138,595.78	$2,361,161.41	$2,627,798.02

Figure 10-12: Adding the Market field and dragging the Region field to the filter area enables you to analyze market revenue for a specific region.

A WORD ABOUT DRAGGING FIELDS FROM ONE AREA TO ANOTHER

When you drag your fields from one area of a pivot table to another, your cursor will turn into a mini pivot table; that is, your cursor turns into an icon that represents your pivot table. As you move your cursor from one area of your actual pivot table to the next, you will notice that different parts of the icon will be shaded. The shaded area corresponds to the area over which you are currently hovering. This enables you to easily discern in which area you are about to drop your field. The key to telling which area you are hovering over is to watch the shaded area of the cursor as shown in Figure 10-13.

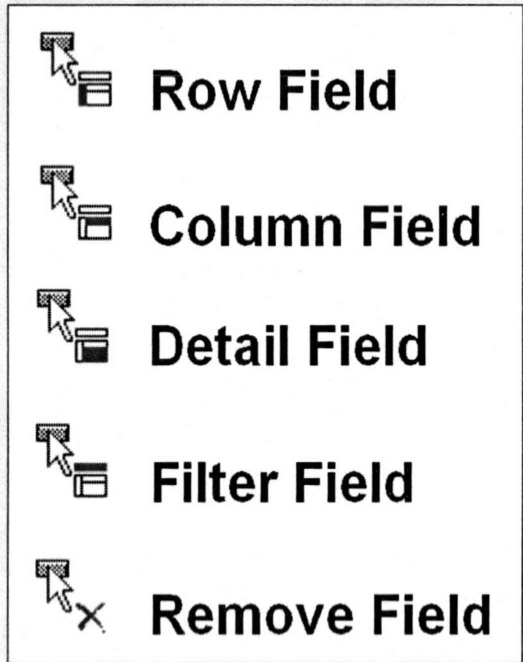

Figure 10-13: Watch the shaded area of the cursor to determine where you are about to drop your field.

TIP **If you need to remove a field from your pivot table, an alternative to dragging it off is to right-click the field name and select Remove.**

Creating an Advanced Pivot Table with Details

This section demonstrates how you can incorporate record details into your pivot table, effectively building an analysis that can drill down to the record level. First create the pivot table shown in Figure 10-14 by following these steps:

1. Start by building the query you see in Figure 10-6, then go to the Design tab and select View → PivotTable View.
2. Drag the Market and Product_Description fields to the row area of the pivot table.
3. Select the Revenue field, then select Data Area from the drop-down box at the bottom of the PivotTable field and click the Add To button.

   Take a moment and look at what you have so far. You've created a basic analysis that reveals the amount of revenue by product for each market. Now you can enhance this analysis by adding customer details to the pivot table. This enables you to drill into a product segment and view all the customers that make up that product's revenue.

4. Select the Customer_Name field, then select Detail Data from the drop-down box at the bottom of the PivotTable field and click the Add To button.
5. Select the Effective_Date field, then select Detail Data from the drop-down box at the bottom of the PivotTable field and click the Add To button.
6. Select the Revenue field, then select Detail Area from the drop-down box at the bottom of the PivotTable field and click the Add To button.

Drop Filter Fields Here

Drop Column Fields Here

Market	Product_Description	Sum of Revenue
⊟ BUFFALO	Cleaning & Housekeeping Services	$66,844.23
	Facility Maintenance and Repair	$69,568.80
	Fleet Maintenance	$86,461.34
	Green Plants and Foliage Care	$34,830.18
	Landscaping/Grounds Care	$65,464.84
	Predictive Maintenance/Preventative Maintenance	$127,309.32
	Total	$450,478.72
⊟ CALIFORNIA	Cleaning & Housekeeping Services	$37,401.55
	Facility Maintenance and Repair	$281,203.86
	Fleet Maintenance	$337,224.62
	Green Plants and Foliage Care	$830,422.28
	Landscaping/Grounds Care	$248,343.46
	Predictive Maintenance/Preventative Maintenance	$520,155.87
	Total	$2,254,751.64
⊟ CANADA	Facility Maintenance and Repair	$294,258.33
	Fleet Maintenance	$273,175.05
	Green Plants and Foliage Care	$15,965.46
	Landscaping/Grounds Care	$76,751.57
	Predictive Maintenance/Preventative Maintenance	$116,097.37
	Total	$776,247.78

Figure 10-14: Build the pivot table shown here.

At this point, it looks as though your pivot table hasn't changed. However, if you click the plus sign next to any one of the product segments, you will see the customer details for every customer that contributed to that segment's total revenue, as shown in Figure 10-15.

TIP **You can show and hide all details at once by right-clicking the field names and selecting Show Details or Hide Details.**

WARNING **Incorporating record details into your pivot tables is a technique that should be limited to smaller datasets. Because the PivotTable component opens a separate ADO recordset for each cell it contains, accessing a large amount of detail through your pivot table can lead to performance issues. If you absolutely need to view all row and column details for a large dataset, you should consider using a query or a form.**

Saving Your Pivot Table

It's important to remember that when you are building your analysis with a pivot table, you are actually working with a query in a PivotTable view. Therefore, when you save your analysis it will save as a query. The next time you open the query it will open in Datasheet view. This doesn't mean your pivot table is lost — just switch back to PivotTable view to see your pivot table.

Market	Product_Description	Customer_Name	Effective_Date	Revenue
BUFFALO	Cleaning & Housekeeping Services	BAUDUS Corp.	1/13/2004	$5,417.95
		CUNUME Corp.	1/19/2004	$3,750.89
		FSULLA Corp.	6/9/2004	$1,250.30
		GOSBOR Corp.	1/7/2004	$3,750.89
		KUYSTU Corp.	1/20/2004	$3,750.89
		LATREB Corp.	1/5/2004	$6,668.24
		LATRUN Corp.	2/2/2004	$2,083.83
		PPGAND Corp.	1/29/2004	$3,750.89
		SPUCAA Corp.	1/8/2004	$10,835.90
		VARGAN Corp.	1/8/2004	$3,750.89
		VUUDUS Corp.	1/12/2004	$5,417.95
		LUXANG Corp.	1/19/2004	$6,668.85
		PRUUUC Corp.	9/27/2004	$1,025.98
		SUNUCA Corp.	1/14/2004	$2,564.94
		THEHAL Corp.	1/21/2004	$3,077.93
		Sum of Revenue		$66,844.23
	Facility Maintenance and Repair	Sum of Revenue		$69,568.80
	Fleet Maintenance	Sum of Revenue		$86,461.34
	Green Plants and Foliage Care	Sum of Revenue		$34,830.18
	Landscaping/Grounds Care	Sum of Revenue		$65,464.84
	Predictive Maintenance/Preventative Maintenance	Sum of Revenue		$127,309.32
	Total	Sum of Revenue		$450,478.72

Figure 10-15: You now have the ability to drill down into the details that make up your revenue totals.

If you want your query to run in PivotTable view by default, change the Default View property of the query. To do this, open your query in Design view. On the Design tab, in the Show/Hide group, select the Property Sheet. Select the Property Sheet button. This opens the Property Sheet dialog box shown in Figure 10-16. Change the Default View property to PivotTable. The next time you open your query, it will open in PivotTable view.

Sending Your Access Pivot Table to Excel

When you are happy with your Access pivot table analysis, you may want to share your pivot table with the world. You can distribute your Access pivot table via Excel. To do so, open your query in PivotTable view. Then go to the Design tab and click the Export to Excel button. This sends your pivot table to Excel, where you can format it and e-mail it as a professional analysis.

The nifty thing about this technique is that only the pivot cache is sent to Excel. That is to say, the raw data behind the pivot table is not sent to the workbook to be placed in a separate sheet. This means a smaller file size and a cleaner-looking workbook.

TIP What if you wanted your users have access to the raw data also? Since Access only transfers the pivot table and not the raw data, are you out of luck? No. To get the raw data, simply double-click on the bottom-right-most Grand Total value of your pivot table. This drills into the pivot cache and outputs the raw data that makes up your pivot table onto a separate worksheet.

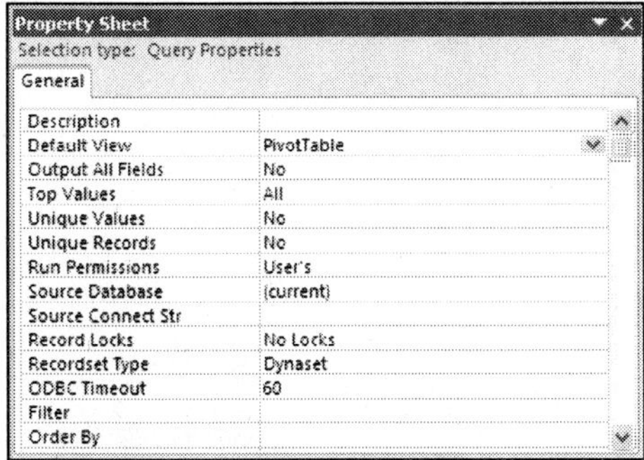

Figure 10-16: Change the Default View property to PivotTable.

Pivot Table Options

You will often find that the pivot tables you create need to be tweaked in order to get the result you're looking for. In this section, I will cover some of the pivot table options you can adjust in order to enhance your analysis. To prepare for the examples in this section, create the pivot table shown in Figure 10-17 by following these steps:

1. Start by building the query you see in Figure 10-6, and then select View → PivotTable View from the Design tab.
2. Drag the Region, Market, and Customer_Name fields to the row area of the pivot table.
3. Select the Revenue field, then select Data Area from the drop-down box at the bottom of the PivotTable field and click the Add To button.
4. Select the TransactionCount field, then select Data Area from the drop-down box at the bottom of the PivotTable field and click the Add To button.

Drop Filter Fields Here

Drop Column Fields Here

Region	Market	Customer_Name	Sum of Revenue	Sum of TransactionCount
⊟ MIDWEST	⊟ DENVER	ADOMSC Corp.	$1,190.30	6
		ADVANC Corp.	$1,709.64	12
		ALLAAN Corp.	$625.25	4
		ALLFAN Corp.	$448.02	4
		ALPANE Corp.	$4,578.26	25
		ALUXAN Corp.	$1,139.76	8
		AMPRUT Corp.	$448.02	4
		AMPUST Corp.	$5,592.04	30
		AMUSYS Corp.	$937.88	6
		ANAQAE Corp.	$1,172.20	8
		ANATUD Corp.	$4,644.84	24
		ANCLEM Corp.	$716.28	6
		ANDALU Corp.	$997.29	7
		ANDART Corp.	$2,421.99	17
		ANDUQU Corp.	$1,318.73	9
		ANDUSS Corp.	$448.02	4
		ANFANA Corp.	$434.06	4
		ANGUSS Corp.	$1,318.73	9

Figure 10-17: Build the pivot table shown here.

Expanding and Collapsing Fields

It's always difficult to perform an effective analysis on a large volume of data. So when you are analyzing a large amount of data in a pivot table such as the one shown in Figure 10-17, it's helpful to see small chunks of data at a time.

For this reason, Access enables you to expand or collapse detail easily by clicking on the plus and minus signs shown in the pivot tables. You can also expand or collapse all values in a field at once. For example, right-click the Market field and select Collapse. As you can see in Figure 10-18, all the customer details for each market are now hidden, which makes this pivot table easier to read. Now you can analyze the customer detail for one market at time clicking the plus sign for that market.

Changing Field Captions

Access often attempts to name aggregated fields with its own name such as Sum of TransactionCount. Of course, labels like this one can be confusing to the consumer. You can customize your field captions by changing the Caption property of the field.

Drop Filter Fields Here

Drop Column Fields Here

Region	Market	Customer_Name	Sum of Revenue	Sum of TransactionCount
⊟ MIDWEST	⊞ DENVER		$645,584.10	4231
	⊞ KANSASCITY		$574,899.15	3784
	⊞ TULSA		$628,407.41	4417
	Total		$1,848,890.66	12432
⊟ NORTH	⊞ BUFFALO		$450,478.72	2625
	⊞ CANADA		$776,247.78	4981
	⊞ MICHIGAN		$678,708.11	3689
	⊞ NEWYORK		$873,580.79	4808
	Total		$2,779,015.40	16103
⊟ SOUTH	⊞ CHARLOTTE		$890,514.49	5389
	⊞ DALLAS		$467,086.11	3392
	⊞ FLORIDA		$1,450,397.76	11486
	⊞ NEWORLEANS		$333,452.80	1920
	Total		$3,141,451.17	22187
⊟ WEST	⊞ CALIFORNIA		$2,254,751.64	13617
	⊞ PHOENIX		$570,254.17	3222
	⊞ SEATTLE		$179,826.42	1053
	Total		$3,004,832.22	17892
Grand Total			$10,774,189.46	68614

Figure 10-18: Collapsing fields makes your pivot tables easier to read.

Right-click the Sum of TransactionCount field heading and select Properties. This activates the Properties dialog box shown in Figure 10-19. Click the Captions tab and enter Count of Transactions in the Caption input box. Close the dialog box and your changes will take effect immediately.

Sorting Data

By default, pivot tables are initially sorted in ascending order. However, you may prefer to present your data in an order that makes more sense in your situation. To change the sort order of a particular field or aggregation, simply right-click the chosen field or aggregation and select Sort, and then select Sort Ascending or Sort Descending.

Grouping Data

A particularly useful feature in pivot tables is the ability to create a new layer of analysis by grouping and summarizing unrelated data items. Imagine that you need to group the products shown in Figure 10-20 into two segments: outside services and inside services — Green Plants and Foliage Care and Landscaping/Grounds Care need to be classified as Inside Services and Outside Services, respectively.

To accomplish this task, hold down the Ctrl key and select both Green Plants and Foliage Care and Landscaping/Grounds Care. Then right-click and select Group Items, as shown in Figure 10-21.

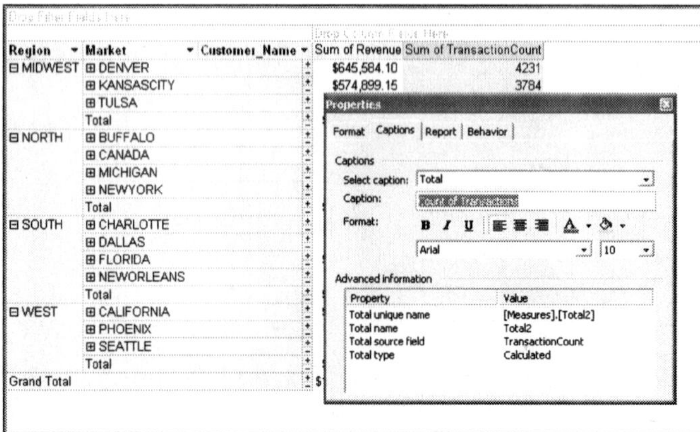

Figure 10-19: You can change a field's name by setting the Caption property of the field.

Drop Filter Fields Here

Product_Description	Sum of Revenue
Cleaning & Housekeeping Services	$1,138,595.78
Facility Maintenance and Repair	$2,361,161.41
Fleet Maintenance	$2,627,798.02
Green Plants and Foliage Care	$1,276,790.55
Landscaping/Grounds Care	$1,190,911.60
Predictive Maintenance/Preventative Maintenance	$2,178,932.11
Grand Total	$10,774,189.46

Figure 10-20: You need to group these products into two groups.

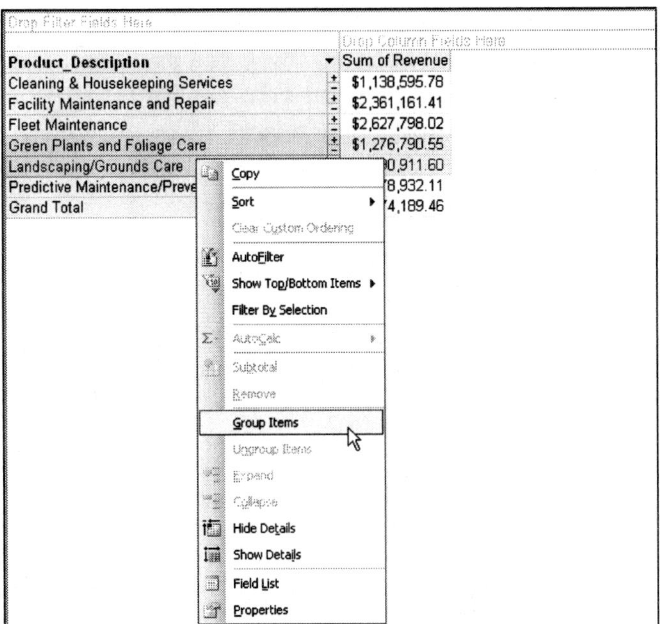

Figure 10-21: Select Group Items.

At this point, your pivot table should look similar to the one shown in Figure 10-22. As you can see, you have essentially created a new field with two data items: Group1 and Other. All that is left to do is to change the captions on these newly created objects. To change the caption of a grouped field, right-click the field name and select Properties. This activates the Properties dialog box where you can click the Caption tab and edit the Caption input box.

Drop Filter Fields Here

Drop Column Fields Here

Product_Description1 ▾	Product_Description	Sum of Revenue
⊟ Group1	Green Plants and Foliage Care	$1,276,790.55
	Landscaping/Grounds Care	$1,190,911.60
	Total	$2,467,702.15
⊟ Other	Cleaning & Housekeeping Services	$1,138,595.78
	Facility Maintenance and Repair	$2,361,161.41
	Fleet Maintenance	$2,627,798.02
	Predictive Maintenance/Preventative Maintenance	$2,178,932.11
	Total	$8,306,487.31
Grand Total		$10,774,189.46

Figure 10-22: Change the caption of a grouped field.

Figure 10-23 illustrates what the final report with a new Product Segment field should look like.

One last note about grouping data. If you activate your field list and drill into the Product_Description field, as shown in Figure 10-24, you will notice that your newly created grouping is listed there as a sub-field. This means you can treat this field as any other in your field list. To delete your grouping, right-click its entry in the field list and select Delete.

Drop Filter Fields Here

Drop Column Fields Here

Product Segment ▾	Product_Description	Sum of Revenue
⊟ Outside Services	Green Plants and Foliage Care	$1,276,790.55
	Landscaping/Grounds Care	$1,190,911.60
	Total	$2,467,702.15
⊟ Inside Services	Cleaning & Housekeeping Services	$1,138,595.78
	Facility Maintenance and Repair	$2,361,161.41
	Fleet Maintenance	$2,627,798.02
	Predictive Maintenance/Preventative Maintenance	$2,178,932.11
	Total	$8,306,487.31
Grand Total		$10,774,189.46

Figure 10-23: In just a few clicks, you have added another layer to your analysis.

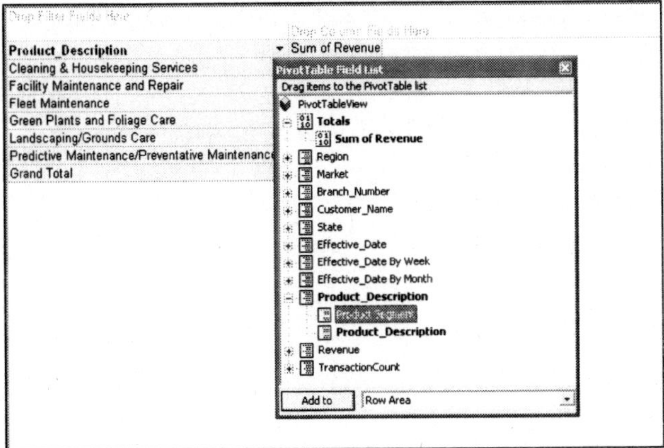

Figure 10-24: To delete your grouping, find it in the PivotTable Field List, then right click on it, and then click Delete.

Using Date Groupings

Note that in Figure 10-25, you see a field called Effective_Date and directly below that field you see Effective_Date by Week and Effective_Date by Month. Unlike Excel where you would have to explicitly create date groupings, Access automatically creates these groupings for any field that is formatted as a date field.

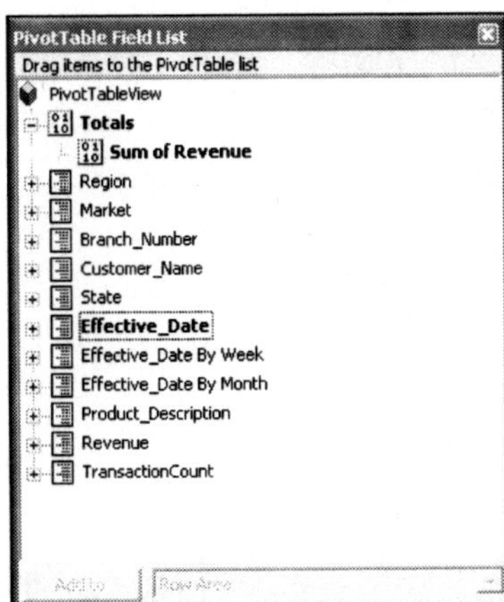

Figure 10-25: Access automatically creates date groupings for any field that is formatted as a date field.

Figure 10-26 illustrates how you can simply drag these date groupings onto your pivot table just as you would any other field.

NOTE **One drawback to using the Access-provided date groupings is that you can't separate them. For example, you cannot drag the Year grouping into the column area then drag the Month grouping into the row area.**

Filtering for Top and Bottom Records

Filtering your pivot table to show the top or bottom *n*th records can be done with just a few clicks of the mouse. In the example illustrated in Figure 10-27, you have a list of customers and want to limit the list to the top 10 customers by sum of revenue. Right-clicking the Customer_Name field heading will expose a shortcut menu where you would select Show Top/Bottom Items → Show only the Top → 10.

As you can see in Figure 10-27, the filtering options also include the ability to filter by percent of records. You can remove the applied filter by right-clicking the field heading and selecting AutoFilter.

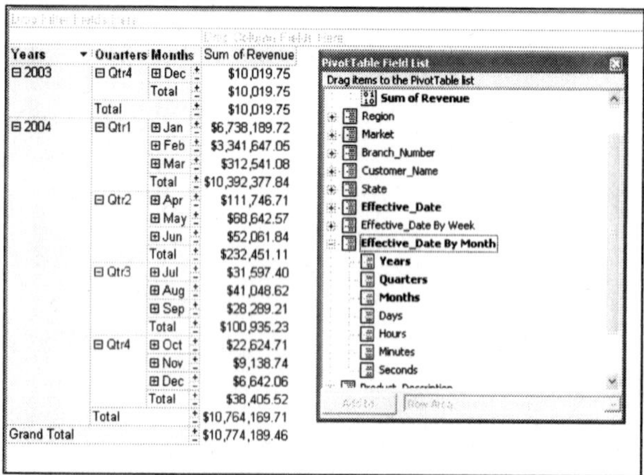

Figure 10-26: Date Groupings in action.

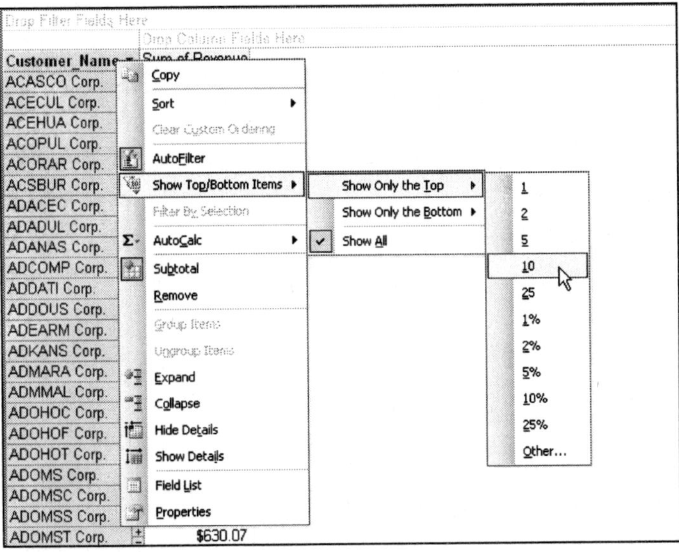

Figure 10-27: An example of how easy it is to filter the top 10 customers.

TIP **There are actually two methods you can use to remove an applied filter from a field.**

- **Method 1: Right-click the field heading and select AutoFilter.**
- **Method 2: Right-click the field heading and select Show Top/Bottom Items → Show All.**

Unlike Method 2, Method 1, highlighted above, enables you to reapply the last known filter to the field at any time by right-clicking the field heading and selecting AutoFilter. Method 2, on the other hand, clears the filter settings altogether.

Adding a Calculated Total

When you create a pivot table, you may find it useful to expand your analysis by performing calculations on summary totals. To demonstrate this, create the pivot table shown in Figure 10-28. This analysis calculates total revenue and total count of transactions. Upon reviewing these results, you determine that you need to get an average dollar amount per transaction.

Market	Sum of Revenue	Sum of TransactionCount
BUFFALO	$450,478.72	2625
CALIFORNIA	$2,254,751.64	13617
CANADA	$776,247.78	4981
CHARLOTTE	$890,514.49	5389
DALLAS	$467,086.11	3392
DENVER	$645,584.10	4231
FLORIDA	$1,450,397.76	11486
KANSASCITY	$574,899.15	3784
MICHIGAN	$678,708.11	3689
NEWORLEANS	$333,452.80	1920
NEWYORK	$873,580.79	4808
PHOENIX	$570,254.17	3222
SEATTLE	$179,826.42	1053
TULSA	$628,407.41	4417
Grand Total	$10,774,189.46	68614

Figure 10-28: You need to calculate the average dollar amount per transaction for each market.

Go to the Design tab and select Formulas → Create Calculated Total. Next, you will notice a new field called New Total in your pivot table, as shown in Figure 10-29. Also, the Properties dialog box for this field opens.

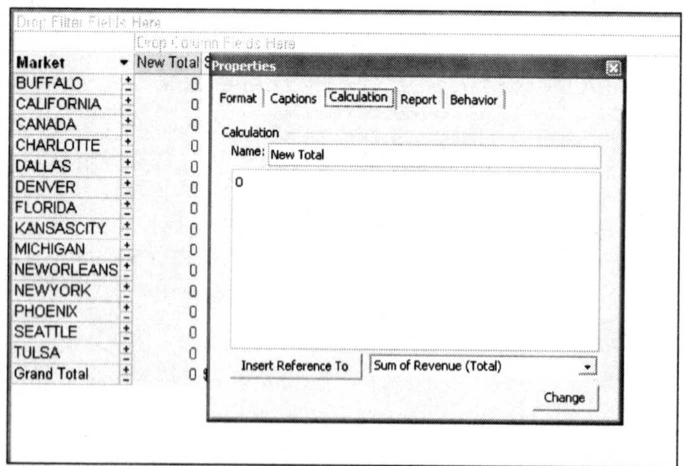

Figure 10-29: Adding a new calculated total will create a new field in your pivot table.

Next, enter the calculation you need into the dialog box.

1. Enter **Dollars per Transaction** into the Name text box.
2. Delete the 0 from the large text box below Name.
3. Select Sum of Revenue (Total) from the drop-down menu, and then click the Insert Reference To button.
4. Type a forward slash (/) to indicate division.
5. Select Sum of TransactionCount (Total) from the drop-down list and then click the Insert Reference To button.

   At this point, your dialog box should look similar to Figure 10-30.

6. Click the Change button.
7. Go to the Format Tab and select Currency from the Number box.

As you can see in Figure 10-31, your new calculation looks and acts like any other Totals field in your pivot table.

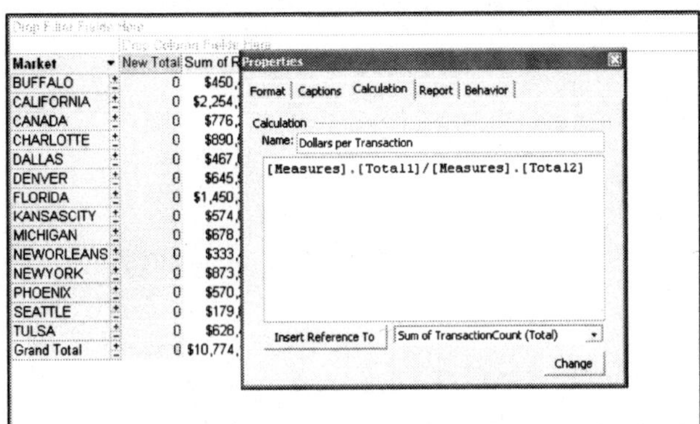

Figure 10-30: Your dialog box should look like this.

Market	Dollars per Transaction	Sum of Revenue	Sum of TransactionCount
BUFFALO	$171.61	$450,478.72	2625
CALIFORNIA	$165.58	$2,254,751.64	13617
CANADA	$155.84	$776,247.78	4981
CHARLOTTE	$165.25	$890,514.49	5389
DALLAS	$137.70	$467,086.11	3392
DENVER	$152.58	$645,584.10	4231
FLORIDA	$126.28	$1,450,397.76	11486
KANSASCITY	$151.93	$574,899.15	3784
MICHIGAN	$183.98	$678,708.11	3689
NEWORLEANS	$173.67	$333,452.80	1920
NEWYORK	$181.69	$873,580.79	4808
PHOENIX	$176.99	$570,254.17	3222
SEATTLE	$170.78	$179,826.42	1053
TULSA	$142.27	$628,407.41	4417
Grand Total	$157.03	$10,774,189.46	68614

Figure 10-31: You have enhanced your analysis with a calculated total.

To adjust the calculation behind your calculated total, right-click the field heading and select Properties. This will open the Properties dialog box where you can change the calculation in the Calculation tab.

To delete your calculated total, right click on its entry in the field list, shown in Figure 10-32, and select Delete.

NOTE **You can also create a Calculated Detail field using the same steps illustrated above. However, it's generally a better idea to perform calculations on details in the actual query as opposed to a pivot table. This way, Microsoft ACE (ACE is the Access 2007 replacement for Microsoft Jet) performs the calculation instead of the PivotTable component, making your PivotTable view perform better.**

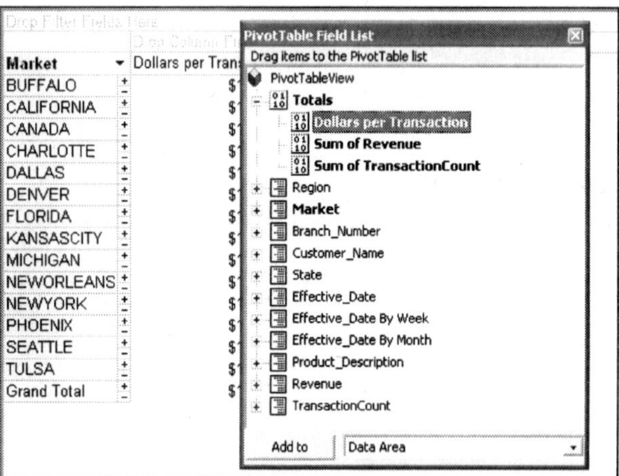

Figure 10-32: To delete your calculated total, find it in the PivotTable Field List, right-click it, and then click Delete.

Working with Pivot Charts in Access

A pivot chart is essentially a pivot table in chart form. When you are familiar with the basics of using a pivot table, you will also be able to handle a pivot chart — it's quite intuitive. However, the anatomy of these two differs slightly. Figure 10-33 shows an empty pivot chart where you can see four distinct areas. Just as in pivot tables, how you choose to utilize these areas defines both the utility and the appearance of your pivot chart.

The Data Area

The data area, identified as Drop Data Fields Here and highlighted in Figure 10-34, is the area that calculates and supplies the data points for your chart.

The Series Area

The series area, identified by the phrase Drop Series Fields Here and highlighted in Figure 10-35, is the area that makes up the *y* axis of your chart. This area is equivalent to the column area of a pivot table. In other words, if you create a pivot table and switch to PivotChart view, the fields in the column area of the pivot table will become the *y* axis series.

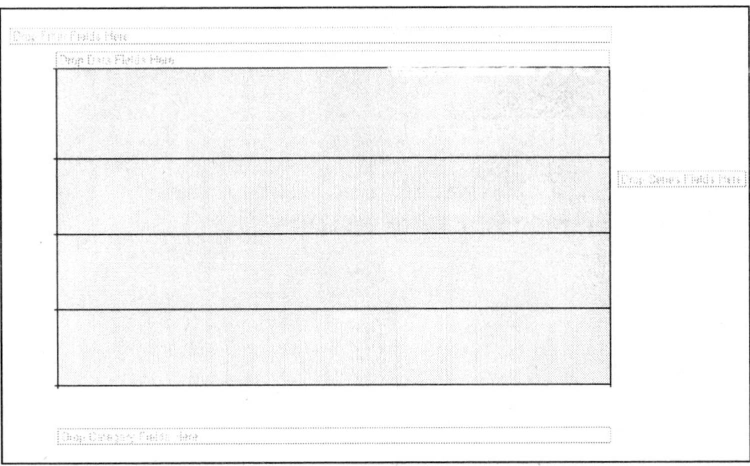

Figure 10-33: An empty pivot chart in Access.

Figure 10-34: The data area supplies the data points for your chart.

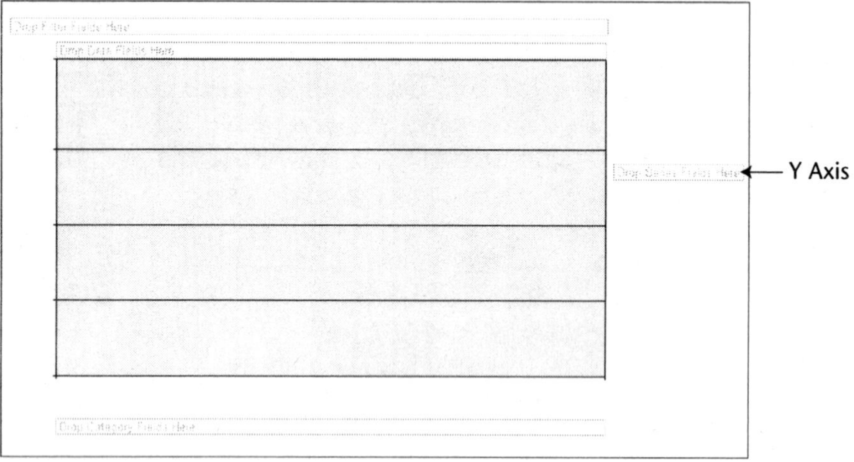

Figure 10-35: The series area makes up the *y* axis of your chart.

The Category Area

The category area, identified by the phrase Drop Category Fields Here and highlighted in Figure 10-36, is the area that makes up the *x* axis of your chart. This area is equivalent to the row area of a pivot table. In other words, if you create a pivot table and switch to PivotChart view, the fields in the row area of the pivot table will become categories in the *x* axis.

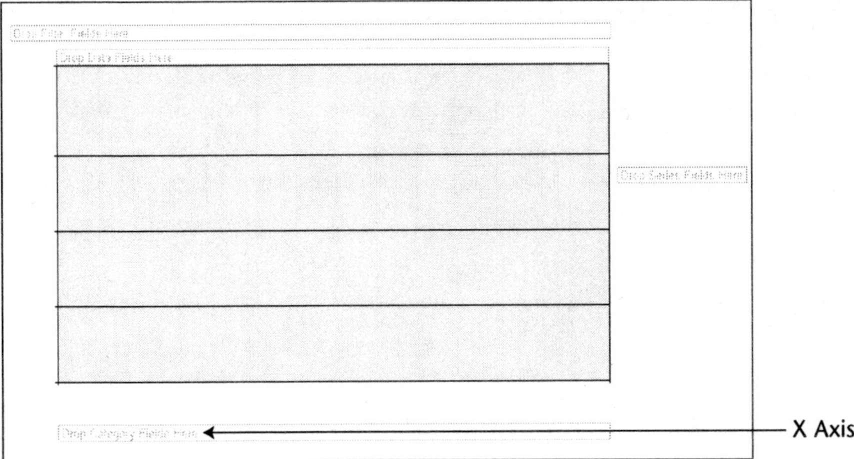

Figure 10-36: The category area makes up the *x* axis of your chart.

The Filter Area

The filter area, identified by the phrase Drop Filter Fields Here and highlighted in Figure 10-37, allows for dynamic filtering of your pivot chart based on a value in a field. This area is identical to the filter area of a pivot table.

Figure 10-37: The filter area enables you to filter your pivot chart.

Creating a Basic Pivot Chart

To create a pivot chart, start by building a query in design view, as shown in Figure 10-38, then go to the Design tab and select View → PivotChart View.

At this point, you will see an empty pivot chart, shown in Figure 10-39, and a list of fields that are in your dataset.

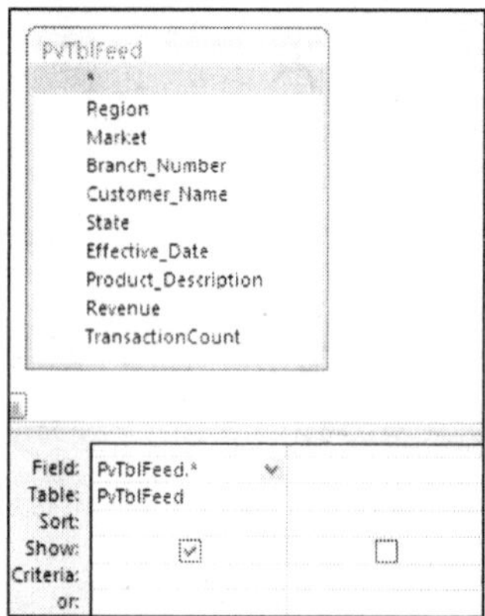

Figure 10-38: Build your query then switch to PivotChart view.

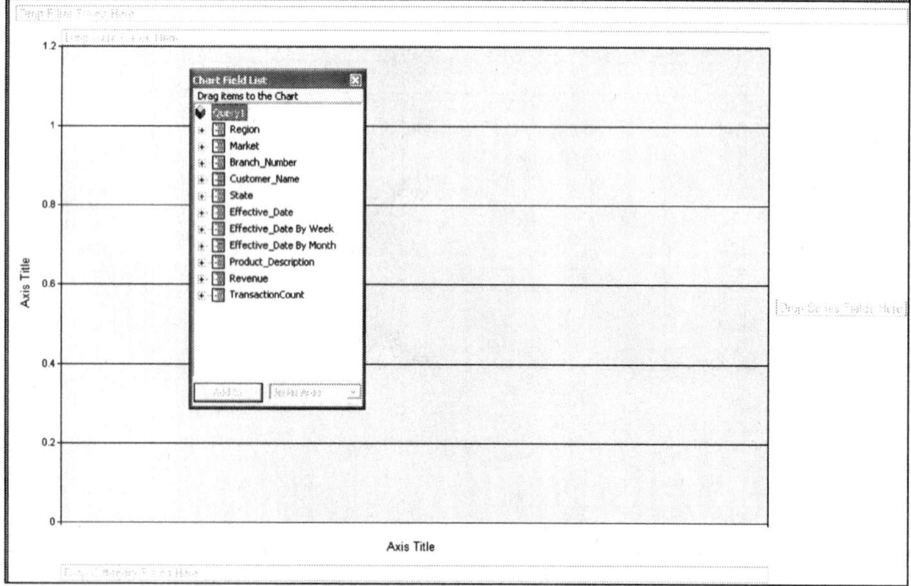

Figure 10-39: You will use the field list to build your pivot table.

Just as in a pivot table, the idea is to drag the fields you need into the pivot chart's drop areas. Build a basic chart by dragging the Revenue field to the data area, then the Market field to the category area. Finally, drag the Region field to the filter area. Your completed chart should look like the one illustrated in Figure 10-40.

NOTE **You may notice that the pivot charts produced by Access are not as polished as those Excel produces. This is because Access uses the old Office Web Component technology that was primarily designed for reporting on the Web. Excel, on the other hand, uses the slick new graphics engine that comes with Office 2007.**

Formatting Your Pivot Chart

The key to formatting a pivot chart in Access is to remember that everything revolves around property settings. Each object on the chart has its own properties that can be adjusted. To demonstrate this, right-click your pivot chart and select Properties. This opens the Properties dialog box shown in Figure 10-41. Go to the General tab.

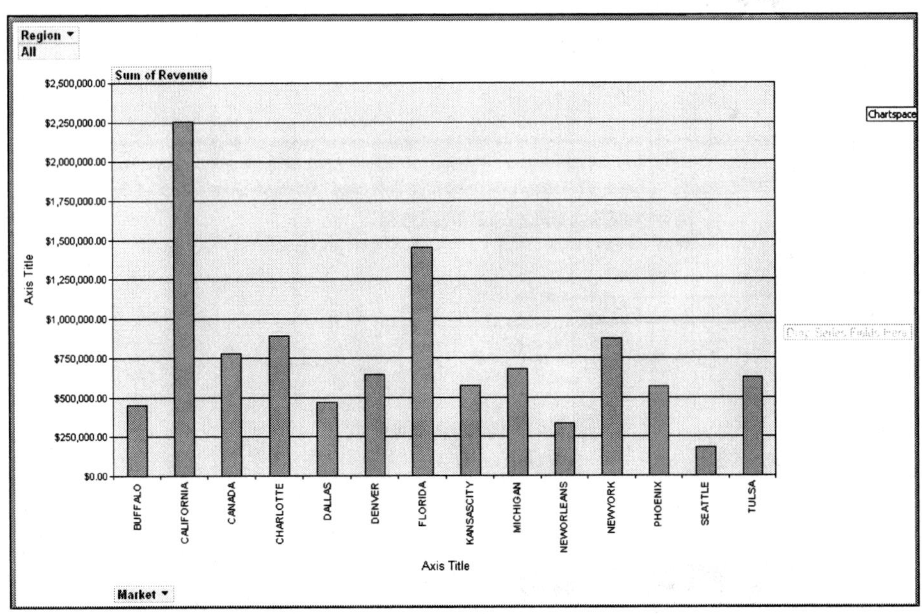

Figure 10-40: You've built your first pivot chart.

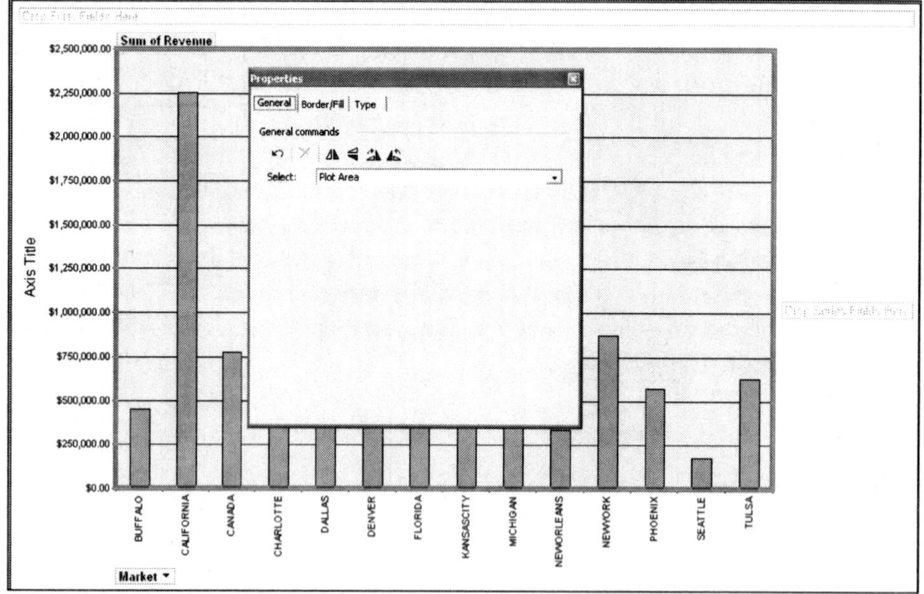

Figure 10-41: Select the General tab of the pivot chart properties dialog box.

Select the object with which you want to work in order to expose the adjustable properties. For example, if you wanted to add labels to your series, you would select Series from the Select drop-down list as demonstrated in Figure 10-42.

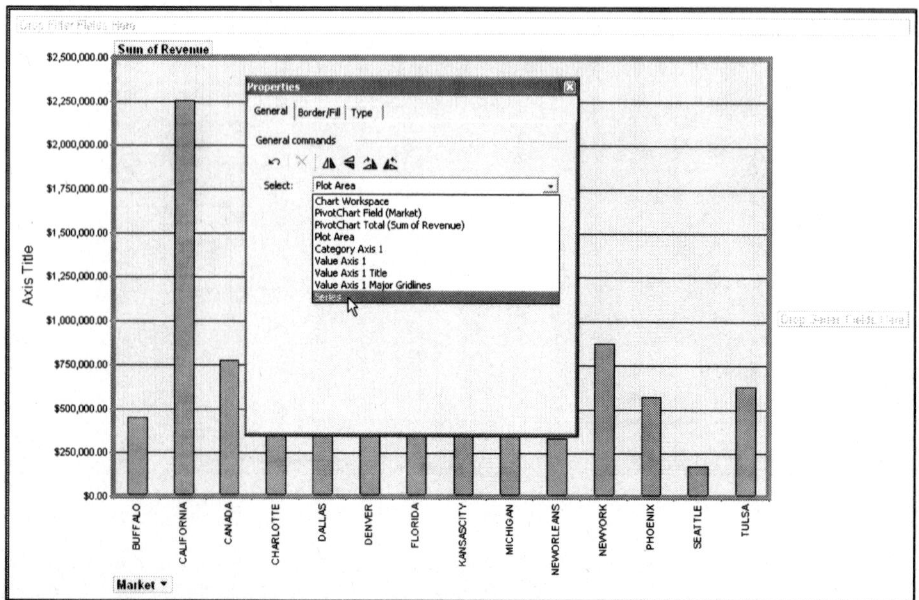

Figure 10-42: Selecting the Series object exposes its modifiable properties.

With the Series properties exposed, you can tailor its properties to suit your needs. In Figure 10-43, you are adding data labels to you pivot chart.

Of course, data labels have properties that can be modified as well. Return to the General tab of the Properties dialog box and select the series data labels you just added. As you can see in Figure 10-44, the Select drop-down list has been updated to include Series Data Labels 1.

Twenty minutes of experimenting with each object's properties will give you a solid level of proficiency at formatting pivot charts in Access.

NOTE **As of this writing, you cannot export pivot charts from Access to Excel. Again, this is due to the fact that Access and Excel use entirely different charting engines.**

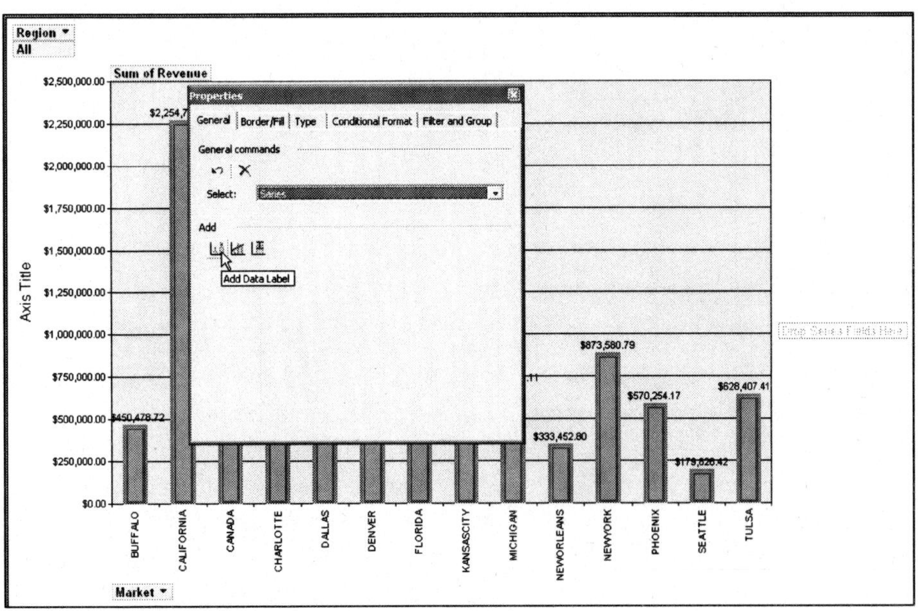

Figure 10-43: Adding Data Labels to your pivot chart.

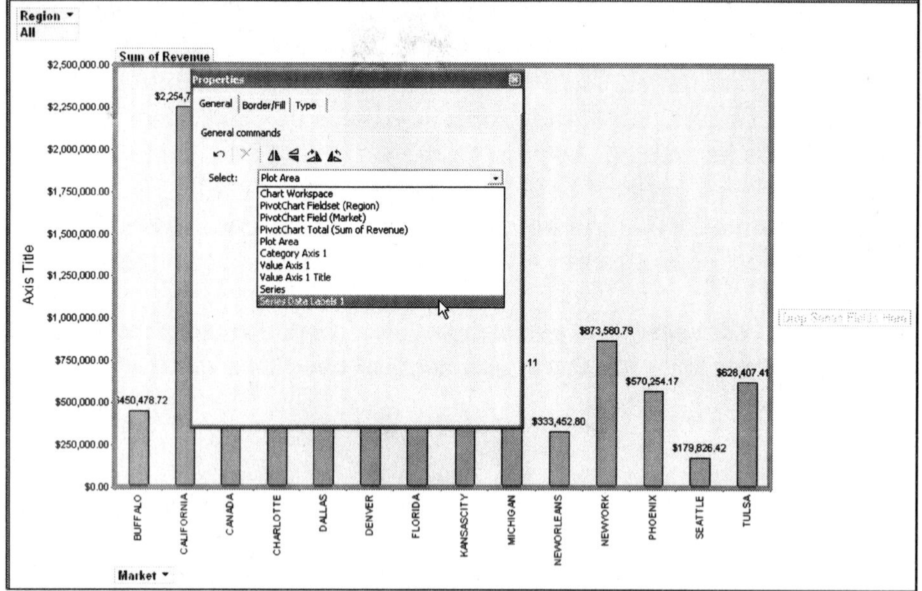

Figure 10-44: The Select drop down list is updated every time you add a new object to your chart.

Summary

From a data analysis point of view, pivot tables and pivot charts are some of the most powerful data-crunching tools found in Access. With a pivot table, you can group, summarize, and perform a wide variety of calculations in a fraction of the time it takes by hand. In addition, you can interactively change the content and shape of your analysis by dragging data fields to one area of the pivot table to another. This enables you to dynamically change your perspective, recalculate totals to fit the current view, and interactively drill down to the detail records. Pivot charts enhance your analytical tools by allowing you to display your pivot tables in chart form. By applying your knowledge of Excel pivot tables to Access, you can completely change the way you analyze your Access data.

Advanced Analysis Techniques

CHAPTER

11

Scheduling and Running Batch Analysis

In the realm of Microsoft Access, the term *automation* actually has two meanings. First, it's used to describe the computerization of a process where Access self-regulates a procedure based on predetermined requirements you supply. It is also used to define the means of manipulating another application's objects with the use of Access Visual Basic for Applications (VBA). In the context of this book, the term automation involves the former.

Access provides you with two key methods of automating your analytical processes: macros and VBA. This chapter focuses on using macros to automate your processes and run batch analysis on your data. Why should you care? Well, leveraging macro functionality is not just a cool way to use Access; it also offers the following advantages:

- **Higher productivity:** Just because you have the skills to analyze data in Access doesn't mean you have the time. With automation, you can have Access carry out redundant analyses and recurring analytical processes, leaving you free to work on other tasks.
- **Quality control:** Human beings make mistakes. The more you touch a set of analyses, the greater the chance there is for errors. Automation takes humans (you) out of the equation.

- **Reproducibility:** There's an old quip among data analysts: "It's okay to produce the wrong answer, as long as you produce the same wrong answer consistently." Although you obviously don't want to produce a wrong answer, the point is you want to be able to reproduce the analysis you have established. If your answer changes from one analysis to the next, you'll find yourself wondering whether you've done something differently. Automating your analytical processes ensures that Access executes your analyses in the same way every time.

Introduction to Access Macros

Access macros are very different from Excel macros. In Excel, macros are used as a way to record actions that can be played back when needed. Excel macros are analogous to programming a phone to dial a specific telephone number when you press a special key. In Access, however, macros are used to execute a set of pre-programmed functions, much like a list of menu options on your TV that can be fired when selected. These pre-programmed functions are called *actions*. The idea behind building a macro in Access is to choose a set of actions you want the macro to carry out when it is executed. Figure 11-1 illustrates an Access macro that carries out three actions when run.

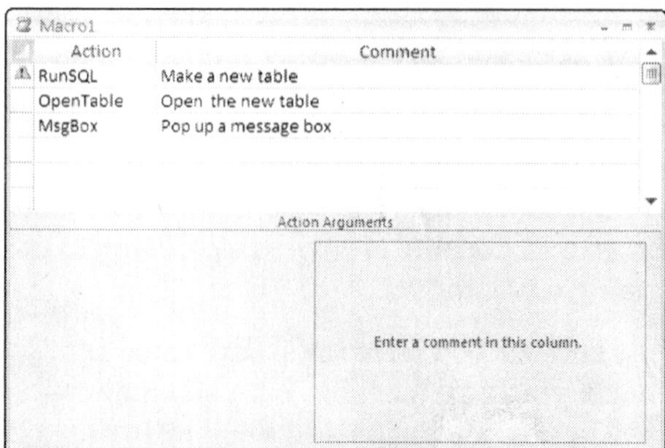

Figure 11-1: This macro runs a SQL statement that makes a new table, opens the new table, and throws up a message box.

Again, none of the actions shown in Figure 11-1 were recorded by the user. They are all actions that came pre-packaged for use in a macro.

Dealing with Access 2007 Security Features

Before jumping into your first macro, it's important to understand the new security features in Access 2007.

Access 2007 comes with over 65 macro actions that you can use in your processes. However, the new security features in Access 2007 prevent 26 of those macro actions from running unless the Access database you are working with is trusted. The term *trusted* means that you have explicitly told Access that the macros within the database are of no threat and can be run freely.

For example, when you open the sample database for this book, you should see a security message directly below the ribbon (see Figure 11-2). This message indicates that because this database is not trusted, certain actions have been disabled.

This means that certain macro actions will not run at all. For example, the macro illustrated in Figure 11-3 contains two SetWarnings macro actions. These macro actions require that the database be trusted before running properly.

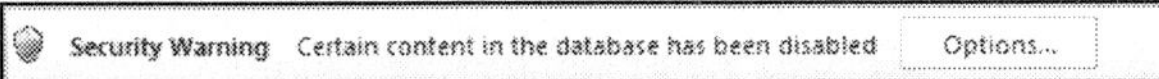

Figure 11-2: Databases that are not trusted will have certain features automatically disabled.

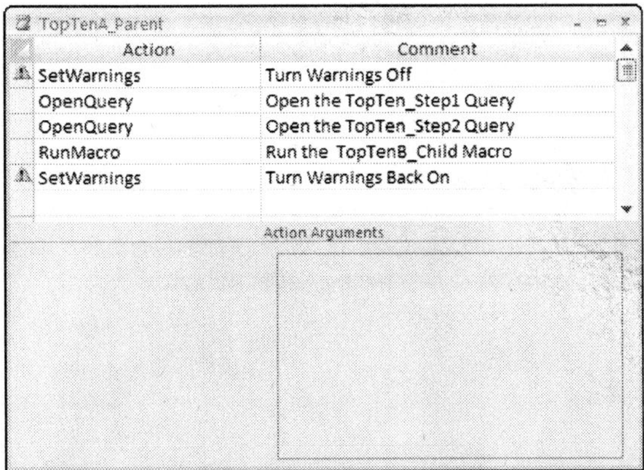

Figure 11-3: The two SetWarnings macro actions will not run in an untrusted database.

NOTE **Note that in Figure 11-3, the two SetWarnings macro actions have a triangle icon next to them. These icons alert you that the action will require a trusted database to run properly.**

Attempting to run this macro in a database that is not trusted will result in a message similar to the one shown in Figure 11-4.

TIP **The following Macro Actions require a trusted database to run: CopyDatabaseFile, CopyObject, DeleteObject, Echo, OpenDataAccessPage, OpenDiagram, OpenFunction, OpenModule, OpenStoredProcedure, OpenView, PrintOut, Quit, Rename, RunApp, RunCommand, RunSavedImportExport, RunSQL, Save, SendKeys, SetValue, SetWarnings, ShowToolbar, TransferDatabase, TransferSharePointList, TransferSpreadsheet, TransferSQLDatabase, and TransferText.**

Note that although the RunCommand macro action does not, in and of itself, require a trusted database to run, many of its arguments do.

The Quick Fix

The easy fix for a disabled database is to manually enable the content. You can do this by clicking the Options button on the security message shown in Figure 11-2. This opens the Microsoft Office Security Options dialog box. Select the Enable this content option, shown in Figure 11-5.

Keep in mind that this is a quick fix that will need to be repeated each time you open the database. For databases that you work with consistently, you will want a longer-term solution.

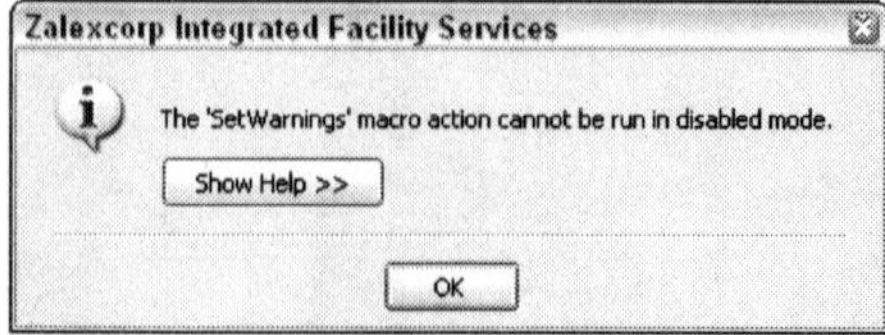

Figure 11-4: Running certain actions in an untrusted database causes an error.

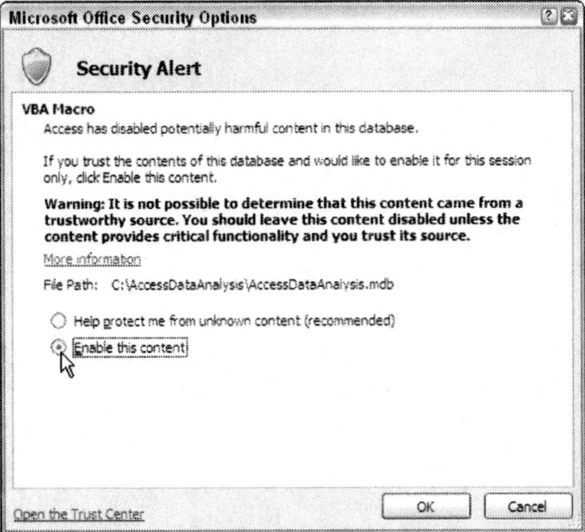

Figure 11-5: When you enable the content in a database, all macros will run fine.

The Long-Term Fix

The best way to work around the security issues in Access 2007 on a long-term basis is to use the database in a *trusted location*, a directory that is deemed a safe zone where only trusted workbooks are placed. A trusted location enables you to work with a database with no security restrictions, as long as the database is in that location.

To set up a trusted location, follow these steps:

1. Select the Office icon in the upper left-hand corner of the application window, and then select the Access Options button.
2. Click the Trust Center button, and then select Trust Center Settings.
3. Select the Trusted Locations button.
4. Select Add New Location.
5. Click Browse to specify the directory that will be considered a trusted location (such as your MyDocuments directory or Documents directory if you're using Vista).

When a trusted location is specified, all databases opened from that location are, by default, opened with macros enabled.

Creating Your First Macro

Start by initializing a new macro. To do this, select the Create tab on the ribbon and then click the Macro button. This activates the Macro window shown in Figure 11-6.

As you can see, this is essentially a grid with three columns (Action, Arguments, and Comment) and many rows. The idea is to fill each row with an action selected from the drop-down box in the Action column.

TIP **Access 2007, by default, hides any macro action that requires a trusted database to run properly. That is to say, these macro actions do not appear in the Action column drop-down boxes. Therefore, before you get started, you will want to click the Show All Actions button on the Design tab of the ribbon. This ensures that all macro actions are displayed in the Action column drop-down boxes, even those that require a trusted database.**

The first action you want to run is a `RunSQL` action, so select RunSQL from the Action drop-down box. When you select your action, you will see some new input boxes in the grey area underneath the grid. These new input boxes are called *action arguments*. Every action comes with a unique set of arguments that you can tailor to fit your needs. As you can see in Figure 11-7, the `RunSQL` action requires two arguments: SQL Statement and Use Transaction.

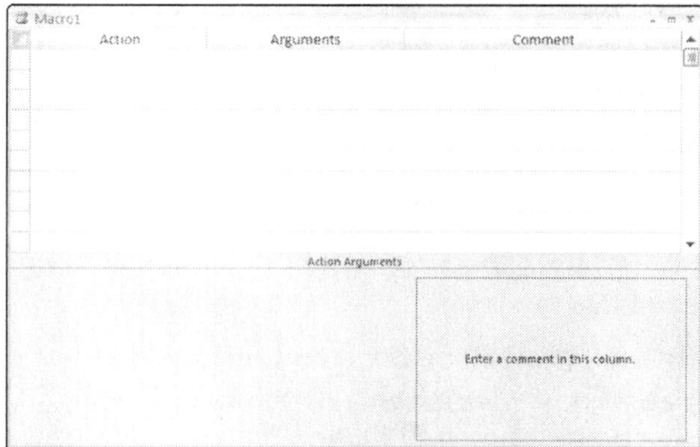

Figure 11-6: The Macro window is essentially a grid where each row defines a specified action to carry out.

Click inside the SQL Statement input field and enter **SELECT Customer_Number INTO MyTable FROM CustomerMaster**. This action runs a make-table query in order to make a new table called MyTable. In addition, enter a comment about this action in the Comment column. Although this is optional, it is generally a good practice to add comments for documentation.

TIP **When you click inside the text box for an action argument, you will see some quick tips for that argument in blue lettering in the lower-right corner of the Macro window. In addition, pressing F1 while the text box is active brings up a help file pertaining to that argument.**

Add the `OpenTable` action and enter **MyTable** in the Table Name field, as shown in Figure 11-8. This action opens the MyTable table.

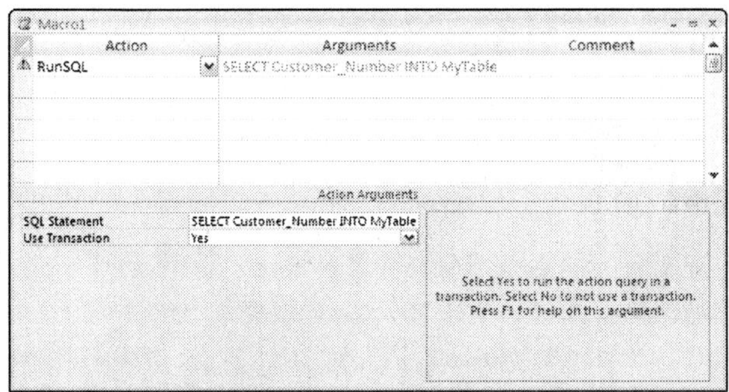

Figure 11-7: Add the `RunSQL` action and specify its arguments.

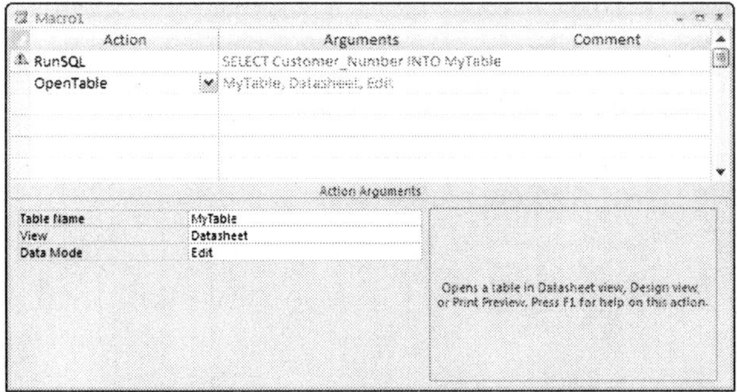

Figure 11-8: Add the `OpenTable` action and specify its arguments.

NOTE **Although there is no table called MyTable currently in the database, there will be when the `RunSQL` action runs. In the meantime, the macro doesn't care that there is no table called MyTable and will save with no problem. This illustrates the fact that, unlike VBA modules, macros don't compile to identify unrecognized objects or other errors.**

Add the `MsgBox` action and enter **Table has been created.** in the Message field, as shown in Figure 11-9. This action activates a message box.

At this point, save and close your newly created macro. Access will prompt you to give your new macro a name. When you name your macro, it will be saved in the Macros collection in your Database window. To run it, simply double-click it. If you built your macro correctly, it should paste 9,253 records into a new table called MyTable, and then open the table and throw up a message box that reads, "Table has been created."

NOTE **To edit any macro, you can simply right-click the macro and select Design View.**

Essential Macro Actions

Trying to determine which macro actions benefit the automation of your data analysis can be overwhelming. A set of 18 macro actions, however, are ideal for automating your analytical processes. When trying to familiarize yourself with the macro actions that are available to you, the actions in this section should be first on your list.

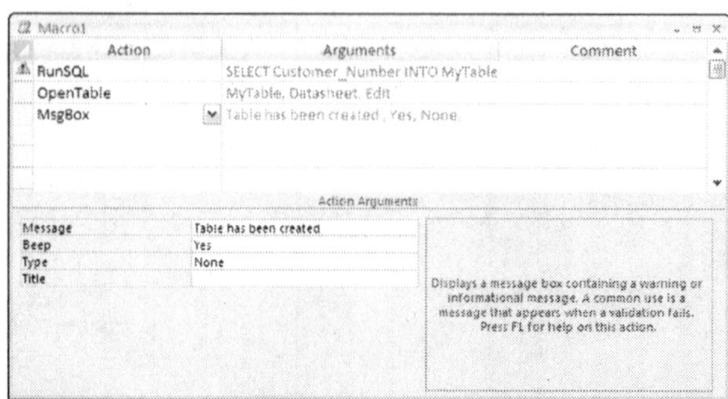

Figure 11-9: Add the `MsgBox` action and specify its arguments.

Manipulating Forms, Queries, Reports, and Tables

The following macro actions manipulate forms, queries, reports, and tables:

- **Close:** The `Close` action closes a specified form, query, report, or table. This is useful when you want to ensure that a particular object is closed before running a process.
- **DeleteObject:** The `DeleteObject` action deletes a specified form, query, report, or table. This action comes in handy when you need to delete temporary tables that you created during an analytical process. Note that this macro action requires a trusted database to run properly.
- **OpenQuery:** The `OpenQuery` action runs a specified query or, if indicated, opens the query in Design view. The action is typically used to string multiple `OpenQuery` actions together in order to run a series of queries, effectively running a batch analysis.
- **OpenForm:** The `OpenForm` action opens a specified form. This action can be used to open a form that supplies the values needed for your analytical process.
- **OpenReport** and **OpenTable:** The `OpenReport` and `OpenTable` actions enable you to open a specified report and table, respectively. These are useful for presenting a final result after your batch analysis.

The Access Environment

The following macro actions affect the Access environment:

- **Quit:** The `Quit` action closes the entire Access application. This action comes in handy when you are running a scheduled process and you want to close the application when the macro has finished executing. Note that this macro action requires a trusted database to run properly.
- **SetWarnings:** The `SetWarnings` action forces an OK or Yes response to all system messages, effectively suppressing message pop-ups while a macro runs. Without the `SetWarnings` action, you would have to be there to click Yes or OK on every confirmation message that popped up while your macro was running. Note that this macro action requires a trusted database to run properly.

Executing Processes

The following macro actions control the execution of processes:

- **RunCode:** The `RunCode` action executes an existing VBA function. This action is ideal when you need to initialize a procedure that can only be accomplished with VBA, such as automating Excel.
- **RunMacro:** The `RunMacro` action executes another macro. This action can be used in a conditional macro where the resulting decision requires that another macro be executed.
- **RunSQL:** The `RunSQL` action executes a valid SQL string. Bear in mind that only `Insert`, `Delete`, `Select...Into`, or `Update` statements are valid in the macro environment. This action comes in handy when you need to run action queries, but you don't want to inundate your database with superfluous query objects. Note that this macro action requires a trusted database to run properly.
- **StopMacro:** The `StopMacro` stops the current macro. You can use this action in a conditional macro where the resulting decision indicates no further processing is needed.

Outputting Data

The following macro actions export or output data:

- **PrintOut:** The `PrintOut` action prints the active datasheet, form, or report. This action is ideal for ensuring that a hardcopy of analytical results are produced. Note that this macro action requires a trusted database to run properly.
- **OutputTo:** The `OutputTo` action outputs a table, query, form, or report to an external document. Output options include outputting to Excel, Word, HTML, or text. Note that this action is memory intensive and does not work well with very large datasets.
- **TransferDatabase:** The `TransferDatabase` action exports and imports data to and from an external database. This action is ideal for backing up your database to an external location. You can even schedule nightly backups of your data using this macro action. Note that this macro action requires a trusted database to run properly.

- **TransferSpreadsheet and TransferText:** The `TransferSpreadsheet` and `TransferText` actions export and import data to and from external spreadsheets and text files, respectively. These actions are equivalent to the Export menu option in Access, saving the data into a file. Note that these macro actions require a trusted database to run properly.
- **SendObject:** The `SendObject` action outputs an object to an Excel, text, or HTML file, then attaches that file to an e-mail message that can be sent to specified addresses with additional text. This action works with any 32-bit e-mail program that conforms to Mail Application Programming Interface (MAPI) standards.

Setting Up and Managing Batch Analysis

An analytical process involves a series of queries that run in a logical order, giving you the needed set of analyses. A batch analysis is nothing more than automating the execution of one or more of your analytical processes. In this section, you learn how to set up and manage your own automated batch analysis.

Getting Organized

Creating a batch analysis is as simple as defining which queries and actions you need to run. This involves pointing your macro to specific objects. However, if your database is inundated with temporary queries and tables, or queries that have no logical name or order, it becomes difficult to determine which object does what, let alone point a macro to the right set of objects. That being said, there are a few things you can do to ensure that you keep your database organized.

Using a Logical Naming Convention

The long-standing guideline on using naming conventions in Access is that you preface each type of object in your database with a prefix describing that object. For example, an appropriate name for a query would be *qryMonthlyRevenue*, a table could be called *tblCustomers*, and a form could be named *frmMain*.

What you are about to read will be considered blasphemy in many Access circles, but the fact is that this is not always the best-naming convention you can use.

The database in Figure 11-10 is a good example. This database contains 15 queries that make up two separate analytical processes. As you can see, it's difficult to determine which query belongs to which process.

Adding *qry* to each query, as shown in Figure 11-11, doesn't help much in this situation.

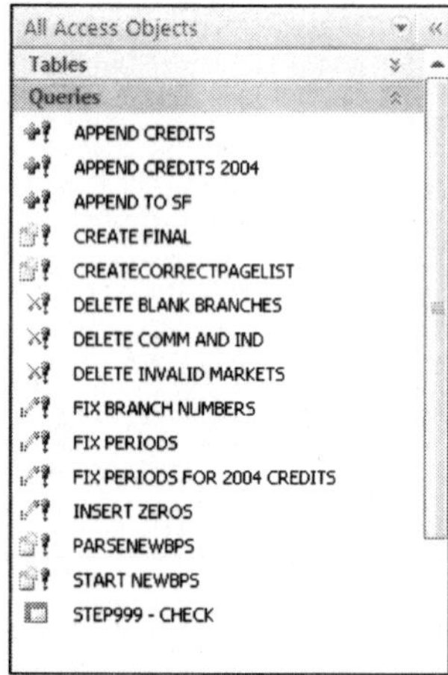

Figure 11-10: It's difficult to determine which query belongs to which analytical process.

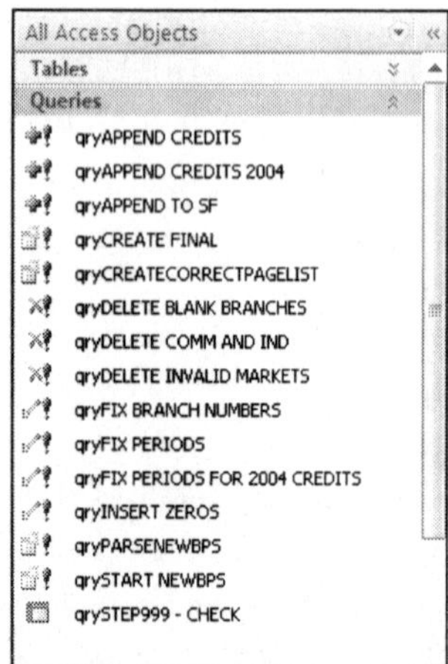

Figure 11-11: Prefixing each query with qry does not clear things up at all.

So, what do you do? In a database that is used primarily for data analysis, the best way to organize your queries is to take advantage of the fact that the default sort order is alphabetical. Preface your query names with text describing the analysis followed by a logical numbering system. For example, instead of AppendCredits, you could use PSmry_2A_AppendCredits. Figure 11-12 demonstrates this naming convention. Keep in mind that there is nothing special about the prefix *PSmry*; it is simply a description that allows for easy recognition of the analyses that have to do with creating the period summary.

NOTE **Note the use of the underscore in place of spaces. It's generally a good practice not to use spaces in your object names in order to avoid complications when writing SQL strings or using VBA code.**

You should also make your object names *upper camel case,* meaning that the first letter of each word is capitalized. This makes your object names easier to read. Figure 11-13 demonstrates this naming convention.

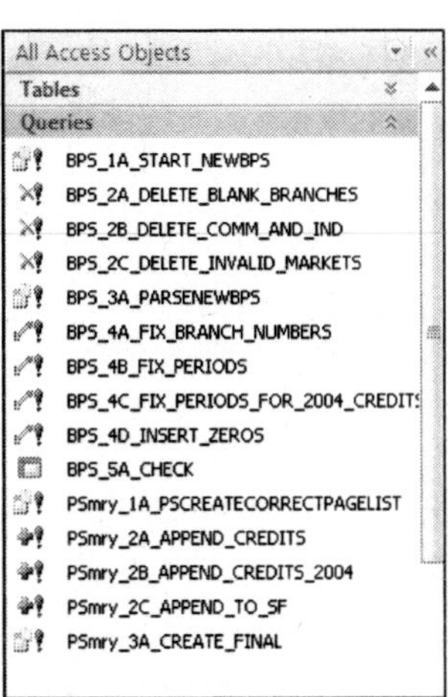

Figure 11-12: With this naming convention, you cannot only distinguish between the two analyses, but you can see the correct order each query should be run.

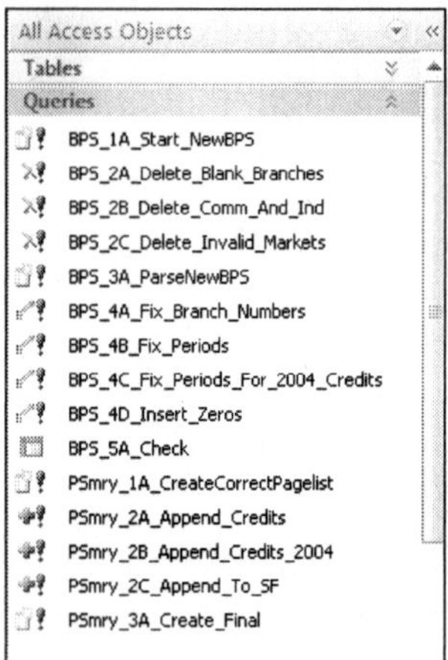

Figure 11-13: Using camel case makes your object names easier to read.

Using the Description Property

Each object has a Description property that you use to describe the object in detail. To adjust an object's Description property, right-click the object and select Properties. This opens a properties dialog box for that object, as shown in Figure 11-14. You can use up to 250 characters to describe the object.

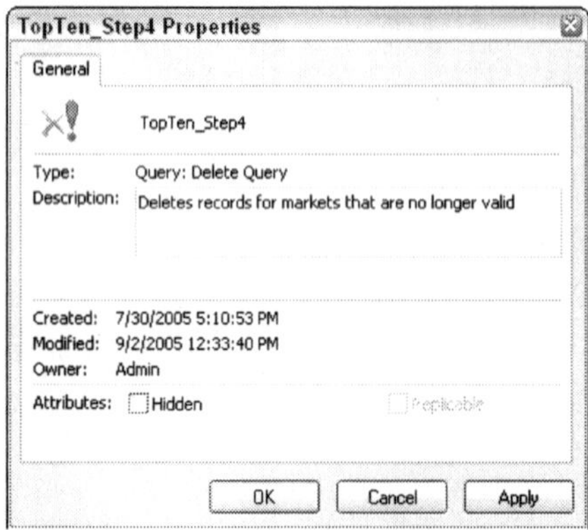

Figure 11-14: Use the Description property to describe the object in detail.

Now you can change your database view to show descriptions along with the names and other details of your Access objects. To do so, right-click the title bar of the navigation pane and select View By → Details as demonstrated in Figure 11-15.

This shows you a series of details to include the description you entered. Figure 11-16 shows a database in Details view.

Setting Up a Basic Batch Analysis

Setting up a basic batch analysis involves little more than creating a macro that executes a set of analytical processes in a logical order conducive to your analysis. For example, the database in Figure 11-17 is used to run three queries that work together to accomplish a set of analytics.

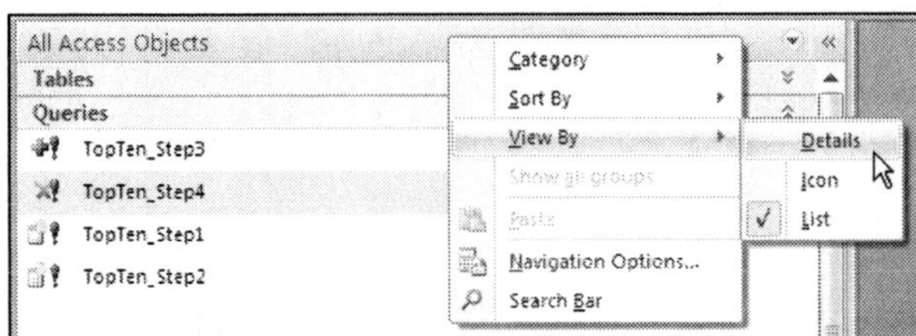

Figure 11-15: Change the view of your navigation pane to show details.

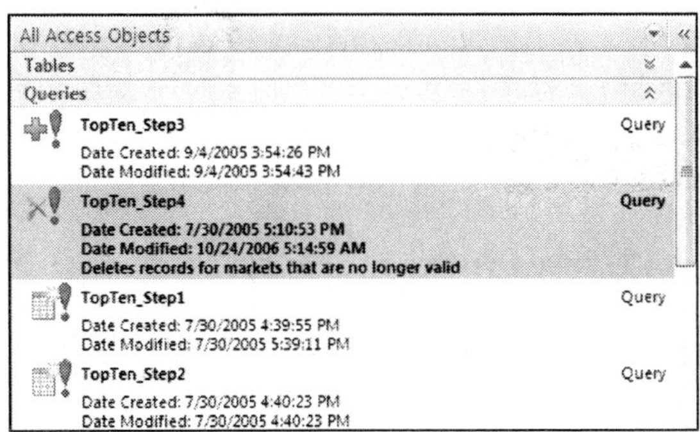

Figure 11-16: You can now see the description you added.

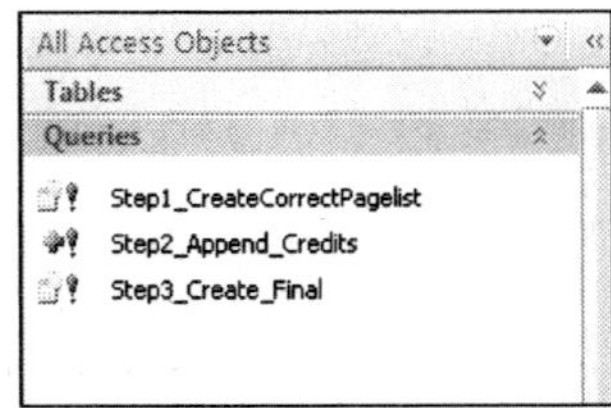

Figure 11-17: These three queries make up a simple analytical process.

The macro being built in Figure 11-18 starts with a `SetWarnings` action to ensure that no system messages interrupt the process. From here, it's simply a question of adding the queries that need to be executed in order.

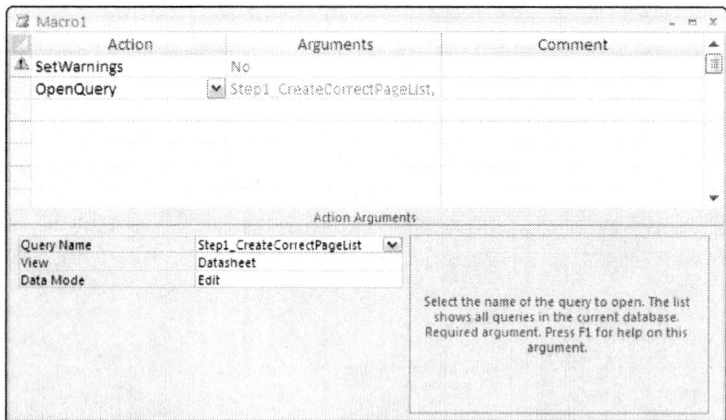

Figure 11-18: Building a macro to automate the execution of the three queries.

TIP **Instead of selecting queries from the argument drop-down list as shown in Figure 11-18, you can drag your queries into the Macro window. This enters an `OpenQuery` action for that query.**

After all queries are added, a second `SetWarnings` action is called to reinstate system messages, and then a `Msgbox` is thrown up to indicate completion of the macro. The completed macro, shown in Figure 11-19, is then saved and run as a batch analysis.

TIP **The Arguments column you see in Figure 11-19 was added to Access 2007 so you can see the arguments of each macro action without having to select each action. You can choose to hide this column by clicking the Arguments button on the Design tab.**

You can even create a macro that runs multiple batch analyses at once. The Big 5 Analysis macro, shown in Figure 11-20, runs five macros, each of which executes its own batch analysis.

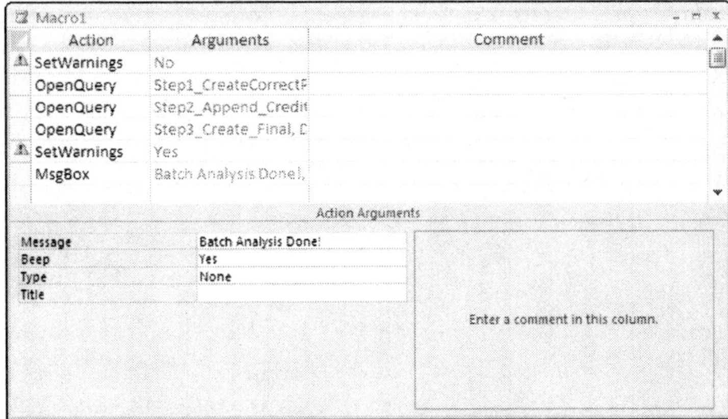

Figure 11-19: When completed and saved, the macro can be run anytime as a batch analysis.

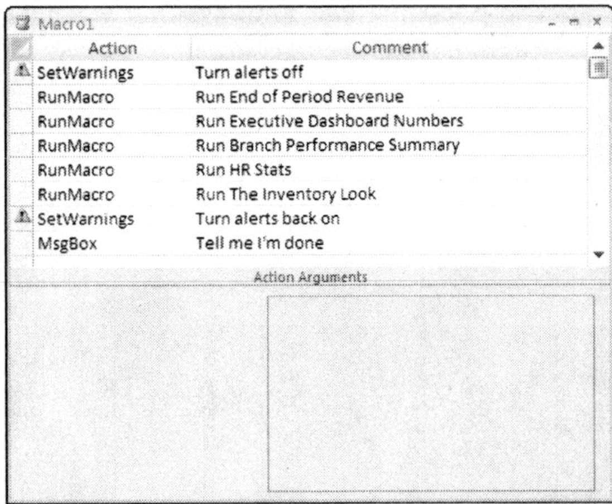

Figure 11-20: You can create a master macro to run all your batch analyses at once.

Building Smarter Macros

Did you know that you can use `If...Then...Else` statements through a macro? Well, not exactly, but you can simulate that decision-making functionality by building conditions into your macros. A *condition* is a logical expression that is evaluated in order to return a `True` or `False` answer. With conditions, you simulate an `If...Then` scenario or even an `If...Then...Else` scenario.

Simulating If...Then

To demonstrate how to build a basic `If...Then` scenario, you will write a simple macro that will analyze a number entered into an Input Box and then make a decision based on that number. Start by building the macro shown in Figure 11-21. Note that the Message argument for the `MsgBox` action is "That number is over 10."

Now go up to the Design tab on the application ribbon and click the Conditions button. At this point, your Macro window should look similar to the one shown in Figure 11-22. As you can see, a column called Condition has been unhidden. The idea is to enter an expression here that will evaluate as `True` or `False`. If the expression evaluates as `True`, then the action next to it will be executed.

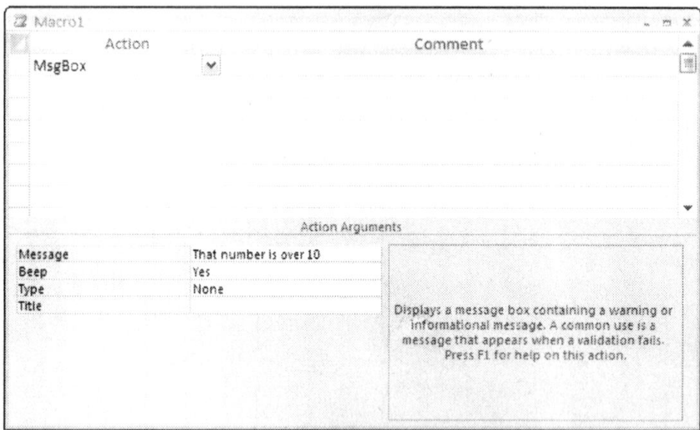

Figure 11-21: Start a new macro with one `MsgBox` action.

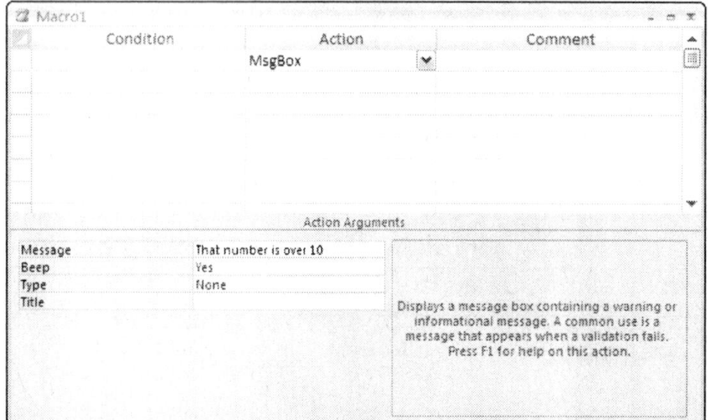

Figure 11-22: The Condition column is hidden by default until you explicitly unhide it.

Enter the following expression: **InputBox("Enter any number")>10**. Your Macro window should look similar to the one shown in Figure 11-23. This expression activates an input box and asks you to enter a number. The number you enter will then be evaluated to determine if it is greater than 10. If the number you enter is greater than 10, the expression returns a `True` answer, otherwise, it will return a `False` answer.

NOTE **The `InputBox` function enables you to get information from a user. You can think of it as a `MsgBox` in reverse. A `Msgbox` function outputs information, whereas an `InputBox` accepts information.**

Close the macro and save it as **Macro1**. When you run the macro, you will see the input box shown in Figure 11-24. If you enter a number less than or equal to 10, nothing will happen. If you enter a number greater than 10, a message will pop up telling you your number is greater than 10.

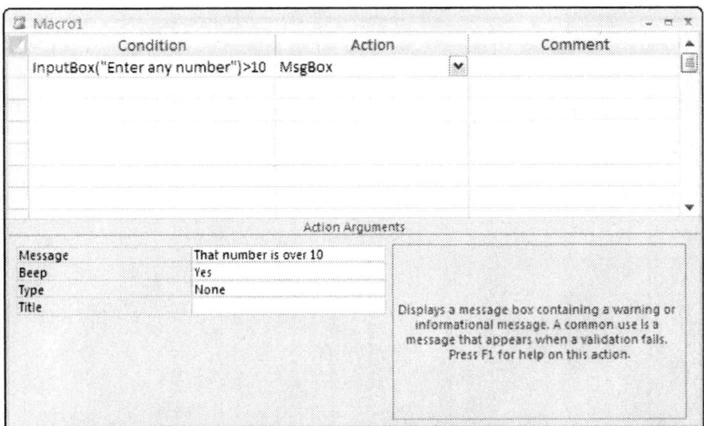

Figure 11-23: This expression evaluates the number you enter to determine whether it is greater than 10.

Figure 11-24: Running the macro activates an input box where you enter your chosen number.

Simulating If...Then...Else

You can expand the scope of your conditions by adding `If... Then...Else` functionality. To demonstrate this, create a new macro and unhide the Condition column. Then, enter the following condition in the first row: **InputBox("Guess How Many Locations There are")=DCount("[Branch_Number]","[LocationMaster]")**.

With this condition, you are comparing the user's input to the number of records in the LocationMaster table. If the two are equal, the expression evaluates as `True`. Select `Beep` as the action, and your Macro window should look similar to Figure 11-25.

On the next two lines, enter three periods (also called an *ellipsis*) as the condition. Any macro action that has an ellipsis as the condition will be run only if the preceding condition evaluated as `True`; otherwise, those actions will be skipped.

Select the `MsgBox` action, and then select the `StopMacro` action. Note that the Message argument for `MsgBox` is "That's Right". At this point, your Macro window should look similar to the one shown in Figure 11-26.

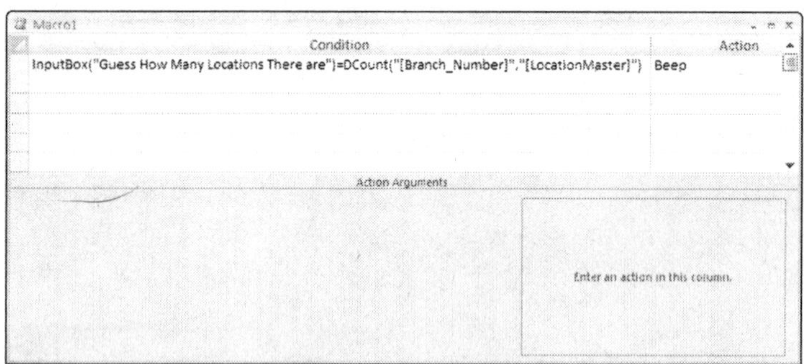

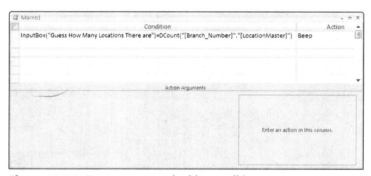

Figure 11-25: Start a macro and add a condition.

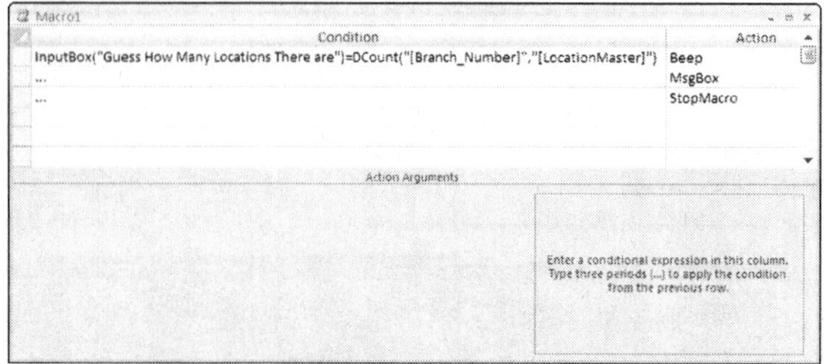

Figure 11-26: Using an ellipsis in the Condition inputs tells the macros to execute the action on that line only if the condition in the preceding line is True.

On the next line, select the `MsgBox` action, and enter "The Answer is 59." in the Message argument. On the line below that, select the `RunMacro` Action and enter "ConditionalMacro" as the Macro Name argument.

At this point, your Macro window should look similar to the one shown in Figure 11-27. Notice that there are no ellipses in the condition inputs of the newly added actions. This is because you don't want these actions to run if the correct answer was selected.

Make sure to save the macro and name it **ConditionalMacro**.

Now take moment to consider what will happen when you run this macro.

1. It will give you an input box where you will guess how many locations there are. It will then compare your answer to the real record count from the LocationMaster table. *If* your answer matches the real record count, *then* it will do steps 2 and 3; or *else* it will skip to step 4. As you can see, this essentially gives you the `IF...THEN...ELSE` effect. *If* your answer matches the actual record count, *then* the macro performs steps 2 and 3; *else* the macro will skip to step 4.
2. If your macro goes to step 2, it means you got the answer right. A message box will be thrown up to tell you so.
3. The macro stops.
4. If your macro goes directly to step 4, it means you got the answer wrong. A message box will be thrown up to tell you the correct answer.
5. The macro is run again to give you another chance.

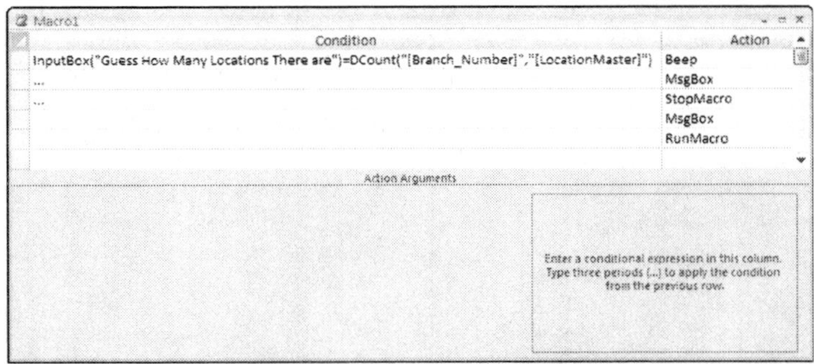

Figure 11-27: Notice that you are not using the ellipsis in the Condition inputs for your newly added actions. This means that these actions will only be run if you did not enter the correct answer in Input Box.

You have successfully built a macro that will execute actions based on a condition. Beyond that, however, this example also demonstrates a functionality that adds even more value to macros: looping.

Looping with Macros

First, your trustworthy author has to confess that the phrase "looping with macros" is admittedly a tad misleading. *Looping* implies that the macro's actions are continuously being run in the same instance of execution. What is really happening is that the macro is being started repeatedly until a condition is met. However, the fact that you can simulate looping behavior through macros does open up some interesting possibilities for those of you who are not yet comfortable with VBA.

To demonstrate the concept of a looping macro, imagine that you have been asked to provide a list of the top ten customers by market at the end of every month. Instead of running a top values query for each market by hand every month, you decide to use macros to automate the process. For this particular scenario, you will need four queries and two macros.

TIP **You can find a working version of the example illustrated here in the sample database for this book at** `www.wiley.com`**. Refer to the sample database if you run into problems.**

1. Create the make-table query shown in Figure 11-28. Name the table being created **TopTenList**. Running this query creates an empty table that will eventually contain the final results. Be sure to save this query as **TopTen_Step1**.

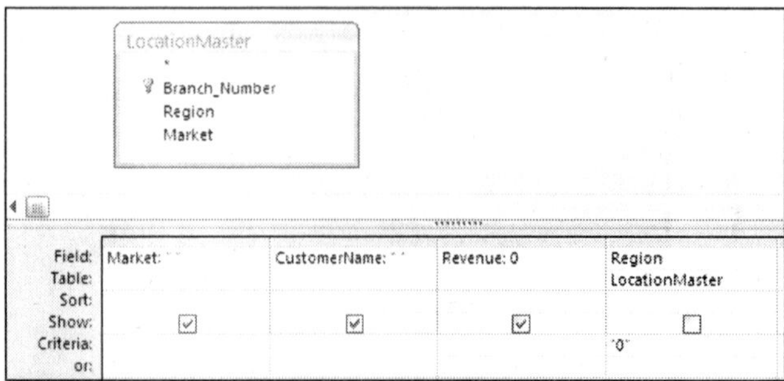

Figure 11-28: Save this make-table query as TopTen_Step1.

NOTE **Run the query you created in Step 1 at least one time. You will need the table it creates for Step 3.**

2. Create the make-table query shown in Figure 11-29. Name the table being created **LoopList**. Running this query will create a list of unique market names that will be used to loop through. Be sure to save this query as **TopTen_Step2**.

NOTE **Run the query you created in Step 2 at least one time. You will need the table it creates for Step 4.**

3. Create the append query shown in Figure 11-30. You will append to the TopTenList table you created in Step 1. Note that the Top Values property has been set to 10 in order to return only the top ten values. Also note the criteria under Market. This criterion ensures that only one market is included in the query: the one whose first letter is closest to the letter A. Be sure to save this query as **TopTen_Step3**.

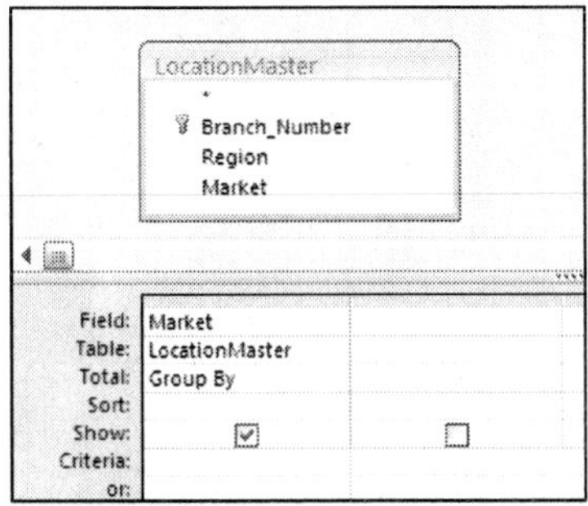

Figure 11-29: Save this make-table query as TopTen_Step2.

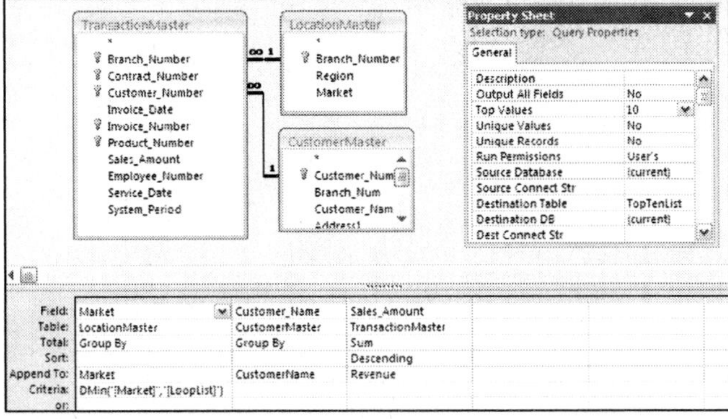

Figure 11-30: Save this append query as TopTen_Step3.

4. Create the delete query shown in Figure 11-31. Running this query deletes the market whose first letter is closest to the letter A from the LoopList. This ensures that the market can never again be used in the TopTen_Step3 query. If you ran this query 14 times, you would eventually run out of markets. Be sure to save this query as **TopTen_Step4**.
5. Start a new macro and add the following actions:
   - **SetWarnings:** Set the Warnings No argument to No.
   - **OpenQuery:** Set the Query Name argument to TopTen_Step1.
   - **OpenQuery:** Set the Query Name argument to TopTen_Step2.
   - **RunMacro:** Set the Macro Name argument to TopTenB_Child.
   - **SetWarnings:** Set the Warnings No argument to Yes.

   This macro does the setup work, creating the tables necessary for the looping action. When the tables are created, it calls the child macro, TopTenB_Child.

   Be sure to save this query as **TopTenA_Parent**. At this point, your Macro window should look similar to the one shown in Figure 11-32.

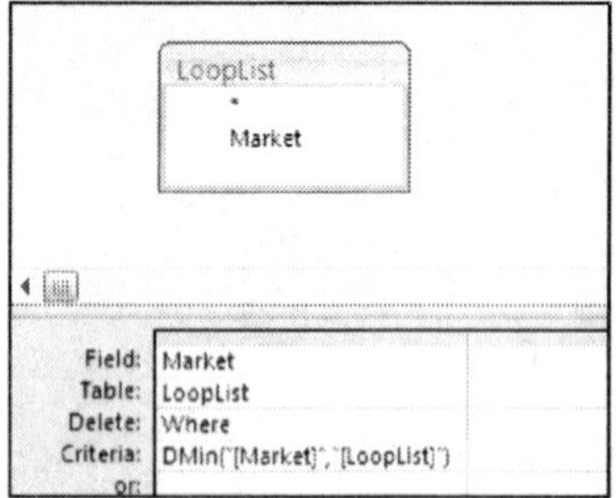

Figure 11-31: Save this delete query as TopTen_Step4.

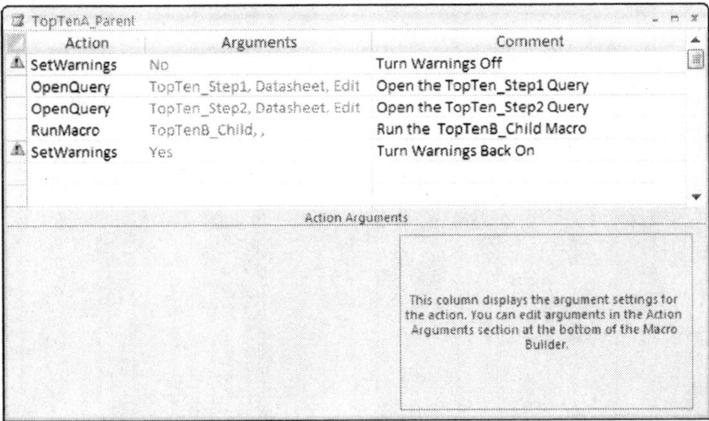

Figure 11-32: Save this macro as TopTenA_Parent.

6. Start a new macro and add the following actions:
   - **Beep:** Set the Condition to DCount("[Market]","[LoopList]")>0. This condition specifies that the record count of the Looplist table must be greater than zero in order to continue with the actions that have the ellipsis condition.
   - **SetWarnings:** Give this action an ellipsis condition. Set the Warnings No argument to No.
   - **OpenQuery:** Give this action an ellipsis condition. Set the Query Name argument to TopTen_Step3.
   - **OpenQuery:** Give this action an ellipsis condition. Set the Query Name argument to TopTen_Step4.
   - **RunMacro:** Give this action an ellipsis condition. Set the Macro Name argument to TopTenB_Child. This action starts the macro over. The idea is that this macro will repeatedly start over until the condition in the first line of the macro is false.
   - **DeleteObject:** This is the first action that runs when the condition in the first line of the macro is false. Set the ObjectType argument to Table and the Object Name argument to LoopList. This action deletes the LoopList table as it is no longer needed.
   - **SetWarnings:** Set the Warnings No argument to Yes.

- **MsgBox:** Set the Message argument to Top Ten Customers by Market can now be found in the TopTenList table.
- **StopMacro:** This action is used as a clean sweep to ensure no rogue macro actions are still executing.

When you are done, your Macro window should look similar to the one shown in Figure 11-33. Be sure to save this query as **TopTenB_Child**.

7. There is nothing left to do but run the macro. Double-click the TopTenA_Parent macro to start the loop. After the macro is done, you will get a message telling you that you can find your results in the TopTenList table. Open the table to see the results.

You may be thinking that this is a lot of work. However, remember that you are not only performing some hefty analytics on 14 markets with a click of the mouse, but now that this process is built, you can run it whenever you need to.

TIP **Instead of using the `OpenQuery` action in your macro, which requires that you create a query object, you can use a SQL statement in a `RunSQL` action. This can help you cut back on the number of superfluous queries in your database.**

Keep in mind that the SQL statements used in `RunSQL` actions cannot be more than 256 characters in length.

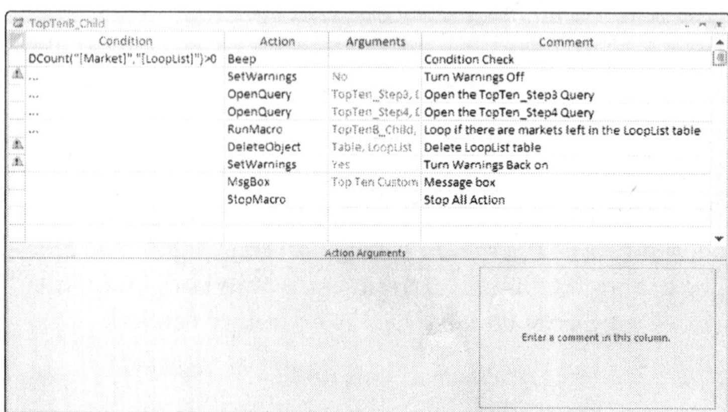

Figure 11-33: Save this macro as TopTenB_Child.

Scheduling Macros to Run Nightly

Although automating a process to run with a click of the mouse is impressive, the ultimate in automation is not even being there. How many times have you heard someone say, "Yeah, I just run a nightly routine" while you nod your head and pretend to know what that means. Meanwhile, you're trudging into work at 5 a.m. to make sure you have the reports ready by eight. The good news is that there is an easy way to schedule your macros to run every night, every Monday, on the 15th of every month, or whenever you like.

Unfortunately, as of Office 2003, Access does not yet have an internal macro scheduler. Until the time it does, you can use the Windows Task Scheduler to schedule a macro to run at specific times. The question is, how do you tell Access which macro to run through a completely unrelated program (Windows Task Scheduler)? You have two options: use an AutoExec macro or use a command-line switch.

Using an AutoExec Macro to Schedule Tasks

If you name a macro AutoExec, that macro will be run automatically when your database is opened. How does that help you? The idea is to create a macro that contains your batch analysis and save it as AutoExec. When the Windows Task Scheduler opens your database at 3:00 a.m., the AutoExec automatically executes your batch analysis.

To demonstrate this, create the macro shown in Figure 11-34. The `MsgBox` action with the Message argument set to read "A bunch of actions are executed" represents a batch analysis. Using the `Quit` action makes certain that the database closes once the macro completes execution. Save your newly created macro as **AutoExec**.

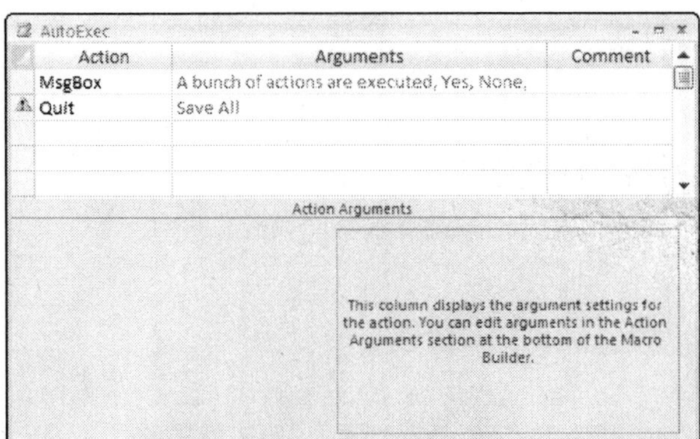

Figure 11-34: Create this macro and save it as AutoExec.

TIP **If you need to run multiple batch analyses, you can create a master macro that runs other macros, and then save it as AutoExec.**

When you save your macro as AutoExec, close the database to test it. When you open your database again, you should see the message box you entered into the AutoExec; then the database closes. Now you are ready to schedule your newly created macro with the Windows Task Scheduler.

TIP **How do you get back into your database? Simply hold down the Shift key while you open the database. This prevents the AutoExec macro from running.**

You may be tempted to remove the `Quit` **action from your macro, but keep in mind that during a nightly routine, you want the database to close automatically. Removing the** `Quit` **action will cause the database to stay open.**

Keep in mind that the Quit action will only run if the database is trusted as per the new security features highlighted earlier in this chapter.

Using the Windows Task Scheduler

Open the Windows Control Panel by clicking the Start button, then selecting Setting, and then Control Panel. Once you are in Control Panel, find and double-click the Scheduled Tasks icon, shown in Figure 11-35.

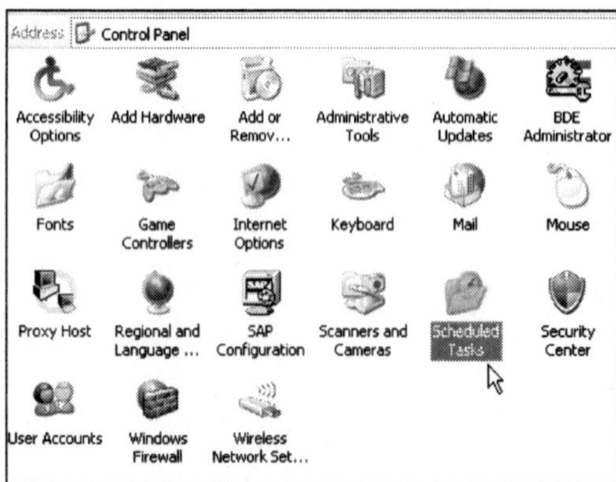

Figure 11-35: Double-click Scheduled Tasks.

NOTE **If your Control Panel is in category view, you can get to Windows Task Scheduler by selecting Performance and Maintenance → Scheduled Tasks.**

When you are in the Scheduled Tasks folder, double-click the Add Scheduled Task icon to activate the Scheduled Task Wizard shown in Figure 11-36, and then click Next.

The next window, shown in Figure 11-37, asks you to select the program you would like to run. Select Microsoft Office Access 2007 from the program list, and then click the Next button.

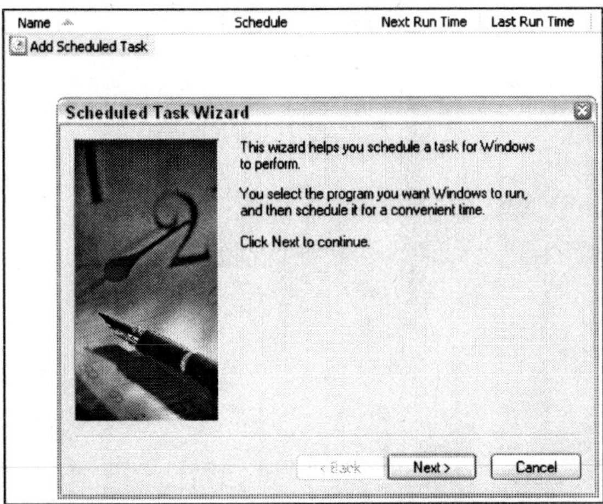

Figure 11-36: Activate the Scheduled Task Wizard and then click the Next button.

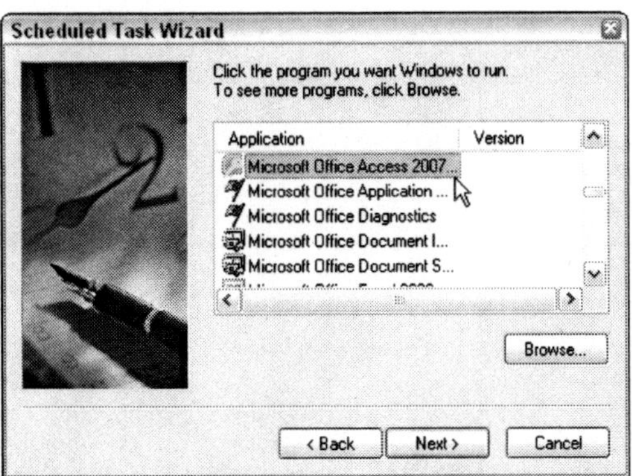

Figure 11-37: Select Microsoft Access from the program list, and then click Next.

At this point, you will see the window shown in Figure 11-38, where you will name your scheduled task and specify when you want the task to be performed. In this example, the task will be performed daily.

In the next window, you will set up the time and interval for the task. In the example illustrated in Figure 11-39, the task will be performed at 3:00 a.m. every day, starting on March 1, 2007.

TIP **Spend some time playing with the controls here. You will quickly realize that you have a wide array of options when scheduling a task.**

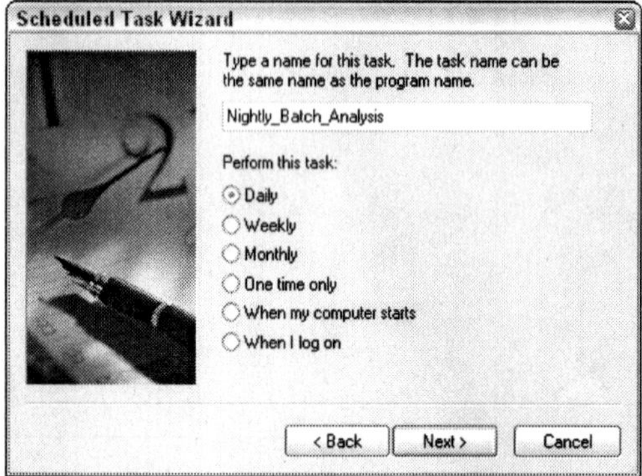

Figure 11-38: Specify when you want the task to be performed, and then click the Next button.

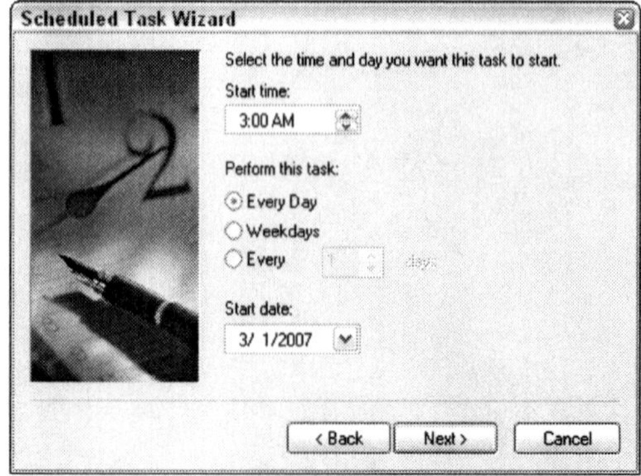

Figure 11-39: Indicate the time and interval you want the task to be performed, and then click Next.

In the next window, shown in Figure 11-40, you will have to enter the user ID and password you use to log in. This is important, as the scheduled task will not run without it.

WARNING **The Windows Task Scheduler does not keep track of expired or changed passwords. You will have to reconfigure your task if you change your password.**

When you get to Figure 11-41, you're almost done. Select the check box Open advanced properties for this task when I click Finish.

TIP **If you accidentally click Finish before selecting the advanced properties check box, you can get back to the advanced properties by simply right-clicking your task and selecting Properties.**

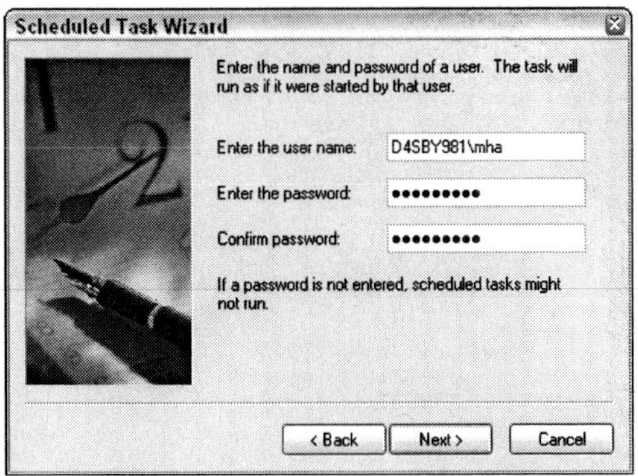

Figure 11-40: Enter your security information, and then click the Next button.

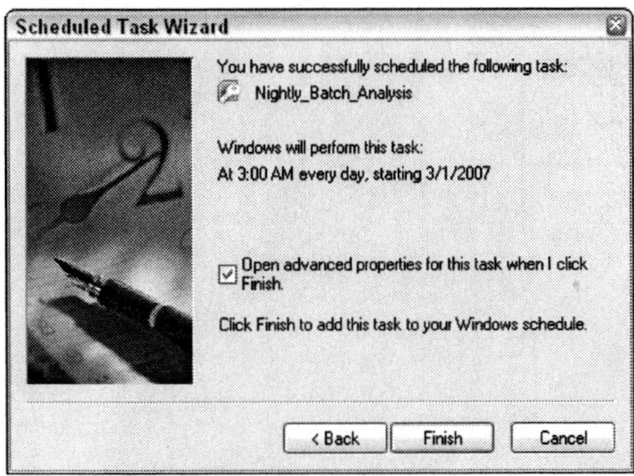

Figure 11-41: Select the advanced properties check box, and then click Finish.

The last step is to click the Browse button, shown in Figure 11-42, and point the Scheduler to the database that contains the AutoExec macro.

NOTE **Be sure to change the Files of Type setting to All Files (*.*) in the Browse dialog box.**

Now you can test the task to make sure it runs properly by right-clicking its name and selecting Run, as demonstrated in Figure 11-43.

Your task is now scheduled. One thing to keep in mind is that the PC on which the task is scheduled obviously must stay on. Also, based on your PC's configuration, you must be logged-in in order for the task to run. That is to say that if you log out, the task may not run. A work-around to this problem is to lock the workstation, which effectively keeps your user ID logged in without compromising security.

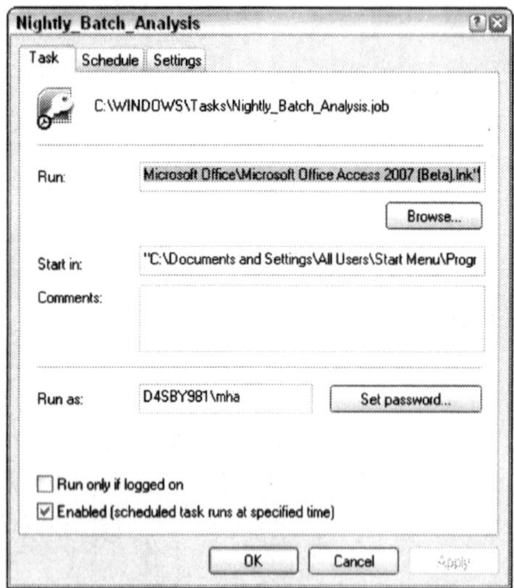

Figure 11-42: Click the Browse button and point the Scheduler to your database.

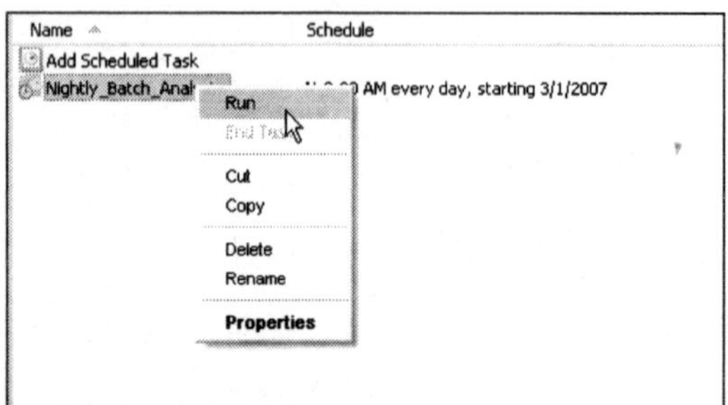

Figure 11-43: Be sure to test your task to make sure it runs properly.

Using Command Lines to Schedule Tasks

Command lines are nothing more than commands you can pass to your Access database to modify its startup process. In other words, you can tell Access to do something on startup. For example, the following command line tells the DB1 database to open exclusively and fire the STATS macro.

```
"C:\Program Files\Microsoft Office\Office\msaccess.exe" ⮐
"C:\Data\DB1.mdb"/Excl/X STATS
```

A command line is made up of three basic parts:

- The path to the msaccess.exe:

  ```
  "C:\Program Files\Microsoft Office\Office\msaccess.exe" ⮐
  "C:\Data\DB1.mdb"/Excl/X STATS
  ```

- The path of the affected database:

  ```
  "C:\Program Files\Microsoft Office\Office\msaccess.exe" ⮐
  "C:\Data\DB1.mdb"/Excl/X STATS
  ```

- The command-line switches used:

  ```
  "C:\Program Files\Microsoft Office\Office\msaccess.exe" ⮐
  "C:\Data\DB1.mdb"/Excl/X STATS
  ```

In this example, the `/Excl` switch tells the database to open exclusively. The `/X STATS` switch tells the database to run the STATS macro upon opening.

NOTE **Here's a quick list of the more useful command line switches:**

- `/excl` **opens the specified database exclusively.**
- `/ro` **opens the specified database as read-only.**
- `/user` **starts Access by using the specified user name.**
- `/pwd` **starts Access by using the specified password.**
- `/profile` **starts Access by using the options in the specified user profile.**
- `/compact` **compacts and repairs the specified database.**
- `/X MacroName` **starts the specified database and runs the specified macro.**
- `/wrkgrp` **starts Access by using the specified workgroup information.**

When to Use Command Lines to Schedule Tasks Instead of AutoExec

Microsoft recommends that you use an AutoExec macro in lieu of command line switches. However, there are situations where a command line makes more sense. Consider the following when deciding which method to use to schedule your batch analysis:

- **AutoExec affects the startup of your database every time you open it.** You already know that holding the Shift key while you open the database bypasses the AutoExec macro. However, working with a database where you constantly have to remember to hold down the Shift key can be quite annoying. In contrast, a command line switch does not become part of the database. This means you can fire it whenever you like. If you regularly work in the same database used to run scheduled tasks, consider using command lines.
- **Each macro can have its own schedule.** The problem with combining all your analytical processes into one AutoExec macro is that you run them *all* when you run AutoExec. If you want to schedule some of your analyses to run on Monday while others run on Wednesday, you'll have to create another database with a separate AutoExec macro. Command lines, on the other hand, enable you to have multiple macros run on different schedules without creating new databases. If you have multiple tasks that need to be scheduled at different time, consider using command lines.

Scheduling a Macro to Run Using a Command Line

To schedule a task using a command line, you follow the steps you performed in the section "Using the Windows Task Scheduler" (shown in Figures 11-35 through 11-42). In the advanced properties dialog box shown in Figure 11-42, enter the following in the Run box:

1. The path to msaccess.exe in quotes. In most cases it will be `"C:\Program Files\Microsoft Office\OFFICExx\msaccess.exe"`, where xx is the version of Office.
2. A space.

3. The path to the database that contains the macro you want to run in quotes.
4. The command line switch for running a macro (`/X MacroName`).

The following is an example of a valid command line switch:

```
"C:\Program Files\Microsoft Office\OFFICE12\msaccess.exe" ↵
"C:\Data\MyDatabase.mdb"/X MyMacro
```

As you can see in Figure 11-44, to use this command line, you would simply enter it into the Run input box.

Your task is now scheduled!

TIP **You can create a new shortcut on your desktop and use a command line as the target. This will enable you to run a macro from a shortcut, compact and repair your database from a shortcut, and so forth.**

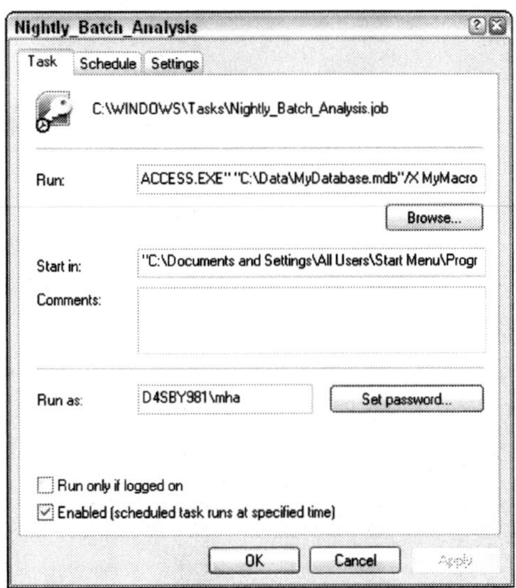

Figure 11-44: Simply enter the command line into the Run input box.

Summary

Access macros are used to execute a set of pre-programmed functions called actions. The idea behind building a macro in Access is to choose a set of actions you want the macro to carry out when it is executed. There are over 65 macro actions in Access, each one performing a certain function. These functions range from manipulating Access objects to executing and outputting data analysis. When you build a macro that automates your analytical processes, you can schedule it to run automatically by using the Windows Task Scheduler. Leveraging macro functionality enables you to automate many of your analytical processes, leading to higher productivity and a reduced chance of human error.

CHAPTER

12

Leveraging VBA to Enhance Data Analysis

Many Access users are not programmers, and it would be fair to say that most do not aspire to be programmers. In fact, most of you are just trying to survive the projects you are juggling now; who has the time to learn VBA?

If you are tempted to take a polite look at this chapter and then move on, you should definitely fight that urge. Leveraging Visual Basic for Applications (VBA) in your analytical processes can make your life easier in the long run. VBA can help you do things faster and more efficiently. In fact, just a few lines of code can save you hours of work, freeing you up to do other things, and increasing your productivity. Consider some of the advantages that VBA offers:

- VBA can help you automate redundant analyses and recurring analytical processes, leaving you free to work on other tasks.
- VBA enables you to process data without the need to create and maintain queries and macros.
- With VBA, you can automate external programs such as Excel to expand the reporting capabilities.
- With VBA, you can perform complex, multi-layered procedures that involve looping, record level testing, and `If...Then...ElseIf` statements.

- You can tailor your own error-handling procedures using VBA, enabling you to anticipate and plan for process flow changes in the event of an error.

This chapter covers some fundamental concepts and techniques that will lay the groundwork for your own ideas about how to enhance your analytical processes with VBA.

TIP **True to its purpose, all the techniques in this chapter involve writing some basic code. In order to keep this chapter focused on the data analysis aspect of these techniques, this chapter does not spend much time explaining the VBA code behind them. If you are new to VBA, you may want to refer to Appendix B, "Access VBA Fundamentals," which will give you a firm understanding of the basic concepts used in this chapter.**

NOTE **Keep in mind that the new security features in Access may prevent you from running the procedures found in the sample file. You will need to enable the content in the database in order to use the VBA. Feel free to revisit Chapter 11 to find out how the new securty features in Access work and how to enable the content in your database.**

Creating and Using Custom Functions

The developers at Microsoft have put in thousands of man-hours developing functions that are expansive enough to fit the needs of most users. In most cases, the functions available in Access more than satisfy user requirements. In fact, many users will never use a majority of the functions available, typically gravitating towards only those that fit their needs.

On the other end of the spectrum, there are those users whose daily operations involve tasks not covered by the functions in Access. These tasks can involve a business-specific calculation or a complex expression that achieves a particular result. In most cases, these tasks would be accomplished by building expressions. For example, suppose that your analysis routinely calls for the last day of the current week. Because no built-in function exists to help you determine the last day of the current week, you would use the following expression wherever you need this data:

```
Date() - WeekDay(Date()) + 7
```

The alternative to using such an expression is to build a custom function (sometimes referred to as a user-defined function). *Custom functions* are VBA procedures that expose your expressions to other objects in your database as a function, much like the built-in Access functions. This essentially means that instead of creating and using expressions in a query or form, you build your expressions into a VBA procedure, and then call it whenever you need it. Why bother with custom functions? Consider the following inherent advantages to converting your expressions into custom functions.

- Expressions, in and of themselves, generally perform operations that are simple and linear in nature. They don't allow for complex operations that involve looping or `If...Then...ElseIf` logic. Building a custom function will give you the flexibility to perform complex, multi-layered procedures that involve looping, record-level testing, and `If...Then...ElseIf` logic.
- Expressions don't enable you to define explicitly what happens in the event of an error. Building a custom function in a VBA environment allows you to include error-handling procedures with your expressions, empowering you to anticipate and plan for process flow changes in the event of an error.
- When you change the definition of an expression, you have to find and modify that expression in every place it is used. A custom function resides in one module; therefore, when there is a change in your expression or procedure, you have to update it in only one location.
- There is an increased risk of error when you are forced to manually type expressions repeatedly. For example, the expression, `Date() - WeekDay(Date()) + 7` contains syntax that could easily be keyed incorrectly or omitted. By using a custom function, you ensure that your expression is performed the same way every time, without the risk of a typing mistake.

Creating Your First Custom Function

For your first custom function, you will build a function that will return the last day of the current week.

1. Start a new module by clicking on the Create tab on the ribbon and selecting Macro → Module as demonstrated in Figure 12-1.

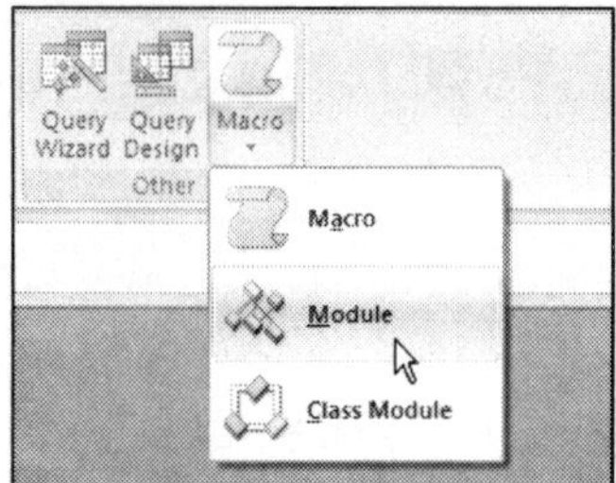

Figure 12-1: Start a new module.

2. Create a new function by entering the following code:

```
Function LastDayThisWeek()
```

NOTE **There is nothing special about the name LastDayThisWeek. It's simply a descriptive name that coincides with the purpose of the function. When creating your own custom function, it a good practice to give your functions simple names that are descriptive and easy to remember.**

3. On the next line, assign the needed expression to the function, giving your custom function its utility.

```
LastDayThisWeek = Date - Weekday(Date) + 7
```

   At this point, your module should look similar to the one shown in Figure 12-2.

4. Save the module and close it.

To test your newly created custom function, create the query you see in Figure 12-3 and run it. In this query, you will first determine the last day of the current week by using your newly created function, and then you will use that value to calculate how many days are left in the current week.

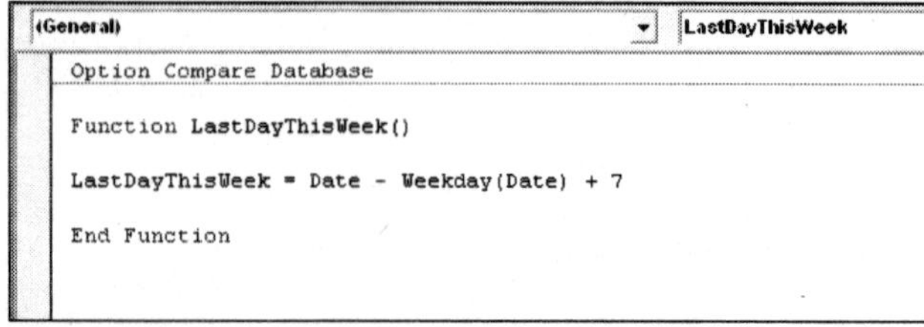

Figure 12-2: You have created your first custom function.

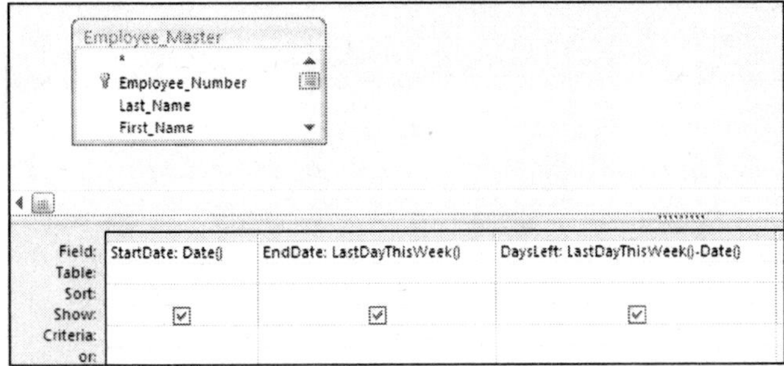

Figure 12-3: This query uses your newly created function to determine how many days are left in the current week.

Creating a Custom Function that Accepts Arguments

Sometimes the operation that is performed by your custom function requires arguments that cannot be supplied internally by Access. In these situations, you will need to create a custom function that accepts arguments. To illustrate this concept, look at the query in Figure 12-6.

In this query, the Revenue field is being annualized — that is, the revenue value of each row is being translated to an annual rate for comparative purposes. The nature of this operation requires three arguments: the value being annualized, the number of periods already completed, and the number of periods that make up an entire year. As you can see in this query, the value being annualized is revenue, the number of periods completed is 8, and the number of periods that make up a year is 12.

In order to convert this expression to a custom function, you will have to allow the user to pass the required arguments. Follow these steps:

1. Press Ctrl+Alt to open the Visual Basic Editor.
2. Select Insert → Module to start a new project.
3. Create and name your new function by entering the following code:

   ```
   Function Annualized()
   ```

4. Inside the parentheses, declare a variable and type for each argument that will be passed to the function.

   ```
   Function Annualized(MyValue As Long, _
   PeriodsCompleted As Integer, PeriodsinYear As Integer)
   ```

5. On the next line, assign the needed expression to the function, giving your custom function its utility. Instead of using hard-coded values, you will use the values passed to the declared variables.

   ```
   Annualized = MyValue / PeriodsCompleted * PeriodsinYear
   ```

TRICKS OF THE TRADE: CREATING A CENTRAL REPOSITORY OF CUSTOM FUNCTIONS

You don't have to create a separate module for each custom function in your database; you can create one module to hold them all. In the sample database that comes with this book, you will see a module called My_Custom_Functions. If you open it, you will see the seven separate custom functions shown in Figure 12-4. These functions can be used separately in various analyses.

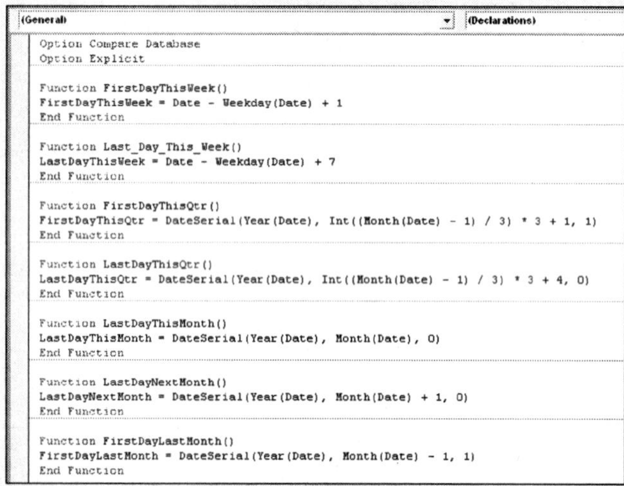

Figure 12-4: Creating one module that holds all your custom functions enables you to quickly find and edit any of your user-defined functions.

This method of storing your custom functions makes finding and editing your functions easy. Figure 12-5 illustrates another advantage of this method. When you activate the Expression Builder, you can drill into all the modules you have created in your database. Having one module that contains all your custom functions provides you a complete list of your functions.

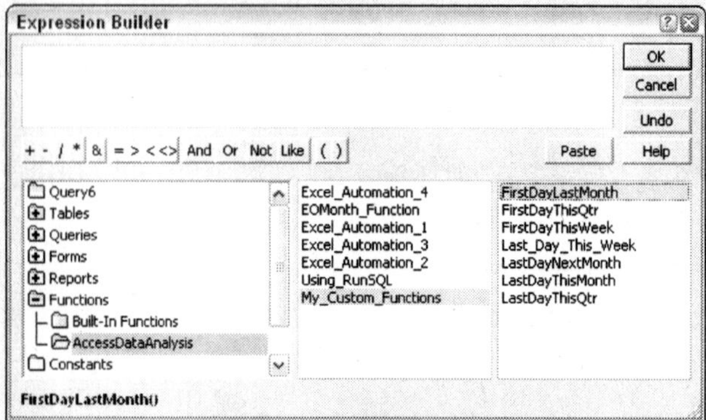

Figure 12-5: Creating one module that holds all your custom functions enables you to quickly find and edit any of your user-defined functions.

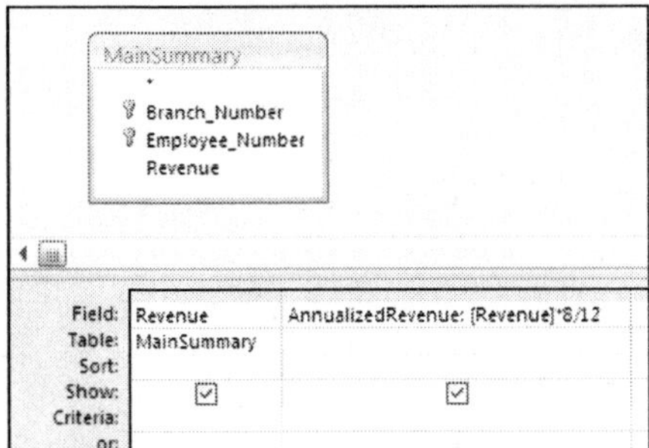

Figure 12-6: This query is using an expression that annualizes a revenue value.

At this point, your module should look similar to the one shown in Figure 12-7.

To test your newly created Annualized function, create the query you see in Figure 12-8, and then run it. Note that you are using your newly created function in an Alias called AnlzdRev.

TIP **You can hard-code selected arguments in your custom function to limit the number of arguments that need to be passed. For example, the following code demonstrates how you can change the procedure for the** `Annualized` **function to hard-code the number of periods in a year:**

```
Function Annualized(MyValue As Long, PeriodsCompleted As Integer)
Annualized = MyValue / PeriodsCompleted * 12
End Function
```

As you can see, the number of periods in a year has been hard-coded to 12, so when using this function you only have to pass two arguments. For example:

```
Annualized([Revenue], 8)
```

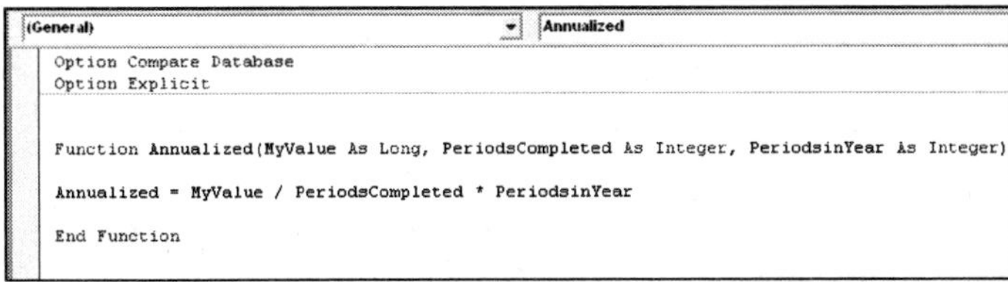

Figure 12-7: This custom function accepts three variables and uses them in an expression.

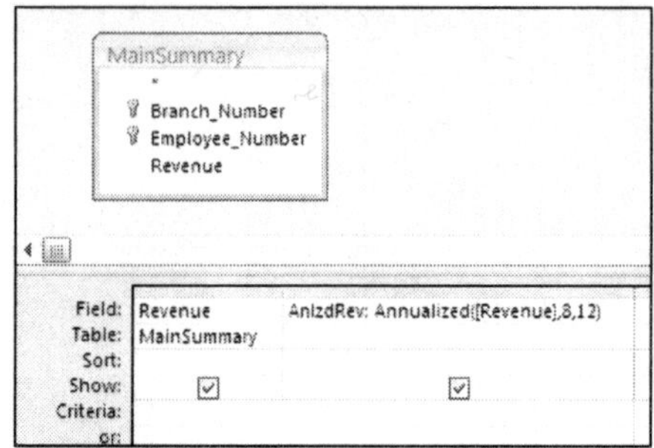

Figure 12-8: This query uses your newly created function to get the annualized revenue for each record.

A WORD ABOUT USING CUSTOM FUNCTIONS

Up to this point, you have tested your custom functions using queries. Although you will most commonly use your custom functions in queries, it is important to note that you can use them anywhere you would use any one of the built-in Access functions. Here are a few examples of how you can utilize your custom functions.

In a query environment, you can use your custom functions in the same ways you would use built-in Access functions. Figure 12-9 demonstrates some of the ways you can use a custom function in a query.

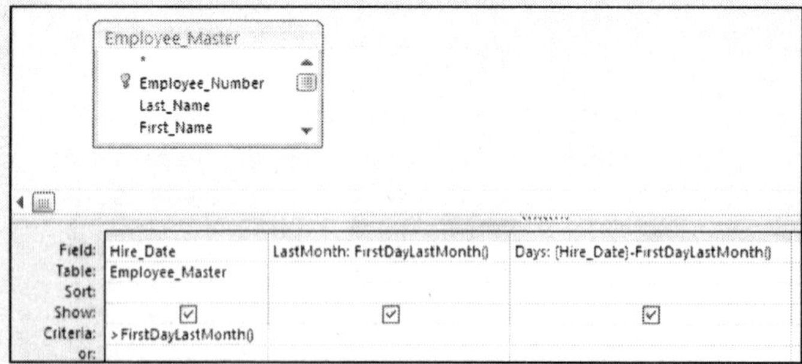

Figure 12-9: Using custom functions in a query.

Figure 12-10 illustrates how in a form, you can tie the Control Source for a text box to one of your custom functions. This same method works in Access reports. In this example, this form will automatically execute the `FirstDayLastMonth` function each time it is opened to provide a value to the assigned text box.

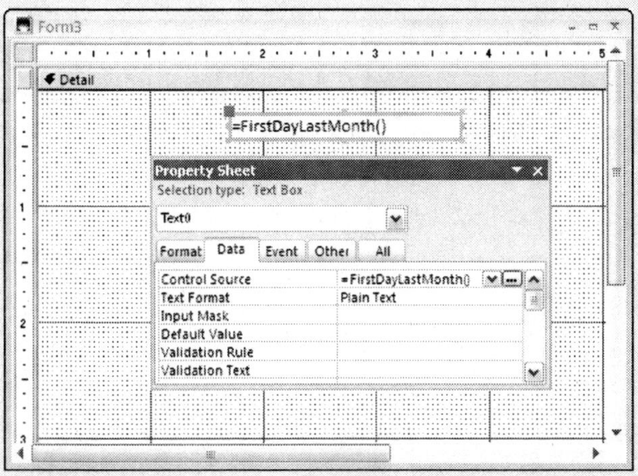

Figure 12-10: Using a custom function in a form.

Figure 12-11 illustrates how your custom functions can be used in other VBA procedures. This procedure uses the `FirstDayLastMonth` function to find the first day of last month and then puts that date into a message box.

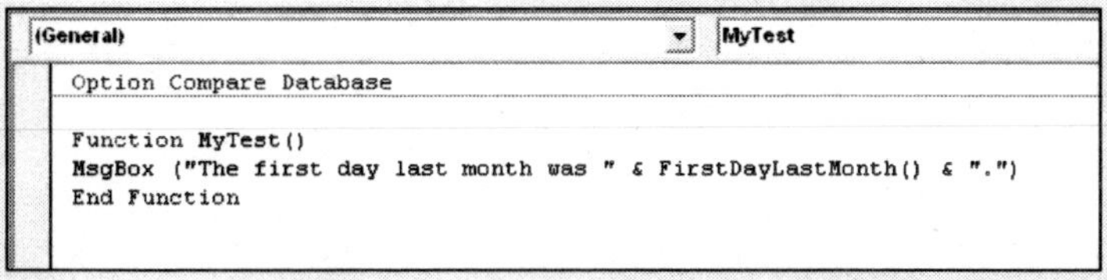

```
Option Compare Database

Function MyTest()
MsgBox ("The first day last month was " & FirstDayLastMonth() & ".")
End Function
```

Figure 12-11: Using a custom function in another VBA procedure.

Controlling Analytical Processes with Forms

An Access form is nothing more than a database object that can accept user input and display data using a collection of controls. Access forms are often thought of as part of the presentation layer of a database, primarily being used as the front-end of an application. Although it is true that the primary purpose of forms is to act as an interface between Access and a user, this does not mean the user cannot be you (the designer of the database). In this section, you will learn how Access forms can be leveraged on the back-end of a database as a data analysis tool that interacts with your analyses and further automates your analytical processes.

The Basics of Passing Data from a Form to a Query

The idea behind passing data from a form to a query is that instead of using parameters in a query to collect the data for your analysis, you collect the data through a form. To get a firm understanding of the basics of passing parameters from a form to a query, perform the following steps:

1. Start by creating a new form. Go to the Create tab on the ribbon and click the Form Design button as demonstrated in Figure 12-12.
2. Go to the Design tab and select the Text Box control as demonstrated in Figure 12-13; then click anywhere on your form. At this point, you should have a form with one text box control.
3. Right-click the text box and select Properties. Click the All tab, and then give the newly created text box a distinctive name by entering **txtParam** as the Name property, as shown in Figure 12-14.

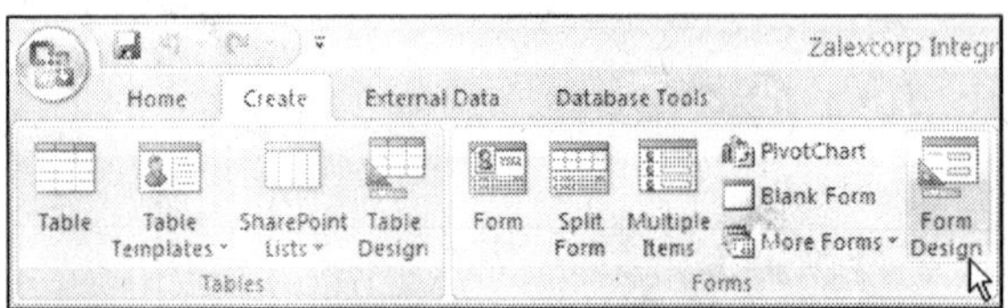

Figure 12-12: Start a new form in Design view.

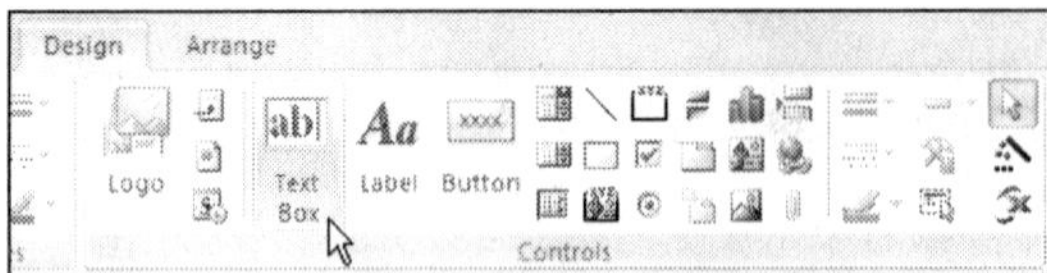

Figure 12-13: Add a text box control to your form.

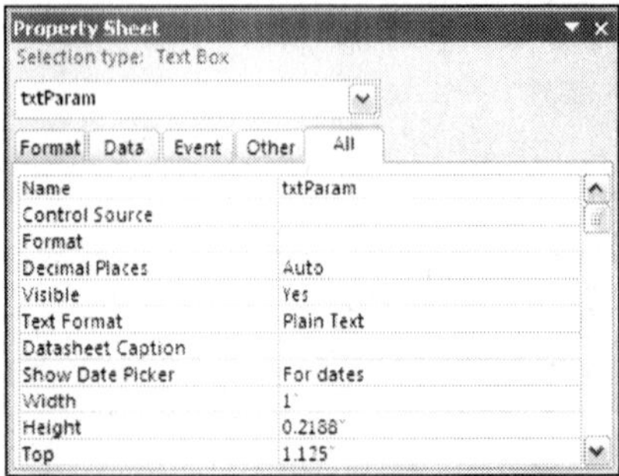

Figure 12-14: Give your text box control a distinctive name.

NOTE **Each control on your form must have a valid name in the Name property. The Name property is a unique identifier that enables Access to reference a control in other parts of your database. Access automatically assigns generic names to newly created controls. However, you should always make it a point to give each of your controls you own descriptive name. This makes referencing and recognizing your controls much easier.**

4. Go back to the Design tab and select the Command Button control, as shown in Figure 12-15, and then click anywhere on your form. This places a command button on your form.

NOTE **If the Command Button Wizard activates, click Cancel to close it. You will not need this wizard for this exercise.**

5. Right-click the newly created command button and select Properties. Click the All tab, and change the Name property of your command button to read **btnRunQuery**. Then change the Caption property to read **Run Query**.
6. Next, while still in the command button's properties, click the Event tab and then select [Event Procedure] from the On Click event, as shown in Figure 12-16. Next, click the ellipsis button (the button next to the drop-down list).

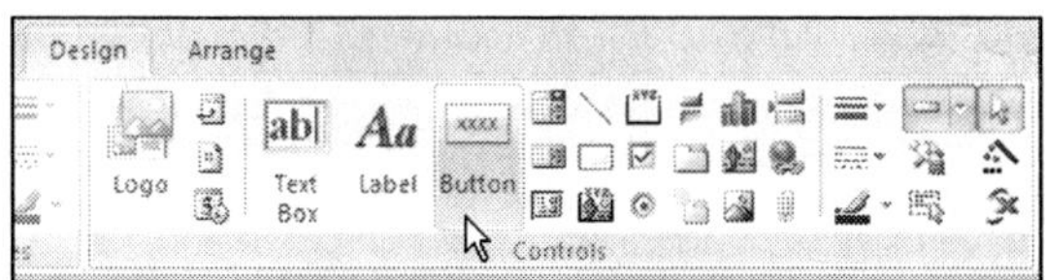

Figure 12-15: Add a command button control to your form.

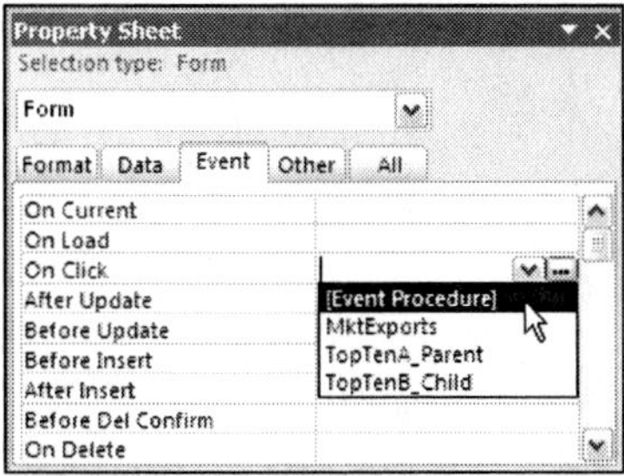

Figure 12-16: Set the On Click event to run an [Event Procedure], and then click the ellipsis button.

7. At this point, you should be inside the VBA editor where you will enter a DoCmd action that will run the query called Chapter12_Example_A. Enter the following code, just as you see in Figure 12-17:

```
DoCmd.OpenQuery "Chapter12_Example_A", acViewNormal
```

NOTE **The** `DoCmd.OpenQuery` **method enables you to execute any saved query from code. This method is perfect for simple automation processes such as this.**

8. When you are done, save your form as **frmMain** and close it.
9. It's time to test. Open the newly created frmMain form and click the Run Query button. If the query runs successfully, you have set up your form correctly. Now you can prepare your query to accept parameters from this form!
10. Open the query Chapter12_Example_A in Design view. Enter **[Forms]![frmMain].[txtParam]** as the criteria for the System_Period field, as shown in Figure 12-18.
11. Save and close the query.

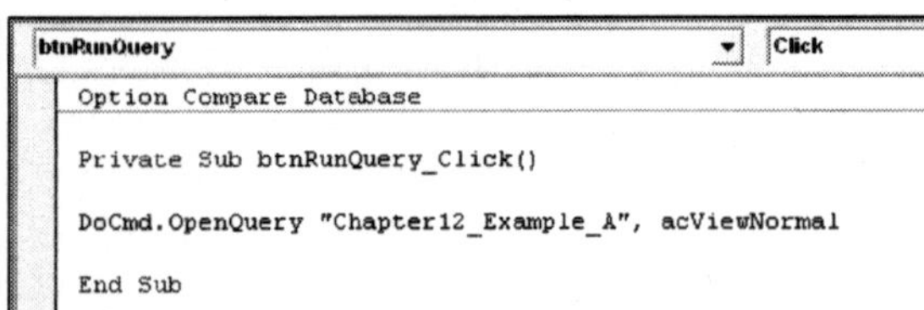

Figure 12-17: Use the Docmd.OpenQuery method to execute the query Chapter 12_Example_A.

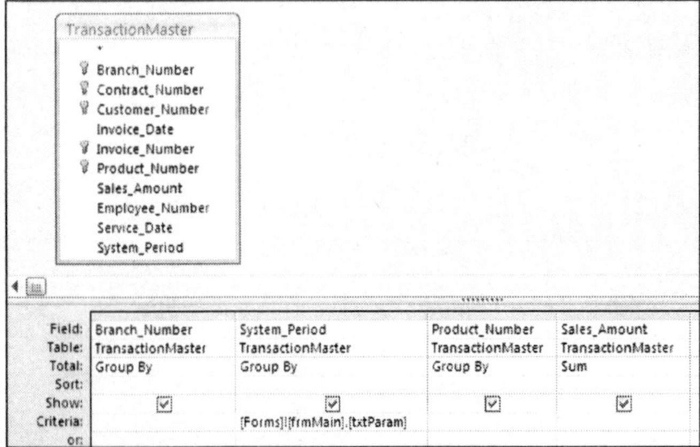

Figure 12-18: This query filters on the System_Period field based on the value of the txtParam text box in the frmMain form.

Now you can open the frmMain form and enter a parameter for your query through a form! Enter 200401 in the text box, as shown in Figure 12-19, and then run the query. This will return all revenues earned in the 200401system period.

NOTE **You will notice that if you leave the text box blank, your query will not return any results. This is the same issue you encounter using parameter queries. One way to get around this problem is to combine your expression with a wildcard so that if the text box is blank, all records will be returned. In this scenario, for example, you would change your expression to read:**

```
Like [Forms]![frmMain].[txtParam] & "*"
```

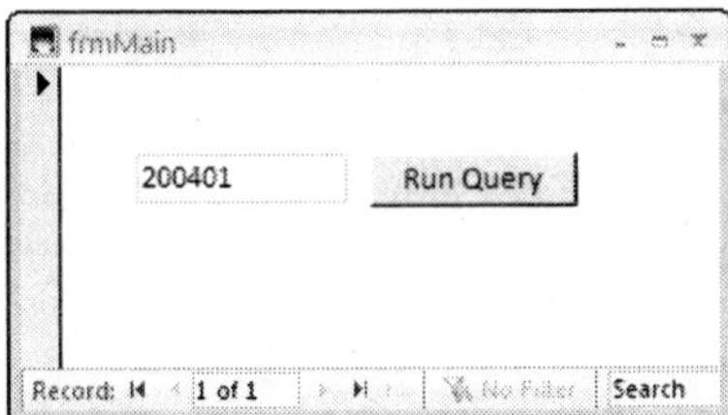

Figure 12-19: Now you can pass your parameters to your query through a form.

UNDERSTANDING THE SYNTAX FOR REFERENCING A FORM

- ***Brackets ([ ])*: Brackets are used to identify the name of an object. For example, if you were referring to the CustomerMaster table, you would refer to it as [CustomerMaster]. If you were referring to a query called TopTen_Step1, you would refer to it as [TopTen_Step1]. This not only helps Access identify objects, but it will also make your code easier to read.**
- ***The collection operator (!)*: The collection operator (sometimes referred to as the bang operator) is used to tell Access that the object with which you are working belongs to a particular collection of objects. For example, if you are working with a form called Main, you would refer to it as [Forms]![Main] because the form [Main] belongs to the Forms collection.**
- ***The dot operator (.)*: The dot operator is used to point to a property belonging to an object. For example, [CustomerMaster] refers to the CustomerMaster table, whereas [CustomerMaster].[City] refers to the City field in the CustomerMaster table. Here is another example. [Forms]![Main] refers to the form Main, whereas [Forms]![Main].[Fname] refers to a control called Fname located in Main.**

TIP **You can reference any form control that has a value property, including combo boxes, list boxes, text boxes, and option groups.**

Enhancing Automation with Forms

Access forms can help you enhance your automated processes using little more than a few controls and some light VBA coding. The idea is to turn your forms into something more than just a tool to pass parameters; you can create a robust central control point for your analysis.

To help illustrate the power of incorporating Access forms into your analysis, open the frmMktRpts form in the sample database, shown in Figure 12-20. The purpose of this form is to control the execution of an analysis that involves creating market reports. The idea is to select a market, run the process that executes a query, and then send the results to an Excel file in the C:\AccessDataAnalysis directory.

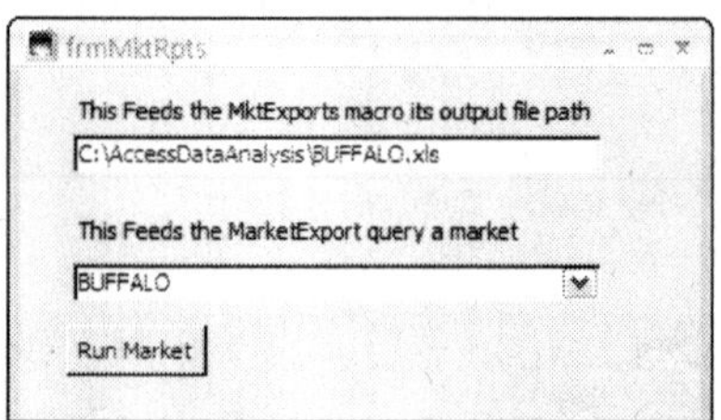

Figure 12-20: This form enables you to control the execution of an analytical process.

Open the form in Design view to see how this works. As you can see, there are three controls on this form.

- **The txtPath text box:** The txtPath text box uses the market value from the combo box to construct a file path. This enables you to dynamically create a separate path for each market. This path is constructed by concatenating two strings and a control reference.
  - **C:\AccessDataAnalysis\:** This is the first part of the file path, pointing to the AccessDataAnalysis directory in the C: drive.
  - **[cboLocations]:** This is the name of the combo box where you select your market. This becomes the file name.
  - **.xls:** This string finishes the path by assigning the file extension that identifies the file as an Excel file.

  If you open the MktExports macro, shown in Figure 12-21, you will notice that the Output File path is referencing this text box. This enables the macro to avoid using a hard-coded file path.

- **The cboLocations combo box**: This combo box helps to accomplish two things. First, it feeds the txtPath text box a market to use in the construction of a file path. Second, it feeds the MarketExports query its parameter. If you open the MarketExports query, shown in Figure 12-22, you will notice that filter criteria for the Market field is referencing this combo box. This allows the query to avoid using a hard-coded market.
- **The btnRunMarket command button:** Right-click this command button and then click Build Event. This will take you to the VBA editor shown in Figure 12-23. As you can see, this button simply runs the MktExports macro, and then throws up a message box announcing the location of your new file.

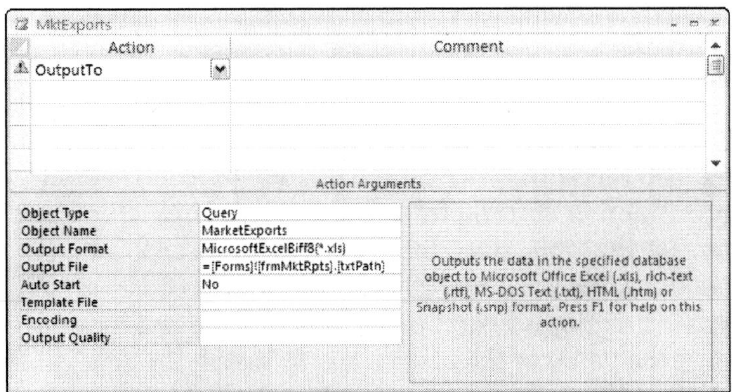

Figure 12-21: You will use the txtPath text box to dynamically feed your macro the Output File path for each market.

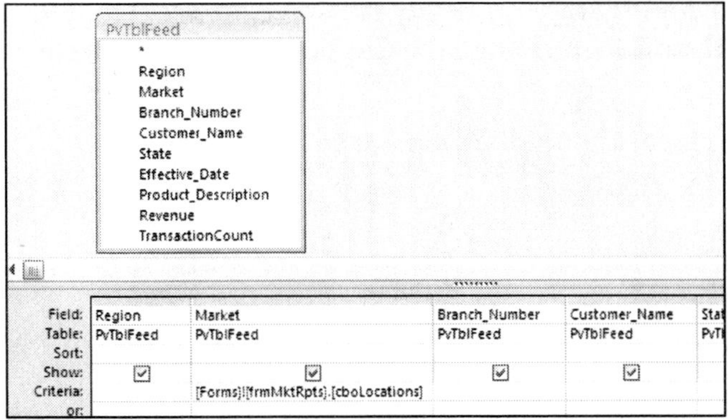

Figure 12-22: You are using the cboLocations combo box as the filter criteria for the Market field.

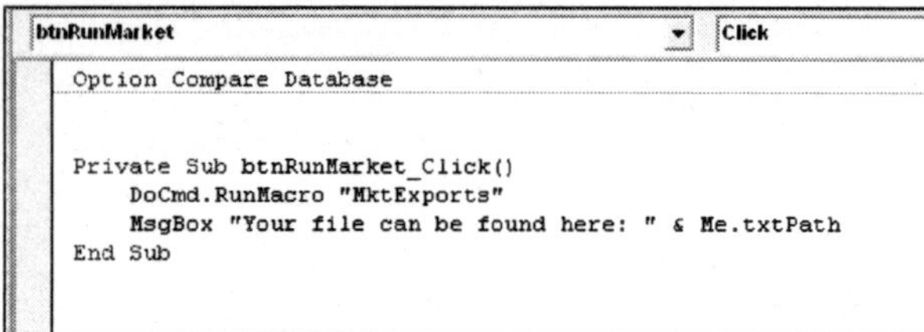

Figure 12-23: When you click the command button, a `DoCmd` action will run the macro and then call a message box.

Now that you have a firm grasp of how this form works, you can enhance it even further. Instead of running one market at a time, wouldn't it be useful to run all markets at once? You can do this by using VBA to enumerate through all the markets in the combo box, running the MktExports as you go.

Enumerating Through a Combo Box

Open the frmMktRpts form and take a look at the combo box on the form. The entries, or rows, you see within the combo box are indexed — that is, each row has an index number starting from 0 and continuing to however many rows there are. For example, the first row is index number 0, the second row is index number 1, the third row is index number 2, and so on. The idea behind enumerating through a combo box is to capture one index at a time, and then change the value of the combo box to match the row value assigned to that index number.

1. Start by opening the frmMktRpts form in Design view and adding a second command button.
2. Adjust the Name property of your newly created command button to read **btnRunAll**, and then change the Caption property to read **Run All**.

   At this point, your form should look similar to Figure 12-24.

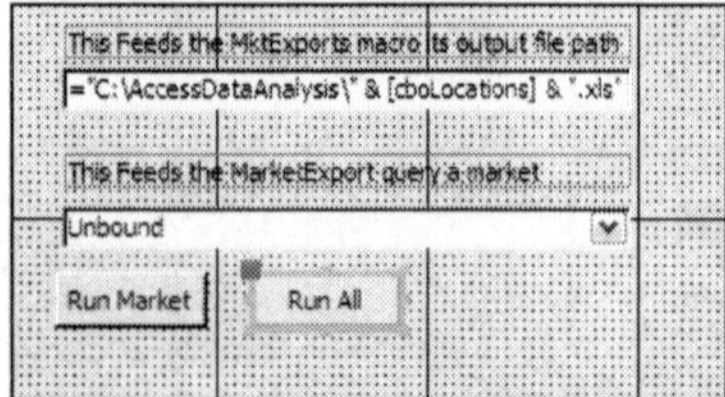

Figure 12-24: Add a second command button called Run All to the form.

3. Right-click the button and select Build Event. Select Code Builder from the Choose Builder dialog box, and then click OK. This opens the VBA Editor. As you can see in Figure 12-25, this creates a separate subprocedure.
4. Start the code by declaring an integer variable called IndexNum. This will be used to trap the index number of each entry of the combo box.

```
Dim IndexNum As Integer
```

5. Initiate a `For...Next` loop with the `IndexNum` variable. This line of code ensures that the procedure runs for each index number in the combo box.

```
For IndexNum = 0 To Me.cboLocations.ListCount - 1
```

NOTE **Why subtract 1 from the combo box's list count? You must do this to adjust for the fact that index numbers of a combo box start at 0. If there are 10 rows in a combo box, the `ListCount` property starts counting at 1, returning a count of 10 rows. However, the index numbers in the same combo box range from 0 to 9. Subtracting 1 from the list count removes the extra number and corrects the discrepancy.**

6. Set the value of the combo box equal to the value of the row assigned to the current index number. After the new value has been set, run the predefined macro.

```
Me.cboLocations.Value = Me.cboLocations.ItemData(IndexNum)
DoCmd.RunMacro "MktExports"
```

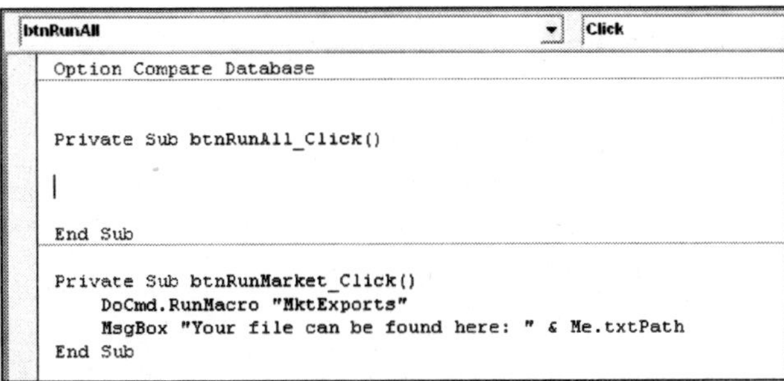

Figure 12-25: Build an On Click event for the newly created btnRunAll command button.

7. Repeat the process for the next index number. The message will alert you when the procedure has completed its execution.

```
Next IndexNum
MsgBox "Your files can be found in the C:\AccessDataAnalysis
directory."
```

If you have done everything correctly, your procedure should look similar to Figure 12-26.

8. Save your form and test the newly created functionality by clicking the Run All button.

When the procedure has completed running, look under the `C:\AccessDataAnalysis` directory to see all the Excel files that were created (see Figure 12-27).

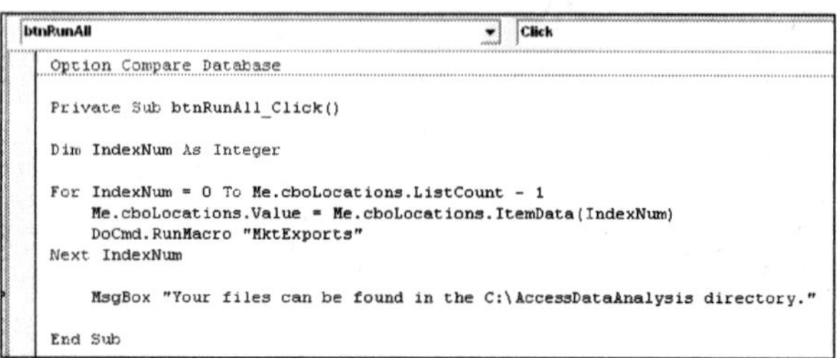

Figure 12-26: This procedure enumerates through a combo box, running a macro for each entry.

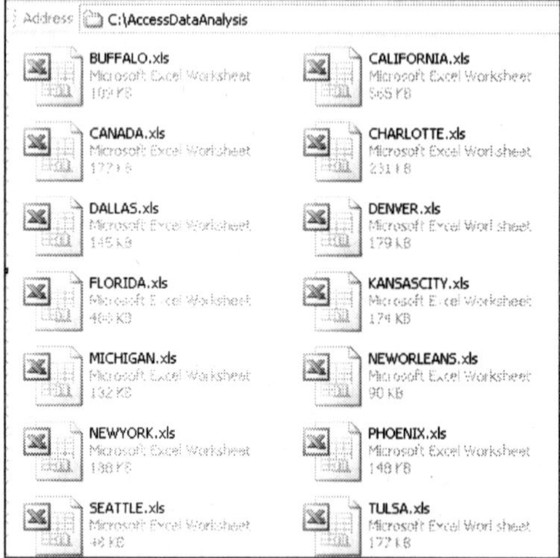

Figure 12-27: All of these Excel files were created with automation.

Needless to say, this example is just one of the hundreds of ways you can enhance your analytical processes using forms. The flexibility and functionality you gain by using a few controls and a handful of code is simply incredible. Even simple techniques such as passing parameters from a form to a query can open the doors to a completely new set of analytical functionality.

Processing Data Behind the Scenes

One of the benefits of using VBA is that you can perform much of your data processing in the background without the use of queries and macros. This can be beneficial in several ways:

- **Reduce the number of query objects in your database:** Every analytical process will have intermediate steps that serve as a means to an end. These steps typically involve action queries that massage and transform the data for the bigger analysis. Too many of these peripheral queries can inundate your database with query objects, making your analytical processes difficult to manage and change. Processing your data in the background using VBA can help you streamline your processes by reducing the number of query objects in your database, making both the management and the maintenance of your analyses more practical.
- **Better organize your analytical processes:** Have you ever seen a process that involves queries that link to forms that, in turn, link to macros that reference tables created by other queries, and so on? You will undoubtedly run into analyses that involve complicated processes, and there is nothing wrong with utilizing the tools Access provides. However, engineering overly elaborate systems that involve macros, queries, and forms can make your processes difficult to manage and maintain. Processing your data in the background using VBA can help you centralize your analysis into one procedure, organizing your tasks in a clearly defined set of instructions that are easy to locate, update, and manage.
- **Protect your processes in shared environments:** Processing your data in the background using VBA can help you protect your analytical processes working in a shared database. Building your processes in VBA can reduce the risk of someone changing your queries or accidentally deleting objects.

- **Enhance your processes with VBA:** The more you integrate your analytical processes into VBA, the more you can take advantage of its many benefits such as looping, record-level testing, and error handling.

Anyone who routinely works with Access knows that there are several different ways to accomplish any given task. Processing data using VBA is no different. Indeed, the beauty of VBA is that its flexibility enables you to perform literally any action in countless ways. That said, it should be obvious that it would be impossible to cover every possible way to process data using VBA. Therefore, you will focus on using `RunSQL` statements here. This technique gives you some fundamental controls over your processes through VBA and will enable you to start moving more of your analyses behind the scenes.

Processing Data with RunSQL Statements

In Chapter 7, you learned that the query objects you are accustomed to using are simply visual representations of SQL statements. What you may not know is that you don't necessarily need to create a query object in order to process data. You can process data directly through a `RunSQL` statement. One of the ways to do this is to use the `RunSQL` method.

The Basics of the RunSQL Method

If you were designing a macro, you would find `RunSQL` in the list of macro actions. In technical terms, `RunSQL` is a method belonging to the `DoCmd` object. Those of you who have been paying attention will have noticed that up until now, you have been using `OpenQuery` when working with a query in a macro environment, and `Docmd.OpenQuery` when working with a query through code. In this light, it's important to note the differences between the `RunSQL` method and `OpenQuery` method.

- The `OpenQuery` method executes a saved query, whereas the `RunSQL` method processes a SQL statement without the need for a saved query.
- The `RunSQL` method only allows you to execute action queries (make-table, append, delete, and update), whereas the `OpenQuery` method enables the execution of any type of saved query, including select queries.
- The `OpenQuery` method is ideal for use in a macro environment. The `RunSQL` method, on the other hand, is better suited for dynamic back-end processes performed in VBA.

NOTE **Among other reasons, `RunSQL` is better suited for VBA because in a macro environment, the `RunSQL` action limits you to SQL statements that do not exceed 256 characters. This obviously restricts the functionality of `RunSQL` in the macro environment. However, there is no such limitation in the VBA environment.**

Using RunSQL Statements

Using `RunSQL` statements in your code is easy. You would simply place each `RunSQL` statement in your VBA procedure as needed. For example, the following procedure runs four actions, demonstrating that you can process data without creating one query:

- Makes a table called tblJobCodes
- Inserts a new record into the tblJobCodes table
- Updates the job code PPL to PPL1
- Deletes the PPL1 job code

```
Function Look_Ma_No_Queries()

DoCmd.RunSQL "SELECT [Job_Code]INTO [tblJobCodes]FROM ⮐
[Employee_Master] GROUP BY [Job_Code]"

DoCmd.RunSQL "INSERT INTO [tblJobCodes] ( [Job_Code] ) SELECT ⮐
'PPL' AS NewCode FROM [Employee_Master] GROUP BY 'PPL'"

DoCmd.RunSQL "UPDATE [tblJobCodes] SET [Job_Code] = 'PPL1' ⮐
WHERE [Job_Code]='PPL'"

DoCmd.RunSQL "DELETE * FROM [tblJobCodes] WHERE [Job_Code]='PPL1'"

End Function
```

NOTE **You will find this procedure in the sample database within the module called Using_RunSQL. Note that each `RunSQL` statement should be one line of code. You see the lines broken up here due to layout specifications.**

TIP **Having trouble creating SQL statements? Here's a handy trick. Create a query in Design view, and then switch to SQL view. Although you will have to adjust the SQL statement a bit, Access will have done most of the work for you.**

THE ANATOMY OF RUNSQL STATEMENTS

DoCmd.RunSQL(SQLStatement, UseTransaction)

RunSQL **is a method of the** DoCmd **object that executes action queries such as append, delete, update, and make-table. This method has the following two arguments:**

- SQLStatement **(required): This is the SQL statement that is to be executed.**
- UseTransaction **(optional): This is a true or false indicator that specifies how Access safeguards your data during the execution of your SQL statement. The default state for this argument is** True, **which ensures that your SQL statement is tested in a temporary log before final execution. You should rarely set this argument to** False.

DoCmd.RunSQL "Delete * from [MyTable]" **deletes all records from MyTable.**

Advanced Techniques Using RunSQL Statements

Now that you have a firm understanding of what RunSQL statements can do, take a look at some of the advanced techniques that will help enhance your behind-the-scenes processing.

Suppressing Warning Messages

As you execute your RunSQL statements, you will notice that Access throws up the same warning messages you would get if you were to run the same actions with stored queries. You can use the SetWarnings method to suppress these messages just as you would in a macro. For example, the following code sets warnings to False, runs the RunSQL statement, and then sets warnings back to True.

```
DoCmd.SetWarnings False
DoCmd.RunSQL "DELETE * FROM [tblJobCodes] WHERE [Job_Code]='PPL1'"
DoCmd.SetWarnings True
```

Passing a SQL Statement as a Variable

One of the biggest challenges in working with the RunSQL method is managing and making sense of giant SQL statements. It's difficult to determine what is going on in your code when your RunSQL statement runs off the page with over 1000 characters in its SQL string. One of the ways to make for easier reading is to pass your SQL statement as a variable. This section demonstrates how passing your SQL statement through a string variable enables you to break up your statement into pieces that are easier to read.

1. Start a procedure and declare a string variable called `MySQL`.

```
Function Passing_SQL_With_Strings()
Dim MySQL As String
```

2. Start assigning the SQL statement to the `MySQL` variable. What you're looking for here is structure, a format that makes the SQL statement easy to read and manage within the VBA editor. The first line starts the string. Each subsequent line is concatenated to the previous line. By the last line, the `MySQL` variable contains the entire SQL string.

```
MySQL = "SELECT TOP 10 Market, Sum(Revenue) AS Rev INTO TopTenList "
MySQL = MySQL & "FROM PvTblFeed "
MySQL = MySQL & "GROUP BY PvTblFeed.Market, PvTblFeed.Customer_Name "
MySQL = MySQL & "ORDER BY Sum(PvTblFeed.Revenue) DESC"
```

3. All that is left to do now is pass the `MySQL` variable to your `RunSQL` statement, as follows:

```
DoCmd.RunSQL MySQL
End Function
```

NOTE **Although there are other ways to concatenate this SQL string without the redundancy of typing *"MySQL = MySQL &..."*, this method creates a visual block of code that unmistakably enables the person reviewing the code to know that all this goes together.**

Passing User-Defined Parameters from a Form to Your SQL Statement

Even when you are processing data behind the scenes, you can pass user-defined parameters from a form to create dynamic SQL statements. Here are some examples of how you would pass data from a form to your SQL statements.

Passing Textual Parameters from a Form

In this example, you are passing a textual criterion from a form. Note that the expression that points to the user-defined parameter on the form must be wrapped in quotes. In addition, because the data type you are passing is textual, the entire expression is wrapped in single quotes.

```
MySQL = "SELECT Market, Customer_Name, EffDate, TransCount "
MySQL = MySQL & "INTO MyResults "
MySQL = MySQL & "FROM MyTable "
MySQL = MySQL & "WHERE Market='" & [Forms]![frmMain].[cboMarket] & "'"
DoCmd.RunSQL MySQL
```

Passing Numeric Parameters from a Form

In this example, you are passing a numeric criterion from a form. Note that the expression that points to the user-defined parameter on the form must be wrapped in quotes.

```
MySQL = "SELECT Market, Customer_Name, EffDate, TransCount "
MySQL = MySQL & "INTO MyResults "
MySQL = MySQL & "FROM MyTable "
MySQL = MySQL & "WHERE TransCount =" & [Forms]![frmMain].[cboCount] & ""
DoCmd.RunSQL MySQL
```

Passing Date Parameters from a Form

In this example, you are passing a date criterion from a form. Note that the expression that points to the user-defined parameter on the form must be wrapped in quotes. In addition, because the data type you are passing is a date, the entire expression is wrapped in a pound sign (#).

```
MySQL = "SELECT Market, Customer_Name, EffDate, TransCount "
MySQL = MySQL & "INTO MyResults "
MySQL = MySQL & "FROM MyTable "
MySQL = MySQL & "WHERE EffDate =#" & [Forms]![frmMain].[cboMarket] & "#"
DoCmd.RunSQL MySQL
```

TRICKS OF THE TRADE: TROUBLESHOOTING SQL STATEMENTS WITH A MESSAGE BOX

Troubleshooting a SQL statement in VBA can be one of the most frustrating exercises you will undertake, primarily for two reasons. First, you are working in an environment where the SQL statement is broken up into pieces. Although this makes it easier to determine what the SQL statement is doing, it makes debugging problematic since you cannot readily see the statement as a whole. Second, the error messages you get when SQL statements fail are often times vague, leaving you to guess what the problem may be.

For example, the SQL string in Figure 12-28 contains an error. When this procedure is run, the error message shown in Figure 12-29 will pop up.

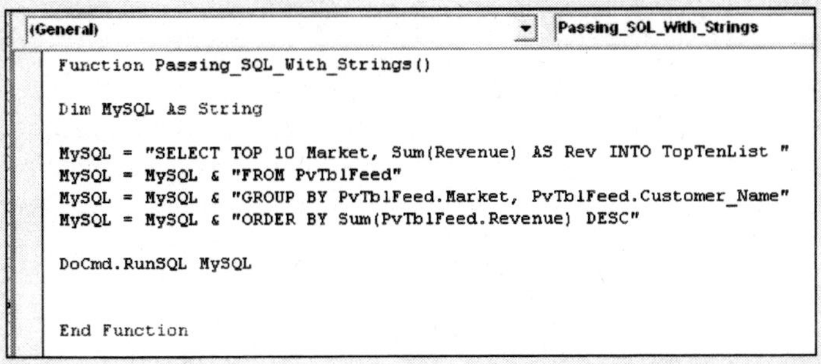

```
(General)                                    Passing_SQL_With_Strings

Function Passing_SQL_With_Strings()

Dim MySQL As String

MySQL = "SELECT TOP 10 Market, Sum(Revenue) AS Rev INTO TopTenList "
MySQL = MySQL & "FROM PvTblFeed"
MySQL = MySQL & "GROUP BY PvTblFeed.Market, PvTblFeed.Customer_Name"
MySQL = MySQL & "ORDER BY Sum(PvTblFeed.Revenue) DESC"

DoCmd.RunSQL MySQL


End Function
```

Figure 12-28: The SQL string in this code contains an error. Can you pick it out?

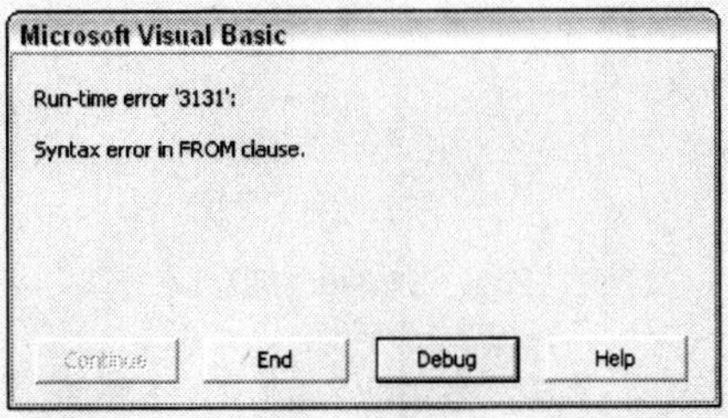

```
Microsoft Visual Basic

Run-time error '3131':

Syntax error in FROM clause.

Continue    End    Debug    Help
```

Figure 12-29: The error message you get when the procedure is run provides little help. Nothing seems to be wrong with the `FROM` clause.

It's obvious that an error lies somewhere, but it's impossible to see it when the SQL string is broken out like this. So how can you see the SQL string in its entirety? Use a message box! Figure 12-30 demonstrates how you can feed the SQL string to a message box before firing the `RunSQL` statement.

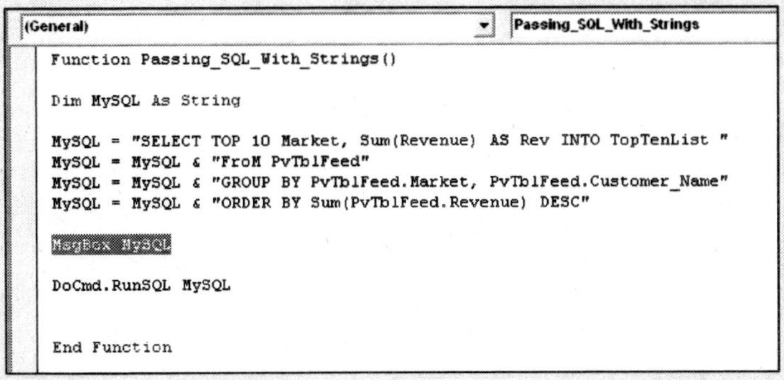

```
(General)                                    Passing_SQL_With_Strings

Function Passing_SQL_With_Strings()

Dim MySQL As String

MySQL = "SELECT TOP 10 Market, Sum(Revenue) AS Rev INTO TopTenList "
MySQL = MySQL & "FroM PvTblFeed"
MySQL = MySQL & "GROUP BY PvTblFeed.Market, PvTblFeed.Customer_Name"
MySQL = MySQL & "ORDER BY Sum(PvTblFeed.Revenue) DESC"

MsgBox MySQL

DoCmd.RunSQL MySQL


End Function
```

Figure 12-30: Use a message box to read the variable that holds your SQL string. This enables you to see a complete SQL statement and possibly pinpoint the error.

(Continued)

TRICKS OF THE TRADE: TROUBLESHOOTING SQL STATEMENTS WITH A MESSAGE BOX *(Continued)*

After running the procedure, the message box pops up with the entire SQL statement. (See Figure 12-31.) How does this help you? Well, the error message stated that the error was in the FROM **clause, so you should look there first. If you look closely, you'll see that there is no space between the words *PvTblFeed* and *GROUP BY*.**

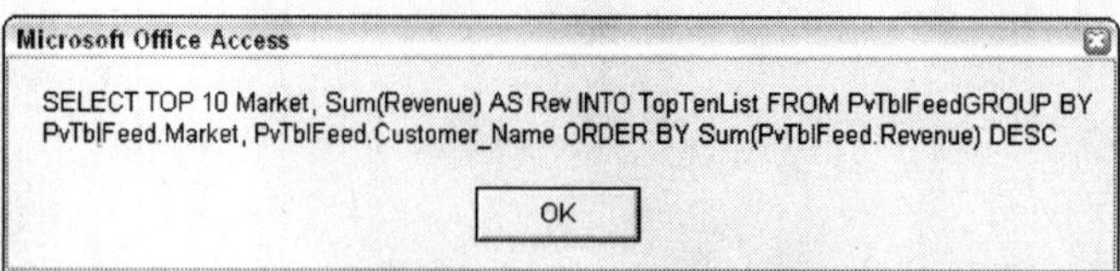
Microsoft Office Access
SELECT TOP 10 Market, Sum(Revenue) AS Rev INTO TopTenList FROM PvTblFeedGROUP BY PvTblFeed.Market, PvTblFeed.Customer_Name ORDER BY Sum(PvTblFeed.Revenue) DESC
OK

Figure 12-31: The message box helped you determine that error was caused by the fact that there is no space between the words *PvTblFeed* and *GROUP BY*.

That's right: One measly space causes the entire SQL statement to fail. Remember, these lines of code are not separate SQL statements; they are actually pieces of one SQL statement that have been broken down into parts. They will be pieced back together when the function is executed. In that light, you have to consider, and include, all syntax that is necessary to create a valid SQL statement, including spaces. This is why you always see a space before the close quotes for each piece of the SQL statement. So the syntax, From PvtTblFeed, should be adjusted to include a space before the close quotes. Figure 12-32 shows the fixed procedure.

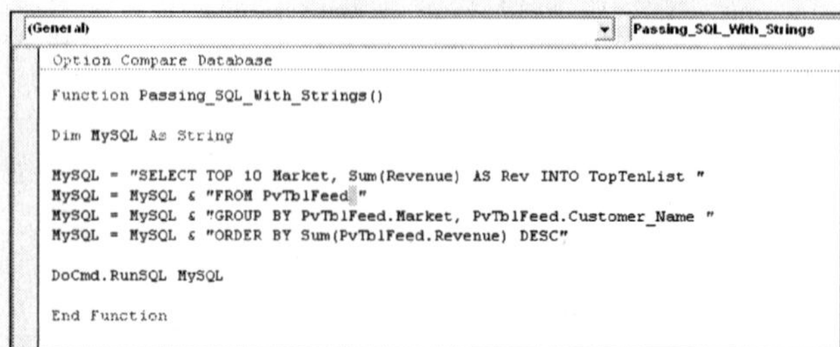
(General)
Passing_SQL_With_Strings
Option Compare Database
Function Passing_SQL_With_Strings()
Dim MySQL As String
MySQL = "SELECT TOP 10 Market, Sum(Revenue) AS Rev INTO TopTenList "
MySQL = MySQL & "FROM PvTblFeed "
MySQL = MySQL & "GROUP BY PvTblFeed.Market, PvTblFeed.Customer_Name "
MySQL = MySQL & "ORDER BY Sum(PvTblFeed.Revenue) DESC"
DoCmd.RunSQL MySQL
End Function

Figure 12-32: Using a message box to troubleshoot the SQL statement helped determine that the error was caused by a missing space after FROM PvtTblFeed.

Summary

Leveraging VBA in your analytical processes can help you automate redundant and recurring analyses, as well as process data without the need to create and maintain queries and macros. Although there are countless ways you can leverage VBA to improve your analytical process, in this chapter, you covered three techniques: building custom functions, incorporating Access Forms in your analysis, and using `RunSQL` commands to run queries behind the scenes.

Custom functions are VBA procedures that expose your expressions to other objects in your database as a function, much like Access's built-in functions. This essentially means that instead of creating and using expressions in a query or form, you build your expressions into a VBA procedure, and then call it whenever you need it. The major advantages to building your own custom functions using VBA is that you have the flexibility to perform complex multi-layered procedures that involve looping, record-level testing, and `If...Then...ElseIf` logical evaluations while ensuring that your expression is performed the same way every time, without the risk of a typing mistake.

Another way to use VBA to enhance analysis is to incorporate Access forms into your analytical processes. An Access form is nothing more than a database object that can accept user input and display data using a collection of controls. Access forms are often thought of as part of the presentation layer of a database, primarily being used as the front-end of an application. Although it is true that the primary purpose of forms is to act as an interface between Access and a user, this does not mean the user cannot be you. Access forms can be leveraged on the back end of a database as a data analysis tool that interacts with your analyses and further automates your analytical processes.

Finally, you can create and run `RunSQL` commands using VBA to process data behind the scenes, without the need for query objects or temporary tables. The advantages of using `RunSQL` commands are: You can reduce the number of query objects in your database; you can centralize your analysis into one procedure, organizing your tasks in a clearly defined set of instructions that are easy manage; and you can protect your processes in shared environments, reducing the risk of someone changing your queries or accidentally deleting objects.

CHAPTER

13

Query Performance, Database Corruption, and Other Final Thoughts

One of the most important aspects of analyzing data with Access is keeping your database healthy. In this chapter, you learn some of the best practices around building and maintaining your database, ensuring that it runs efficiently and free of error. In addition, this chapter teaches you how to get help in Access when you need a push in the right direction.

Optimizing Query Performance

When you are analyzing a few thousand records, query performance is not an issue. Analytical processes run quickly and smoothly with few problems. However, when you are moving and crunching hundreds of thousands of records, performance becomes a huge issue. There is no getting around the fact that the larger the volume of data, the slower your queries run. That said, there are steps you can take to optimize query performance and reduce the time it takes to run your large analytical processes.

Understanding the Access Query Optimizer

Most relational database programs have a built-in optimizer to ensure efficient performance, even in the face of large volumes of data. Access also has a built-in query optimizer. Have you ever noticed that when you build a query, close it, and then open it again, Access sometimes shuffles your criteria and expressions around? This is because of its built-in query optimizer.

The query optimizer is charged with the task of establishing a query execution strategy. The query execution strategy is a set of instructions given to the Microsoft Access database engine (ACE) that tells it how to run the query in the quickest, most cost-effective way possible. The Access query optimizer bases its query execution strategy on the following factors:

- The size of the tables used in the query
- Whether indexes exist in the tables used in the query
- The number of tables and joins used in the query
- The presence and scope of any criteria or expressions used in the query

This execution strategy is created when the query is first run, and it is recompiled each time you save a query or compact your database. After a query execution strategy has been established, the ACE database engine simply refers to it each time the query is run, effectively optimizing the execution of the query.

Steps You Can Take to Optimize Query Performance

You've heard the phrase *garbage in, garbage out,* referring to the fact that the results you get out of a database are only as good as the data you put in. This concept also applies to the Access query optimizer. Since the Access optimization functionality largely depends on the make-up and utility of your tables and queries, poorly designed tables and queries can limit the effectiveness of the Access query optimizer. To that end, there are actions you can take to help maximize query optimization.

Normalizing Your Database Design

Many users who are new to Access build one large flat table and call it a database. This structure seems attractive because you don't have to deal with joins and you only have to reference one table when you build your queries. However, as the volume of data grows in a structure such as this one, query performance will take a nosedive.

When you normalize your database to take on a relational structure, you break up your data into several smaller tables. This has two effects. First, you inherently remove redundant data, giving your query less data to scan. Second, you can query only the tables that contain the information you need, preventing you from scanning your entire database each time you run a query.

Using Indexes on Appropriate Fields

Imagine that you have a file cabinet that contains 1,000 records that are not alphabetized. How long do you think it would take you to pull out all the records that start with S? You would definitely have an easier time pulling out records in an alphabetized filing system. Indexing fields in an Access table is analogous to alphabetizing records in a file cabinet.

When you run a query where you are sorting and filtering on a field that has not been indexed, Access has to scan and read the entire dataset before returning any results. As you can imagine, on large datasets, this can take a very long time. By contrast, queries that sort and filter on fields that have been indexed run much more quickly because Access uses the index to check positions and restrictions.

You can create an index on a field in a table by going into the table's design view and adjusting the Indexed property. Figure 13-1 demonstrates how this is done.

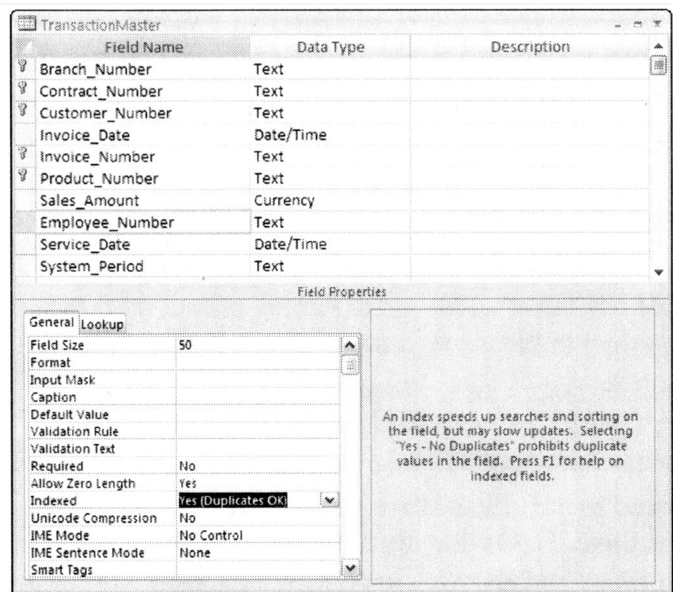

Figure 13-1: Create an index by changing the Indexed property.

NOTE Fields that are tagged as primary keys are already indexed. You can index fields that have duplicate values by setting the Indexed property of the field to Yes(Duplicates OK). Each table in your database can have up to 32 separate indexes.

Now before you go out and start creating an index on every field in your database, there is one caveat to indexing. Although indexes do speed up Select queries dramatically, they significantly slow down action queries such as Update, Delete, and Append. This is because when you run an action query on indexed fields, Access has to update each index in addition to changing the actual table. To that end, it's important that you limit the fields that you index. A best practice is to limit your indexes to the following types of fields:

- Fields where you will routinely filter values using criteria
- Fields you anticipate using as joins on other tables
- Fields where you anticipate sorting values regularly

TIP See Chapter 2, "Access Basics", for a refresher on indexes.

Optimizing by Improving Query Design

You would be surprised how a few simple choices in query design can improve the performance of your queries. Take a moment to review some of the actions you can take to speed up your queries and optimize your analytical processes.

- Avoid sorting or filtering fields that are not indexed.
- Avoid building queries that select "*" from a table. For example, **"SELECT * FROM MyTable"**. This forces Access to look up the field names from the system tables every time the query is run.
- When creating a totals query, include only the fields needed to achieve the query's goal. The more fields you include in the GROUP BY clause, the longer the query will take to execute.
- Sometimes you need to include fields in your query design only to set criteria against them. Fields that are not needed in the final results should be set to "not shown". In other words, clear the check box in the Show row of the query design grid.
- Avoid using open-ended ranges such as > or <. Instead, use the `Between...And` statement.

- Use smaller temporary tables in your analytical processes instead of your large core tables. For example, instead of joining two large tables together, consider creating smaller temporary tables that are limited to only the relevant records, then joining those two. You will often find that your processes run faster even with the extra steps of creating and deleting temporary tables.
- Use fixed column headings in Crosstab queries whenever possible. This way, Access does not have to take the extra step of establishing column headings in your Crosstab queries.
- Avoid using calculated fields in subqueries or domain aggregate functions. Subqueries and domain aggregate functions already come with an inherent performance hit. Using calculated fields in them compounds your query's performance loss considerably.

NOTE **Subqueries and domain aggregate queries are discussed in detail in Chapter 8.**

Compacting and Repairing Your Database Regularly

Over time, your database changes because it is used frequently. The number of tables may have increased or decreased, you may have added and removed several temporary tables and queries, you may have abnormally closed the database once or twice, and the list goes on. All this action may change your table statistics, leaving your previously compiled queries with inaccurate query execution plans. When you compact and repair your database, you force Access to regenerate table statistics and re-optimize your queries so that they will be recompiled the next time the query is executed. This ensures that Access runs your queries using the most accurate and efficient query execution plans.

TIP **You can set your database to automatically compact and repair each time you close it by doing the following:**

1. **Click the Office icon on the upper left-hand corner of the ribbon.**
2. **Click the Access Options button. This activates the Access Options dialog box.**
3. **When in the Access Options dialog box, select Current Database to display the configuration settings for the current database. It is here that you will see the Compact on Close setting.**
4. **Select the option Compact on Close and click the OK button to confirm the change.**

Handling Database Corruption

Corruption is a state where an error occurs in your Access database and causes unpredictable behavior or, in worst-case scenarios, renders your database unusable. To understand why corruption happens, you need to understand how the ACE database engine manages data.

ACE administers your data in a series of blocks, each consisting of 4,096 bytes of data. When you see a table in a database, you see it as a solid object, but it's actually made of blocks of data. Depending on the size of the table, a table can be made of one block of data or many blocks that point to each other. Most corruption is caused by errors that occur when writing to one or more of these blocks. In fact, small-scale corruption happens all the time; you just don't know it because ACE usually resolves these corruption issues during the course of reading and writing data. However, sometimes ACE cannot resolve the issue on its own. In these cases, the database is considered corrupted.

Signs and Symptoms of a Corrupted Database

There are many reasons why a database would become corrupted. The database may have encountered errors while writing data, table definitions may have been degraded over time, some VBA code or macro may have caused a fatal error, and the list goes on. The point being made here is that since corruption can be caused by a wide range of nebulous issues, the signs and symptoms of a corrupted database are just as expansive and just as nebulous. You will never see a message explicitly stating that your database is corrupt. So the question is, how do you know if your database has been corrupted?

Databases that fall victim to corruption can generally be separated into two categories: those that you can open and work with, and those that will not open at all.

Watching for Corruption in Seemingly Normal Databases

The dangerous thing about corrupted databases that are still usable is that you may never know that you are working with a corrupted database. It can be quite difficult to spot the signs of this type of corruption. That being said, there are some reasonably clear indicators that strongly suggest corruption:

- You get an error message stating "Invalid field data type" when trying to open a table in either Data view or Design view or when viewing the relationships window.
- You get an error message stating "Could not find field Description" when trying to compact and repair the database.
- When you try to open a table, a query, a form, a report, or a data access page, you get one of the following messages:
  - "MSAccess can't open the table in datasheet view"
  - "Record is deleted."
  - "Unable to carry out the command."
  - "There was an error executing the command."
- You get an error message stating, "Table 'TempMSysAccessObjects' already exists" when trying to compact and repair the database.
- Nothing happens when you try to open or delete a linked table.
- Access unexpectedly closes and then tries to send an error report.
- You get an error message *falsely* stating that "The changes you requested to the table were not successful because they would create duplicate values in the index, primary key, or relationship."
- #DELETED# starts appearing in your tables.
- Access starts to drop records randomly.
- You get an error message stating "Invalid argument" when clicking on a record.
- All fields for a specific record show #Error when you run a query against that record or view it in a form.

Common Errors Associated with Database Corruption

A tell-tale sign that a database has become corrupted is when the database will not open at all. The following error messages are the most common ones associated with a corrupted database that will not open:

- AOIndex is not an index in this table.
- Could not use; file already in use.
- Enter database password (when none has been set).
- Failure to open/failure to show error.

- Microsoft Access has encountered a problem and needs to close.
- Microsoft Access has encountered a problem and needs to close. We are sorry for the inconvenience.
- Microsoft ACE database engine could not find object MSysDB. Make sure the object exists and that you spell its name correctly and the path name correctly.
- MSysCompactError. Make sure the object exists and that you spell its name correctly and the path name correctly.
- Operation failed too many indexes reduce the number and try again.
- Operation invalid without current index.
- The database databasename.accdb needs to be repaired or isn't a Microsoft Access database file.
- The database has been placed in a state by user <*X*> on machine <*M*> that prevents it from being opened or locked.
- The instruction at 0x???????? referenced memory at 0x????????. The memory could not be written.
- The Microsoft ACE database engine cannot find the input table or query MSysAccessObjects. Make sure it exists and that its name is spelled correctly
- The Microsoft ACE database engine cannot open the file.
- The Microsoft ACE database engine could not find the object <*File name*>. Make sure the object exists and that you spell its name and path name correctly.
- The Microsoft ACE database engine could not find the object.
- The Microsoft ACE database engine stopped the process because you and another user are attempting to change the same data at the same time.
- The VBA project in the database is corrupt.
- This database has been converted from a prior version of Microsoft Access by using the DAO CompactDatabase method instead of the Convert Database command on the Tools menu (Database Utilities submenu). This has left the database in a partially converted state. If you have a copy of the database in its original format, use the Convert Database command on the Tools menu (Database Utilities submenu) to convert it. If the original database is no longer available, create a new database and import your tables and queries to preserve your data. Your other database objects can't be recovered.

- This database is in an unrecognized format. The database may have been created with a later version of Microsoft Access than the one you are using. Upgrade your version of Microsoft Access to the current one, then open this database.
- Unexpected Error 35012.
- Unrecognized database format.
- The VBA project in this database is corrupt.
- You do not have the necessary permissions to open this object. Please contact your system administrator.

Recovering a Corrupted Database

If you have determined that your database is indeed corrupt, there are actions you can take to attempt recovery. Keep in mind that your ability to fix a corrupted database depends on the nature and extent of the corruption. The idea is to follow these steps until your issue is resolved.

1. **Make a backup copy of the corrupt database.** Any recovery attempts come with the possibility of permanently disabling the database. You will definitely want a backup in case this happens.
2. **Try working in another environment.** Try opening and using the database on several local machines (especially if you are working with the database through a network). If this resolves your issue, the problem is probably not a corruption issue. Look for other hardware or software issues.
3. **Delete the .laccdb file associated with the database.** When you open an Access database, a .laccdb file is created. This file is the mechanism that allows for multi-user operations. Deleting the associated .laccdb file will ensure that no rogue instances of the database are left hanging around. If you cannot delete the file, use the windows task manager and end all instances of MSAccess or any other process that could be logged into the database. In some cases, this action can actually resolve your issue.
4. **Import your database into a new .laccdb file.** Start a new database and attempt to import your tables, queries, forms, reports, macros, data access pages, and modules from the corrupted database. In most cases, all of your data and code can be salvaged using this method.

5. **Restore the database from a previously backed up version.** If you have a backup of your database, you may want to use it to help restore some of the data you have lost.
6. **Use an Access Repair Service.** The last resort is to use an Access repair service. These services use specialized software to restore databases; with a success rate close to 99 percent. This will cost you between $50 and $200, depending on the company you use and the complexity of your issue. You can find a plethora of these services by entering "corrupt Access database" into any of the major search engines.

Steps You Can Take to Prevent Database Corruption

Unfortunately, there isn't a clear set of warnings alerting you to the fact that your database is on the verge of corruption. By the time you know that you have a corrupted database, it's too late. In that light, remember that preparation is a lot better that desperation. Get into the habit of taking a few simple measures that will minimize the chance of corruption and prepare you for the event of a corrupted database.

Backing Up Your Database on a Regular Basis

Having a backup of your database is like having a spare tire. There is no better safeguard against loosing data than having a spare copy of it stored away. When you choose a backup plan, you will want to consider two things: when and where. You will want to choose a backup schedule that directly relates to your threshold of data loss. For example, if you cannot lose more than one day of data, make a backup of your database every day. If daily backups are excessive, make a weekly backup. Where should you back up your database? You will want to choose a location that is safe, accessible, and not in the same folder as your working database.

Compacting and Repairing Your Database on a Regular Basis

There are certain things that happen through the natural course of using a database. For example, the data blocks in the database become fragmented, the table statistics become outmoded, and the database grows in size. Although none of these occurrences directly lead to a corrupt database, they can contribute to one if left unchecked. Many Access users think that the compact and repair utility simply releases disk space, but several important actions are performed with a compact and repair procedure.

The compact and repair utility:

- Reclaims disk space and ensures the prevention of database bloat.
- Defragments the blocks of data that make up table pages, improving performance and making efficient use of the read ahead cache.
- Resets AutoNumber fields, ensuring that the next value allocated will be one more than the highest value in the remaining records.
- Regenerates table statistics used by the query optimizer to create query execution strategies.
- Flags all queries, indicating a recompile the next time the query is executed.

These actions can play a big part in keeping your database streamlined and efficient. You can set your database to automatically compact and repair each time you close it. To do this, follow these steps:

1. Click the Office Icon in the upper left-hand corner of the ribbon.
2. Click the Access Options button. This opens the Access Options dialog box.
3. In the Access Options dialog box, select Current Database to display the configuration settings for the current database. It is here that you will see the Compact on Close setting.
4. Select the Compact on Close check box and click the OK button to confirm the change.

Avoiding Interruption of Service while Writing to Your Database

The most common cause of corruption is interruption while writing to your database. Interrupted write processes can lead to a host of issues from incomplete table definitions to lost indexes. In that vein, be sure to avoid any type of abnormal or abrupt termination of Access. Following these general guidelines will help you avoid corruption due to interrupted processes:

- Always wait until all queries, macros, and procedures have completed execution before closing Access.
- Avoid using the Task Manager to shut down Access.
- Never place your Access database on a file server that is regularly shut down or rebooted.
- Avoid power loss while working with your database. If your database is on a file server, make sure the server has protection against power surges or power outages.

Never Working with a Database from Removable Media

When you work with an Access database, additional disk space is needed for the .laccdb file and for the normal database bloat that comes with using Access. If you open an Access database on removable media such as a memory stick or a ZIP disk, you run the risk of corruption due to disk space errors. A good practice is to copy the database to your hard drive, work with the database there, and then copy it back to the removable media when you are done.

Getting Help in Access

As you experiment with new functions and tools in Access, you may sometimes need a little help or a simple push in the right direction. The first place you should look is the Access Help system. It is true that the Help system in Access has its flaws. To a new user, the Access Help system may seem like a clunky add-in that returns a perplexing list of topics that has nothing to do with the original topic being searched. However, it is often the fastest and easiest way to get help on a topic. The following sections provide some tips that will help you get the most out of the Access Help system.

Location Matters When Asking for Help

You may remember the Help system in Access 97 being a lot more user-friendly and more effective than newer versions of Access. Rest assured that you are not just imagining it. The fact is that Microsoft did fundamentally change the mechanics of the Access Help system. In Access 97, when you entered a key word in the search index, Access did a global search, throwing your search criteria against all the topics within Access.

In the later versions of Access, however, there are actually two Help systems: one providing help on Access features and another on VBA programming topics. Instead of doing a global search with your criteria, Access throws your search criteria only against the help system that is relevant to your current location. This essentially means that the help you get is determined by the area of Access in which you are working. In that vein, if you require help on a topic that involves VBA programming, you will need to be in the VBA Editor while performing your search. On the other hand, if you need help on building a query, it's best to be in the Query Design view. This ensures that your key word search is performed on the correct help system.

Online Help Is Better than Off-Line Help

When you search for help on a topic, Access checks to see if there is an Internet connection available. If there is, Access returns help results based on online content from the Microsoft web site. If there is no Internet connection available, Access uses the help files that are locally stored with Microsoft Office. One way to maximize the help you are getting in Access is to use the online help. Online help is generally better than off-line help because often the content you find with online help is more detailed and includes updated information as well as links to other resources not available off-line.

Diversifying Your Knowledgebase with Online Resources

Familiarize yourself with a handful of web sites and forums dedicated to Access. These resources can serve as supplemental help, not only for basic Access topics, but also for situation-specific tips and tricks. The following list of sites should get you started. These sites are free to use and are particularly helpful when you need an extra push in the right direction.

- Access topics and general help:

  `www.allenbrowne.com`

  `www.mvps.org/access/`

- Access tutorials and samples:

  `www.fontstuff.com`

  `www.datapigtechnologies.com`

- Access discussion groups and forums:

  `www.microsoft.com/office/community/en-us/default.mspx`

  `www.utteraccess.com`

Summary

As your database grows in size and complexity, you must take precautionary measure to guard against a loss in performance and database corruption. In this chapter, you covered some of the simple steps you can take to optimize query performance and protect against database corruption.

The performance of your analytical processes largely depends on the make-up and utility of your tables and queries. That is to say, poorly designed tables and queries can limit the efficiency and speed of your queries. To that end, there are actions you can take to help maximize query optimization: normalize your database design, use indexes on appropriate fields, and Compact and Repair your database frequently.

Database corruption can cause a wide range of serious issues from deleted records to a loss of entire databases. However, just as there are actions to protect against a loss in performance, there are actions you can take to avoid database corruption and loss of data. To mention a few: you can create regular backups of your database, Compact and Repair your database frequently, and avoid interruption of service while writing to your database.

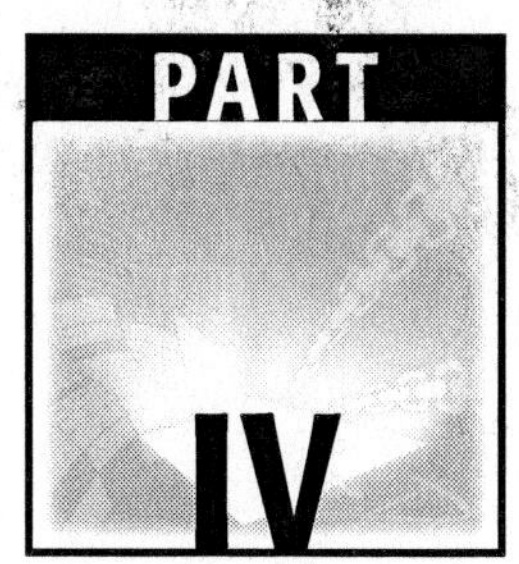

Automating Data Analysis

APPENDIX

A

Data Analyst's Function Reference

Access 2007 has over 140 built-in functions that perform a wide variety of tasks.

The list outlined in this appendix is designed to provide a solid reference to the functions that are most relevant to the realm of data analysis. Several of these functions have been covered in detail throughout the chapters in this book.

TIP **You can learn more about the functions that have not been covered here by using the Access Help system.**

Abs

Purpose

The `Abs` function is a math function that returns a value that represents the absolute value of the number. That is, the magnitude of the number without the positive or negative sign. For example, `Abs(-5)` would return 5.

Arguments

```
Abs(number)
```

Number (required): This is the numeric expression you are evaluating. In a query environment, you can use the name of a field to specify that you are evaluating all the row values of that field.

Asc

Purpose

The `Asc` function is a conversion function used to convert a string to its ASCII code. For example, `Asc("A")` would return 65 because 65 is the ASCII code for the uppercase letter A. If you pass a whole word to the `Asc` function, it will only return the ASCII code for the first letter of the word.

Arguments

```
Asc(String)
```

String (required): This is the string you are evaluating. If the string you are passing to the function contains no characters, the function will fail and produce a runtime error.

Atn

Purpose

The `Atn` function is a math function that allows you to calculate the arctangent of a number.

Arguments

```
Atn(number)
```

Number (required): This is the numeric expression you are evaluating.

Choose

Purpose

The `Choose` function is a program flow function that allows you to return a value from a list of choices based on a given position. For example: `Choose(3, "Microsoft", "Access", "Data", "Analysis")` would return Data, because Data is in the third position in the list of values.

Arguments

```
Choose(PositionNumber, List of Values Separated by Commas)
```

PositionNumber (required): This is the numeric expression or field that results in a value between 1 and the number of available choices. If this argument's value is less than 1 or greater than the number of choices in the function, a Null value will be returned.

List of Values Separated by Commas (required): This is a variant expression that contains a list of one or more values.

Chr

Purpose

The `Chr` Function is a conversion function that is used to convert a string to its associated ASCII code. For example, `Chr(65)` would return A.

Arguments

```
Chr(Number)
```

Number (required): This is the number value that represents an ASCII character code. If the number you are passing to the function is not a valid ASCII character code, the function will fail and produce a runtime error.

Cos

Purpose

The `Cos` function is a math function that allows you to calculate the cosine of an angle.

Arguments

```
Cos(number)
```

Number (required): This is the numeric expression that represents an angle in radians.

Date

Purpose

The `Date` function returns today's date based on your PC's current system date. The `Date` function is key to performing any analysis that involves a time comparison in relation to today's date. There are no required arguments for this function; to use it, simply enter `Date()`.

DateAdd

Purpose

The `DateAdd` function returns a date to which a specified interval has been added. In other words, the `DateAdd` function allows you to calculate a date by adding 30 days to it, subtracting 3 weeks from it, adding 4 months to it, or so on. For example:

- `DateAdd("ww",1,#11/30/2004#)` adds 1 week, returning 12/7/2004.
- `DateAdd("m",2,#11/30/2004#)` adds 2 months, returning 1/30/2005.
- `DateAdd("yyyy",-1,#11/30/2004#)` subtracts 1 year, returning 11/30/2003.

Arguments

```
DateAdd(Interval, Number, Date)
```

Interval (required): This is the interval of time you want to use. The intervals available are:

"yyyy" - Year
"q" - Quarter
"m" - Month
"y" - Day of year
"d" - Day
"w" - Weekday
"ww" - Week
"h" - Hour
"n" - Minute
"s" - Second

Number (required): This is the number of intervals to add. A positive number will return a date in the future, whereas a negative number will return a date in the past.

Date (required): This is the date value with which you are working. In a query environment, you can use the name of a field to specify that you are evaluating all the row values of that field.

DateDiff

Purpose

The `DateDiff` function returns the difference between two dates based on a specified time interval. For example, `DateDiff('yyyy', #5/16/1972#, #5/16/2005#)` returns 33 because there is a difference of 33 years between the two dates.

Arguments

```
DateDiff(Interval, Date1, Date2, FirstDayOfTheWeek, FirstWeekOfTheYear)
```

Interval (required): This is the interval of time you want to use. The intervals available are:

"yyyy" - Year
"q" - Quarter
"m" - Month
"y" - Day of year
"d" - Day
"w" - Weekday
"ww" - Week
"h" - Hour
"n" - Minute
"s" - Second

Date1 (required): This is one of the two dates you want to calculate the difference between. In a query environment, you can use the name of a field to specify that you are evaluating all the row values of that field.

Date2 (required): This is one of the two dates you want to calculate the difference between. In a query environment, you can use the name of a field to specify that you are evaluating all the row values of that field.

FirstDayOfTheWeek (optional): This specifies which day you want to count as the first day of the week. Enter 1 in this argument to make the first day Sunday, 2 for Monday, 3 for Tuesday, and so on. If this argument is omitted, the first day is a Sunday by default.

FirstWeekOfTheYear (optional): This specifies the first week of the year. In most cases, you would omit this argument. This uses the first week that includes January 1 as the default. However, you can alter this setting by using one of the following values.

0 - Use the NLS(National Language Support) API setting.

1 - Use the first week that includes January 1.

2 - Use the first week that has at least four days.

3 - Use the first week that has seven days.

DatePart

Purpose

The `DatePart` function allows you to evaluate a date and return a specific interval of time represented in that date. For example, `DatePart("q",#6/4/2004#)` returns 2 (as in second quarter) which is the quarter that is represented in that date.

Arguments

```
DatePart(Interval, ValidDate, FirstDayOfTheWeek, FirstWeekOfTheYear)
```

Interval (required): This is the interval of time you want to use. The intervals available are:

"yyyy" - Year

"q" - Quarter

"m" - Month

"y" - Day of year

"d" - Day

"w" - Weekday

"ww" - Week

"h" - Hour

"n" - Minute

"s" - Second

ValidDate (required): This is the date value with which you are working. In a query environment, you can use the name of a field to specify that you are evaluating all the row values of that field.

FirstDayOfTheWeek (optional): This specifies which day you want to count as the first day of the week. Enter 1 in this argument to make the first day Sunday, 2 for Monday, 3 for Tuesday, and so on. If this argument is omitted, the first day is a Sunday by default.

FirstWeekOfTheYear (optional): This specifies the first week of the year. In most cases, you would omit this argument. This uses the first week that includes January 1 as the default. However, you can alter this setting by using one of the following values.

0 - Use the NLS API setting.

1 - Use the first week that includes January 1.

2 - Use the first week that has at least four days.

3 - Use the first week that has seven days.

DateSerial

Purpose

The `DateSerial` function allows you to construct a date value by combining given year, month, and day components. This function is perfect for converting disparate strings that, together, represent a date, into an actual date. For example, `DateSerial(2004, 4, 3)` returns April 3, 2004.

Arguments

```
DateSerial(Year, Month, Day)
```

Year (required): Any number or numeric expression from 100 to 9999.

Month (required): Any number or numeric expression.

Day (required): Any number or numeric expression.

DateValue

Purpose

The `DateValue` function enables you to convert a string or expression that represents a valid date, time, or both into a date value. For example, `DateValue("October 31, 2004")` returns 10/31/2004.

Arguments

```
DateValue(Expression)
```

Expression (required): Any string or valid expression that can represent a valid date, time, or both.

Day

Purpose

The `Day` function is a conversion function that converts a valid date to a number from 1 to 31, representing the day of the month for a given date. For example, `Day(#5/16/1972#)` returns 16.

Arguments

```
Day(ValidDate)
```

ValidDate (required): This is any value that can represent a valid date. In a query environment, you can use the name of a field to specify that you are evaluating all the row values of that field.

DDB

Purpose

The DDB function is a financial function that calculates the depreciation of an asset for a specific period using the double-declining balance method or another specified method.

Arguments

```
DDB(Cost, Salvage, Life, Period, Factor)
```

Cost (required): This is the initial cost of the asset; must be a positive number.

Salvage (required): This is the value of the asset at the end of its useful life; must be a positive number.

Life (required): This is the length of the useful life of the asset.

Period (required): This is the period for which asset depreciation is calculated.

Factor (optional): This is the rate at which the balance declines. The default setting for this argument is the double-declining method (a factor of 2).

Domain Aggregate Functions

Purpose

Domain aggregate functions enable you to extract and aggregate statistical information from an entire dataset (a domain). These functions differ from an Aggregate query in that an Aggregate query groups data before evaluating the values whereas a domain aggregate function evaluates the values for the entire dataset. There are 12 different domain aggregate functions, but they all have the same arguments.

Arguments

```
("Field Name]","[Dataset Name]", "[Criteria]")
```

Field Name (required): This expression identifies the field containing the data with which you are working. This argument must be in quotes.

Dataset Name (required): This expression identifies the table or query you are working with; also known as the domain. This argument must be in quotes.

Criteria (optional): This expression is used to restrict the range of data on which the domain aggregate function is performed. If omitted, the domain aggregate function is performed against the entire dataset. This argument must be in quotes.

Additional Remarks

The 12 different domain aggregate functions are:

DSum: The `DSum` function returns the total sum value of a specified field in the domain. `DSum("[Sales_Amount]", "[TransactionMaster]")` gives you the total sum of sales amount in the TransactionMaster table.

DAvg: The `DAvg` function returns the average value of a specified field in the domain. `DAvg("[Sales_Amount]", "[Transaction Master]")` gives you the average sales amount in the Transaction-Master table.

DCount: The `DCount` function returns the total number of records in the domain. `DCount("*", "[TransactionMaster]")` gives you the total number of records in the TransactionMaster table.

DLookup: The `DLookup` function returns the first value of a specified field that matches the criteria you define within the `DLookup` function. If you don't supply a criterion, the `DLookup` function returns a random value in the domain. `DLookup` functions are particularly useful when you need to retrieve a value from an outside dataset.

`DLookUp("[Last_Name]","[Employee_Master]", "[Employee_Number]='42620' ")` returns the value in the Last_Name field of the record where the Employee_Number is '42620'.

DMin, DMax: The `DMin` and `DMax` functions return the minimum and maximum values in the domain, respectively. `DMin("[Sales_Amount]", "[TransactionMaster]")` returns the lowest sales amount in the TransactionMaster, whereas `DMax("[Sales_Amount]", "[TransactionMaster]")` returns the highest sales amount.

DFirst, DLast: The `DFirst` and `DLast` functions return the first and last values in the domain, respectively. `DFirst("[Sales_Amount]", "[TransactionMaster]")` returns the first sales amount in the TransactionMaster table, whereas `DLast("[Sales_Amount]", "[TransactionMaster]")` returns the last.

DStdev, Dstdevp, DVar, Dvarp: You can use the `DStdev` and the `DStdevp` functions to return the standard deviation across a population sample and a population respectively. The `Dvar` and the `Dvarp` functions similarly return the variance across a population sample and a population.

Exp

Purpose

The `Exp` function is a math function that raises the base of natural logarithms (2.718282) number to a power you specify.

Arguments

```
Exp(Number)
```

Number (required): This is the numeric expression that is used as the power to raise 2.718282.

FormatCurrency

Purpose

The `FormatCurrency` function is a conversion function that converts an expression to a currency using the currency symbol defined by your computer's regional settings.

Arguments

```
FormatCurrency(Number,TrailingDigits,LeadingDigits,NegativeParens,Group)
```

Number (required): This is the number value you want to convert. In a query environment, you can use the name of a field to specify that you are evaluating all the row values of that field.

TrailingDigits (optional): This is the number of digits to the right of the decimal you want displayed.

LeadingDigits (optional): This indicates whether a leading zero is displayed for fractional values. The settings for this argument are -1 for True, 0 for False, or -2 to use the computer's regional/default settings.

NegativeParens (optional): This specifies if negative values should be wrapped in parentheses. The settings for this argument are -1 for True, 0 for False, or -2 to use the computer's regional settings FormatNumber.

Group (optional): This indicates whether or not numbers are grouped using the group delimiter specified in the computer's regional settings. The settings for this argument are -1 for True, 0 for False, or -2 to use the computer's regional settings.

FormatDateTime

Purpose

The `FormatDateTime` function is a conversion function that converts an expression to a date or time.

Arguments

```
FormatDateTime(Date,NamedFormat)
```

Date (required): This is the date/time expression you want to convert. In a query environment, you can use the name of a field to specify that you are evaluating all the row values of that field.

NamedFormat (optional): This is the format code specifying the date/time format you would like to use. The settings for this argument are as follows:

0 - Display date as a short date and time as a long time.

1 - Display a date using the long date format specified in your computer's regional settings.

2 - Display a date using the short date format specified in your computer's regional settings.

3 - Display a time using the time format specified in your computer's regional settings.

4 - Display a time using the 24-hour format (hh:mm).

FormatNumber

Purpose

The `FormatNumber` function is a conversion function that converts a numeric expression to a formatted number.

Arguments

```
FormatNumber(Number,TrailingDigits,LeadingDigits,NegativeParens,Group)
```

Number (required): This is the number value you want to convert. In a query environment, you can use the name of a field to specify that you are evaluating all the row values of that field.

TrailingDigits (optional): This is the number of digits to the right of the decimal you want displayed.

LeadingDigits (optional): This indicates whether a leading zero is displayed for fractional values. The settings for this argument are -1 for True, 0 for False, or -2 to use the computer's regional/default settings.

NegativeParens (optional): This specifies if negative values should be wrapped in parentheses. The settings for this argument are -1 for True, 0 for False, or -2 to use the computer's regional settings.

Group (optional): This indicates whether or not numbers are grouped using the group delimiter specified in the computer's regional settings. The settings for this argument are -1 for True, 0 for False, or -2 to use the computer's regional settings.

FormatPercent

Purpose

The `FormatPercent` function is a conversion function that converts a numeric expression to a formatted percentage with a trailing percent (%) character.

Arguments

```
FormatPercent(Number,TrailingDigits,LeadingDigits,NegativeParens,Group)
```

Number (required): This is the number value you want to convert. In a query environment, you can use the name of a field to specify that you are evaluating all the row values of that field.

TrailingDigits (optional): This is the number of digits to the right of the decimal you want displayed.

LeadingDigits (optional): This indicates whether a leading zero is displayed for fractional values. The settings for this argument are 1 for True, 0 for False, or 2 to use the computer's regional settings.

NegativeParens (optional): This specifies if negative values should be wrapped in parentheses. The settings for this argument are 1 for True, 0 for False, or 2 to use the computer's regional settings.

Group (optional): This indicates whether or not numbers are grouped using the group delimiter specified in the computer's regional settings. The settings for this argument are 1 for True, 0 for False, or 2 to use the computer's regional settings.

FV

Purpose

The `FV` function is a financial function that allows you to calculate an annuity's future value. An annuity is a series of fixed cash payments normally made against a loan over a period of time.

Arguments

```
FV(Rate, PaymentPeriods, PaymentAmount, PresentValue, Type)
```

Rate (required): This is the average interest rate per period.

PaymentPeriods (required): This is the total number of payment periods in the annuity.

PaymentAmount (required): This is the payment amount, usually consisting of principal and interest.

PresentValue (optional): This is the present value of future payments. If omitted, 0 is assumed.

Type (optional): This argument specifies when payments are due. A value of 0 means that payments are due at the end of the payment period, whereas a value of 1 means that payments are due at the beginning of the payment period. If omitted, 0 is assumed.

Hour

Purpose

The `Hour` function is a conversion function that converts a valid time to a number from 0 to 23, representing the hour of the day. For example, `Hour(#9:30:00 PM#)` returns 21.

Arguments

```
Hour(ValidTime)
```

ValidTime (required): This is any combination of values that can represent valid time. In a query environment, you can use the name of a field to specify that you are evaluating all the row values of that field.

IIf

Purpose

The `IIf` function is a program flow function that allows you to create an `If...Then...Else` statement, returning one value if a condition evaluates to True, and another value if it evaluates to False.

Arguments

```
IIf(Expression, TrueAnswer, FalseAnswer)
```

Expression (required): This is the expression you want to evaluate.

TrueAnswer (required): This is the value to return if the expression is true.

FalseAnswer (required): This is the value to return if the expression is false.

InStr

Purpose

The `InStr` function is a text function that searches for a specified string in another string and returns its position number. For example: `InStr("Alexander, Mike","x")` would returns 4 because the "x" is character number 4 in this string.

Arguments

```
InStr(Start, SearchString, FindString, Compare)
```

Start (optional): This is the character number to start the search; default is 1.

SearchString (required): This is the string to be searched.

FindString (required): This is the string to search for.

Compare (optional): This specifies the type of string comparison.

Additional Remarks

The Compare argument can have the following values:

-1 - Performs a comparison using the setting of the Option Compare statement.

0 - Performs a binary comparison.

1 - Performs a textual comparison.

2 - Microsoft Access only. Performs a comparison based on information in your database.

InStrRev

Purpose

The `InStrRev` function is a text function that searches for a specified string in another string and returns its position number from the end of the string.

Arguments

```
InstrRev(SearchString, FindString, Start, Compare)
```

SearchString (required): This is the string to be searched.

FindString (required): This is the string to search for.

Start (optional): This is the character number to start the search; default is 1.

Compare (optional): This specifies the type of string comparison.

Additional Remarks

The Compare argument can have the following values:

-1 - Performs a comparison using the setting of the Option Compare statement.

0 - Performs a binary comparison.

1 - Performs a textual comparison.

2 - Microsoft Access only. Performs a comparison based on information in your database.

IPmt

Purpose

The `IPmt` function is a financial function that allows you to calculate the interest paid within a specified period during the life of an annuity. An annuity is a series of fixed cash payments normally made against a loan over a period of time.

Arguments

```
IPmt(Rate, Period, PaymentPeriods, PresentValue, FutureValue, Type)
```

Rate (required): This is the average interest rate per period.

Period (required): This is the specified payment period in question.

PaymentPeriods (required): This is the total number of payment periods in the annuity.

PresentValue (required): This is the present value of future payments.

FutureValue (optional): This is the future value or final balance on a loan or an investment upon making the last payment. If omitted, 0 is assumed.

Type (optional): This argument specifies when payments are due. A value of 0 means that payments are due at the end of the payment period, whereas a value of 1 means that payments are due at the beginning of the payment period. If omitted, 0 is assumed.

IRR

Purpose

The `IRR` function is a financial function that calculates the internal rate of return based on serial cash flow, payments, and receipts.

Arguments

```
IRR(IncomeValues, Guess)
```

IncomeValues (required): These values make up an array that represent the periodic cash flow values. Within this array, there must be at least one negative number and one positive number.

Guess (optional): This argument allows you to estimate the percent of total investment that will be returned. If this is omitted, 10 percent is used.

IsError

Purpose

The `IsError` function is an inspection function that determines if an expression is evaluates as an error. This function returns a True or False answer.

Arguments

```
IsError(Expression)
```

Expression (required): This is any value or expression. In a query environment, you can use the name of a field to specify that you are evaluating all the row values of that field.

IsNull

Purpose

The `IsNull` function is an inspection function that determines if a value contains no valid date. This function returns a True or False answer.

Arguments

```
IsNull(Expression)
```

Expression (required): This is any value or expression. In a query environment, you can use the name of a field to specify that you are evaluating all the row values of that field.

IsNumeric

Purpose

The `IsNumeric` function is an inspection function that determines if an expression evaluates as a numeric value. This function returns a True or False answer.

Arguments

```
IsNumeric(Expression)
```

Expression (required): This is any value or expression. In a query environment, you can use the name of a field to specify that you are evaluating all the row values of that field.

LCase

Purpose

The `LCase` function converts a string to lowercase letters.

Arguments

```
LCase(String)
```

String (required): This is the string to be converted. In a query environment, you can use the name of a field to specify that you are converting all the row values of that field.

Left

Purpose

The `Left` function returns a specified number of characters starting from the left most character of the string. For example, `Left("Nowhere", 3)` returns Now.

Arguments

```
Left(String, NumberofCharacters)
```

String (required): This is the string to be evaluated. In a query environment, you can use the name of a field to specify that you are evaluating all the row values of that field.

NumberofCharacters (required): This is the number of characters you want returned. If this argument is greater than or equal to the number of characters in a string, the entire string is returned.

Len

Purpose

The `Len` function returns a number identifying the number of characters in a given string. This function is quite useful when you need to dynamically determine the length of a string. For example, `Len("Alexander")` returns 9.

Arguments

```
Len(String or Variable)
```

String or Variable (required): This is the string or variable to be evaluated. In a query environment, you can use the name of a field to specify that you are evaluating all the row values of that field.

Log

Purpose

The `Log` function is a math function that calculates the natural logarithm of a number.

Arguments

```
Log(Number)
```

Number (required): This is the numeric expression that is to be evaluated; must be greater than zero.

Mid

Purpose

The `Mid` function returns a specified number of characters starting from a specified character position. The required arguments for the `Mid` function are: The text you are evaluating, the starting position, and the number of characters you want returned. For example: `Mid("Lonely", 2, 3)` captures 3 characters starting from character number 2 in the string, returning *one*.

Arguments

```
Mid(String, StartPosition, NumberofCharacters)
```

String (required): This is the string to be evaluated. In a query environment, you can use the name of a field to specify that you are evaluating all the row values of that field.

StartPosition (required): This is the position number of the character you want to start your capture.

NumberofCharacters (required): This is the number of characters you want returned. If this argument is greater than or equal to the number of characters in a string, the entire string is returned.

Minute

Purpose

The Minute function converts a valid time to a number from 0 to 59, representing the minute of the hour. For example, `Minute(#9:30:00 PM#)` returns 30.

Arguments

```
Minute(ValidTime)
```

ValidTime (required): This is any combination of values that can represent valid time. In a query environment, you can use the name of a field to specify that you are evaluating all the row values of that field.

MIRR

Purpose

The `MIRR` function is a financial function that calculates the internal rate of return based on serial cash flow, payments, and receipts that are financed at different rates.

Arguments

```
MIRR(IncomeValues, FinanceRate, ReinvestRate)
```

IncomeValues (required): These values make up an array that represents the periodic cash flow values. Within this array, there must be at least one negative number and one positive number.

FinanceRate (required): This is the interest rate paid as the cost of investing. The values of this argument must be represented as decimal values.

ReinvestRate (required): This is the interest rate received on gains from cash reinvestment. The values of this argument must be represented as decimal values.

Month

Purpose

The `Month` function converts a valid date to a number from 1 to 12, representing the month for a given date. For example, `Month(#5/16/1972#)` returns 5.

Arguments

```
Month(ValidDate)
```

ValidDate (required): This is any value that can represent valid date. In a query environment, you can use the name of a field to specify that you are evaluating all the row values of that field.

MonthName

Purpose

The `MonthName` function converts a numeric month designation (1 to 12) to a month name. For example, `MonthName(8)` returns August. Values less than 1 or greater than 12 will cause an error.

Arguments

```
MonthName(NumericMonth, Abbreviated)
```

NumericMonth (required): This is a number from 1 to 12 that represents a month. 1 represents January, 2 represents February, and so on.

Abbreviated (optional): This specifies whether the month is abbreviated or not. If this argument is omitted, the month is not abbreviated. Enter 1 to return abbreviated months.

Now

Purpose

The Now function returns today's date and time based on your PC's current system date and time. There are no required arguments for this function; to use it, simply enter Now().

NPer

Purpose

The NPer function is a financial function that specifies the number of periods for an annuity based on periodic, fixed payments at a fixed interest rate. An annuity is a series of fixed cash payments normally made against a loan over a period of time.

Arguments

```
NPer(Rate, PaymentAmount, PresentValue, FutureValue, Type)
```

Rate (required): This is the average interest rate per period.

PaymentAmount (required): This is the payment amount, usually consisting of principal and interest.

PresentValue (required): This is the present value of future payments and receipts.

FutureValue (optional): This is the future value or final balance on a loan or an investment upon making the last payment. If omitted, 0 is assumed.

Type (optional): This argument specifies when payments are due. A value of 0 means that payments are due at the end of the payment period, whereas a value of 1 means that payments are due at the beginning of the payment period. If omitted, 0 is assumed.

NPV

Purpose

The NPV function is a financial function that calculates the net present value or the current value of a future series of payments and receipts based on serial cash flow, payments, receipts, and a discount rate.

Arguments

```
NPV(DiscountRate, IncomeValues)
```

DiscountRate (required): This is the discount rate received over the length of the period. The values of this argument must be represented as decimal values.

IncomeValues (required): These values make up an array that represents the periodic cash flow values. Within this array, there must be at least one negative number and one positive number.

NZ

Purpose

The `NZ` function enables you to tell Access to recognize Null values as another value, preventing your null values from propagating through an expression.

Arguments

```
NZ(Variant, ValueIfNull)
```

Variant (required): This is the data you are working with.

ValueIfNull (required in the query environment): This is the value you want returned if the Variant is null.

Partition

Purpose

The `Partition` function is a database function that identifies the particular range in which numbers fall and returns a string describing that range. This function is useful when you need to create a quick and easy frequency distribution.

Arguments

```
Partition(Number, Range Start, Range Stop, Interval)
```

Number (required): This is the number you are evaluating. In a query environment, you typically use the name of a field to specify that you are evaluating all the row values of that field.

Range Start (required): This is a whole number that is to be the start of the overall range of numbers. Note that this number cannot be less than zero.

Range Stop (required): This is a whole number that is to be the end of the overall range of numbers. Note that this number cannot be equal to or less than the Range Start.

Interval (required): This is a whole number that is to be the span of each range in the series from Range Start to Range Stop. Note that this number cannot be less than one.

Pmt

Purpose

The `Pmt` function is a financial function that calculates the payment for an annuity based on periodic, fixed payments at a fixed interest rate. An annuity is a series of fixed cash payments normally made against a loan over a period of time.

Arguments

```
Pmt(Rate, PaymentPeriods, PresentValue, FutureValue, Type)
```

Rate (required): This is the average interest rate per period.

PaymentPeriods (required): This is the total number of payment periods in the annuity.

PresentValue (required): This is the present value of future payments and receipts.

FutureValue (optional): This is the future value or final balance on a loan or an investment upon making the last payment. If omitted, 0 is assumed.

Type (optional): This argument specifies when payments are due. A value of 0 means that payments are due at the end of the payment period, while a value of 1 means that payments are due at the beginning of the payment period. If omitted, 0 is assumed.

PPmt

Purpose

The `PPmt` function is a financial function that allows you to calculate the principal payment for a specified period during the life of an annuity. An annuity is a series of fixed cash payments normally made against a loan over a period of time.

Arguments

```
PPmt(Rate, Period, PaymentPeriods, PresentValue, FutureValue, Type)
```

Rate (required): This is the average interest rate per period.

Period (required): This is the specified payment period in question.

PaymentPeriods (required): This is the total number of payment periods in the annuity.

PresentValue (required): This is the present value of future payments and receipts.

FutureValue (optional): This is the future value or final balance on a loan or an investment upon making the last payment. If omitted, 0 is assumed.

Type (optional): This argument specifies when payments are due. A value of 0 means that payments are due at the end of the payment period, whereas a value of 1 means that payments are due at the beginning of the payment period. If omitted, 0 is assumed.

PV

Purpose

The `PV` function is a financial function that allows you to calculate an annuity's present value. An annuity is a series of fixed cash payments normally made against a loan over a period of time.

Arguments

```
PV(Rate, PaymentPeriods, PaymentAmount, FutureValue, Type)
```

Rate (required): This is the average interest rate per period.

PaymentPeriods (required): This is the total number of payment periods in the annuity.

PaymentAmount (required): This is the payment amount, usually consisting of principal and interest.

FutureValue (optional): This is the future value or final balance on a loan or an investment upon making the last payment. If omitted, 0 is assumed.

Type (optional): This argument specifies when payments are due. A value of 0 means that payments are due at the end of the payment period, whereas a value of 1 means that payments are due at the beginning of the payment period. If omitted, 0 is assumed.

Rate

Purpose

The `Rate` function is a financial function that enables you to calculate the interest rate per period for an annuity. An annuity is a series of fixed cash payments normally made against a loan over a period of time.

Arguments

```
Rate(Periods, PaymentAmount, PresentValue, FutureValue, Type, Guess)
```

Periods (required): This is the total number of payment periods in the annuity.

PaymentAmount (required): This is the payment amount, usually consisting of principal and interest.

PresentValue (required): This is the present value of future payments and receipts.

FutureValue (optional): This is the future value or final balance on a loan or an investment upon making the last payment. If omitted, 0 is assumed.

Type (optional): This argument specifies when payments are due. A value of 0 means that payments are due at the end of the payment period, whereas a value of 1 means that payments are due at the beginning of the payment period. If omitted, 0 is assumed.

Guess (optional): This argument allows you to estimate the percent of total investment that will be returned. If this is omitted, 10 percent is used.

Replace

Purpose

The `Replace` function enables you to replace a specified substring with another substring. This function has the same effect as the Find and Replace functionality. For example, `Replace("Pear", "P", "B")` would return Bear.

Arguments

```
Replace(String, Find, Replace, Start, Count, Compare)
```

String (required): This is the full string you are evaluating. In a query environment, you can use the name of a field to specify that you are evaluating all the row values of that field.

Find (required): This is the substring you need to find and replace.

Replace (required): This is the substring used as the replacement.

Start (optional): The position within the substring to begin the search; default is 1.

Count (optional): Number of occurrences to replace; default is all occurrences.

Compare (optional): The kind of comparison to use.

Additional Remarks

The Compare argument can have the following values:

-1 - Performs a comparison using the setting of the Option Compare statement.

0 - Performs a binary comparison.

1 - Performs a textual comparison.

2 - Microsoft Access only. Performs a comparison based on information in your database.

Right

Purpose

The `Right` function returns a specified number of characters starting from the right most character of the string. For example, `Left("Nowhere", 4)` returns here.

Arguments

```
Right(String, NumberofCharacters)
```

String (required): This is the string to be evaluated. In a query environment, you can use the name of a field to specify that you are evaluating all the row values of that field.

NumberofCharacters (required): This is the number of characters you want returned. If this argument is greater than or equal to the number of characters in a string, the entire string is returned.

Rnd

Purpose

The `Rnd` function is a math function that generates and returns a random number that is greater than or equal to 0 but less than 1.

Arguments

```
Rnd(number)
```

Number (optional): This numeric expression determines how the random number is generated. The `Rnd` function follows these rules:

- If the Number argument is omitted from the function, the next random number in the sequence is generated.
- If the Number argument is less than zero, the same number is generated every time.
- If the Number argument is greater than zero, the next random number in the sequence is generated.
- If the Number argument equals zero, the most recently generated number is returned.

Round

Purpose

The `Round` function is a math function that allows you to round a number to a specified number of decimal places. For example, `Round(456.7276)` returns 457.

Arguments

```
Round(Number, DecimalPlaces)
```

Number (required): This is the numeric expression you want to evaluate. In a query environment, you typically use the name of a field to specify that you are evaluating all the row values of that field.

DecimalPlaces (optional): This is the number of places to the right of the decimal that are included in the rounding. If omitted, the Round function returns an integer with zero decimal places.

Second

Purpose

The `Second` function converts a valid time to a number from 0 to 59, representing the second of the minute. For example, `Second(#9:00:35 PM#)` returns 35.

Arguments

```
Second(ValidTime)
```

ValidTime (required): This is any combination of values that can represent valid time. In a query environment, you can use the name of a field to specify that you are evaluating all the row values of that field

Sgn

Purpose

The `Sgn` function is a math function that returns an integer code associated with the sign of a given number. If the given number is less than zero (has a negative designation), the `Sgn` function returns -1. If the given number equals zero, the `Sgn` function returns 0. If the given number is greater than zero (has a positive designation), the `Sgn` function returns 1.

Arguments

```
Sgn(Number)
```

Number (required): This is the numeric expression you are evaluating.

Sin

Purpose

The `Sin` function is a math function that allows you to calculate the sine of an angle.

Arguments

```
Sin(Number)
```

Number (required): This is any numeric expression that expresses an angle in radians.

SLN

Purpose

The `SLN` function is a financial function that calculates the straight-line depreciation of an asset for one period.

Arguments

```
SLN(Cost, Salvage, Life)
```

Cost (required): This is the initial cost of the asset; must be a positive number.

Salvage (required): This is the value of the asset at the end of its useful life; must be a positive number.

Life (required): This is the length of the useful life of the asset.

Space

Purpose

The `Space` function enables you to create a string with a specified number of spaces to a string. This function comes in handy when you need to clear data in fixed-length strings. For example, you can use the `Space` function within an expression such as `Space(5) & "Access"`. This changes the string "Access" to " Access".

Arguments

```
Space(Number)
```

Number (required): This is the number of spaces to include in the string.

SQL Aggregate Functions

Purpose

SQL aggregate functions are the most commonly used functions in Access. These functions perform either mathematical calculations or value evaluations against a given expression. These functions are typically used in a query environment where the Expression argument refers to a field in a table where you are evaluating all the row values of that field.

Sum(Expression): `Sum` calculates the total value of the all the records in the designated field or grouping. This function will only work with the following data types: AutoNumber, Currency, Date/Time, and Number.

Avg(Expression): `Avg` calculates the average of all the records in the designated field or grouping. This function will only work with the following data types: AutoNumber, Currency, Date/Time, and Number.

Count(Expression): `Count` simply counts the number of entries within the designated field or grouping. This function works with all data types.

StDev(Expression): `StDev` calculates the standard deviation across all records within the designated field or grouping. This function only works with the following data types: AutoNumber, Currency, Date/Time, and Number.

Var(Expression): `Var` calculates the amount by which all the values within the designated field or grouping vary from the average value of the group. This function only works with the following data types: AutoNumber, Currency, Date/Time, and Number.

Min(Expression): `Min` returns the value of the record with the lowest value in the designated field or grouping. This function only works with the following data types: AutoNumber, Currency, Date/Time, Number, and Text.

Max(Expression): `Max` returns the value of the record with the highest value in the designated field or grouping. This function only works with the following data types: AutoNumber, Currency, Date/Time, Number, and Text.

First(Expression): `First` returns the value of the first record in the designated field or grouping. This function works with all data types.

Last(Expression): `Last` returns the value of the last record in the designated field or grouping. This function works with all data types.

Sqr

Purpose

The `Sqr` function is a math function that calculates the square root of a given number.

Arguments

```
Sqr(Number)
```

Number (required): This is the numeric expression you are evaluating.

Str

Purpose

The `Str` function is a conversion function that converts a numeric value into a string representation of the number. For example, `Str(2304)` would return " 2304". Note that positive numbers converted with `Str` always have a leading space to represent the positive sign. Negative numbers have a negative sign as the leading character.

Arguments

```
Str(Number)
```

Number (required): This is the number you want to convert to a string. In a query environment, you can use the name of a field to specify that you are evaluating all the row values of that field.

StrConv

Purpose

The `StrConv` function enables you to convert a string to a specified conversion setting such as uppercase, lowercase, or proper case. For example, `StrConv("my text",3)` is converted to proper case, reading My Text.

Arguments

```
StrConv(String, ConversionType, LCID)
```

String (required): This is the string to be converted. In a query environment, you can use the name of a field to specify that you are converting all the row values of that field.

ConversionType (required): The conversion type specifies how to convert the string. The following constants identify the conversion type.

1 - Converts the string to uppercase characters.

2 - Converts the string to lowercase characters.

3 - Converts the first letter of every word in the string to uppercase.

64 - Converts the string to Unicode using the default system code page.

128 - Converts the string from Unicode to the default system code page.

LCID (optional): This is the LocaleID you want to use. The system LocaleID is the default.

String

Purpose

The `String` function allows you to return a character string of a certain length. For example, `String(4, "0")` would return 0000.

Arguments

```
String(LengthOfString, StringCharacter)
```

LengthOfString (required): This is the number of times you want to repeat the StringCharacter.

StringCharacter (required): This is the character that will make up your string. If you enter a series of characters, only the first character will be used.

StrReverse

Purpose

The `StrReverse` function returns an expression in reverse order. For instance, `StrReverse("ten")` returns net. This works with numbers too; `StrReverse(5432)` returns 2345.

Arguments

```
StrReverse(Expression)
```

Expression (required): This is the expression that contains the characters you want reversed.

Switch

Purpose

The `Switch` function is a program flow function allowing you to evaluate a list of expressions and return the value associated with the expression determined to be true. To use the `Switch` function, you must provide a minimum of one expression and one value.

Arguments

```
Switch(Expression, Value)
```

Expression (required): This is the expression you want to evaluate.

Value (required): This is the value to return if the expression is true.

Additional Remarks

To evaluate multiple expressions, simply add another Expression and Value to the function. For example:

```
Switch(Expression1, Value 1, Expression2, Value2, Expression3, Value3)
```

When the `Switch` function is executed, each expression is evaluated. If an expression evaluates to True, the value that follows that expression is returned. If more than one expression is true, the value for the first true expression is returned.

SYD

Purpose

The `SYD` function is a financial function that calculates the sum-of-years' digits depreciation of an asset for a specified period.

Arguments

```
SYD(Cost, Salvage, Life, Period)
```

Cost (required): This is the initial cost of the asset; must be a positive number.

Salvage (required): This is the value of the asset at the end of its useful life; must be a positive number.

Life (required): This is the length of the useful life of the asset.

Period (required): This is the period for which asset depreciation is calculated.

Tan

Purpose

The `Tan` function is a math function that allows you to calculate the tangent of an angle.

Arguments

```
Tan(Number)
```

Number (required): This is any numeric expression that expresses an angle in radians.

Time

Purpose

The `Time` function returns today's time based on your PC's current system time. This function is ideal for time stamping transactions. There are no required arguments for this function; to use it, simply enter `Time()`.

TimeSerial

Purpose

The `TimeSerial` function essentially builds a time value based on the given hour, minute, and second components. Keep in mind that this function works on a 24-hour clock, so the expression `TimeSerial(18,30,0)` would return 6:30:00 PM. This function is perfect for converting disparate strings that represent a time when combined, into an actual time.

Arguments

```
TimeSerial(Hour, Minute, Second)
```

Hour (required): This is any number or numeric expression that has a value between 0 and 23, inclusive. In a query environment, you can use the name of a field to specify that you are evaluating all the row values of that field; this is true for all the arguments in this function.

Minute (required): This is any number or numeric expression. If the number specified for this argument exceeds the normal range for minutes in an hour, the function increments the hour as appropriate. For example, `TimeSerial(7,90,00)` returns 8:30:00 AM.

Second (required): This is any number or numeric expression. If the number specified for this argument exceeds the normal range for seconds in a minute, the function increments the minutes as appropriate. For example, `TimeSerial(7,10, 75)` returns 7:11:15 AM.

TimeValue

Purpose

The `TimeValue` function converts a string representation of a time to an actual time value. For example, `TimeValue("4:20:37 PM")` returns 4:20:37 PM. The function also works on a 24-hour clock.

Arguments

```
TimeValue(String)
```

String (required): This is any string or expression that represents a time ranging from 0:00:00 and 23:59:59. The string can be either a 12-hour clock entry, or a 24-hour clock entry. In a query environment, you can use the name of a field to specify that you are evaluating all the row values of that field.

Trim, LTrim, RTrim

Purpose

The `Trim` function effectively removes both the leading and trailing spaces from a string. The `LTrim` function removes only the leading spaces, whereas the `RTrim` function removes only the trailing spaces. These functions come in handy when cleaning up data received from a mainframe source.

Arguments

```
Trim(String)
LTrim(String)
RTrim(String)
```

String (required): This is the string you are working with. In a query environment, you can use the name of a field to specify that you are evaluating all the row values of that field.

TypeName

Purpose

The `TypeName` function is an inspection function that returns the type information of a variable. For example, `TypeName("Michael")` returns String.

Arguments

```
TypeName(Variable)
```

Variable (required): This is the variable you want to evaluate. In a query environment, you can use the name of a field to specify that you are evaluating all the row values of that field.

Additional Remarks

The string returned by the `TypeName` function can be any one of the following:

"Object type" (an object whose type is *objecttype*)

"Byte" (a Byte value)

"Integer" (an Integer type)

"Long" (a Long integer type)

"Single" (a Single-precision floating-point number)

"Double" (a Double-precision floating-point number)

"Currency" (a Currency value)

"Decimal" (a Decimal value)

"Date" (a Date value)

"String" (a String type)

"Boolean" (a Boolean value)

"Error" (an error value)

"Empty" (variable has not been initialized)

"Null" (variable contains no valid data; a Null value)

"Object" (an object)

"Unknown" (an object whose type is unknown)

"Nothing" (an Object variable that does not refer to an object)

UCase

Purpose

The `UCase` function converts a string to uppercase letters.

Arguments

```
UCase(String)
```

String (required): This is the string to be converted. In a query environment, you can use the name of a field to specify that you are converting all the row values of that field.

Val

Purpose

The `Val` function is a conversion function that extracts the numeric part of a string. For example, `Val("5400 Legacy Drive")` returns 5400. One caveat to the Val function is that it stops reading the string as soon as it hits a textual character. Therefore, the number you are extracting needs to be at the beginning of the string.

Arguments

```
Val(String)
```

String (required): This is the string you want to evaluate. In a query environment, you can use the name of a field to specify that you are evaluating all the row values of that field.

VarType

Purpose

The `VarType` function is an inspection function that returns the subtype code associated with a variant's character type. For example, `VarType("Michael")` returns 8, because this is the subtype code for a string.

Arguments

```
VarType(Variant)
```

Variant (required): This is the variant you want to evaluate. In a query environment, you can use the name of a field to specify that you are evaluating all the row values of that field.

Additional Remarks

The following is a list of the subtype codes that the `VarType` function can return.

0 - Empty (uninitialized)

1 - Null (no valid data)

2 - Integer

3 - Long integer

4 - Single-precision floating-point number

5 - Double-precision floating-point number

6 - Currency value

7 - Date value

8 - String

9 - Object

10 - Error value

11 - Boolean value

12 - Variant (used only with arrays of variants)

13 - A data access object

14 - Decimal value

17 - Byte value

36 - Variants that contain user-defined types

8192 - Array

Weekday

Purpose

The `Weekday` function returns a number from 1 to 7 representing the day of the week for a given date; 1 represents Sunday, 2 represents Monday, and so on. For example, `Weekday (#12/31/1997#)` will return 4.

Arguments

```
Weekday(ValidDate, FirstDayOfTheWeek)
```

ValidDate (required): This is any value that can represent a valid date. In a query environment, you can use the name of a field to specify that you are evaluating all the row values of that field.

FirstDayOfTheWeek (optional): This specifies which day you want to count as the first day of the week. Enter 1 in this argument to make the first day Sunday, 2 for Monday, 3 for Tuesday, and so on. If this argument is omitted, the first day is a Sunday by default.

WeekdayName

Purpose

The `WeekdayName` function converts a numeric weekday designation (1 to 7) to a weekday name. For example, `WeekdayName(7)` returns Saturday. Values less than 1 or greater than 7 will cause an error.

Arguments

```
WeekdayName(WeekdayNumber, Abbreviated, FirstDayOfTheWeek)
```

WeekdayNumber (required): This is a number from 1 to 7 that represents a weekday; 1 represents Sunday, 2 represents Monday, and so on.

Abbreviated (optional): This specifies whether the weekday is abbreviated or not. If this argument is omitted, the weekday is not abbreviated. Enter 1 for this argument to return abbreviated weekdays.

FirstDayOfTheWeek (optional): This specifies which day you want to count as first day of the week. Enter 1 in this argument to make the first day Sunday, 2 for Monday, 3 for Tuesday, and so on. If this argument is omitted, the first day is a Sunday by default.

Year

Purpose

The `Year` function returns a whole number representing the year for a given date. For example, `Year(#5/16/1972#)` returns 1972.

Arguments

```
Year(ValidDate)
```

ValidDate (required): This is any value that can represent a valid date. In a query environment, you can use the name of a field to specify that you are evaluating all the row values of that field.

APPENDIX

B

Access VBA Fundamentals

If you haven't worked much with Visual Basic for Applications (VBA), you may want to brush up on some of the basics before tackling the latter chapters in this book. The purpose of this appendix is to provide a high-level overview of some of the fundamental concepts and techniques demonstrated in the later chapters. Bear in mind that because the focus of this book is on data analysis, this appendix is written to provide only an introductory look at VBA. If you are interested in more of an in-depth look at programming Access VBA, consider one of the following titles:

Beginning Access 2007 VBA by Denise Gosnell (ISBN: 0-470-04684-8)

Access 2007 VBA Programming For Dummies by Alan Simpson (ISBN: 0-470-04653-8)

These books offer a solid introduction to VBA that is ideal for novice Access programmers.

Covering the Basics in 10 Steps

There is no better way to learn than hands-on experience. So instead of reading paragraph after paragraph of terms and definitions, you will cover some of the basics of VBA in 10 steps!

Step 1: Creating a Standard Module

Have you ever found code on the Internet where you could supposedly copy the code and paste it into Access to do something wonderful, but you didn't know where to paste it? Well, knowing where to put your code is the first step in programming. In Access, VBA code is contained in a *module*.

Here are the types of modules you can use:

- **Standard Modules:** This type is the most common, letting you store code that can be used anywhere within your database.
- **Form and Report Modules:** These types of modules store code that can be used only within the form or report to which they belong.
- **Class Modules:** These modules are for hardcore programmers who want to create and define their own custom objects.

To create a module, do the following:

1. Start a new standard module by going to the application ribbon and selecting the Create tab.
2. From there, select the Macro drop-down menu, and then select Module. At this point, your screen should look similar to Figure B-1.

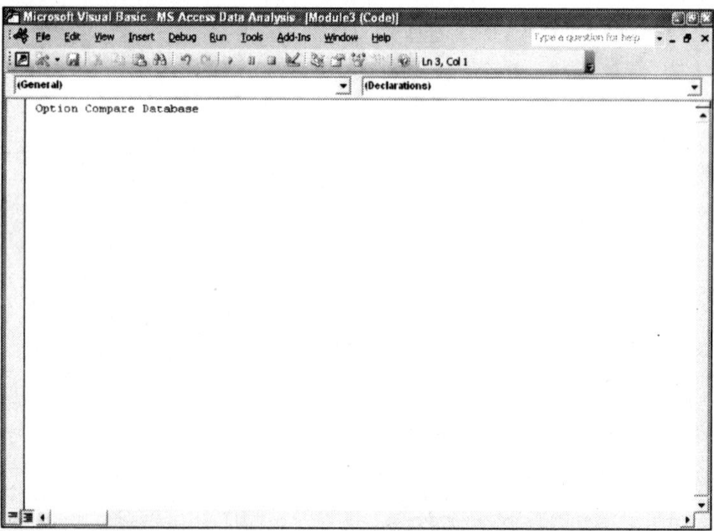

Figure B-1: A module is the container that will hold your code and expose it to other parts of your database.

Step 2: Creating a Function

A *function* is a set of procedures that returns a value. You can think of a function as a defined task that contains the individual actions that Access needs to perform to reach an answer or goal.

To create a function, go to the first empty line and type:

```
Function MyFirstFunction
```

This creates a new function named MyFirstFunction. After you press Enter on your keyboard, Access adds a few things to your code. As you can see in Figure B-2, a set of parentheses and the words End Function are added automatically.

Step 3: Giving Your Function Purpose with a Procedure

A function's utility and purpose in life is defined in large part by its procedures. *Procedures* (sometimes called *routines*) are the actions Access takes to accomplish an objective.

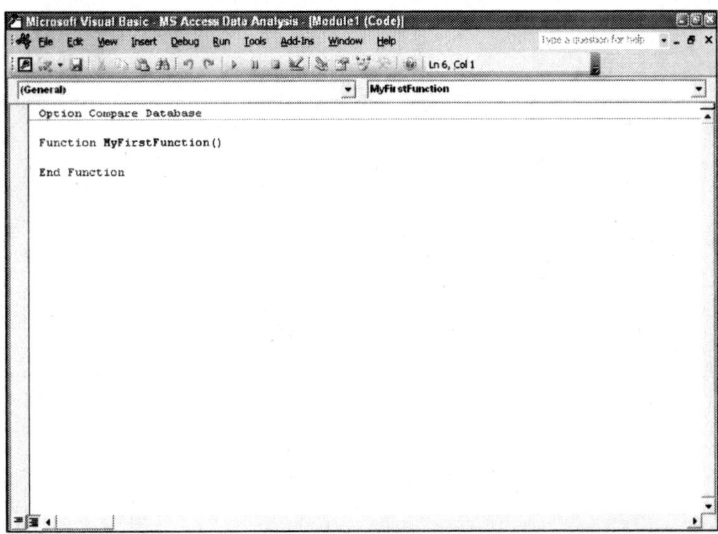

Figure B-2: Create a function that will provide the steps for your task.

For your first procedure, you call a message box. Type **MsgBox** within the function:

```
Function MyFirstFunction()
MsgBox
End Function
```

After you press the space key on your keyboard, you see a tooltip pop up, shown in Figure B-3, which shows you the valid arguments for `MsgBox`. This useful functionality, called *IntelliSense*, is a kind of cheat sheet that enables you to quickly grasp the methods, properties, and arguments that are involved in the object or function you are working with. IntelliSense is typically activated when you enter an object or a function and then follow it with a space, open parenthesis, period, or equal sign.

Finish the `MsgBox` function by typing **"I am blank years old."** At this point, your function should look like the one shown in Figure B-4.

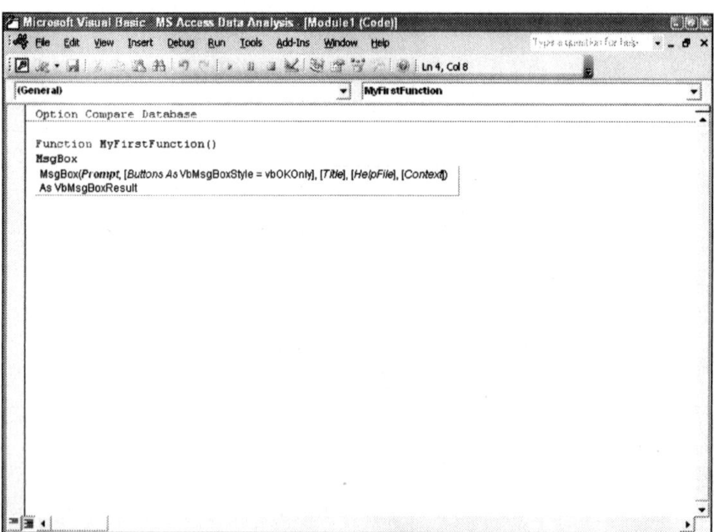

Figure B-3: IntelliSense is an invaluable tool when working with VBA.

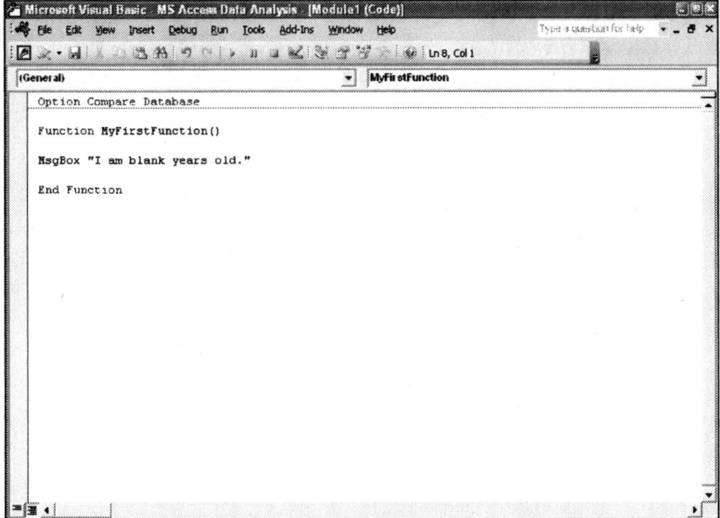

Figure B-4: Your function is ready to play.

Step 4: Testing Your Function

To test your function, simply place your cursor anywhere inside the function and press the F5 key on your key board. If all goes well, you should see the message box shown in Figure B-5.

Step 5: Declaring a Variable

A *variable* is a placeholder for a data type. When you declare a variable, you are telling Access to set aside memory to store a value. The amount of memory that is allocated depends on the data type.

TIP **To get a list of the data types available to you along with the amount of memory that each data type requires, activate Access Help and enter *Data Type Summary* in the Search for text box.**

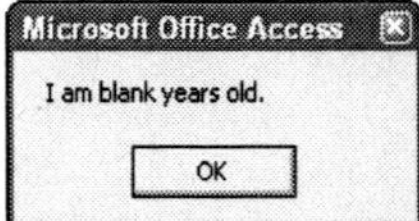

Figure B-5: You have successfully written your first function!

Your next question should be, "How do I know which data type to use?" The data type itself depends on what you are trying to accomplish with the variable. For example, in this scenario, you want to declare a variable that will capture your age. Since age is a number, you will use the `Integer` data type.

In order to declare a variable, you must use a `Dim` statement. `Dim`, short for dimension, explicitly lets Access know that you are declaring a variable. It is good programming practice to declare all your variables before you start your procedure.

Declare a new variable called `MyAge` as an `Integer` data type:

```
Function MyFirstFunction()
Dim MyAge as Integer
MsgBox "I am blank years old."
End Function
```

Step 6: Assigning a Value to a Variable

When you have memory set aside for a variable, you can assign a value to it. To assign a value to a variable, simply indicate the value to which it is equal. Here are some examples:

- **MyVariable = 1:** This assigns a 1 to the variable called `MyVariable`.
- **MyVariable = "Access":** This assigns the word Access to `MyVariable`.
- **MyVariable = [Forms]![MainForm].[TextBox1]:** This sets the value of `MyVariable` to equal the value in the TextBox1 control in the form called `MainForm`.
- **MyVariable = InputBox("User Input"):** This sets the value of `MyVariable` to equal the value of a user's input using an `InputBox`.

In this scenario, you will use an `InputBox` to capture an age from a user and then pass that age to the `MyAge` variable. You will then pass the `MyAge` variable to the message box. You can see the distinct flow of information from a user to an Access message box. Your code should look similar to the code shown here.

```
Function MyFirstFunction()
Dim MyAge as Integer
MyAge = InputBox("Enter your Age")
MsgBox "I am " & MyAge & " years old."
End Function
```

NOTE **Note that the MsgBox is broken into three sections separated by ampersands (&):**

- **"I am " (The first two words in the message)**
- **MyAge (The variable that will return your age)**
- **" years old." (The last two words in the message)**

Go ahead and test your function. To do so, place your cursor anywhere inside the function and press F5. If you did everything correctly, you should see the input dialog box, shown in Figure B-6, asking you for your age.

Step 7: Compiling Your Newly Created Function

You should get into the habit of compiling your code after you create it. Compiling has two major benefits. First, when you compile a procedure, Access checks your code for errors. Second, Access translates your code from the text you can read and understand to a machine language that your computer can understand. To compile your code, go to the application menu and select Debug → Compile *xxxx* (where *xxxx* is the name of your project).

Step 8: Saving Your Newly Created Function

Now that you have built your first function, you would like to save it. Go to the application menu and select File → Select Save *xxxx* (where *xxxx* is the name of your project).

If your module is new, you'll see a dialog box asking you to give your module a name. Keep the default name ("Module1") and click OK. Close your module and look in the Navigation Pane, shown in Figure B-7, to see it in the Modules collection.

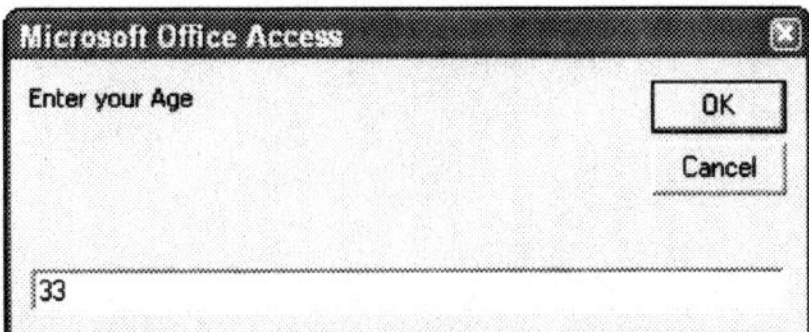

Figure B-6: This input box captures your age and passes it to the `MyAge` variable.

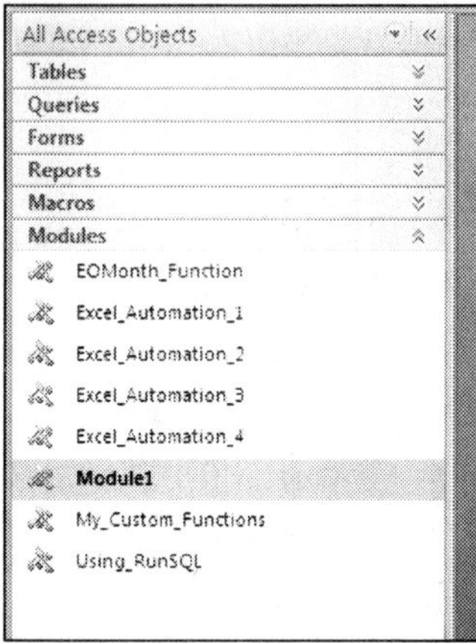

Figure B-7: When you save a module, you can see it in the Database Window in the Modules collection.

Step 9: Running Your Function in a Macro

The benefit of building your VBA procedures in standard modules is that you can run them from anywhere within your database. For example, you can run your newly created function in a macro by simply calling your function using the `RunCode` macro action.

Create a new macro and add the `RunCode` macro action. The function name you are calling is `MyFirstFunction()`. When your Macro window looks like the one shown in Figure B-8, save the macro and run it.

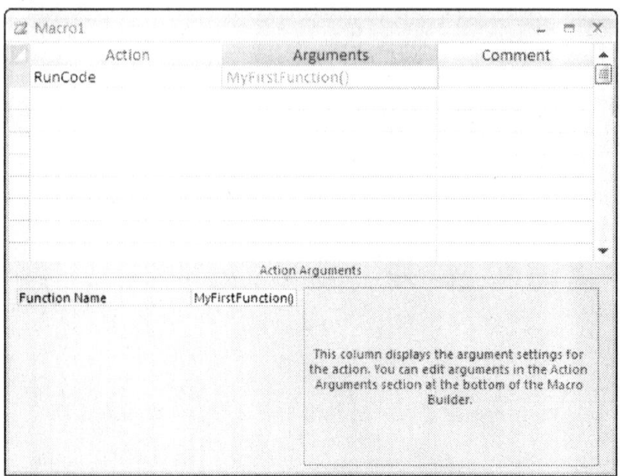

Figure B-8: You can run your VBA procedures as part of a macro process.

Step 10: Running Your Function from a Form

You can also call your functions from a form. Start by creating a new form. You can do this by selecting Blank Form on the Create tab, as demonstrated in Figure B-9.

On the Formatting tab, select View → Design View. This activates the toolbox shown in Figure B-10. Select CommandButton and then click anywhere on your form. This places a command button on your form.

NOTE **If the Command Button Wizard pops up, click Cancel to close it. You do not need the wizard for this exercise.**

Right-click your newly created command button and select Build Event. This activates the Choose Builder dialog box. Select Code Builder, and you are taken to the form module, shown in Figure B-11. A form module serves as a container for event procedures managed and executed by the form or its controls.

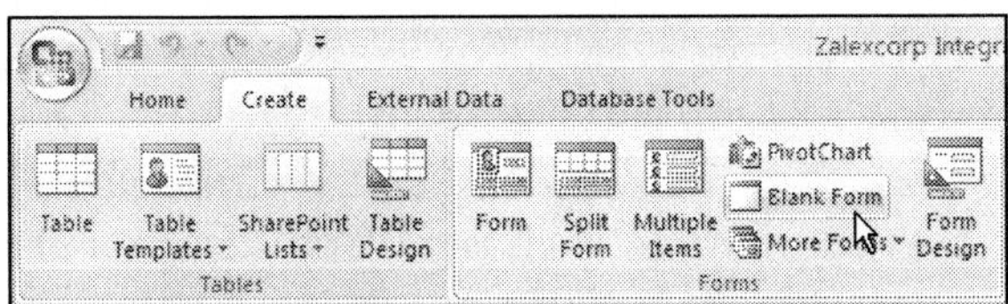

Figure B-9: Start a new form in Design view.

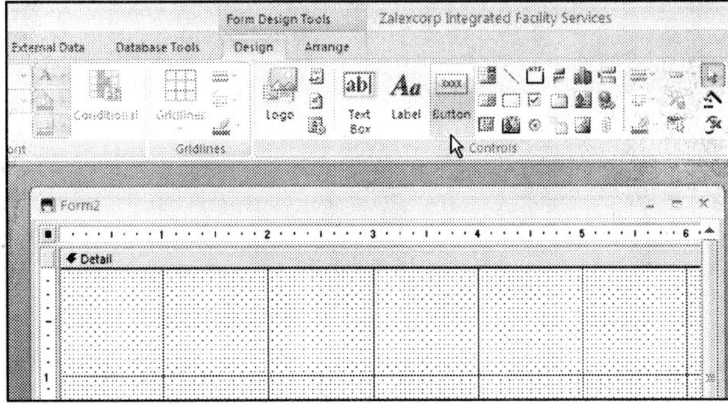

Figure B-10: Add a CommandButton control to your form.

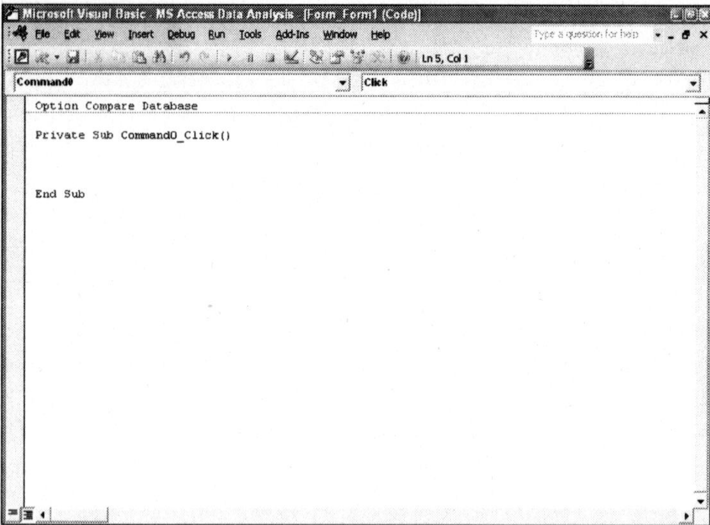

Figure B-11: Create a new event using the Code Builder.

Access is an event-driven environment, which means that procedures are executed with the occurrence of certain events. For example, in Figure B-11, you will notice the procedure's name is `Command0_Click()`. This means that you are building a procedure for a control called Command0, and this procedure will fire when the control is clicked. You can execute your function from here by calling it. Figure B-12 demonstrates how this is done.

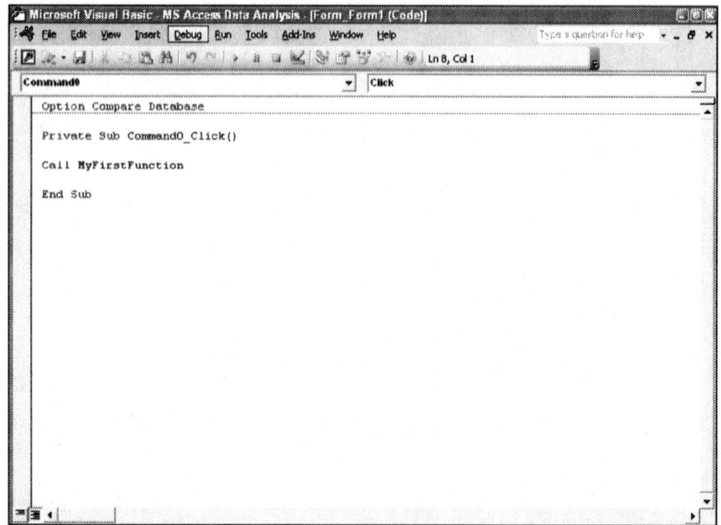

Figure B-12: Call your function from the command button's event procedure.

Finally, close the VBA editor and select View → Form View from the application menu. Then click your command button to execute your function.

Letting Access Teach You VBA

One of the most beneficial functionalities in Access is the ability to convert a macro to VBA code. To demonstrate how this is done, click Macros in the Database Window and highlight the TopTenB_Child macro, as shown in Figure B-13.

Go to the application menu and select Office Icon → Save As. This activates the Save As dialog box. Here, you can indicate that you want to save this macro as a module and give it a name. Figure B-14 demonstrates how to fill in this dialog box.

Next, the dialog box shown in Figure B-15 gives you the options of adding comments and error handling. In this case, you want both, so simply click the Convert button.

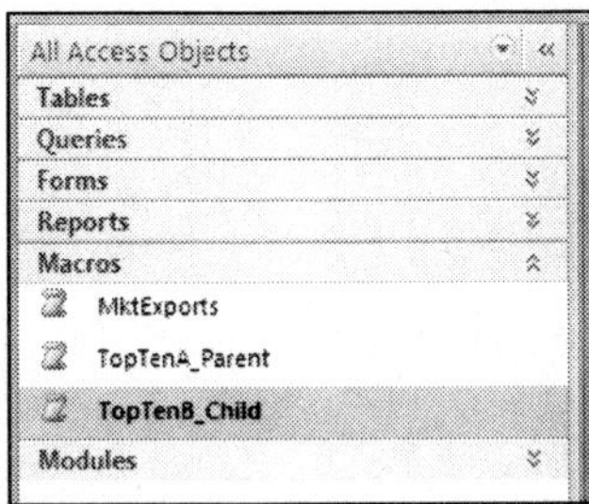

Figure B-13: Highlight the macro you want to convert.

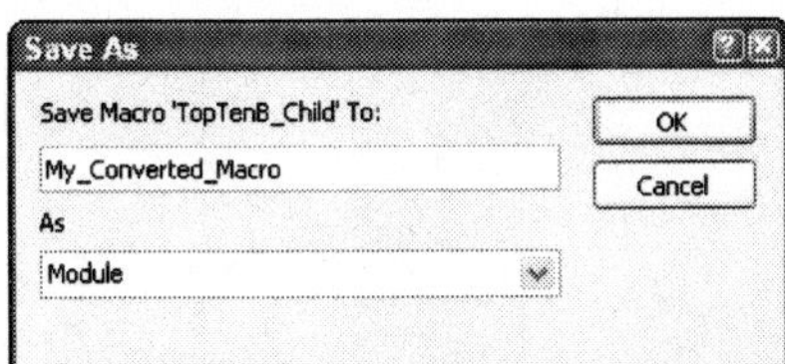

Figure B-14: Indicate that you want to save this macro as a module and then name the module.

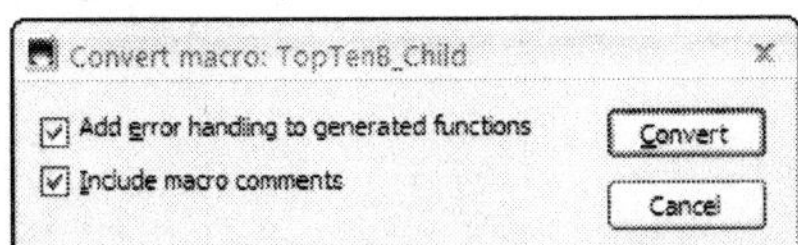

Figure B-15: Tell Access to add comments and include error handling.

When the conversion is complete, select Modules in the Database window and click the module named Converted Macro- TopTenB_Child as shown in Figure B-16.

As you can see in Figure B-17, Access has converted all the macro actions in the TopTenB_Child macro to a VBA function complete with comments and error handling.

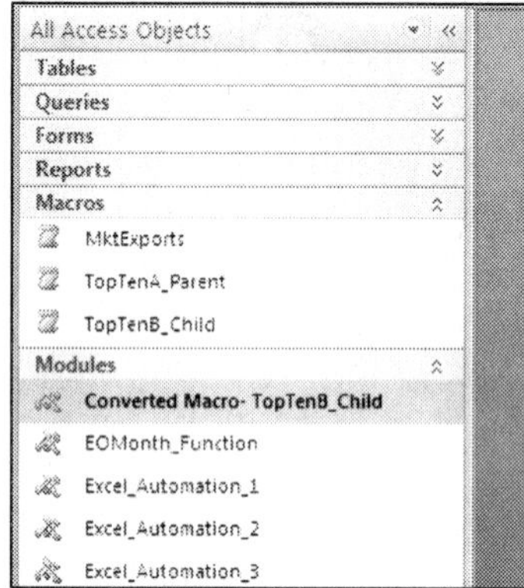

Figure B-16: You can find your converted VBA code in the Modules collection of the Database Window.

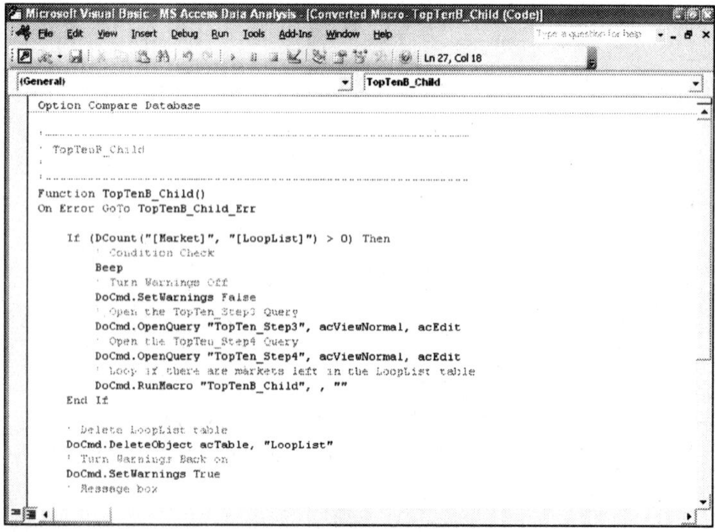

Figure B-17: Your macro has been converted to a VBA function.

Keep in mind that this is not just a cool way to get out of writing code. This is a personal tutor! Look at Figure B-17 again. With this one converted macro, you get a first-hand look at how an `If` statement works, how to call queries from code, how to call macros from code, and how to handle errors. You can create a wide variety of macros and then convert them to VBA to learn about the syntax that is used for each action and to experiment by adding your own functionality to them. For many Access developers, this experimentation eventually led to successful programming careers.

APPENDIX

C

Error Message Reference

Analyzing data in Access is a trial-and-error endeavor. You will undoubtedly encounter many errors on your path to Access proficiency. The purpose of this appendix is to introduce you to some of the errors you will be likely to come across while working within the context of data analysis.

The Top 10 Query Errors

Table C-1 lists the 10 most common errors new users are likely to encounter while working with queries. Ironically, although these are the most common errors in a query environment, they are also the least descriptive. This leaves many new Access users scratching their heads.

Table C-1: Top Ten Query Errors

ERROR	DESCRIPTION
6	Overflow This message usually means that the number you are using is outside the range of the data type you are assigning it to. In other words, the number you are using is either too big or too small for the data type.
7	Out of memory This means that the query or procedure you are running requires more memory than is available on your system. Try closing any other applications you have open. You can also try breaking up the query or procedure into steps.
11	Division by zero When you divide a number by zero you get this message.
13	Type mismatch You would typically get this message when you are trying to join two fields with different data types, that is a Text field and a Number field. Make sure any fields you are joining are the same data type.
16	Expression too complex This typically means that you have too many nested expressions or subqueries in your query. Try breaking up your query into steps.
3001	Invalid Argument This error is most often raised when your database has reached the 2 GB limit. When this error is thrown, you should check the current size of the database. If your database has reached 2 GB (or close to it), perform a Compact and Repair. This will resolve the error.
3060	Wrong data type for parameter `<Parameter Name>`. This means that you are feeding a parameter the wrong type of data.
3068	Not a valid alias name. This means that you have either used a reserved word for your alias name, or your alias name contains invalid characters.

Table C-1 *(continued)*

ERROR	DESCRIPTION
3073 3326	Operation must use an updatable query. This Recordset is not updatable. These two error messages can be thrown when any of the following applies: Your query is using a join to another query. To work around this issue, create a temporary table that you can use instead of the joined query. Your query is based on a crosstab query, an aggregate query, a union query, or a subquery that contains aggregate functions. To work around this issue, create a temporary table that you can use instead of the query. Your query is based on three or more tables and there is a many-to-one-to-many relationship. To work around this issue, create a temporary table that you can use without the relationship. Your query is based on a table where the Unique Values property is set to Yes. To work around this issue, set the Unique Values property of the table to No. Your query is based on a table on which you do not have Update Data permissions, or is locked by another user. To work around this issue, ensure you have permissions to update the table, and that the table is not in Design view or locked by another user Your query is based on a table in a database that is open as read-only or is located on a read-only drive. To work around this issue, obtain write access to the database or drive. Your query is based on a linked ODBC table with no unique index or a Paradox table without a primary key. To work around this issue, add a primary key or a unique index to the linked table Your query is based on a SQL pass-through query. To work around this issue, create a temporary table that you can use instead of the query.

Common Parsing Errors

As you start experimenting with different functions and expressions, you will undoubtedly make mistakes. The errors in Table C-2 are parsing errors — that is, errors that are caused by syntax or structure mistakes. These errors are quite descriptive, for the most part telling you what exactly went wrong. If you are new to Access, you should take some time to read some of these errors to get advanced notice about some of the possible mistakes you could make when building your analyses.

Table C-2: Common Parsing Errors to Watch For

ERROR	DESCRIPTION
2420	The expression you entered has an invalid number.
2421	The expression you entered has an invalid date value.
2422	The expression you entered has an invalid string. A string can be up to 2048 characters long, including opening and closing quotation marks.
2423	The expression you entered has an invalid . (dot) or ! operator or invalid parentheses. You may have entered an invalid identifier or typed parentheses following the Null constant.
2424	The expression you entered has a field, control, or property name that *<Database Name>* can't find.
2425	The expression you entered has a function name that *<Database Name>* can't find.
2426	The function you entered can't be used in this expression. You may have used a `DoEvents`, `LBound`, `UBound`, `Spc`, or `Tab` function in an expression. You may have used an aggregate function, such as `Count`, in a design grid or in a calculated control or field.
2427	You entered an expression that has no value. The expression may refer to an object that has no value, such as a form, a report, or a label control.
2428	You entered an invalid argument in a domain aggregate function. A field in the string expression may not be in the domain. A field specified in the criteria expression may not be in the domain.
2429	The `In` operator you entered requires parentheses.
2430	You did not enter the keyword `And` in the `Between...And` operator.
2431	The expression you entered contains invalid syntax. You may have entered a comma without a preceding value or identifier.
2432	The expression you entered contains invalid syntax, or you need to enclose your text data in quotes. You may have entered an invalid comma or omitted quotation marks. For example, if the Default Value property of a text field is "Huey, Louie, and Dewey," it must be enclosed in quotes if you mean it as a literal text string. This avoids the confusion with the expression "Huey Louie" And "Dewey".
2433	The expression you entered contains invalid syntax. You may have entered an operator, such as the + operator, in an expression without a corresponding operand.
2434	The expression you entered contains invalid syntax. You may have entered an operand without an operator.

Table C-2 *(continued)*

ERROR	DESCRIPTION
2435	The expression you entered has too many closing parentheses.
2436	The expression you entered is missing a closing parenthesis, bracket (]), or vertical bar (|).
2437	The expression you entered has invalid vertical bars (|).
2438	The expression you entered contains invalid syntax. You omitted an operand or operator, you entered an invalid character or comma, or you entered text without surrounding it in quotation marks.
2439	The expression you entered has a function containing the wrong number of arguments.
2440	You must enclose `IIf` function arguments in parentheses.
2442	The expression you entered has invalid parentheses. You may have used the parenthesis syntax for an identifier in a query.
2443	You can use the Is operator only in an expression with Null or Not Null.
2445	The expression you entered is too complex.
2446	There isn't enough memory available to perform this calculation. Close unneeded programs, and try again. For more information on freeing memory, search the Microsoft Windows Help index for "memory, troubleshooting".
2447	There is an invalid use of the `.` (dot) or `!` operator or invalid parentheses. You may have entered an invalid identifier or typed parentheses following the Null constant.
2448	You can't assign a value to this object. The object may be a control on a read-only form. The object may be on a form that is open in Design view. The value may be too large for this field.
2449	There is an invalid method in an expression. For example, you may have tried to use the `Print` method with an object other than Report or Debug.
2450	*<Database Name>* can't find the form *<Form Name>* referred to in a macro expression or Visual Basic code. The form you referenced may be closed or may not exist in this database. *<Database Name>* may have encountered a compile error in a Visual Basic module for the form.
2451	The report name *<Report Name>* you entered is misspelled or refers to a report that isn't open or doesn't exist.

(continued)

Table C-2 *(continued)*

ERROR	DESCRIPTION
2452	The expression you entered has an invalid reference to the Parent property. For example, you may be using the Parent property with a control on a main form or report rather than with a control on a subform or subreport.
2453	The control name *<Control Name>* you entered in your expression is misspelled or refers to a control on a form or report that isn't open or doesn't exist.
2454	The object name *<Object Name>* you entered following the ! operator in the expression is invalid. For example, you may have tried to enter an identifier with two control names separated by the ! operator.
2455	You entered an expression that has an invalid reference to the property *<Property Name>*. The property may not exist or may not apply to the object you specified.

Errors that May Indicate Database Corruption

The errors in Table C-3 are those errors that are commonly associated with database corruption. As you look through these errors, you will notice that many of them are vague or their descriptions point to some other type of problem not related to database corruption. The problem with database corruption is that it can be caused by a wide range of nebulous issues. Therefore, you will rarely see a message explicitly stating that your database is corrupt. However, the errors listed here in Table C-3 are key indicators that point to the possibility that your database could be corrupted.

Table C-3: Errors Commonly Associated with Database Corruption

ERROR	DESCRIPTION
2239	*<Database Name>* has detected that this database is in an inconsistent state, and cannot attempt to recover the database because the file is read-only. To allow Access to recover the database, close the database and set the file to read/write, and then open the database.

Table C-3 *(continued)*

ERROR	DESCRIPTION
2572	This database is in an unexpected state and *<Database Name>* cannot open it. This database has been converted from a prior version of *<Database Name>* by using the DAO CompactDatabase method instead of the Convert Database command (click the Microsoft Office Button and then click Convert). Converting by using the DAO CompactDatabase method has left the database in a partially converted state. If you have a copy of the database in its original format, click the Microsoft Office Button and then click Convert to convert it. If the original database is no longer available, create a new database and import your tables and queries to preserve your data and try again. Your other database objects cannot be recovered.
3011	The Microsoft Office Access database engine could not find the object *<Object Name>*. Make sure the object exists and that you spell its name and the path name correctly.
3019	Operation invalid without a current index.
3033	You do not have the necessary permissions to use the *<Object Name>* object. Have your system administrator or the person who created this object establish the appropriate permissions for you.
3045	Could not use *<File Name>*; file already in use.
3049	Cannot open database *<Database Name>*. It may not be a database that your application recognizes, or the file may be corrupt.
3051	The Microsoft Office Access database engine cannot open or write to the file *<File Name>*. It is already opened exclusively by another user, or you need permission to view and write its data.
3078	The Microsoft Office Access database engine cannot find the input table or query *<Query Name>*. Make sure it exists and that its name is spelled correctly.
3197	The Microsoft Office Access database engine stopped the process because you and another user are attempting to change the same data at the same time.
3340	Query *<Query Name>* is corrupt.
3343	Unrecognized database format *<Object Name>*.
3428	A problem occurred in your database. Correct the problem by repairing and compacting the database.
3626	The operation failed. There are too many indexes on table *<Table Name>*. Delete some of the indexes on the table and try the operation again.

(continued)

Table C-3 *(continued)*

ERROR	DESCRIPTION
3734	The database has been placed in a state by user *<User Name>* on machine *<Machine Name>* that prevents it from being opened or locked.
3800	*<Name>* is not an index in this table.
7801	This database is in an unrecognized format. The database may have been created with a later version of *<Database Name>* than the one you are using. Upgrade your version of *<Database Name>* to the current one, then open this database.
29063	The Visual Basic for Applications project in the database is corrupt.
29072	*<Database Name>* has detected corruption in this file. To try to repair the corruption, first make a backup copy of the file. Click the Microsoft Office Button, point to Manage and then click Compact and Repair Database. If you are currently trying to repair this corruption, you need to recreate this file or restore it from a previous backup.

Other Access Database Engine Errors

Table C-4 lists some of the other Microsoft Office Access database engine errors you can encounter while working with Access.

Table C-4: Access Database Engine Errors You May Encounter

ERROR	DESCRIPTION
2001	You canceled the previous operation.
2002	You tried to perform an operation involving a function or feature that was not installed in this version of *<Database Name>*.
2004	There isn't enough memory to perform this operation. Close unneeded programs and try the operation again.
2005	There isn't enough free memory to start *<Database Name>*. Close unneeded programs and try again. For information on freeing memory, search the Microsoft Windows Help index for "memory, troubleshooting".
2006	The object name *<Object Name>* you entered doesn't follow *<Database Name>* object-naming rules. For more information about naming objects, click Help.

Table C-4 *(continued)*

ERROR	DESCRIPTION
2007	You already have an open database object named *<Database Name>*. Use a different name for each database object of the same type. If you want this object to replace the original object, close the original object, and then save this object using the same name. For more information on renaming a database object, click Help.
2008	You can't delete the database object *<Object Name>* while it's open. Close the database object, and then delete it.
2009	You can't rename the database object *<Object Name>* while it's open. Close the database object, and then rename it.
2010	You can't delete the database object *<Object Name>* while it's open. Close the database object, and then delete it.
2011	The password you entered is incorrect.
2014	You have given this *<Object Name>* the same name as an existing *<Object>* in your database. You can't give a table and a query the same name. Give this object a name that isn't already used by another table or query.
2015	There are no registered wizards of this type. Rerun *<Database Name>* or Microsoft Office Setup to reinstall the wizards. If you want to preserve your security or custom settings, back up the *<Database Name>* workgroup information file. For more information on backing up files, search the Microsoft Windows Help index for "backing up files".
2016	You can't modify the attributes of System Tables.
2017	Microsoft helps protect this Visual Basic for Applications Project with a password. You must supply the password in the Visual Basic Editor before you can perform this operation.
2018	The data access page name *<Page Name>* you entered is misspelled or refers to a data access page that isn't open or doesn't exist.
2019	The number you used to refer to the data access page is invalid. Use the Count property to count the open data access pages and make sure that the page number is not greater than the number of open data access pages minus one.
2021	One or more operators in the filter expression are invalid. For a valid list of operators refer to the help file.
2022	You entered an expression that requires a data access page to be the active window.

(continued)

Table C-4 *(continued)*

ERROR	DESCRIPTION
2024	The report snapshot was not created because you don't have enough free disk space for temporary work files. To fix this, free up disk space (for example, empty the Recycle Bin or delete unnecessary files).
2025	The file is not in the correct format for a <*Database Name*> project
2027	This operation is not supported for <*Database Name*> 1.*x* databases.
2028	<*Database Name*> was unable to close the database object.
2029	Microsoft Office applications cannot suspend while you have documents open from a network location. Exit the applications or close the open documents and try again.
2030	The <*Database Name*> project will be opened read-only because one of the following occurred: Either the file is locked for editing by another user, the file (or the folder in which it is located) is marked as read-only, or you specified that you wanted to open the file read-only.
2031	You can't convert or enable an MDE file.
2033	Name conflicts with existing module, project, or object library.
2034	Cannot Compile Project.
2035	Cannot Load Project of wrong version.
2037	<*Database Name*> could not perform name AutoCorrect during this operation. The Log name AutoCorrect option is set, but the Data and Misc. Objects are not checked out.
2038	The file <*File Name*> cannot be opened because it has been locked by another user.
2040	<*Database Name*> can't run.
2041	<*Database Name*> couldn't find file <*File Name*>. This file is required for startup.
2042	A system error occurred, or there isn't enough free memory to start <*Database Name*>. Close unneeded programs and try again.
2043	<*Database Name*> can't find the database file <*File Name*>. Make sure you entered the correct path and file name.
2044	You can't exit <*Database Name*> now. If you're running a Visual Basic module that is using OLE or DDE, you may need to interrupt the module.

Table C-4 *(continued)*

ERROR	DESCRIPTION
2045	The command line you used to start <*Database Name*> contains an option that <*Database Name*> doesn't recognize. Exit and restart <*Database Name*> using valid command line options.
2046	The command or action <*Command Name*> isn't available now. You may be in a read-only database or an unconverted database from an earlier version of <*Database Name*>. The type of object the action applies to isn't currently selected or isn't in the active view. Use only those commands and macro actions that are currently available for this database.
2048	There isn't enough free memory to open the file <*File Name*>. Close unneeded programs and try again. For more information on freeing memory, search the Microsoft Windows Help index for "memory, troubleshooting".
2050	Enter an OLE/DDE Timeout setting from 0 through 300 seconds.
2051	The object name <*Name or Value*> can't be longer than <*Number*> characters according to <*Database Name*> object-naming rules.
2052	There isn't enough free memory to update the display. Close unneeded programs and try again.
2053	The command name can't be blank. Please choose a name.
2054	<*Database Name*> is unable to load the Visual Basic for Applications dynamic-link library (DLL) Vbe6. Rerun the <*Database Name*> Setup program.
2055	The expression <*Expression Name*>you entered is invalid.
2056	<*Database Name*> can't supply context-sensitive Help.
2057	There isn't enough stack memory left to perform the operation. The operation is too complicated. Try simplifying the operation.
2058	The file <*File Name*> is incompatible. <*Database Name*> needs to be reinstalled. Run Setup to reinstall <*Database Name*>. If you want to preserve your security or custom settings, back up the <*Database Name*> workgroup information file. For more information on backing up files, search the Microsoft Windows Help index for backing up files.
2059	<*Database Name*> cannot find the object <*Object Name*>. Make sure the object exists and that you spell its name correctly.
2060	You can't create a field list based on the action query <*Query Name*>. Action queries don't have fields. A form or report must be based on a table, or on a select or crosstab query. Change the `RecordSource` property for the form or report, or open the action query and change it to a select query.

(continued)

Table C-4 *(continued)*

ERROR	DESCRIPTION
2061	Enter a zero or greater-than-zero number for this option.
2062	The command name must be shorter than 255 Characters. Please choose a name.
2063	*<Database Name>* can't create, open, or write to the index file *<File Name>*; the information (.inf) file it uses to keep track of dBASE indexes. The index file may be damaged, or you may not have read/write permission for the network drive you're trying to link to. You can link to the dBASE file without specifying any dBASE indexes, but the existing indexes will not be used with the linked table.
2064	The menu bar value *<Data Value>* is invalid. You supplied an argument to the `DoMenuItem` method that refers to a menu bar that is invalid. Use an intrinsic constant or numeric value that refers to a valid menu bar value, such as `acFormbar`.
2065	The name for the menu, command, or subcommand you entered is invalid. You supplied an argument to the `DoMenuItem` method that refers to a menu name, command, or subcommand that is invalid. Use an intrinsic constant or numeric value that refers to a valid menu, command, or subcommand value, such as `acRecordsMenu`.
2067	A menu bar macro can only be run if the menu bar macro name is the setting used by particular properties or options. You tried to run a menu bar macro containing the `AddMenu` action. Set one of the following properties or options to the name of the menu bar macro: The `MenuBar` property of a form or report. The `ShortcutMenuBar` property of a form, report, or control. The Menu Bar or Shortcut Menu Bar option in the Startup dialog box. This error also occurs if *<Database Name>* attempts to run a menu bar macro containing an `AddMenu` action that follows an action that makes some other object the active object. For example, the `OpenForm` action.
2068	The selected item is customized and doesn't have context-sensitive Help. For more information on creating custom Help for a form, report, or control, click Help.
2069	The key or key combination *<Value>* in *<Object Name>* has invalid syntax or is not allowed. Use the SendKeys syntax to specify the key or key combinations. For the allowed key or key combinations, click Help.
2070	You already assigned the key or key combination *<Value>* in *<Object Name>* to another macro. Only the first key or key combination will be used.
2071	The Docking property can't be set to *<Value>* at this time. If you want to set the Docking property to *<Value>*, move the toolbar from its current position and try again.

Table C-4 *(continued)*

ERROR	DESCRIPTION
2072	All objects were imported successfully.
2073	Successfully exported *<Object Name>*.
2074	This operation is not supported within transactions.
2075	This operation requires an open database.
2076	Successfully linked *<Object Name>*.
2077	This Recordset is not updatable.
2078	Help isn't available due to lack of memory or improper installation of Microsoft Windows or *<Database Name>*. For more information on troubleshooting a low memory problem, search the Microsoft Windows Help index for "memory, troubleshooting". If you need to reinstall *<Database Name>*, you may want to preserve your security or custom settings. To do so, back up the *<Database Name>* workgroup information file. For more information on backing up files, search the Microsoft Windows Help index for "backing up files".
2079	Form is read-only, because the Unique Table property is not set.
2080	The toolbar or menu *<Menu Name>* already exists. Do you want to replace the existing toolbar or menu?
2081	The Create From Macro command only works when a macro is selected in the Navigation Pane.
2083	The database *<Database Name>* is read-only. You can't save changes made to data or object definitions in this database.
2084	Field *<Field Name>* is based on an expression and can't be edited.
2085	The ODBC Refresh Interval setting must be from 1 through 32,766 seconds.
2086	Recordset requires a form to be updatable.
2087	*<Database Name>* can't display the Add-ins submenu. The Add-ins submenu expression *<Expression Name>*you entered exceeds the 256-character limit. Shorten the macroname or functionname expression in the Menu Add-ins key of the Windows Registry setting, and then restart *<Database Name>*. For more information on customizing *<Database Name>* settings in the Windows Registry, click Help.
2088	*<Database Name>* can't display the Add-ins submenu *<Menu Name>* because a setting you entered in the Windows Registry is missing a macro name or function name expression. Supply the missing expression in the Menu Add-ins key of the Windows Registry, and then restart *<Database Name>*. For more information on customizing *<Database Name>* settings in the Windows Registry, click Help.

(continued)

Table C-4 *(continued)*

ERROR	DESCRIPTION
2089	*<Database Name>* can't display the same menu more than once in a menu bar.
2090	An action within the current global menu's macro group can't change the global menu bar. *<Database Name>* can't display the global menu bar because the macro called when you first set the global menu includes another action that tries to reset the global menu. Check your menu bar macros, and make sure that you set the global menu bar only once.
2091	*<Name>* is an invalid name.
2092	The value you specified for the Setting argument in the `SetOption` method is not the correct type of Variant for this option. You specified a string when *<Database Name>* expected a number. See the Access Options dialog box (click the Microsoft Office Button, and then click Access Options) to see what type of data is required to set this particular option. For example, the setting for the Default Database Folder option must be a string. To see what type of Variant you passed to the `SetOption` method, use the `VarType` function. For more information, search the Help index for "Variant data type" and "VarType function".
2093	The numeric value for the `Setting` argument in the `SetOption` method does not correspond to any list box or option group settings in the Access Options dialog box. Valid settings are 0 (the first item in the list) through *<Object Name>* (the last item in the list).
2094	*<Database Name>* cannot find the toolbar *<Toolbar Name>*. You tried to run a macro that includes a `ShowToolbar` action or a VBA procedure that includes a `ShowToolbar` method. The toolbar name might be misspelled or might refer to a legacy toolbar that is no longer available. This action might refer to a custom toolbar that was deleted from or renamed in the current database. This action might refer to a custom toolbar that exists in a different database.
2097	The table for which you tried to create an import/export specification was created in an earlier version of *<Database Name>*. To convert this database to the current version of *<Database Name>*, click the Microsoft Office Button, and then click Convert.
2098	The operation could not be completed because the Smart Tag *<Tag Name>* is not recognized by your system.
2100	The control or subform control is too large for this location. The number you entered for the Left, Top, Height, or Width property is too large or is a negative number. Reduce the size of the control or subform control, or enter a positive number.

Table C-4 *(continued)*

ERROR	DESCRIPTION
2101	The setting you entered isn't valid for this property. To see the valid settings for this property, search the Help index for the name of the property.
2102	The form name *<Form Name>* is misspelled or refers to a form that doesn't exist. If the invalid form name is in a macro, an Action Failed dialog box will display the macro name and the macro's arguments after you click OK. Open the Macro window, and enter the correct form name.
2103	The report name *<Report Name>* you entered in either the property sheet or macro is misspelled or refers to a report that doesn't exist. If the invalid report name is in a macro, an Action Failed dialog box will display the macro name and the macro's arguments after you click OK. Open the Macro window, and enter the correct report name.
2104	You entered the control name *<Control Name>* which is already in use. You already have a control on the form with this name, or an existing control has its name mapped to this name for Visual Basic. Visual Basic maps spaces in control names to underscores. For example, My Control and My_Control are treated as duplicate names.
2105	You can't go to the specified record. You may be at the end of a recordset.
2106	*<Number>* errors occurred when you loaded the form or report. You loaded a form or report that has controls or properties that *<Database Name>* doesn't recognize and will ignore.
2107	The value you entered does not meet the validation rule defined for the field or control. To see the validation rule, switch to Design view, click the appropriate field, and then, if the property sheet is not open, press F4. Then, click the Data tab in the property sheet. Enter a value that meets the validation rule, or press ESC to undo your changes.
2108	You must save the field before you execute the `GoToControl` action, the `GoToControl` method, or the `SetFocus` method. You tried to move the focus to another control using the `SetFocus` method, `GoToControl` action, or the `GoToControl` method. Set the macro or method to the `AfterUpdate` property instead of the `BeforeUpdate` property so it saves the field before changing the focus.
2109	There is no field named *<Field Name>* in the current record.

(continued)

Table C-4 *(continued)*

ERROR	DESCRIPTION
2110	*<Database Name>* can't move the focus to the control *<Control Name>*. The control may be a type that can't receive the focus, such as a label. The control's Visible property may be set to No. The control's Enabled property may be set to No.
2111	The changes you made can't be saved. The save operation may have failed due to the temporary locking of the records by another user. Click OK to try again. You may need to click OK several times (or wait until the other user closes the table). Click Cancel if repeated attempts to save your changes fail.
2112	The item on the Clipboard can't be pasted into this control.
2113	The value you entered isn't valid for this field. For example, you may have entered text in a numeric field or a number that is larger than the FieldSize setting permits.
2114	*<Database Name>* doesn't support the format of the file *<File Name>* or file is too large. Try converting the file to BMP format.
2115	The macro or function set to the `BeforeUpdate` or `ValidationRule` property for this field is preventing *<Database Name>* from saving the data in the field. If this is a macro, open the macro in the Macro window and remove the action that forces a save (for example, `GoToControl`). If the macro includes a `SetValue` action, set the macro to the `AfterUpdate` property of the control instead. If this is a function, redefine the function in the Module window.
2116	The value violates the validation rule for the field or record. For example, you might have changed a validation rule without verifying whether the existing data matches the new validation rule. Click Undo to restore the previous value, or enter a new value that meets the validation rule for the field or record.
2117	*<Database Name>* has canceled the Paste operation. The text on the Clipboard is too long to paste into the form. For example, you may have pasted too much text into a label or entered too much text in the `ColumnWidths` property. Paste smaller sections. For labels, you must paste fewer than 2,048 characters.
2118	You must save the current field before you run the `Requery` action. If you are running a macro from the Navigation Pane, save the field first, and then run the macro. If the macro name is the setting of the `BeforeUpdate` property in a Visual Basic function, set the `AfterUpdate` property to the name of the macro instead.
2119	The `Requery` action can't be used on the control *<Control Name>*. Certain controls, such as labels and rectangles, can't receive the focus; therefore, you can't apply a `Requery` action to them.

Table C-4 *(continued)*

ERROR	DESCRIPTION
2120	To create a form, report, or data access page using this wizard, you must first select the table or query on which the form, report, or data access page will be based.
2121	*<Database Name>* can't open the form *<Form Name>*. It contains data that *<Database Name>* doesn't recognize. Re-create the form or, if you maintain backup copies of your database, retrieve a copy of the form.
2122	You can't view a form as a continuous form if it contains a subform, an ActiveX control, or a bound chart. Set the `DefaultView` property of the form to Single Form, Datasheet, PivotTable, or PivotChart.
2123	The control name you entered doesn't follow *<Database Name>* object-naming rules.
2124	The form name you entered doesn't follow *<Database Name>* object-naming rules.
2125	The setting for the FontSize property must be from 1 through 127.
2126	The setting for the ColumnCount property must be from 1 through 255.
2127	The setting for the BoundColumn property can't be greater than the setting for the ColumnCount property.
2128	*<Database Name>* encountered errors while importing *<Object Name>*. For more detailed error information, see the file *<File Name>*.
2129	The setting for the DefaultEditing property must be Allow Edits, Read Only, Data Entry, or Can't Add Records. Enter 1, 2, 3, or 4 for the DefaultEditing property.
2130	The settings for the GridX and GridY properties must be from 1 through 64.
2131	An expression can't be longer than 2,048 characters.
2132	The setting for the DecimalPlaces property must be from 0 through 15, or 255 for Auto (default).
2133	You can't place a form (or report) within itself. Select or enter a different form or report to serve as the subform or subreport.
2134	The setting for the Width property must be from 0 through 22 inches (55.87 cm).
2135	This property is read-only and can't be set.

(continued)

Table C-4 *(continued)*

ERROR	DESCRIPTION
2136	To set this property, open the form or report in Design view. For more information on this property, search the Help index for the name of the property.
2137	You can't use Find or Replace now. The fields are not searchable due to one of the following: The fields are controls (such as buttons or OLE objects); the fields have no data; or there are no fields to search.
2138	You can't search the field for the specified value. Resolve the error given in the previous error message before you attempt to search again.
2139	You can't replace the current value of the field with the replacement text. Resolve any errors before making further replacements.
2140	<*Database Name*> cannot save the change you made to the record in the Replace operation for the reason shown in the previous message. Click Undo or enter a new value in the field.
2141	<*Database Name*> can't find the text you specified in the Find What box.
2142	The FindRecord action requires a Find What argument. You tried to run a macro set to one of the current field's properties, but you left the Find What argument blank. When you click OK, an Action Failed dialog box will display the macro name and the macro's arguments. In the Macro window, enter text or an expression for the Find What argument, and try the Search operation again.
2143	You didn't specify search criteria with a `FindRecord` action. In the Macro window, insert a `FindRecord` action before the `FindNext` action.
2144	The setting for the ListRows property must be from 1 through 255.
2145	The `ColumnWidths` property setting must be a value from 0 through 22 inches (55.87 cm) for each column in a list box or a combo box. If there is more than one column, separate the numbers with either a semicolon or the list separator character. List separator characters are defined in the Regional Settings section of Windows Control Panel.
2147	You must be in Design view to create or delete controls.
2148	The number you used to refer to the form or report section is invalid. Make sure that the number is less than the number of sections in the form or report.
2149	The constant you entered for the control type is invalid. For a list of valid constants you can use to create a control, click Help.

Table C-4 *(continued)*

ERROR	DESCRIPTION
2150	This type of control can't contain other controls.
2151	The parent control can't contain the type of control you selected. For example, you used the `CreateControl` function to designate an option group as the parent of a text box.
2152	You can set group levels for reports only, not for forms.
2153	You can't specify more than 10 group levels.
2154	You can't call this function when the Group, Sort, and Total Pane is open.
2157	The sum of the top margin, the bottom margin, the height of the page header, and the height of the page footer is greater than the length of the page you are printing on.
2158	You can use the `Print` method and the report graphics methods (`Circle`, `Line`, `PSet`, and `Scale`) only in an event procedure or a macro set to the `OnPrint`, the `OnFormat`, or the `OnPage` event property.
2159	There isn't enough memory to initialize the `Print` method or one of the report graphics methods (`Circle`, `Line`, `PSet`, `Scale`). Close unneeded programs and try again to print or preview the report. For more information on freeing memory, search the Microsoft Windows Help index for "memory, troubleshooting".
2160	*<Database Name>* couldn't create the graphic or text. An error occurred while initializing the Print method or one of the report graphics methods (Circle, Line, PSet, Scale). Close unneeded programs and try again to print or preview the report. For more information on freeing memory, search the Microsoft Windows Help index for "memory, troubleshooting".
2161	The text or expression you entered doesn't match the type of data you are searching for. Redefine the text or expression, or search in a different field.
2162	A macro set to one of the current field's properties failed because of an error in a `FindRecord` action argument. In the Macro window, change the Search As Formatted argument to Yes. If you want the argument setting to remain No, do all of the following: Select No for the Match Case argument; select Yes for the Only Current Field argument; and make sure you are searching in a bound control.
2163	The page number you used as an argument for the `GoToPage` action or method doesn't exist in this form.
2164	You can't disable a control while it has the focus.

(continued)

Table C-4 *(continued)*

ERROR	DESCRIPTION
2165	You can't hide a control that has the focus.
2166	You can't lock a control while it has unsaved changes.
2167	This property is read-only and can't be modified.
2169	You can't save this record at this time. <*Database Name*> may have encountered an error while trying to save a record. If you close this object now, the data changes you made will be lost. Do you want to close the database object anyway?
2170	There isn't enough memory to retrieve data for the list box. Close unneeded programs. Then close and reopen the active form, and click the list box again. For more information on freeing memory, search the Microsoft Windows Help index for "memory, troubleshooting".
2171	You can't have more than seven nested subforms in a main form. Remove the eighth nested subform.
2172	You can't use a pass-through query or a non-fixed-column crosstab query as a record source for a subform or subreport. Before you bind the subform or subreport to a crosstab query, set the query's ColumnHeadings property.
2173	The control <*Control Name*> the macro is attempting to search can't be searched. Try one of the following: Add a GoToControl action before the FindRecord action; for the FindRecord action, change the Only Current Field action argument from Yes to No; or change the focus to a searchable control.
2174	You can't switch to a different view at this time. Code was executing when you tried to switch views. If you are debugging code, you must end the debugging operation before switching views.
2175	There isn't enough free memory to continue the Search operation. Close unneeded programs. Then try the Search operation again. For more information on freeing memory, search the Microsoft Windows Help index for "memory, troubleshooting".
2176	The setting for this property is too long. You can enter up to either 255 or 2,048 characters for this property, depending on the data type.
2177	You can't insert a report into a form. A report can be inserted only into a report.
2178	You can't add another section now. The maximum total height for all sections in a report, including the section headers, is 200 inches (508 cm). Remove or reduce the height of at least one section, and then add the new section.

Table C-4 *(continued)*

ERROR	DESCRIPTION
2181	You can't sort on a calculated field in a form. You can sort on a calculated field only in a query. Create a calculated field in a query, sort the field, and then base the form on the query. Because the query must execute before the form opens, the form will open more slowly.
2182	You can't sort on this field.
2183	*<Database Name>* can't create an object of the type requested. You are trying either to create a form from a report that has been saved as text, or to create a report from a saved form.
2184	The value you used for the `TabIndex` property isn't valid. The correct values are from 0 through *<Value>*.
2185	You can't reference a property or method for a control unless the control has the focus. Try one of the following: Move the focus to the control before you reference the property. In Visual Basic code, use the `SetFocus` method. In a macro, use the `GoToControl` action. Reference or set the property from a macro or event procedure that runs when the `GotFocus` event for the control occurs.
2186	This property isn't available in Design view. Switch to Form view to access this property, or remove the reference to the property.
2187	This property is available only in Design view.
2188	The object you attempted to load from text has an invalid value for the property *<Property Name>* on a *<Object>*.
2189	The code contains a syntax error, or a *<Database Name>* function you need is not available. If the syntax is correct, check the Control Wizards subkey or the Libraries key in the *<Database Name>* section of the Windows Registry to verify that the entries you need are listed and available. If the entries are correct, either you must correct the *<Database Name>* Utility Add-in, or the file acWzlib or this wizard has been disabled. To re-enable this wizard, run *<Database Name>* or Microsoft Office Setup again to reinstall *<Database Name>*. Before you reinstall *<Database Name>*, delete the Windows Registry keys for the *<Database Name>* Utility Add-in and acWzlib.
2190	This property has been replaced by a new property; use the new property instead.
2191	You can't set the *<Property Name>* property in print preview or after printing has started. Try setting this property in the `OnOpen` event.

(continued)

Table C-4 *(continued)*

ERROR	DESCRIPTION
2192	The bitmap you specified is not in a device-independent bitmap (.dib) format. You tried to set the `PictureData` property of a form, report, button, or image control.
2193	The left margin, right margin, or both margins are wider than the paper size specified in the Print Setup dialog box.
2194	You can't set the `PictureData` property in Datasheet view. To see the valid settings for this property, search the Help index for "PictureData property".
2195	The section name you entered doesn't follow *<Database Name>* object-naming rules.
2196	*<Database Name>* can't retrieve the value of this property. The property isn't available from the view in which you're running the macro or Visual Basic code, or *<Database Name>* encountered an error while retrieving the value of the property. To see the valid settings for this property, search the Help index for the name of the property.
2197	You can't set a subform control's `SourceObject` property to a zero-length string if you're displaying the main form in Form view. You can set this property to a zero-length string from Design view, Datasheet view, or Print Preview.
2200	The number you entered is invalid.
2201	There was a problem retrieving printer information for the *<Object Name>* on *<Printer Name>*. The object may have been sent to a printer that is unavailable.
2202	There are currently no printers installed on your computer. To use this feature, you must first install a printer in Windows. For more information about how to install a printer, search for "install printer" in Windows Help.
2203	The dynamic-link library Commdlg failed: error code 0x. The printer driver for the selected printer may be incorrectly installed. For information on selecting another printer or reinstalling this printer from Microsoft Windows, search the Windows Help index for "printer setup".
2204	The default printer driver isn't set up correctly. For information on setting a default printer, search the Microsoft Windows Help index for "default printer, setting".
2205	The default printer driver isn't set up correctly. For information on setting a default printer, search the Microsoft Windows Help index for "default printer, setting".

Table C-4 *(continued)*

ERROR	DESCRIPTION
2206	The page number you entered is invalid. For example, it may be a negative number or an invalid range, such as 6 to 3.
2207	*<Database Name>* can't print macros. You tried to use the `PrintOut` action or method, but the active object is a macro. If you want to print an object other than a macro, use the `SelectObject` action or method to select the desired object before you run the `PrintOut` action.
2210	*<Database Name>* can't print or preview the page because the page size you selected is larger than 22.75 inches.
2211	*<Database Name>* can't print or preview the Debug window.
2212	*<Database Name>* couldn't print your object. Make sure that the specified printer is available. For information on setting a default printer, search the Windows Help index for "default printer, setting".
2213	There was a problem retrieving printer information for this object. The object may have been sent to a printer that is unavailable.
2214	There was a problem retrieving information from the printer. New printer has not been set.
2215	*<Database Name>* cannot print this PivotTable because its *<Component Part>* exceed(s) 22.75 inches. Reduce the *<Component Part>* by making changes to the formatting or included data of the PivotTable view, and then try to print again.
2220	*<Database Name>* can't open the file *<File Name>*.
2221	The text is too long to be edited.
2222	This control is read-only and can't be modified.
2223	The file name *<File Name>* is too long. Enter a file name that's 256 characters or less.
2225	*<Database Name>* couldn't open the Clipboard. The Clipboard isn't responding, probably because another application is using it. Close all other applications and try the operation again.
2226	The Clipboard isn't responding, so *<Database Name>* can't paste the Clipboard's contents. Another application may be using the Clipboard. There may not be enough free memory for the paste operation. Close all other applications, and then copy and paste again.
2227	The data on the Clipboard is damaged, so *<Database Name>* can't paste it. There may be an error in the Clipboard, or there may not be enough free memory. Try the operation again.

(continued)

Table C-4 *(continued)*

ERROR	DESCRIPTION
2229	*<Database Name>* can't start the OLE server. You tried to use a form, report, or datasheet that contains an OLE object, but the OLE server (the application used to create the object) may not be registered properly. Reinstall the OLE server to register it correctly.
2234	*<Database Name>* can't paste the OLE object.
2237	The text you entered isn't an item in the list. Select an item from the list, or enter text that matches one of the listed items.
2243	The data in the Clipboard isn't recognizable; *<Database Name>* can't paste the OLE object.
2244	The file name you specified in the Picture property for a command button or toggle button can't be read. The file you specified may be corrupted. Restore the file from a backup copy or re-create the file. The disk where the file is located may be unreadable.
2245	The file you specified doesn't contain valid icon data. Specify a valid icon file.
2260	An error occurred while sending data to the OLE server (the application used to create the object). You may have tried to send too much data. If you're creating a chart and the chart is based on a query, modify the query so that it selects less data. If the chart is based on a table, consider basing it on a query instead so that you can limit the data. You may be using an OLE server that doesn't accept the Clipboard format. You may not be able to start the OLE server because it's not properly registered. Reinstall it to register it. Your computer may be low on memory. Close other application windows to free up memory.
2262	This value must be a number.
2263	The number is too large.
2264	*<Database Name>* didn't recognize the unit of measurement. Type a valid unit, such as inches (in) or centimeters (cm).
2265	You must specify a unit of measurement, such as inches (in) or centimeters (cm).
2266	*<Name* or *Value>* may not be a valid setting for the RowSourceType property, or there was a compile error in the function. For information on valid settings for the RowSourceType property, click Help.
2267	There is not enough disk space to create a temporary buffer file for printing. Free up some disk space to make room for the temporary buffer file.

Table C-4 *(continued)*

ERROR	DESCRIPTION
2269	Some library databases couldn't be loaded because too many were specified. To change library database references, click References on the Tools menu.
2272	The setting for the Update Retry Interval must be from 0 through 1,000 milliseconds.
2273	The setting for Update Retries must be from 0 through 10.
2274	The database *<Database Name>* is already open as a library database.
2275	The string returned by the builder was too long. The result will be truncated.
2276	The custom builder you're using caused an error by changing the focus to a different window while you were using it. Enter a value without using the custom builder.
2277	There was a font initialization error.
2278	*<Database Name>* can't save your changes to this bound OLE object. Either you don't have permission to write to the record in which the object is stored, or the record is locked by another user. Copy the object to the Clipboard (select the object and click Copy on the Edit menu), and click Undo Current Record on the Edit menu. Then open the application you used to create the object, paste the object from the Clipboard, and save it.
2279	The value you entered isn't appropriate for the input mask *<Mask Name>* specified for this field.
2280	You have added more output formats to the Windows Registry than *<Database Name>* can initialize. Some output formats will not be available. Remove those formats that you never or least often use.
2281	Output format information is missing. There appears to be a problem with your *<Database Name>* installation. Please reinstall *<Database Name>* or contact your system administrator or help desk representative.
2282	The format in which you are attempting to output the current object is not available. Either you are attempting to output the current object to a format that is not valid for its object type, or the formats that enable you to output data as a Microsoft Excel, rich-text format, MS-DOS text, or HTML file are missing from the Windows Registry. Run Setup to reinstall *<Database Name>* or, if you're familiar with the settings in the Registry, try to correct them yourself. For more information on the Registry, click Help.

(continued)

Table C-4 *(continued)*

ERROR	DESCRIPTION
2283	The format specification for *<Object Name>* is invalid. You can't save output data to a file in this format until you correct the setting for the format in the Windows Registry. Run Setup to reinstall *<Database Name>* or, if you're familiar with the settings in the Registry, try to correct them yourself. For more information on the Registry, click Help.
2284	*<Database Name>* can't write to the file. The network may not be working. Wait until the network is working, and then try again. You may be out of memory. Close one or more *<Database Name>* windows, close other applications, and then try again.
2285	*<Database Name>* can't create the output file. You may be out of disk space on the destination drive. The network may not be working. Wait until the network is working, and then try again. You may be out of memory. Close one or more *<Database Name>* windows, close other applications, and then try again.
2286	*<Database Name>* can't close the file. The network may not be working. Wait until the network is working, and then try again. You may be out of memory. Close one or more *<Database Name>* windows, close other applications, and then try again.
2287	*<Database Name>* can't open the mail session. Check your e-mail application to make sure that it's working properly.
2288	*<Database Name>* can't load the *<Format Name>* format. The setting for this format in the Windows Registry is incorrect. You can't save the output data to a file in this format until you correct the setting in the Registry. Run Setup to reinstall *<Database Name>* or, if you're familiar with the settings in the Registry, try to correct them yourself. For more information on the Registry, click Help.
2289	*<Database Name>* can't output the module in the requested format.
2290	There were too many message recipients; the message was not sent.
2291	There are too many message attachments; the message was not sent.
2292	The message text is too long, so it was not sent.
2293	*<Database Name>* can't send this e-mail message. Before attempting to send an e-mail message from *<Database Name>*, resolve the problem identified in the previous message, or configure your computer to send and receive e-mail messages.
2294	*<Database Name>* can't attach the object; the message was not sent. The network may not be working. Wait until the network is working, and then try again. You may be out of memory. Close one or more *<Database Name>* windows, close other applications, and then try again.

Table C-4 *(continued)*

ERROR	DESCRIPTION
2295	Unknown message recipient(s); the message was not sent.
2296	The password is invalid; the message wasn't sent.
2297	*<Database Name>* can't open the mail session. You may be out of memory. Close one or more *<Database Name>* windows, close other applications, and then try again. You may also want to check your mail application to ensure that it's working properly.
2298	*<Database Name>* can't start the wizard, builder, or add-in. The library database containing the wizard, builder, or add-in may not be installed. Point to Add-ins on the Tools menu, and then click Add-in Manager to see if the library database is installed. The wizard, builder, or add-in code may not be compiled and *<Database Name>* can't compile it. There may be a syntax error in the code. The key for the add-in in the Windows Registry file may be incorrect.
2299	*<Database Name>* can't open the Zoom box. The *<Database Name>* Utility add-in is missing or was modified. Rerun *<Database Name>* or Microsoft Office Setup to reinstall *<Database Name>* and the *<Database Name>* Utility add-in.
2300	*<Database Name>* can't output because there are too many controls selected that have different styles, such as color and font. Select fewer controls, and then try again.
2301	There are not enough system resources to output the data. Close one or more *<Database Name>* windows and close other applications. Then try to output the data again.
2302	*<Database Name>* can't save the output data to the file you've selected. The file may be open. If so, close it, and then save the output data to the file again. If you are using a template, check to make sure the template exists. If the file isn't open, check to make sure that you have enough free disk space. Make sure that the file exists on the path specified. Check to make sure you have permission to write to the specified folder.
2303	*<Database Name>* can't output data now. The network may not be working. Wait until the network is working, and then try again. You may be out of disk space. Free up disk space and try again.
2304	*<Database Name>* can't save output data to the specified file. Make sure that you have enough free disk space on your destination drive.
2305	There are too many columns to output, based on the limitation specified in the output format or by *<Database Name>*.
2306	There are too many rows to output, based on the limitation specified by the output format or by *<Database Name>*.

(continued)

Table C-4 *(continued)*

ERROR	DESCRIPTION
2308	The file <*File Name*> already exists. Do you want to replace the existing file?
2309	There is an invalid add-in entry for <*Object Name*>. There is an error in the Windows Registry for this add-in. Correct the setting and restart <*Database Name*>. For information on the Registry, click Help.
2311	There isn't enough memory to run the NotInList event procedure.
2312	The shortcut <*Shortcut Name*> must be re-created. The file may be missing, damaged, or in an older format that can't be read.
2313	<*Database Name*> can't find the shortcut databases <*Database 1*> or <*Database 2*>. Re-create the shortcut with the correct locations of the databases.
2314	<*Database Name*> can't find the shortcut database <*Database Name*>. Re-create the shortcut with the correct location of the database.
2315	The input string is too long.
2316	This table or query can't be opened because it has no visible fields. This can result if the table or query has only system fields, and the Show System Objects option is off. To turn on the Show System Objects option, click Options on the Tools menu, click the View tab, and select the System Objects check box.
2317	The database <*Database Name*> can't be repaired or isn't a <*Database Name*> database file.
2320	<*Database Name*> can't display the field for which you entered Where in the Total row. Clear the Show check box for that field. If you want this field to appear in the query's results, add it to the design grid twice. For the field that will appear in the query's results, don't specify Where in the Total row, and make sure the Show check box is checked.
2321	You can't set criteria before you add a field or expression to the Field row. Either add a field from the field list to the column and enter an expression, or delete the criteria.
2322	You can't sort on the asterisk (*). Because the asterisk represents all fields in the underlying table or query, you can't sort on it. Add the asterisk to the query design grid, along with the specific fields you want to sort on. Clear the Show check box for the sorting fields, and then specify a sort order.
2323	You can't specify criteria for the asterisk (*). Because the asterisk represents all the fields in the underlying table or query, you can't specify criteria for it. Add the asterisk to the query design grid, along with the field(s) you want to set criteria for, and then enter criteria for the specific fields. In the query design grid, clear the Show check box for the criteria field(s), before you run the query.

Table C-4 *(continued)*

ERROR	DESCRIPTION
2324	You can't calculate totals on the asterisk (*). Because the asterisk represents all the fields in the table, you can't calculate totals on it. Remove the asterisk from the query design grid. Add the fields you want to use to the design grid, and then select the total you want to calculate for specific fields.
2325	The field name you entered exceeds the 64-character limit of the LinkMasterFields property. When you use the Relationships command (on the Database Tools tab, click Relationships) to define a relationship between the tables underlying a form and subform, <*Database Name*> links the form and subform automatically and sets the LinkChildFields and LinkMasterFields properties.
2326	You can't specify Group By, Expression, or Where in the Total row for this column. Specify an aggregate function, such as Sum or Count, for the field or expression you designate as the Value in the crosstab query. For more information on aggregate functions, click Help.
2327	You must enter Group By in the Total row for a field that has Column Heading in the Crosstab row. The values derived from the field or expression that you designate as the Column Heading are used to group data in the crosstab query.
2328	You can't run an update query on the asterisk (*). Because the asterisk represents all the fields in the table, you can't update it. Remove the asterisk from the query design grid. Add the fields you want to update to the design grid.
2329	To create a crosstab query, you must specify one or more Row Heading(s) options, one Column Heading option, and one Value option.
2330	<*Database Name*> can't represent the join expression <*Expression*> in Design view. One or more fields may have been deleted or renamed. The name of one or more fields or tables specified in the join expression may be misspelled. The join may use an operator that isn't supported in Design view, such as > or <.
2331	You must enter Group By in the Total row for at least one of the Row Heading options you enter in the Crosstab row.
2332	<*Database Name*> can't match the fields you added using the asterisk (*) in the append query. Because the asterisk represents all the fields in the underlying table or query, you can't append an asterisk to one field or expression, and you can't append a single field or expression to an asterisk. Append an asterisk to an asterisk (for example, a table to a table), or append specific fields.

(continued)

Table C-4 *(continued)*

ERROR	DESCRIPTION
2333	You must enter the name of the table you are creating or appending records to. You tried to define a make-table or append query without specifying a destination table.
2334	*<Database Name>* can't print *<Object Name>* because it is an action query. Because action queries don't produce a recordset, you can't print a Datasheet view of them. Note that an exclamation point (!) joined to a query icon in the Navigation Pane marks an action query. To print a Datasheet view of the records that will be selected by the query, display the query in Design view, click the Datasheet button, and then click the Print button.
2335	You must specify the same number of fields when you set the LinkChildFields and LinkMasterFields properties. You entered a different number of fields for one property than you did for the other. If you use the Relationships command (on the Database Tools tab, click Relationships) to define a relationship between the tables underlying the form and subform, *<Database Name>* will link the form and subform automatically and then set the LinkChildFields and LinkMasterFields properties.
2337	You can't specify criteria on the same field for which you entered *Value* in the Crosstab row. You tried to display a crosstab query after entering *Value* in the Crosstab row and criteria in the Criteria row. If you want this field to supply the cross-tabulated values in the crosstab query, delete the entry in the Criteria row. If you want this to be a criteria field, leave the Crosstab row blank.
2338	*<Database Name>* truncated the expression you entered. The expression *<Expression Name>* exceeds the 1,024-character limit for the query design grid.
2339	*<Database Name>* can't create a temporary link. You reached the limit for the number of links in your database. *<Database Name>* needs to create a temporary link in order to import your ODBC table. Remove all unneeded links or tables.
2340	The expression you entered exceeds the 1,024-character limit for the query design grid.
2342	A RunSQL action requires an argument consisting of a SQL statement. For example, an action query that appends records starts with INSERT INTO. A data-definition query that creates a table starts with CREATE TABLE.
2343	The value you entered exceeds the Alias property's 64-character limit.
2344	For the TopValues property in the query property sheet, you must enter an integer greater than zero.

Table C-4 *(continued)*

ERROR	DESCRIPTION
2345	For the TopValues property in the query property sheet, you must enter a percentage from 1 through 100.
2346	For the TopValues property in the query property sheet, you must enter a number greater than zero.
2347	*<Database Name>* can't find the file name you entered for the DestinationDB property in an action query's property sheet. You may have misspelled the database file name, or the file may have been deleted or renamed.
2348	You can't leave the Alias property blank.
2349	For the TopValues property in the query property sheet, you must enter a number smaller than 2,147,483,647.
2350	*<Database Name>* can't save the query. The query is a pass-through query and can't be represented as a simple SQL string. Save the query as a named query from the Query Builder. When you close the Query Builder, *<Database Name>* will fill the RecordSource or RowSource property with the saved query name. Make sure the query doesn't have a SQL syntax error.
2351	*<Database Name>* can't represent an implicit VALUES clause in the query design grid. Edit this in SQL view.
2352	You can't modify this query because it has been deleted or renamed by another user.
2353	Bad query parameter *<Parameter Value>*.
2354	This query or table has an expression that is failing to evaluate.
2355	You can select up to *<Number>* values in a column filter for a multi-valued field. Remove some values, and then try again.
2356	You cannot assign a multi-valued or Attachment field to the Link Master Fields or Link Child Fields properties.
2360	A field name is missing. You have defined a data type or a description for a field without specifying the field name. Enter a name for the field, or delete the row.
2361	*<Database Name>* can't save this table. There are no fields in this table. Define at least one field by entering a field name and selecting a data type.
2362	You already have a field named *<Field Name>*.
2363	*<Database Name>* allows only one AutoNumber field per table. Use the Number data type for similar fields.

(continued)

Table C-4 *(continued)*

ERROR	DESCRIPTION
2364	*<Database Name>* can't open the table in Datasheet view.
2366	*<Database Name>* was unable to save the field ordering. All other changes were saved successfully. Click the Microsoft Office Button, point to Manage, and then click Compact and Repair Database.
2370	Removing or changing the index for this field would require removal of the primary key. If you want to delete the primary key, select that field and click the Primary Key button.
2371	*<Database Name>* can't create a primary key. Your changes weren't saved.
2372	The field name is not valid. Make sure that the name doesn't contain a period (.), exclamation point (!), bracket ([]), leading space, or non-printable character such as a carriage return. If you have pasted the name from another application, try pressing ESC and typing the name again.
2373	The setting for the FieldSize property must be from 0 through 255.
2374	You can't create an index or primary key on more than 10 fields.
2375	You can't paste beyond the end of a table. You have attempted to paste fields beyond the 255th row in a table in Design view.
2376	*<Database Name>* can't create a primary key. You have selected too many fields for a multiple-field primary key.
2377	Once you enter data in a table, you can't change the data type of any field to AutoNumber, even if you haven't yet added data to that field. Add a new field to the table, and define its data type as AutoNumber. *<Database Name>* then enters data in the AutoNumber field automatically, numbering the records consecutively starting with 1.
2378	This table is read-only. Use a different name in the Save As dialog box to save your changes.
2379	You can't create a primary key on a field of this data type. You can't define a primary key on fields with an OLE Object, Memo, Attachment, or Multi-valued lookup field.
2380	*<Database Name>* can't create a primary key because no fields have been selected. You have selected a row with no fields defined. Place the insertion point somewhere in the row of the field you want to define as the primary key.
2381	*<Database Name>* can't create a primary key because the field doesn't have a name. Name the field, and then define it as a primary key field.

Table C-4 *(continued)*

ERROR	DESCRIPTION
2382	You can't switch to Datasheet view and you can't return to Design view. Another user has opened this table or a query, form, or report that is bound to this table.
2383	<*Database Name*> can't change the data type. There isn't enough disk space or memory.
2384	You cannot change one field from an AutoNumber data type and add another AutoNumber field at the same time. Do the following: 1. Delete the AutoNumber field you just added, click the Microsoft Office Button, and then click Save. 2. Add the new AutoNumber field, and then save the table again.
2385	Errors were encountered during the save operation.
2386	<*Database Name*> was unable to create the table.
2387	You can't delete the table <*Table Name*>; it is participating in one or more relationships. If you want to delete this table, first delete its relationships in the Relationships window.
2388	You can't change the primary key. This table is the primary table in one or more relationships. If you want to change or remove the primary key, first delete the relationship in the Relationships window.
2389	You can't delete the field <*Field Name*>. It is part of one or more relationships. If you want to delete this field, first delete its relationships in the Relationships window.
2390	You can't change the data type or field size of this field; it is part of one or more relationships. If you want to change the data type of this field, first delete its relationships in the Relationships window.
2391	Field <*Field Name*> doesn't exist in destination table <*Table Name*>. <*Database Name*> was unable to complete the append operation. The destination table must contain the same fields as the table you are pasting from.
2392	You can't set the Unique property of a primary key to No. A primary key, by definition, contains only unique values. If you want to allow nonunique values in this field, remove the primary key definition by setting the Primary property to No.
2393	You can't set the IgnoreNulls property of a primary key to Yes. A primary key, by definition, can't allow null values. If you want null values in this field, remove the primary key definition by setting the Primary property to No.
2394	The index name is invalid. The index name may be too long (over 64 characters) or contain invalid characters.

(continued)

Table C-4 *(continued)*

ERROR	DESCRIPTION
2395	Indexes must have names.
2396	*<Database Name>* can't create an index or primary key. One or more field names are missing. Enter or select at least one field in the Field Name column for each index you name.
2397	You already have an index named *<Name>*.
2398	The primary key has been changed. This table is the primary table in one or more relationships. Changes to the primary key won't be saved.
2399	The setting for the FieldSize property must be from 1 through 8000.
2400	The row you inserted in the grid exceeds the limit of 255 rows (fields) for a table or 1,000 rows (actions) for a macro.
2401	You can't delete the *<Column Name>* column at this time. The *<Column Name>* column is part of the primary key for the *<Table Name>* table. It is used to identify and store the rows in your table in the database. You cannot delete a primary key while using Datasheet view. To delete the primary key, open the table in Design view and remove the primary key field.
2491	The action or method is invalid because the form or report isn't bound to a table or query. You tried to use the ApplyFilter or SearchForRecord action or method. However, the form or report you applied the filter to is not based on a table or query, so the form or report doesn't have any records to apply a filter to. Use the SelectObject action or method to select the desired form or report before you run the ApplyFilter action. To base a form or report on a table or query, open the form or report in Design view, and enter the table or query name in the RecordSource property.
2492	*<Database Name>* can't find the macro *<Macro Name>* in the macro group *<Group Name>*. You used the macrogroupname. macroname syntax to specify a macro. You then tried to run the macro (directly or indirectly), or you used the RunMacro method to run the macro. However, the macro you specified isn't in this macro group. Create the macro in the macro group, specify the correct macro group, or specify the correct macro name.
2493	This action requires an Object Name argument.
2494	The action or method requires a Form Name argument. You tried to use the OpenForm action or method, but you left the Form Name argument blank. In the Form Name argument, enter the name of a form in the current database.

Table C-4 *(continued)*

ERROR	DESCRIPTION
2495	The action or method requires a Table Name argument. You tried to use the OpenTable, TransferSpreadsheet, or TransferText action or method, but you left the Table Name argument blank. In the Table Name argument, enter the name of a table that is in the current database.
2496	The action or method requires a Query Name argument. You tried to use the OpenQuery action or method, but you left the Query Name argument blank. In the Query Name argument, enter a query name.
2497	The action or method requires a Report Name argument. You tried to use the OpenReport action or method, but you left the Report Name argument blank. In the Report Name argument, enter the name of a report.
2498	An expression you entered is the wrong data type for one of the arguments. You tried to run a macro or use a method to carry out an action, but an expression evaluated to the wrong data type. For example, for the Close method you specified a string for the Object Type argument, but this argument can be set only to certain intrinsic constants or their numeric equivalents.
2499	You can't use the GoToRecord or SearchForRecord action or method on an object in Design view. Try one of the following: Switch to Form or Datasheet view for a form. Switch to Datasheet view for a query or table. If you are running a macro or Visual Basic procedure containing an action that opens the object, set the View argument to the correct view before you carry out the GoToRecord action.
2500	You must enter a number greater than zero for a Repeat Count argument. You tried to use the RunMacro action or method, but you entered a value less than zero (or an expression that evaluates to less than zero) in the Repeat Count argument. To run the macro once, leave this argument blank.
2501	The *<Operation Name>* action was canceled. You used a method of the DoCmd object to carry out an action in Visual Basic, but then clicked Cancel in a dialog box. For example, you used the Close method to close a changed form, then clicked Cancel in the dialog box that asks if you want to save the changes you made to the form.
2502	The action or method requires a Macro Name argument. You tried to use the RunMacro action or method, but you left the Macro Name argument blank. *<Database Name>* tried to create a custom menu bar for a form or report, but the Menu Macro Name argument of the AddMenu action is blank. In the Menu Macro Name argument, enter the name of a macro or macro group that is in the current database.

(continued)

Table C-4 *(continued)*

ERROR	DESCRIPTION
2503	You can't use this action with the DoCmd object. For a list of the actions that the DoCmd object doesn't support and some alternatives to using these actions, click Help. Any actions that aren't in this list can be used with the DoCmd object.
2504	The action or method requires at least <*Number*> argument(s). You tried to run a macro containing an action or used a method or action with the DoCmd object, but you didn't set the required number of arguments. For example, if you use the MoveSize action, you must set at least one of the four arguments.
2505	An expression in argument <*Argument Name*> has an invalid value. You tried to run a macro or used the DoCmd object in Visual Basic. The argument number above is the position of the argument as it appears in the Macro window, the Action Failed dialog box, or the Object Browser (if you're using the DoCmd object). Try one of the following: Select a setting from the drop-down list box in each argument. Use an intrinsic constant equating to a valid object type. Substitute the correct corresponding expression.
2506	A value you entered for the Transfer Type argument is invalid. An expression in the Transfer Type argument doesn't evaluate to a valid numeric value. Valid values for the Transfer Type argument are as follows: 0, 1, and 2 for the TransferDatabase action. 0, 1, and 2 for the TransferSpreadsheet action. 0 through 6 for the TransferText action.
2507	The <*Type Name*> type isn't an installed database type or doesn't support the operation you chose. You used the TransferDatabase method, but an expression in the databasetype argument doesn't evaluate to a valid database type for importing, exporting, or linking. For information on valid database types, click Help.
2508	A value you entered for the spreadsheettype argument is invalid. You used the TransferSpreadsheet method, and an expression in the spreadsheettype argument doesn't evaluate to a valid numeric value. Valid values are 0, 2, 3, 4, 5, 6, 7, and 8. Note that 1 is an invalid value; you can't import or export to a Lotus .wks format file.
2509	The setting for the Range argument can't be longer than 255 characters.
2510	The expression you entered in the Specification Name argument exceeds the 64-character limit. Select one of the existing specification names from the argument list box when you use the TransferText action in a macro, or enter a name in Visual Basic that follows <*Database Name*> object-naming rules.

Table C-4 *(continued)*

ERROR	DESCRIPTION
2511	The action or method requires a Specification Name argument. You tried to use the TransferText action or method and you specified a Transfer Type argument but left the Specification Name argument blank. In the Specification Name argument, enter an existing specification name from the argument list box.
2512	*<Database Name>* can't parse the expression: *<Expression>*. Click OK to return to the action argument or conditional expression where this expression appears, and then correct the syntax.
2513	The Macro Name argument can't be longer than 64 characters according to *<Database Name>* object-naming rules.
2514	The action or method requires a Control Name argument. You tried to use the GoToControl action or method, but you left the control name blank. In the Control Name argument, enter a control or field name from the active form or datasheet.
2515	*<Database Name>* can't open the macro *<Macro Name>* because it was saved using a different version of *<Database Name>*. Re-create the macro in the current version of *<Database Name>*.
2516	*<Database Name>* can't find the module *<Module Name>*. You tried to use the OpenModule action or method, but *<Database Name>* can't find the module you specified in the Module Name argument. Enter a valid module name from the current database.
2517	*<Database Name>* can't find the procedure *<Procedure Name>*. You may have used the Run method in Visual Basic but entered an invalid procedure name, or you used the Run method without first opening a database. You tried to use the OpenModule action or method, but you used an invalid procedure name.
2520	The action or method requires a Module or Procedure Name argument. You tried to use the OpenModule action or method, but you didn't enter a name in either the Module Name or the Procedure Name argument in the Macro window. Enter a valid name in one of these arguments.
2521	You have specified a Transfer Type that doesn't support the HTML Table Name argument. Leave the HTML Table Name argument blank unless you are using the Import HTML or Link HTML Transfer Types.
2522	The action or method requires a File Name argument. You tried to use the TransferSpreadsheet or TransferText action or method. In the File Name argument, enter a file name.
2523	The value you entered for the show argument is invalid. You used the ShowToolbar method. Valid values for this argument are acToolbarYes, acToolbarWhereApprop, acToolbarNo, or the corresponding numeric values 0, 1, and 2.

(continued)

Table C-4 *(continued)*

ERROR	DESCRIPTION
2524	*<Database Name>* can't invoke the application using the RunApp action. The path to the application is invalid, or a component of the application is missing. Check the path in Windows Explorer or File Manager.
2525	A macro can call itself a maximum of 20 times. Your macro contains a RunMacro action that calls the same macro more than 20 times. Use a condition to stop the macro after it has been run 20 times, or call another macro with the RunMacro action.
2526	The SendKeys action requires the *<Database Name>* Utility Add-in to be loaded. Rerun *<Database Name>* or Microsoft Office Setup to reinstall *<Database Name>* and the *<Database Name>* Utility Add-in.
2527	Lotus .wks file formats aren't supported in the current version of *<Database Name>*. Convert your .wks file to a more recent format, such as .wk1.
2528	The RunCommand macro action argument is missing, or you entered an invalid command ID for the RunCommand method.
2529	The Toolbar argument can't be longer than 64 characters.
2530	The SelectObject method can't be used on a report that is currently printing.
2531	Your HTML file does not contain any tabular data that *<Database Name>* can import.
2532	*<Database Name>* can't find the macro or sub procedure *<Procedure Name>*. The specified macro, macro group, or sub procedure doesn't exist. Note that when you enter the macrogroupname.macroname syntax in an argument, you must specify the name the macro's macro group was last saved under. Also, ensure that the referenced macro has been saved, or that the referenced sub procedure expects 0 arguments.
2533	The ApplyFilter action requires that either the Filter Name or Where Condition argument is set. You tried to run a macro containing an ApplyFilter action, but you didn't set the required arguments.
2534	The action or method requires a data access page Name argument. You tried to use the OpenDataAccessPage action or method, but you left the data access page Name argument blank. In the data access page Name argument, enter the name of a data access page in the current database.
2535	The ApplyFilter action contains a Filter Name that cannot be applied. The filter name is not a valid argument in the ApplyFilter action in Client Server.

Table C-4 *(continued)*

ERROR	DESCRIPTION
2537	The feature *<Feature Name>* is not available while the database is opened in disabled mode.
2538	The *<Operation Name>* macro action cannot be run in disabled mode.
2540	The file *<File Name>* you tried to replace is a *<Database Name>* system file that is in use and can't be replaced or deleted.
2541	The contents of the Clipboard have been deleted and can't be pasted. Some applications do not put large objects on the Clipboard. Instead, they put a pointer to the object on the Clipboard. The pointer may vanish before the paste happens.
2542	Specify the database name in the command line so that *<Database Name>* can find the macro.
2543	You can't paste a database object onto itself.
2545	The CopyObject action requires you to specify a different destination database or a new name to copy from the current database. The macro you are running includes a CopyObject action. Open the macro in the Macro window, and select the CopyObject action. Enter a destination database or a new name in the appropriate argument box.
2546	Select a database object in the Navigation Pane before you run the macro containing the *<Operation Name>* action.
2547	The database *<Database Name>* you tried to delete and replace is read-only and can't be deleted or replaced. Enter a different name for the new database.
2548	*<Database Name>* can't run the Security Wizard because this database is open in exclusive mode. Do you want *<Database Name>* to open the database in shared mode and run the Security Wizard?
2549	*<Database Name>* can't delete *<Object Name>* after compacting it. The compacted database has been named *<Name>*. If you compact a database using the same name, *<Database Name>* creates a new compacted database and then deletes the original database. In this case, however, the original database wasn't deleted because it is read-only. If you can, remove the read-only status, delete the original database, and then rename the new database using the original name. If you can't remove the read-only status, inform your workgroup administrator.

(continued)

Table C-4 *(continued)*

ERROR	DESCRIPTION
2550	*<Database Name>* can't delete *<Object Name>* after encoding it. The encoded database has been named *<Name>*. If you encode a database using the same name, *<Database Name>* creates a new encoded database, and then deletes the original database. In this case, however, the original database can't be deleted because it is read-only. If you can, remove the read-only status, delete the original database, and then rename the new database using the original name. If you can't remove the read-only status, inform your workgroup administrator.
2551	*<Database Name>* can't delete *<Object Name>* after decoding it. The decoded database has been named *<Name>*. If you decode a database using the same name, *<Database Name>* creates a new decoded database, and then deletes the original database. In this case, however, the original database can't be deleted because it is read-only. If you can, remove the read-only status, delete the original database, and then rename the new database using the original name. If you can't remove the read-only status, inform your workgroup administrator.
2552	You can't encode a database that you didn't create or don't own. See the owner of the database or your workgroup administrator.
2553	You can't decode a database that you didn't create or don't own. See the owner of the database or your workgroup administrator.
2554	You can't find the database you specified, or you didn't specify a database at all. Specify a valid database name in the command line, and include a path if necessary.
2556	*<Database Name>* can't run the Security Wizard because the database uses a password. Remove the database password by clicking Unset Database Password in the Database Tools group on the Database Tools tab.
2557	The database you tried to convert was either created in or was already converted to the requested version of *<Database Name>*.
2559	*<Database Name>* was unable to refresh the linked table *<Table Name>* in database *<Database Name>* during conversion. Try to refresh the links manually by using the Linked Table Manager command in the Database Tools group on the Database Tools tab.
2560	*<Database Name>* is unable to load the Database Properties.
2561	*<Database Name>* can't display the Database Properties dialog box.
2562	*<Database Name>* is unable to save the Database Properties.
2564	You can't hide the document *<Document Name>* while it is open. Close the database object first, and then hide it.

Table C-4 *(continued)*

ERROR	DESCRIPTION
2565	You can't unhide the database object *<Object Name>* while it is open. Close the database object first, and then unhide it.
2566	*<Database Name>* is unable to set the application's icon to the file *<File Name>*. Make sure the file is a valid icon (.ico) file. If you're using Microsoft Windows, you can also use .bmp files.
2567	*<Database Name>* can't open or convert this previous version database. The database was created in an earlier version of *<Database Name>*. You don't have appropriate security permissions to open or convert databases created in earlier versions.
2568	*<Database Name>* can't undo this operation. An object with the same name already exists. Another user might have created an object named *<Object Name>* after you had performed this operation on an object with the same name.
2571	You cannot modify objects created in an earlier version of *<Database Name>*. To convert this database to the current version of *<Database Name>*, close the database, click the Microsoft Office Button, and then click Convert.
2573	This database is a replica created in a different version of Access. You can only convert this replica by synchronizing with its Design Master. Convert the Design Master of this replica set then synchronize the replica with the Design Master.
2574	You can't create another *<Database Name>* database with the same name and location as an existing database. You carried out the Make MDE File command, but tried to give the new database the same extension as the old one. Accept the default .mde extension for your new MDE database.
2575	You can't create a *<Database Name>* MDE database from a database replica.
2577	The database *<Database Name>* is already open. Close the database before carrying out the Make MDE File command.
2578	*<Database Name>* was unable to create the .accde, .mde, or .ade file.
2579	Local forms, reports, macros, and modules in this replica will not be converted. To retain these objects, please be sure to import them into the Design Master from the original replica.
2580	The record source *<Source Name>* specified on this form or report does not exist. The name of the recordsource may be misspelled, the recordsource was deleted or renamed, or the recordsource exists in a different database. In the Form or Report's Design view, display the property sheet by clicking the Properties button, and then set the RecordSource property to an existing table or query.

(continued)

Table C-4 *(continued)*

ERROR	DESCRIPTION
2581	You must define a sort field or expression for the group header or footer in the report you tried to preview or print.
2582	You cannot set the GroupInterval property to 0 when the GroupOn property is set to Interval. Click the Sorting and Grouping Design tab and try one of the following: Change the GroupInterval property setting to a number higher than 0. Change the GroupOn property setting to Each Value.
2583	The ApplyFilter action or method can be carried out only from an Open macro or Open event procedure. You may have tried to run a macro or procedure containing the ApplyFilter action or method from a report property other than the OnOpen property. You may have tried to run a macro or event procedure on a report that is already open. To use the ApplyFilter action in a report, set the OnOpen property to the name of the macro, close the report, and then reopen it.
2584	You can't use aggregate functions in a page header or footer. The page header or footer of the report you tried to preview contains a calculated control with an aggregate function in its expression. If you want to show the result of an aggregate function in a page header or footer, create a hidden calculated control in an appropriate section of the report. Then create an unbound text box in the page header or footer. If you are running a macro, use the SetValue action to set the unbound text box value to the value in the hidden control.
2585	This action can't be carried out while processing a form or report event. A macro specified as the OnOpen, OnLoad, OnClose, OnFormat, OnRetreat, OnPage, or OnPrint property setting contains an invalid action for the property. When you click OK, an Action Failed dialog box will display the name of the macro that failed and its arguments.
2586	*<Database Name>* changed the MoveLayout and NextRecord properties to True from False. The macro or Visual Basic function run by the OnFormat property of one of the sections of the report set both the MoveLayout and NextRecord properties to False. Having both properties set to False can make the report print continuously. Revise the macro or function so that it sets these properties to the values you want.
2587	*<Database Name>* can't complete the Output operation. The Visual Basic code you entered contains a syntax error or the Output procedures are not available. Make sure there isn't a syntax error in your code. If the syntax is correct, run Setup to reinstall *<Database Name>*. If you want to preserve your security or custom settings, back up the *<Database Name>* workgroup information file. For information on backing up files, search the Microsoft Windows Help index for "backing up files".

Table C-4 *(continued)*

ERROR	DESCRIPTION
2588	You must select a form to save as a report.
2589	The expression <*Expression Name*>is invalid. Aggregate functions are only allowed on output fields of the Record Source.
2590	The Var and VarP aggregate functions are not supported in an Access project.
2591	You can't change printer properties in the OnOpen event of a report.
2593	This feature is not available in an MDB or ACCDB.
2594	You cannot Filter By Form when form record source is a recordset object.
2595	<*Database Name*> cannot set this property when DefaultSize property is set to True.
2596	Printer object is not available on subforms and subreports.
2597	Unable to bind the report to the specified recordset because the shape does not match the sorting and grouping specified on the report.
2599	Report view is not available for this report.
2600	Verify the new password by retyping it in the Verify box and clicking OK.
2601	You don't have permission to read <*Object Name*>. To read this object, you must have Read Design permission for it. For more information on permissions and who can set them, click Help.
2602	You don't have permission to modify <*Object Name*>. To modify this object, you must have Modify Design permission for it. If the object is a table, you must also have Delete Data and Update Data permissions for it. For more information on permissions and who can set them, click Help.
2603	You don't have permission to run <*Object Name*>. To run this object, you must have Open/Run permission for it. For more information on permissions and who can set them, click Help.
2604	You can't view this object's permissions. To view or change permissions for this object, you must have Administer permission for it. For more information on permissions and who can set them, click Help.
2605	You can't remove this user account from group <*Object Name*>. You may have tried to remove a user account from the default Users group. <*Database Name*> automatically adds all users to the default Users group. To remove a user account from the Users group, you must first delete the account. You may have tried to remove all users from the Admins group. There must be at least one user in the Admins group.

(continued)

Table C-4 *(continued)*

ERROR	DESCRIPTION
2606	The object type is invalid.
2607	You don't have permission to cut <*Object Name*>. To cut this object, you must have Modify Design permission for it. If the object is a table, you must also have Delete Data permission for it. For more information on permissions and who can set them, click Help.
2608	You don't have permission to copy <*Object Name*>. To copy this object, you must have Read Design permission for it. If the object is a table, you must also have Read Data permission for it. For more information on permissions and who can set them, click Help.
2609	You don't have permission to delete <*Object Name*>. To delete this object, you must have Modify Design permission for it. If the object is a table, you must also have Delete Data permission for it. For more information on permissions and who can set them, click Help.
2610	You must enter a personal identifier (PID) consisting of at least 4 and no more than 20 characters and digits. <*Database Name*> uses the combination of the user or group name and the PID to identify the user or group. Note that <*Database Name*> hides the PID after you create it, so make sure to write down the exact user or group account name and the PID entries. If you ever have to re-create the account, you must supply the same name and PID entries.
2611	<*Database Name*> can't find the workgroup file <*File Name*>. Would you like to use the default workgroup file?
2613	You don't have permission to rename <*Object Name*>. To rename a database object, you must have Modify Design permission for the object. For more information on permissions and who can set them, click Help.
2614	You don't have permission to insert this form into another form. To insert a form into another form as a subform, you must have Read Design permission for the form being inserted. For more information on permissions and who can set them, click Help.
2615	You don't have permission to change the owner of <*Object Name*>. To change the owner of a database object, you must have Administer permission for it. For more information on permissions and who can set them, click Help.
2616	You can't change permissions for <*Object Name*>. To change permissions for this object, you must have Administer permission for it. For more information on permissions and who can set them, click Help.
2617	You don't have permission to import, export, or link to <*Object Name*>. To import, export, or link to this object, you must have Read Design and Read Data permissions for it. For more information on permissions and who can set them, click Help.

Table C-4 *(continued)*

ERROR	DESCRIPTION
2618	You must have the database open for exclusive use to set or remove the database password. To open the database exclusively, close the database, and then reopen it by clicking the Microsoft Office Button and using the Open command. In the Open dialog box, click the arrow next to the Open button, and then select Open Exclusive.
2619	You can't change permissions for *<Object Name>* in a replica. Permissions may only be changed in the Design Master for the replica set.
2620	The password you entered in the Old Password box is incorrect. Please enter the correct password for this account.
2621	That password isn't valid. You may have used a semicolon.
2622	You cannot save *<Object* Name> because it is read-only. To save, switch to Design View, click the Microsoft Office Button, point to Save As, and enter a new name.
2624	An error has occurred while changing workgroup database.
2625	Workgroup Administrator couldn't create the workgroup information file. Make sure that you have specified a valid path and file name, that you have adequate permissions to create the file, and that you have enough disk space on the destination drive.
2626	Reserved error *<Object Name>*; there is no message for this error.
2627	There's not enough disk space.
2628	One of your parameters is invalid.
2629	Could not open workgroup file. This is a directory.
2630	The specified path is invalid.
2631	The specified path is too long.
2632	Change Workgroup cannot proceed without your Name, PIN, and a path to the new Workgroup Information File.
2633	*<Database Name>* cannot change the password for the logon account *<Account Name>* because the current connection is using Microsoft Windows NT integrated security.
2634	The new password doesn't match the verify password value.
2635	*<Database Name>* is unable to change the password because the old password doesn't match the password of the currently logged in user.
2636	Workgroup file already exists.

(continued)

Table C-4 *(continued)*

ERROR	DESCRIPTION
2637	Unable to start SQL Server service. To restart the SQL Server service, double-click the SQL Server System Manager icon in the system tray and click Start/Continue. When the service is started, in Microsoft Office Access, click the Microsoft Office Button, point to Server Tasks, click Connection, and then click OK.
2638	Unable to start SQL Server service. To restart the SQL Server service, double-click the SQL Server System Manager icon in the system tray and click Start/Continue. If the service fails to start, go to the Services console and verify that the MSSQLServer service Log On information is correct. When the service is started, in *<Database Name>*, click the Microsoft Office Button, point to Server Tasks, click Connection, and then click OK.
2639	*<Database Name>* cannot open *<Object Name>* due to security restrictions. Security settings restrict access to the file because it is not digitally signed.
2646	*<Database Name>* can't create this relationship and enforce referential integrity. Data in the table *<Table Name>* violates referential integrity rules. For example, there may be records relating to an employee in the related table, but no record for the employee in the primary table. Edit the data so that records in the primary table exist for all related records. If you want to create the relationship without following the rules of referential integrity, clear the Enforce Referential Integrity check box.
2649	*<Database Name>* can't enforce referential integrity for this relationship. Make sure the fields you drag are primary key fields or uniquely indexed and that the unique index or primary key is correctly set. If you want to create the relationship without following the rules of referential integrity, clear the Enforce Referential Integrity check box.
2650	*<Database Name>* can't create this relationship and enforce referential integrity. The fields you chose may have different data types. The fields may have the Number data type but not the same FieldSize property setting. Try one of the following: Select fields with the same data type. Open the tables in Design view, and change the data types and field sizes so that the fields match. If you want to create the relationship without following the rules of referential integrity, clear the Enforce Referential Integrity check box.
2651	You can't create a relationship between fields with the Memo, OLE Object, Yes/No, or Hyperlink data type. You tried to enforce referential integrity for a relationship, but one or more of the fields you chose have the Memo, OLE Object, Yes/No, or Hyperlink data type. Select fields in the grid that don't have these data types, or open the tables in Design view and change data types.

Table C-4 *(continued)*

ERROR	DESCRIPTION
2652	You can't delete a relationship inherited from a linked database.
2680	The form or report includes more OLE objects than *<Database Name>* can display at one time. Delete some of the bound or unbound object frames.
2683	There is no object in this control.
2684	The OLE object is empty. You can't edit a bound object frame if the field in the underlying table doesn't contain an OLE object. Right-click the field, click Insert Object, and use the dialog box to locate and add the object to the field.
2685	The object doesn't have an OLE object data type. The bound object frame containing the object you tried to edit isn't bound to a field with the OLE object data type. If you want to display an OLE object, set the ControlSource property for the bound object frame to a field with the OLE object data type. Or use a different control, such as a text box, to display the data.
2686	*<Database Name>* is unable to save the *<Object Name>* object. Your computer ran out of disk space while *<Database Name>* was saving the OLE object. For information on freeing disk space, search the Microsoft Windows Help index for "disk space, freeing".
2690	A system resource necessary for displaying the *<Object Name>* object isn't available. Your computer may be low on memory. Close unneeded programs, and try the operation again. For more information on freeing memory, search the Microsoft Windows Help index for "memory, troubleshooting".
2691	*<Database Name>* can't communicate with the OLE server. The OLE server may not be registered. To register the OLE server, reinstall it.
2694	The Clipboard isn't available. The Clipboard may be in use by another application, or your computer may be low on memory. If your computer is low on memory, close unneeded programs, and then try the operation again. For more information on freeing memory, search the Microsoft Windows Help index for "memory, troubleshooting".
2695	*<Database Name>* is unable to display the converted *<Object Name>* object. Delete the object in the bound object frame, and then re-create it.
2696	*<Database Name>* can't read the OLE object. Delete the object in the bound object frame, and then re-create it.
2697	There was a problem loading the *<Object Name>* object. The object you tried to create or edit is not a valid OLE object. Re-create the object, and then embed or link it again.

(continued)

Table C-4 *(continued)*

ERROR	DESCRIPTION
2698	The *<Object Name>* object you tried to create or edit is too large to save. Your database may not contain enough space for the object. Your computer may be out of disk space. For information on freeing disk space, search the Microsoft Windows Help index for "disk space, freeing".
2699	The connection with the OLE server was lost, or the OLE server encountered an error while you were using it. Restart the OLE server, and then try the operation again.
2700	*<Database Name>* can't find an OLE server or a dynamic-link library (DLL) required for the OLE operation. The OLE server or DLL may not be registered. To register the OLE server or DLL, reinstall it.
2701	The OLE server for the OLE object you tried to create is already open. Switch to the OLE server window and close it. Then try to create or edit the OLE object again.
2702	The *<Object Name>* object isn't registered. The object may be calling an application that isn't installed. To register the application, reinstall it.
2703	*<Database Name>* can't read the *<Object Name>* object, because communication was interrupted. If the OLE server application is located on a network server, make sure your computer is connected to it.
2704	The *<Object Name>* object you tried to edit doesn't have any displayable information.
2707	*<Database Name>* can't open the file containing the OLE object. You may have specified an invalid file name or an invalid unit of data (such as a range of cells from a worksheet) within the file for the OLE object. The file you specified may not be available because it's locked by another user or you don't have permission to use it. Try one of the following: Make sure the file is available and that you used the correct file name. Check the OLE server's documentation for information about the syntax to use when specifying an OLE object's data.
2711	The file name argument in the GetObject function of the Visual Basic procedure you ran is invalid. You may not have entered, or may have misspelled, the file name. The unit of data (such as a range of cells from a worksheet) may not be valid. Try one of the following: Make sure the file is installed on your computer and that you used the correct file name. Check the OLE server's documentation for information about the syntax to use when specifying an OLE object's data.

Table C-4 *(continued)*

ERROR	DESCRIPTION
2713	A problem occurred when *<Database Name>* tried to access the *<Object Name>* object. You may have specified an invalid file name or an invalid unit of data (such as a range of cells from a worksheet) within the file for the OLE object. The file you specified may not be available because it's locked by another user or you don't have permission to use it. Try one of the following: Make sure that the file is installed on your computer and that you used the correct file name. Check the OLE server's documentation for information about the syntax to use when specifying an OLE object's data.
2714	The *<Object Name>* object doesn't support verbs that can be performed on an OLE object, such as play or edit. Check the OLE server's documentation for information on the verbs the OLE object supports, or use the ObjectVerbs property or the ObjectVerbsCount property to find the verbs supported by an OLE object.
2715	The index for the Action or the Verb property for the *<Object Name>* object is invalid. The setting you entered may be a negative number or may be too large.
2717	The *<Object Name>* object has no information that can be displayed. You tried to perform an operation on a bound or unbound object frame containing an OLE object, but the OLE object is empty. Right-click the frame, click Insert Object, and then use the dialog box to locate and either add or link to an object from a file that is not empty.
2719	A problem occurred while accessing the *<Object Name>* object. The OLE server may not be available because it's on a network server and you lost the connection. Try re-establishing the connection. The OLE object may be stored in a linked file, but the file isn't available. Activate the OLE server outside of *<Database Name>*, and then open the file containing the OLE object to verify that it still exists and can be accessed.
2723	The *<Object Name>* object doesn't support the attempted operation. The OLE object was changed to a picture, or the link to the object was broken. If you want to perform the operation, delete the OLE object, and then embed or link it again.
2724	One or more dynamic-link libraries required for using OLE objects are an incorrect versions. Run Setup to reinstall *<Database Name>*. If you want to preserve your security or custom settings, back up the *<Database Name>* workgroup information file. For information on backing up files, search the Microsoft Windows Help index for " ".
2725	The OLE server isn't registered. To register the OLE server, reinstall it.

(continued)

Table C-4 *(continued)*

ERROR	DESCRIPTION
2726	*<Database Name>* can't perform the OLE operation because it was unable to read the Windows Registry where the OLE server is registered. Reinstall the OLE server, and then try the operation again. If problems continue, reinstall Microsoft Windows and the other applications on your computer. If you reinstall *<Database Name>*, you may want to back up your *<Database Name>* workgroup information file first to preserve any custom settings. For information on backing up files, search the Microsoft Windows Help index for "backing up files". For information on the Windows Registry, search the Microsoft Windows Help index for "registry".
2727	*<Database Name>* can't perform the OLE operation because it was unable to write to the Windows Registry where the OLE server is registered. Reinstall the OLE server, and then try the operation again. If problems continue, reinstall Microsoft Windows and the other applications on your computer. If you reinstall *<Database Name>*, you may want to back up your *<Database Name>* workgroup information file first to preserve any custom settings. For information on backing up files, search the Microsoft Windows Help index for "backing up files". For information on the Windows Registry, search the Microsoft Windows Help index for "registry".
2729	The OLE object you tried to edit is busy. Try again later.
2730	There was a problem communicating with the OLE server. Try again later. If you still can't access the object, try one or more of the following: Free up system memory. For information on freeing memory, search the Microsoft Windows Help index for "memory, troubleshooting". Reinstall the OLE server to make sure it's registered. Check the OLE server's documentation for information about the syntax to use when specifying an OLE object's data.
2731	An error occurred while accessing the OLE server. The OLE server may not be registered. To register the OLE server, reinstall it.
2732	*<Database Name>* can't read the *<Object Name>* object. Communication between *<Database Name>* and the OLE server was interrupted. Make sure your computer is connected to the network server on which the OLE server is located.
2733	The OLE object you tried to edit can't be accessed. You don't have permission to change the object, or another user opened and locked the object.
2734	You can't save the *<Object Name>* object now. The OLE server is running an operation, or another user opened and locked the object. Try to save the object again later.
2735	This disk is write-protected. You can't save the *<Object Name>* object to it.

Table C-4 *(continued)*

ERROR	DESCRIPTION
2737	*<Database Name>* can't find the file containing the linked OLE object you tried to update using the OLE/DDE Links command. You may have misspelled the file name, or the file may have been deleted or renamed. If the file has been moved to a different location, use the OLE/DDE Links command to change the source. Or delete the object, and create a new linked object.
2738	There isn't enough memory to complete the operation. Close unneeded programs and try the operation again. For more information on freeing memory, search the Microsoft Windows Help index for "memory, troubleshooting".
2739	An error occurred during the operation with an OLE object. The object is in use.
2741	Your computer ran out of disk space while *<Database Name>* was saving the changes you made to the *<Object Name>* object. For information on freeing disk space, search the Microsoft Windows Help index for "disk space, freeing".
2742	*<Database Name>* was unable to create more files. Your computer may be low on memory or disk space. Close unneeded programs and try the operation again. For information on freeing memory or disk space, search the Microsoft Windows Help index for "memory, troubleshooting" or "disk space, freeing".
2743	The *<Object Name>* object is stored in a format that is incompatible with the version of OLE on your computer.
2744	*<Database Name>* can't find the OLE server. The setting for the SourceDoc property may be invalid, or the file may have been deleted, renamed, or moved.
2745	Share exe or Vshare.386 is missing from your computer; OLE support needs these files to work correctly. Rerun *<Database Name>* or Microsoft Office Setup to reinstall *<Database Name>*, the Share program, and Vshare.386. If you want to preserve your security or custom settings, back up the *<Database Name>* workgroup information file. Then restore the file to its original location. For information on backing up files, search the Microsoft Windows Help index for "backing up files".
2746	You can't switch to Design view because your form contains too many OLE objects. Close other applications, close the form, and then open the form again in Design view. Then delete some of the OLE objects or move them to a different form.

(continued)

Table C-4 *(continued)*

ERROR	DESCRIPTION
2747	The OLE server can't display the *<Object Name>* object. There is a problem with the file containing the OLE object, or there isn't enough memory available. Open the OLE server outside of *<Database Name>*, and then open the OLE object file. If you can do this, then your computer may be low on memory. Close other programs, and then try the operation again. For more information on freeing memory, search the Microsoft Windows Help index for "memory, troubleshooting".
2748	The Automation object operation isn't available for the *<Object Name>* object. Check the component's documentation for information on which operations are available for an Automation object.
2749	There isn't enough memory to complete the Automation object operation on the *<Object Name>* object. Close unneeded programs and try the operation again. For more information on freeing memory, search the Microsoft Windows Help index for "memory, troubleshooting".
2750	The operation on the *<Object Name>* object failed. The OLE server may not be registered. To register the OLE server, reinstall it.
2751	The Exit or Update operation failed. You pressed the ESC key (or another key used in the OLE server to stop an operation) while *<Database Name>* was saving the changes you made to an OLE object in a form or report. Try to exit or update again.
2753	A problem occurred while *<Database Name>* was communicating with the OLE server or ActiveX Control. Close the OLE server and restart it outside of *<Database Name>*. Then try the original operation again in *<Database Name>*.
2754	A problem occurred while *<Database Name>* was communicating with the OLE server. Try one or more of the following: Make sure you're connected to the network server where the OLE server application is located. Close the OLE server and restart it outside of *<Database Name>*. Then try the original operation again from within *<Database Name>*. Reinstall the OLE server to ensure that it's registered.
2755	There was a problem referencing a property or method of the object. You tried to run a Visual Basic procedure that references an object property or method. Try one or more of the following: Make sure the component is properly registered. Make sure your computer is connected to the network server where the component is located. Close the component and restart it outside of *<Database Name>*. Then try again to run the procedure in *<Database Name>*.

Table C-4 *(continued)*

ERROR	DESCRIPTION
2756	A problem occurred when *<Database Name>* tried to access the OLE object. Close the *<Database Name>* form or report that displays the OLE object, and close the OLE server. Then reopen the form or report to see if it can display the OLE object.
2757	There was a problem accessing a property or method of the OLE object. Try one or more of the following: Verify that the OLE server is registered correctly by reinstalling it. Make sure your computer is connected to the server on which the OLE server application resides. Close the OLE server and restart it outside of *<Database Name>*. Then try the original operation again from within *<Database Name>*.
2759	The method you tried to invoke on an object failed. You may have specified too many or too few arguments for a property or method of an object. Check the component's documentation for information on the properties and methods it makes available for Automation operations. There may not be enough memory to run the procedure. Close unneeded programs and try to run the procedure again. For more information on freeing memory, search the Microsoft Windows Help index for "memory, troubleshooting".
2760	An error occurred while referencing the object. You tried to run a Visual Basic procedure that improperly references a property or method of an object.
2761	There was a problem referencing a property or method of an object. Check the component's documentation for information on the properties and methods it makes available for Automation operations.
2762	*<Object Name>* returned an error while referencing a property of an object. Check the component's documentation for information on the properties and methods it makes available for Automation operations.
2763	*<Object>* returned the error: *<Error Message>*. Check the component's documentation for information on the properties and methods it makes available for Automation operations.
2764	The object's property or method can't be set. You tried to run a Visual Basic procedure to set a property or apply a method for an object. However, the property or method doesn't support named arguments. Check the component's documentation for information on the properties and methods it makes available to Automation operations.

(continued)

Table C-4 *(continued)*

ERROR	DESCRIPTION
2765	Visual Basic can't convert the data type of one of the arguments you entered. You tried to run a Visual Basic procedure that executes a method or sets a property of an object. Check the component's documentation for information on the properties and methods it makes available for Automation operations.
2766	The object doesn't contain the Automation object *<Object Name>*. You tried to run a Visual Basic procedure to set a property or method for an object. However, the component doesn't make the property or method available for Automation operations. Check the component's documentation for information on the properties and methods it makes available for Automation operations.
2767	The object doesn't support American English; it was developed using a different language. Use a version of the object developed in Visual Basic that supports the language you are using.
2768	The number you used to reference an element in the array is outside the bounds of the array. For example, the array is from 0 through 10, and you entered a -1 or an 11. Check the component's documentation for information on the properties and methods it makes available for Automation operations.
2769	A property of the Automation object requires or returns a data type that isn't supported by Visual Basic. You tried to run a Visual Basic procedure that references an Automation object's property. However, the value of the property isn't supported by Visual Basic. Check the component's documentation for information on the properties and methods it makes available for Automation operations.
2770	The object you referenced in the Visual Basic procedure as an OLE object isn't an OLE object.
2771	The bound or unbound object frame you tried to edit does not contain an OLE object. Right-click the frame, click Insert Object, and then use the dialog box to locate and either add or link to an object from a file that is not empty.
2774	The component doesn't support Automation. You tried to run a Visual Basic procedure that references an Automation object. Check the component's documentation for information on whether it supports Automation.
2775	You specified too many arguments in the Visual Basic procedure, or there isn't enough memory to run the procedure. Specify fewer arguments, or close unneeded programs, and then try to run the procedure again. For more information on freeing memory, search the Microsoft Windows Help index for "memory, troubleshooting".

Table C-4 *(continued)*

ERROR	DESCRIPTION
2777	The class argument in the CreateObject function of the Visual Basic procedure you're trying to run is invalid. Try one of the following: Make sure the file is installed on your computer and that you used the correct file name. Check the OLE server's documentation for information about the syntax to use when specifying an OLE object's data.
2778	*<Database Name>* tried to create an OLE link, but there was no source document for this object.
2782	You must specify a property or method for the object. You tried to run a Visual Basic procedure that references and sets a property or method for the object. Enter a property or method for the object.
2783	You entered an invalid setting for the Action property. Use one of the *<Database Name>* intrinsic constants for the Action property. For a list of valid settings you can use with the Action property, click Help.
2784	The path you entered for the SourceDoc property setting for a linked OLE object is too long. Move the file to a location with a shorter path.
2785	The OLE server wasn't able to open the object. The OLE server may not be installed. You may have specified an invalid setting for the SourceDoc or SourceItem property in a property sheet, a macro, or a Visual Basic procedure. To see the valid settings for either of these properties, search the Help index for the property topic.
2786	The OLE server doesn't support linking. You tried to run a Visual Basic procedure using the Action property. However, you provided insufficient information to establish a link.
2788	The *<Object Name>* object isn't a linked object. The property you tried to set in Visual Basic applies only to linked objects.
2790	You can't embed an OLE object into a bound or unbound object frame if the OLETypeAllowed property for the bound or unbound object frame is set to Linked. Insert a linked object, or set the OLETypeAllowed property to Embedded or Either, and then embed the object.
2791	*<Database Name>* can't link the OLE object or the bound or unbound object frame. The OLETypeAllowed property for the bound or unbound object frame is set to Embedded. Embed the object, or set the OLETypeAllowed property to Linked or Either, and then link the object.
2792	You can't save a locked OLE object.

(continued)

Table C-4 *(continued)*

ERROR	DESCRIPTION
2793	*<Database Name>* can't perform the operation specified in the Action property of the Visual Basic procedure you're trying to run. The object frame may be locked or disabled. Set the Locked property to No and the Enabled property to Yes.
2794	The ActiveX control you tried to insert isn't registered. For information on registering an ActiveX control, click Help.
2797	This OLE object was created in an earlier version of OLE so it can't be displayed as an icon. For an effect similar to displaying an object as an icon, add an image control to your form, and add the icon for the application to the image control. Then set the image control's OnDblClick property to a Visual Basic procedure that opens the OLE object.
2798	You can't use the Action property to delete a bound OLE object from its underlying table or query. You tried to run a Visual Basic procedure that deletes the object in a bound object frame by setting the Action property to acOLEDelete. Delete the object in a different way, such as with the DAO Delete method in Visual Basic.
2799	The OLE object can't be activated upon receiving the focus. If you selected an OLE object or a chart, and the AutoActivate property for that control is set to GetFocus, the OLE object or chart should be activated automatically when it receives the focus. However, the ActiveX component doesn't support this operation. Check the component's documentation for information on the properties and methods it makes available to Automation operations.
2800	This object is locked. Any changes you make will be discarded when the form is closed. Click the Microsoft Office Button, point to Save As, and save the object under a different name.
2801	The OLE object isn't loaded because the unbound ActiveX control hasn't been initialized.
2802	You can't insert an ActiveX control in a bound or unbound object frame. ActiveX controls are automatically contained in ActiveX control frames.
2803	You don't have the license required to use this ActiveX control. You tried to open a form containing an OLE object or an ActiveX control or you tried to create an ActiveX control. To obtain the appropriate license, contact the company that provides the licensed OLE object or ActiveX control.
2804	You can't create an ActiveX control in an unbound object frame. ActiveX controls are automatically contained in ActiveX control frames.

Table C-4 *(continued)*

ERROR	DESCRIPTION
2805	There was an error loading an ActiveX control on one of your forms or reports. Make sure all the controls that you are using are properly registered. For information on registering an ActiveX control, click Help.
2806	<*Database Name*> doesn't support this ActiveX control.
2807	You can't paste this object as the type you specified. Choose another object type.
2808	<*Database Name*> can't find the Active Accessibility dynamic-link library (DLL) OleAcc. Rerun the <*Database Name*> Setup program.
2811	<*Database Name*> is unable to create the data access page.
2817	<*Database Name*> is unable to save (or send) the data access page.
2818	<*Database Name*> is unable to retrieve the file: <*File Name*>. Either the file is not available, or you do not have enough disk space to copy the file.
2819	<*Database Name*> is unable to open the data access page.
2820	<*Database Name*> is unable to change the BASE HREF for your document.
2821	File in use.
2822	<*Database Name*> encountered an unexpected error while attempting to recover from a failed save (or send). Your data access page may not be in a usable state. Please attempt to save to a different location.
2823	The <*Database Name*> data access page name <*Page Name*> is misspelled or refers to a Page that doesn't exist. If the invalid Page name is in a macro, an Action Failed dialog box will display the macro name and the macro's arguments after you click OK. Open the Macro window, and enter the correct Page name.
2838	<*Database Name*> is unable to preview the selected theme.
2842	<*Database Name*> encountered an error after saving (or sending) your data access page.
2845	<*Database Name*> is unable to open the data access page from the mail envelope.
2854	<*Database Name*> was unable to parse the document properties for this data access page. They may be corrupted.
2855	<*Database Name*> could not delete one or more files related to the page.

(continued)

Table C-4 *(continued)*

ERROR	DESCRIPTION
2859	Access could not load the e-mail envelope. This could be caused by a network connection problem or a problem with your Office installation.
2860	You cannot insert a bound field to a caption or record navigation section.
2861	<*Database Name*> is unable to preview the selected web page.
2870	<*Database Name*> encountered an error synchronizing the HTML from the Microsoft Script Editor. Please check the HTML for syntax errors and try again.
2871	<*Database Name*> is unable to create a data access page using the codepage selected in Web Options. The codepage may not be installed on your system. Please install the codepage, or select a different one in Web Options.
2874	Cannot move or paste the grouping field <*Field Name*> into a section at a higher group level.
2876	The data definition of this data access page has been corrupted and can't be repaired. You must recreate the page. Save has been disabled.
2877	In a <*Database Name*> database (.mdb), you can't group on a control bound to a field that has a Memo or OLE Object data type. In a <*Database Name*> project (.adp), you can't group on a control bound to a field that has an Image or Text data type.
2878	You cannot add a bound field to a caption or record navigation section.
2879	Caption and record navigation sections cannot contain bound fields.
2880	Can't edit pages that contain framesets.
2881	This web page contains XML namespaces that may conflict with Access namespaces. You should edit the HTML source to ensure that all namespaces have a unique prefix.
2883	A supporting file path for this data access page has been altered outside of Access. Please save this page to a different location and ensure that all supporting files are maintained.
2884	Cannot find the database or some database objects that this page refers to. Update the connection information of the page, or fix the references to the missing database objects.
2885	This page uses a database that is not supported. You will not be able to make data changes until you connect to a supported database.
2886	Components necessary for data access pages are not installed.

Table C-4 *(continued)*

ERROR	DESCRIPTION
2888	*<Database Name>* detects some HTML elements between the banner and the section of your data access page. Saving this page in Access will corrupt it. Close the page without saving it, and then edit the page in another HTML editor to remove these elements.
2889	This section cannot be deleted.
2890	You cannot edit this page because it contains frames. The data access page designer cannot edit pages with frames.
2892	You can't move the group filter control to another section. Delete the group filter control from the current section and create it in a different section.
2893	A link to this data access page could not be created because the database cannot be exclusively locked. To create the link later, open the page by selecting Edit web page that already exists, and then save.
2894	The link to the data access page specified could not be updated because the database cannot be exclusively locked. To update the link, open this page again when you are the only person using the database.
2895	This page was designed with a version of the Microsoft Office Web Components that is not currently installed on this machine. If you have not been prompted to install those components on this page, please contact the page author for the installation location.
2896	The operation is only valid on a data access page opened in Design view. Please switch the page to Design view and try the operation again.
2897	You have opened a page that was last modified using Access 2000. To be able to edit the page, you must save it using a more recent version of the Microsoft Office Web Components. Do you want Access to convert this page by saving it using a more recent version of the Microsoft Office Web Components?
2898	*<Database Name>* has created a backup copy of your original page. This page can be used if you want to revert to the Office 2000 Web Components. The backup page name is: *<Page Name>*
2899	*<Database Name>* could not create a backup copy of your original page. This page cannot be opened.
2900	*<Database Name>* could not upgrade the Office Web Components on your page. This page cannot be opened.
2901	Error loading ActiveX control *<Control Name>* on form or report *<Name>*.

(continued)

Table C-4 *(continued)*

ERROR	DESCRIPTION
2902	Access is unable to save the *<Object Name>* object because it does not support persistence, or your computer may have run out of disk space.
2903	Do you want to set this folder as the default location for data access pages?
2904	You must match each field on the left with a field on the right.
2905	You must choose a linking field for every parameter.
2906	*<Table Name>* contains no fields that can participate in a relationship. The contents of the RecordSource property may be invalid, or the RecordSource may contain only fields that are not acceptable for use in a join. Correct the RecordSource property for this form or report and try your field operation again.
2907	Do you want to revert to the saved *<Object Name>*?
2908	The Control ID *<ID Value>* is already in use. Specify a different ID for the control.
2909	This relationship is not valid because the fields in the first table do not match the fields in the second table. To repair the relationship, select at least one field from each table.
2910	This connection file refers to a provider not supported by data access pages. Please select a different connection file.
2911	You cannot change the data access page path while it is open. Please close the page and try again.
2912	If you create a data access page in this version of Access, you cannot open it in Design view in Access 2000. If you have installed the Microsoft Office XP Web Components, however, you can open this page in Page view in Access 2000. Don't show this warning again.
2913	Cannot save to a URL address with a bookmark. Please specify a valid path.
2914	*<Database Name>* could not link to a connection file. A connection string will be embedded in the page.
2915	*<Database Name>* is unable to connect to the data source specified in the connection string of this page. The server may not exist on the network, or there may be an error in the connection string information for this page.
2916	You cannot edit HTML pages created using PowerPoint in *<Database Name>*.
2917	Invalid HTML color value.

Table C-4 *(continued)*

ERROR	DESCRIPTION
2918	Unable to open or read this connection file. Either the file has been damaged or the file format is not valid.
2919	You can't place this control in the section you specified.
2920	*<Database Name>* is unable to load the database schema. Save has been disabled. Either repair or reinstall Microsoft Office.
2921	*<Database Name>* cannot open this page because it was created using a newer version of Access. Try opening the page using a newer version of *<Database Name>*.
2922	*<Database Name>* has created a backup copy of your original page. This page can be used if you want to revert to the Office XP Web Components. The backup page name is: *<Page Name>*
2923	You do not have the correct permissions. Contact the server administrator.
2924	You cannot compact a file that was opened from a Web Server.
2925	You cannot encrypt a file that was opened from a Web Server.
2926	Because of your security settings and current security policy, this control is disabled. To modify your policy and enable the database, use the Message Bar.
3000	Reserved error (<Error Identifier>); there is no message for this error.
3002	Could not start session.
3003	Could not start transaction; too many transactions already nested.
3005	*<Name>* is not a valid database name.
3006	Database *<Database Name>* is exclusively locked.
3007	Cannot open library database *<Database Name>*.
3008	The table *<Table Name>* is already opened exclusively by another user, or it is already open through the user interface and cannot be manipulated programmatically.
3009	You tried to lock table *<Table Name>* while opening it, but the table cannot be locked because it is currently in use. Wait a moment, and then try the operation again.
3010	Table *<Table Name>* already exists.
3012	Object *<Object Name>* already exists.
3013	Could not rename installable ISAM file.
3014	Cannot open any more tables.

(continued)

Table C-4 *(continued)*

ERROR	DESCRIPTION
3015	Index not found.
3016	Field will not fit in record.
3017	The size of a field is too long.
3018	Could not find field.
3020	Update or CancelUpdate without AddNew or Edit.
3021	No current record.
3022	The changes you requested to the table were not successful because they would create duplicate values in the index, primary key, or relationship. Change the data in the field or fields that contain duplicate data, remove the index, or redefine the index to permit duplicate entries and try again.
3023	AddNew or Edit already used.
3024	Could not find file *<File Name>*.
3025	Cannot open any more files.
3026	Not enough space on disk.
3027	Cannot update. Database or object is read-only.
3028	Cannot start your application. The workgroup information file is missing or opened exclusively by another user.
3029	Not a valid account name or password.
3030	*<Name>* is not a valid account name.
3031	Not a valid password.
3032	Cannot perform this operation.
3034	You tried to commit or rollback a transaction without first beginning a transaction.
3035	System resource exceeded.
3036	Database has reached maximum size.
3037	Cannot open any more tables or queries.
3038	System resource exceeded.
3039	Could not create index; too many indexes already defined.
3040	Disk I/O error during read.
3041	Cannot open a database created with a previous version of your application.

Table C-4 *(continued)*

ERROR	DESCRIPTION
3042	Out of MS-DOS file handles.
3043	Your network access was interrupted. To continue, close the database, and then open it again.
3044	*<Path String>* is not a valid path. Make sure that the path name is spelled correctly and that you are connected to the server on which the file resides.
3046	Could not save; currently locked by another user.
3047	Record is too large.
3048	Cannot open any more databases.
3050	Could not lock file.
3052	File sharing lock count exceeded. Increase MaxLocksPerFile registry entry.
3053	Too many client tasks.
3054	Too many Memo, OLE, or Hyperlink Object fields.
3055	Not a valid file name.
3056	Could not repair this database.
3057	Operation not supported on linked tables.
3058	Index or primary key cannot contain a Null value.
3059	Operation canceled by user.
3061	Too few parameters. Expected *<Number>*.
3062	Duplicate output alias *<Alias Name>*.
3063	Duplicate output destination *<Field Name>*.
3064	Cannot open action query *<Query Name>*.
3065	Cannot execute a select query.
3066	Query must have at least one destination field.
3067	Query input must contain at least one table or query.
3069	The action query *<Query Name>* cannot be used as a row source.
3070	The Microsoft Office Access database engine does not recognize *<Field Name>* as a valid field name or expression.
3074	Cannot repeat table name *<Table Name>* in FROM clause.
3075	*<Error Value>* in query expression *<Expression>*.

(continued)

Table C-4 *(continued)*

ERROR	DESCRIPTION
3076	*<Error Value>* in criteria expression.
3077	*<Error Value>* in expression.
3079	The specified field *<Field Name>* could refer to more than one table listed in the FROM clause of your SQL statement.
3080	Joined table *<Table Name>* not listed in FROM clause.
3081	Cannot join more than one table with the same name *<Object Name>*.
3082	JOIN operation *<Operation Name>* refers to a field that is not in one of the joined tables.
3083	Cannot use internal report query.
3084	Cannot insert data with action query.
3085	Undefined function *<Function Name>* in expression.
3086	Could not delete from specified tables.
3087	Too many expressions in GROUP BY clause.
3088	Too many expressions in ORDER BY clause.
3089	Too many expressions in DISTINCT output.
3090	Resultant table not allowed to have more than one AutoNumber field.
3091	HAVING clause *<Object Name>* without grouping or aggregation.
3092	Cannot use HAVING clause in TRANSFORM statement.
3093	ORDER BY clause *<Object Name>* conflicts with DISTINCT.
3094	ORDER BY clause *<Object Name>* conflicts with GROUP BY clause.
3095	Cannot have aggregate function in expression *<Object Name>*.
3096	Cannot have aggregate function in WHERE clause *<Object Name>*.
3097	Cannot have aggregate function in ORDER BY clause *<Object Name>*.
3098	Cannot have aggregate function in GROUP BY clause *<Object Name>*.
3099	Cannot have aggregate function in JOIN operation *<Object Name>*.
3100	Cannot set field *<Field Name>* in join key to Null.
3101	The Microsoft Office Access database engine cannot find a record in the table *<Table Name>* with key matching field(s) *<Object Name>*.

Table C-4 *(continued)*

ERROR	DESCRIPTION
3102	Circular reference caused by *<Object Name>*.
3103	Circular reference caused by alias *<Alias Name>* in query definition's SELECT list.
3104	Cannot specify fixed column heading *<Object Name>* in a crosstab query more than once.
3105	Missing destination field name in SELECT INTO statement *<Object Name>*.
3106	Missing destination field name in UPDATE statement *<Object Name>*.
3107	Record(s) cannot be added; no insert permission on *<Object Name>*.
3108	Record(s) cannot be edited; no update permission on *<Object Name>*.
3109	Record(s) cannot be deleted; no delete permission on *<Object Name>*.
3110	Could not read definitions; no read definitions permission for table or query *<Query Name>*.
3111	Could not create; no modify design permission for table or query *<Query Name>*.
3112	Record(s) cannot be read; no read permission on *<Object Name>*.
3113	Cannot update *<Object Name>*; field not updatable.
3114	Cannot include Memo, OLE, or Hyperlink Object when you select unique values *<Object Name>*.
3115	Cannot have Memo, OLE, or Hyperlink Object fields in aggregate argument *<Object Name>*.
3116	Cannot have Memo, OLE, or Hyperlink Object fields in criteria *<Object Name>* for aggregate function.
3117	Cannot sort on Memo, OLE, or Hyperlink Object *<Object Name>*.
3118	Cannot join on Memo, OLE, or Hyperlink Object *<Object Name>*.
3119	Cannot group on Memo, OLE, or Hyperlink Object *<Object Name>*.
3120	Cannot group on fields selected with '' *<Object Name>*.
3121	Cannot group on fields selected with ''.
3122	You tried to execute a query that does not include the specified expression *<Expression Name>* as part of an aggregate function.
3123	Cannot use '' in crosstab query.
3124	Cannot input from internal report query *<Object Name>*.

(continued)

Table C-4 *(continued)*

ERROR	DESCRIPTION
3125	*<Object Name>* is not a valid name. Make sure that it does not include invalid characters or punctuation and that it is not too long.
3126	Invalid bracketing of name *<Object Name>*.
3127	The INSERT INTO statement contains the following unknown field name: *<Object Name>*. Make sure you have typed the name correctly, and try the operation again.
3128	Specify the table containing the records you want to delete.
3129	Invalid SQL statement; expected 'DELETE', 'INSERT', 'PROCEDURE', 'SELECT', or 'UPDATE'.
3130	Syntax error in DELETE statement.
3131	Syntax error in FROM clause.
3132	Syntax error in GROUP BY clause.
3133	Syntax error in HAVING clause.
3134	Syntax error in INSERT INTO statement.
3135	Syntax error in JOIN operation.
3136	The LEVEL clause includes a reserved word or argument that is misspelled or missing, or the punctuation is incorrect.
3137	Missing semicolon (;) at end of SQL statement.
3138	Syntax error in ORDER BY clause.
3139	Syntax error in PARAMETER clause.
3140	Syntax error in PROCEDURE clause.
3141	The SELECT statement includes a reserved word or an argument name that is misspelled or missing, or the punctuation is incorrect.
3142	Characters found after end of SQL statement.
3143	Syntax error in TRANSFORM statement.
3144	Syntax error in UPDATE statement.
3145	Syntax error in WHERE clause.
3146	ODBC—call failed.
3151	ODBC—connection to *<Object Name>* failed.
3154	ODBC—could not find DLL *<Object Name>*.
3155	ODBC—insert on a linked table *<Table Name>* failed.

Table C-4 *(continued)*

ERROR	DESCRIPTION
3156	ODBC–delete on a linked table <*Table Name*> failed.
3157	ODBC–update on a linked table <*Table Name*> failed.
3158	Could not save record; currently locked by another user.
3159	Not a valid bookmark.
3160	Table is not open.
3161	Could not decrypt file.
3162	You tried to assign the Null value to a variable that is not a Variant data type.
3163	The field is too small to accept the amount of data you attempted to add. Try inserting or pasting less data.
3164	Field cannot be updated.
3165	Could not open .inf file.
3166	Cannot locate the requested Xbase memo file.
3167	Record is deleted.
3168	Invalid .inf file.
3169	The Microsoft Office Access database engine could not execute the SQL statement because it contains a field that has an invalid data type.
3170	Could not find installable ISAM.
3171	Could not find network path or user name.
3172	Could not open Paradox.net.
3173	Could not open table 'MSysAccounts' in the workgroup information file.
3174	Could not open table 'MSysGroups' in the workgroup information file.
3175	Date is out of range or is in an invalid format.
3176	Could not open file <*File Name*>.
3177	Not a valid table name.
3179	Encountered unexpected end of file.
3180	Could not write to file <*File Name*>.
3181	Invalid range.
3182	Invalid file format.

(continued)

Table C-4 *(continued)*

ERROR	DESCRIPTION
3183	The query cannot be completed. Either the size of the query result is larger than the maximum size of a database (2 GB), or there is not enough temporary storage space on the disk to store the query result.
3184	Could not execute query; could not find linked table.
3185	SELECT INTO on a remote database tried to produce too many fields.
3186	Could not save; currently locked by user <*User Name*> on machine <*Machine Name*>.
3187	Could not read; currently locked by user <*User Name*> on machine <*Machine Name*>.
3188	Could not update; currently locked by another session on this machine.
3189	Table <*Table Name*> is exclusively locked by user <*User Name*> on machine <*Machine Name*>.
3190	Too many fields defined.
3191	Cannot define field more than once.
3192	Could not find output table <*Table Name*>.
3196	The database <*Database Name*> is already in use by another person or process. When the database is available, try the operation again.
3198	Could not start session. Too many sessions already active.
3199	Could not find reference.
3200	The record cannot be deleted or changed because table <*Table Name*> includes related records.
3201	You cannot add or change a record because a related record is required in table <*Table Name*>.
3202	Could not save; currently locked by another user.
3203	Subqueries cannot be used in the expression <*Object Name*>.
3204	Database already exists.
3205	Too many crosstab column headers <*Object Name*>.
3206	Cannot create a relationship between a field and itself.
3207	Operation not supported on a Paradox table with no primary key.
3208	Invalid Deleted setting in the Xbase key of the Windows Registry.
3210	The connection string is too long. The connection string cannot exceed 255 characters.

Table C-4 *(continued)*

ERROR	DESCRIPTION
3211	The database engine could not lock table <*Table Name*> because it is already in use by another person or process.
3212	Could not lock table <*Table Name*>; currently in use by user <*User Name*> on machine <*Object Name*>.
3213	Invalid Date setting in the Xbase key of the Windows Registry.
3214	Invalid Mark setting in the Xbase key of the Windows Registry.
3215	Too many Btrieve tasks.
3216	Parameter <*Parameter Value*> specified where a table name is required.
3217	Parameter <*Parameter Value*> specified where a database name is required.
3218	Could not update; currently locked.
3219	Invalid operation.
3220	Incorrect collating sequence.
3221	Invalid settings in the Btrieve key of the Windows Registry.
3222	Query cannot contain a Database parameter.
3223	<*Object Name*> is invalid because it is too long, or contains invalid characters.
3224	Cannot read Btrieve data dictionary.
3225	Encountered a record locking deadlock while performing a Btrieve operation.
3226	Errors encountered while using the Btrieve DLL.
3227	Invalid Century setting in the Xbase key of the Windows Registry.
3228	Selected collating sequence not supported by the operating system.
3229	Btrieve–cannot change field.
3230	Out-of-date Paradox lock file.
3231	ODBC–field would be too long; data truncated.
3232	ODBC–could not create table.
3234	ODBC–remote query timeout expired.
3235	ODBC–data type not supported on server.
3238	ODBC–data out of range.

(continued)

Table C-4 *(continued)*

ERROR	DESCRIPTION
3239	Too many active users.
3240	Btrieve–missing Btrieve engine.
3241	Btrieve–out of resources.
3242	Invalid reference in SELECT statement.
3243	None of the import field names match fields in the appended table.
3244	Cannot import password-protected spreadsheet.
3245	Could not parse field names from the first row of the import table.
3246	Operation not supported in transactions.
3247	ODBC–linked table definition has changed.
3248	Invalid NetworkAccess setting in the Windows Registry.
3249	Invalid PageTimeout setting in the Windows Registry.
3250	Could not build key.
3251	Operation is not supported for this type of object.
3252	Cannot open a form whose underlying query contains a user-defined function that attempts to set or get the form's RecordsetClone property.
3254	ODBC – Cannot lock all records.
3256	Index file not found.
3257	Syntax error in WITH OWNERACCESS OPTION declaration.
3258	The SQL statement could not be executed because it contains ambiguous outer joins. To force one of the joins to be performed first, create a separate query that performs the first join and then include that query in your SQL statement.
3259	Invalid field data type.
3260	Could not update; currently locked by user *<Object Name>* on machine *<Object Name>*.
3261	Table *<Table Name>* is exclusively locked by user *<Object Name>* on machine *<Object Name>*.
3262	Could not lock table.
3263	Invalid Database object.
3264	No field defined – cannot append TableDef or Index.
3265	Item not found in this collection.

Table C-4 *(continued)*

ERROR	DESCRIPTION
3266	Cannot append a Field that is already a part of a Fields collection.
3267	Property can be set only when the Field is part of a Recordset object's Fields collection.
3268	Cannot set this property once the object is part of a collection.
3269	Cannot append an Index that is already a part of an Indexes collection.
3270	Property not found.
3271	Invalid property value.
3272	Object is not a collection.
3273	Method not applicable for this object.
3274	External table is not in the expected format.
3275	Unexpected error from external database driver <*Object Name*>.
3276	Invalid database object reference.
3277	Cannot have more than 10 fields in an index.
3278	The Microsoft Office Access database engine has not been initialized.
3279	The Microsoft Office Access database engine has already been initialized.
3280	Cannot delete a field that is part of an index or is needed by the system.
3281	Cannot delete this index or table. It is either the current index or is used in a relationship.
3282	Operation not supported on a table that contains data.
3283	Primary key already exists.
3284	Index already exists.
3285	Invalid index definition.
3286	Format of memo file does not match specified external database format.
3287	Cannot create index on the given field.
3288	Paradox index is not primary.
3289	Syntax error in CONSTRAINT clause.
3290	Syntax error in CREATE TABLE statement.

(continued)

Table C-4 *(continued)*

ERROR	DESCRIPTION
3291	Syntax error in CREATE INDEX statement.
3292	Syntax error in field definition.
3293	Syntax error in ALTER TABLE statement.
3294	Syntax error in DROP INDEX statement.
3295	Syntax error in DROP TABLE or DROP INDEX.
3296	JOIN expression not supported.
3297	Could not import table or query. No records found, or all records contain errors.
3298	There are several tables with that name. Please specify owner in the format 'owner.table'.
3299	ODBC Specification Conformance Error <*Object Name*>. Report this error to the developer of your application.
3300	Cannot create a relationship.
3301	Cannot perform this operation; features in this version are not available in databases with older formats.
3302	Cannot change a rule while the rules for this table are in use.
3303	Cannot delete this field. It is part of one or more relationships.
3304	You must enter a personal identifier (PID) consisting of at least 4 and no more than 20 characters and digits.
3305	Invalid connection string in pass-through query.
3306	You have written a subquery that can return more than one field without using the EXISTS reserved word in the main query's FROM clause. Revise the SELECT statement of the subquery to request only one field.
3307	The number of columns in the two selected tables or queries of a union query do not match.
3308	Invalid TOP argument in select query.
3309	Property value is too large.
3310	This property is not supported for external data sources or for databases created with a previous version of Microsoft Office Access.
3311	Property specified already exists.
3312	Validation rules and default values cannot be placed on system or linked tables.

Table C-4 *(continued)*

ERROR	DESCRIPTION
3313	Cannot place this validation expression on this field.
3314	You must enter a value in the <*Object Name*> field.
3315	Field <*Field Name*> cannot be a zero-length string.
3317	One or more values are prohibited by the validation rule <*Rule Name*> set for <*Object Name*>. Enter a value that the expression for this field can accept.
3318	Values specified in a TOP clause are not allowed in delete queries or reports.
3319	Syntax error in union query.
3320	<*Error Value*> in table-level validation expression.
3321	No database specified in connection string or IN clause.
3322	Crosstab query contains one or more invalid fixed column headings.
3323	The query cannot be used as a row source.
3324	The query is a DDL query and cannot be used as a row source.
3325	Pass-through query with ReturnsRecords property set to True did not return any records.
3327	Field <*Field Name*> is based on an expression and cannot be edited.
3328	Table <*Table Name*> is read-only.
3329	Record in table <*Table Name*> was deleted by another user.
3330	Record in table <*Table Name*> is locked by another user.
3331	To make changes to this field, first save the record.
3332	Cannot enter value into blank field on 'one' side of outer join.
3333	Records in table <*Table Name*> would have no record on the 'one' side.
3334	Can be present only in version 1. 0 format.
3335	DeleteOnly called with non-zero cbData.
3336	Btrieve: Invalid IndexDDF option in initialization setting.
3337	Invalid DataCodePage option in initialization setting.
3338	Btrieve: Xtrieve options are not correct in initialization setting.
3339	Btrieve: Invalid IndexDeleteRenumber option in initialization setting.

(continued)

Table C-4 *(continued)*

ERROR	DESCRIPTION
3341	The current field must match the join key <*Object Name*> in the table that serves as the 'one' side of one-to-many relationship. Enter a record in the 'one' side table with the desired key value, and then make the entry with the desired join key in the 'many-only' table.
3342	Invalid Memo, OLE, or Hyperlink Object in subquery <*Query Name*>.
3344	The database engine does not recognize either the field <*Field Name*> in a validation expression, or the default value in the table <*Table Name*>.
3345	Unknown or invalid field reference <*Object Name*>.
3346	Number of query values and destination fields are not the same.
3347	Cannot add record(s); primary key for table <*Table Name*> not in recordset.
3348	Cannot add record(s); join key of table <*Table Name*> not in recordset.
3349	You cannot record your changes because a value you entered violates the settings defined for this table or list (for example, a value is less than the minimum or greater than the maximum). Correct the error and try again.
3350	Object is invalid for operation.
3351	The ORDER BY expression <*Object Name*> includes fields that are not selected by the query. Only those fields requested in the first query can be included in an ORDER BY expression.
3352	No destination field name in INSERT INTO statement <*Object Name*>.
3353	Btrieve: Cannot find file Field.ddf.
3354	At most one record can be returned by this subquery.
3355	Syntax error in default value.
3356	You attempted to open a database that is already opened exclusively by user <*User Name*> on machine <*Machine Name*>. Try again when the database is available.
3357	This query is not a properly formed data-definition query.
3358	Cannot open the Microsoft Office Access database engine workgroup information file.
3359	Pass-through query must contain at least one character.
3360	Query is too complex.
3361	Unions not allowed in a subquery.

Table C-4 *(continued)*

ERROR	DESCRIPTION
3362	Single-row update/delete affected more than one row of a linked table. Unique index contains duplicate values.
3363	Record(s) cannot be added; no corresponding record on the 'one' side.
3364	Cannot use Memo, OLE, or Hyperlink Object field <*Field Name*> in the SELECT clause of a union query.
3365	Property value not valid for REMOTE objects.
3366	Cannot append a relation with no fields defined.
3367	Cannot append. An object with that name already exists in the collection.
3368	Relationship must be on the same number of fields with the same data types.
3370	Cannot modify the design of table <*Table Name*>. It is in a read-only database.
3371	Cannot find table or constraint.
3372	No such index <*Name*> on table <*Table Name*>.
3373	Cannot create relationship. Referenced table <*Table Name*> does not have a primary key.
3374	The specified fields are not uniquely indexed in table <*Table Name*>.
3375	Table <*Table Name*> already has an index named <*Name*>.
3376	Table <*Table Name*> does not exist.
3377	No such relationship <*Relationship Name*> on table <*Table Name*>.
3378	There is already a relationship named <*Object Name*> in the current database.
3379	Cannot create relationships to enforce referential integrity. Existing data in table <*Table Name*> violates referential integrity rules in table <*Table Name*>.
3380	Field <*Field Name*> already exists in table <*Table Name*>.
3381	There is no field named <*Object Name*> in table <*Table Name*>.
3382	Size of field <*Field Name*> is too long.
3383	Cannot delete field <*Field Name*>. It is part of one or more relationships.
3384	Cannot delete a built-in property.

(continued)

Table C-4 *(continued)*

ERROR	DESCRIPTION
3385	User-defined properties do not support a Null value.
3386	Property *<Property Name>* must be set before using this method.
3387	Cannot find TEMP directory.
3388	Unknown function *<Function Name>* in validation expression or default value on *<Object Name>*.
3389	Query support unavailable.
3390	Account name already exists.
3391	An error has occurred. Properties were not saved.
3393	Cannot perform join, group, sort, or indexed restriction. A value being searched or sorted on is too long.
3394	Cannot save property; property is a schema property.
3396	Cannot perform cascading operation. Since related records exist in table *<Table Name>*, referential integrity rules would be violated.
3397	Cannot perform cascading operation. There must be a related record in table *<Table Name>*.
3398	Cannot perform cascading operation. It would result in a null key in table *<Table Name>*.
3399	Cannot perform cascading operation. It would result in a duplicate key in table *<Table Name>*.
3400	Cannot perform cascading operation. It would result in two updates to field *<Field Name>* in table *<Table Name>*.
3401	Cannot perform cascading operation. It would cause field *<Field Name>* to become Null, which is not allowed.
3402	Cannot perform cascading operation. It would cause field *<Field Name>* to become a zero-length string, which is not allowed.
3403	Cannot perform cascading operation: *<Operation Name>*.
3404	Cannot perform cascading operation. The value entered is prohibited by the validation rule *<Rule Name>* set for *<Object Name>*.
3405	Error *<Name>* in validation rule.
3406	The expression you are trying to use for the DefaultValue property is invalid because *<Object Name>*. Use a valid expression to set this property.
3407	The server's MSysConf table exists, but is in an incorrect format. Contact your system administrator.

Table C-4 *(continued)*

ERROR	DESCRIPTION
3408	Too many FastFind Sessions were invoked.
3409	Invalid field definition *<Name>* in definition of index or relationship.
3411	Invalid entry. Cannot perform cascading operation in table *<Table Name>* because the value entered is too large for field *<Field Name>*.
3412	Cannot perform cascading update on the table because it is currently in use by another user.
3413	Cannot perform cascading operation on table *<Table Name>* because it is currently in use by user *<User Name>* on machine *<Machine Name>*.
3414	Cannot perform cascading operation on table *<Table Name>* because it is currently in use.
3415	Zero-length string is valid only in a Text or Memo field.
3417	An action query cannot be used as a row source.
3418	Cannot open *<Object>*. Another user has the table open using a different network control file or locking style.
3419	Cannot open this Paradox 4.x or 5.x table because ParadoxNetStyle is set to 3.x in the Windows Registry.
3420	Object invalid or no longer set.
3421	Data type conversion error.
3422	Cannot modify table structure. Another user has the table open.
3423	You cannot use ODBC to import from, export to, or link an external Microsoft Office Access or ISAM database table to your database.
3424	Cannot create database because the locale is invalid.
3425	This method or property is not currently available on this Recordset.
3426	This action was cancelled by an associated object.
3427	Error in DAO automation.
3429	Incompatible version of an installable ISAM.
3430	While loading the Microsoft Excel installable ISAM, OLE was unable to initialize.
3431	This is not a Microsoft Excel 5.0 file.
3432	Error opening a Microsoft Excel 5.0 file.

(continued)

Table C-4 *(continued)*

ERROR	DESCRIPTION
3433	Invalid setting in Excel key of the Engines section of the Windows Registry.
3434	Cannot expand named range.
3435	Cannot delete spreadsheet cells.
3436	Failure creating file.
3437	Spreadsheet is full.
3438	The data being exported does not match the format described in the Schema.ini file.
3439	You attempted to link or import a Microsoft Word mail merge file. Although you can export such files, you cannot link or import them.
3440	An attempt was made to import or link an empty text file. To import or link a text file, the file must contain data.
3441	Text file specification field separator matches decimal separator or text delimiter.
3442	In the text file specification *<Name>*, the *<Option Name>* option is invalid.
3443	The fixed width specification *<Name>* contains no column widths.
3444	In the fixed width specification *<Name>*, column *<Column Name>* does not specify a width.
3445	Incorrect version of the DLL file *<File Name>* was found.
3446	The VBA file (VBAJET.dll for 16-bit versions, or VBAJET32.dll for 32-bit versions) is missing. Try reinstalling the application that returned the error.
3447	The VBA file (VBAJET.dll for 16-bit versions, or VBAJET32.dll for 32-bit versions) failed to initialize when called. Try reinstalling the application that returned the error.
3448	A call to an OLE system function was not successful. Try reinstalling the application that returned the error.
3449	No country/region code found in connection string for a linked table.
3450	Syntax error in query. Incomplete query clause.
3451	Illegal reference in query.
3452	You cannot make changes to the design of the database at this replica.
3453	You cannot establish or maintain an enforced relationship between a replicated table and a local table.

Table C-4 *(continued)*

ERROR	DESCRIPTION
3455	Cannot make the database replicable.
3456	Cannot make the <*Object* Name> object in <*Object* Name> container replicable.
3457	You cannot set the KeepLocal property for an object that is already replicated.
3458	The KeepLocal property cannot be set on a database; it can be set only on the objects in a database.
3459	After a database has been replicated, you cannot remove the replication features from the database.
3460	The operation you attempted conflicts with an existing operation involving this member of the replica set.
3461	The replication property you are attempting to set or delete is read-only and cannot be changed.
3462	Failure to load a DLL.
3463	Cannot find the .dll <*Object Name*>.
3464	Data type mismatch in criteria expression.
3465	The disk drive you are attempting to access is unreadable.
3468	Access was denied while accessing dropbox folder <*Folder Name*>.
3469	The disk for dropbox folder <*Folder Name*> is full.
3470	Disk failure accessing dropbox folder <*Folder Name*>.
3471	Failure to write to the Synchronizer log file.
3472	Disk full for path <*Path Name*>.
3473	Disk failure while accessing log file <*File Name*>.
3474	Cannot open the log file <*File Name*> for writing.
3475	Sharing violation while attempting to open log file <*File Name*> in Deny Write mode.
3476	Invalid dropbox path <*Path Name*>.
3477	Dropbox address <*Value*> is syntactically invalid.
3478	The replica is not a partial replica.
3479	Cannot designate a partial replica as the Design Master for the replica set.

(continued)

Table C-4 *(continued)*

ERROR	DESCRIPTION
3480	The relationship <*Relationship Name*> in the partial filter expression is invalid.
3481	The table name <*Table Name*> in the partial filter expression is invalid.
3482	The filter expression for the partial replica is invalid.
3483	The password supplied for the dropbox folder <*Folder Name*> is invalid.
3484	The password used by the Synchronizer to write to a destination dropbox folder is invalid.
3485	The object cannot be replicated because the database is not replicated.
3486	You cannot add a second Replication ID AutoNumber field to a table.
3487	The database you are attempting to replicate cannot be converted.
3488	The value specified is not a ReplicaID for any member in the replica set.
3489	The object specified cannot be replicated because it is missing a necessary resource.
3490	Cannot create a new replica because the <*Object Name*> object in <*Container Name*> container could not be replicated.
3491	The database must be opened in exclusive mode before it can be replicated.
3492	The synchronization failed because a design change could not be applied to one of the replicas.
3493	Cannot set the specified Registry parameter for the Synchronizer.
3494	Unable to retrieve the specified Registry parameter for the Synchronizer.
3495	There are no scheduled synchronization's between the two Synchronizers.
3496	Replication Manager cannot find the ExchangeID in the MSysExchangeLog table.
3497	Unable to set a schedule for the Synchronizer.
3499	Cannot retrieve the full path information for a member of the replica set.
3500	You cannot specify two different Synchronizers to manage the same replica.

PART

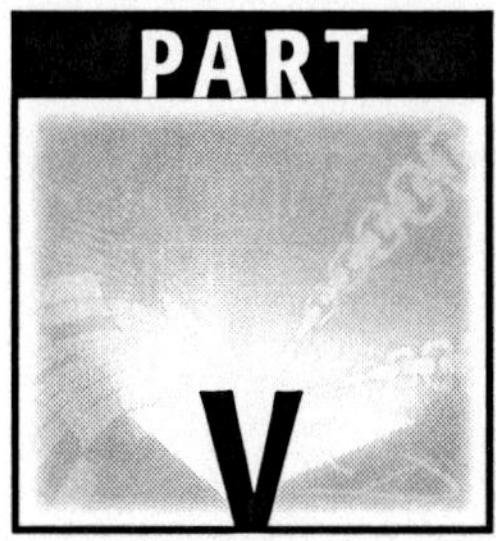

Appendixes

Index

Index

B

C

D

F

G

H

I

J

K

L

M

N

Q

S

U

V

CPSIA information can be obtained at www.ICGtesting.com
Printed in the USA
BVOW03n1506180713

326111BV00001B/1/P